Wounds of the Heart

Joseph Keely

PAGE PUBLISHING, INC.
Conneaut Lake, PA

First originally published by Page Publishing 2020

ISBN 978-1-6624-1953-9 (pbk)
ISBN 978-1-6624-1954-6 (digital)

Printed in the United States of America

This is for my children and my children's children so that they may know that their father/grandfather served his country, along with 2,909,918 other men and woman in uniform, in Vietnam. Most of these men and woman remained loyal to their oath as military personnel and served with honor and distinction. I want them to know that our efforts and sacrifices were undermined at every turn of the event by the American people, the American press, and self-centered politicians through lies, propaganda, and treason on a scale so large it was unstoppable and finally forced the government to abandon its troops on the field of battle to fend for themselves. That they may also see the real truth surrounding the Vietnam War and the war that has raged within me these past fifty-plus years.

FOREWORD

THE HEART IS DEFINED AS a hollow muscular organ that pumps blood around the body in humans situated in the center of the chest with its apex directed to the left. The human heart is also considered as the source and center of emotional life, where the deepest and sincerest feelings are located and an individual is most vulnerable to pain.

It is a deep-rooted pain unlike any other. It is not the pain one feels when one injures themselves. Over the years, I would say that all of us, at one time or another, have felt that emotional pain to the heart. I know I have. Most of the time, that pain has dissipated with time; however, there is one aspect of my life—a one-year-eight-months-and-four-day tour of duty spent in a little Southeast Asian country known as Vietnam—that will not heal.

Although I never had to be medevacked for physical wounds, it was in the early part of my tour in this danger zone that I received that first emotional wound to my heart. In the years since then, many more have followed. These wounds are invisible to the naked eye, and the Purple Heart is never presented. As a Marine, I was taught to suck it up, saddle up, and move out.

It was February 1966, and I was sitting in one of the communication bunkers on Hill 34 approximately three miles south of the Dan-Nang air base, adjacent to the northern edge of Phong-Bac hamlet. The communication bunkers were better fortified than the bunkers on the perimeter. They wanted to make sure that the communication was well protected. It was about 0400 hours when I heard the newscast over the armed forces radio network announce that troops returning to stateside from Vietnam were being cursed at by demonstrators and had dog feces thrown at them. I remember looking at the radio in total bewilderment and saying to myself, "Our people were throwing dog shit at our guys?" (*And I am sitting here less than fifty yards away from someone who wants to kill me.)* This would be the first of many wounds of the heart that I would receive over the next fifty-plus years.

There are many things that have been said and done over these past years that has prompted me to pursue this project of writing a book. There were deeds and words that have evoked the emotions of anger, hurt, sadness, and depression, none of which were a result of my service in the corps or my service in the Nam. The emotions are evoked by the actions and words of my fellow countrymen. Or are they my fellow countrymen, that is? These words and deeds that were said and done, whether intended to hurt or not, have done just that. Time and time again, the name-calling—baby bomber, murderer, the demonstrations that affected our mission, me and my fellow veterans being accused of atrocities that we did not commit—hurt us.

I have heard a lot of reasons why guys have joined the service: "I had a fight with my father and I wanted to get away from him," "I needed a job and didn't know where to go," "It was join the military or go to jail," or "I wanted to get an education." These reasons I consider invalid and unwise. The military will accept you no matter what reason you use to join. However, the military, no matter what country you are from, exists for one reason and one reason only: to defend its nation. To believe otherwise is foolish. I say this because the reason you do something determines your outlook of the situation you put yourself in. When one joins the service, he or she should join knowing that they may very well have to forfeit their life for that decision. I joined knowing just that. I also felt obligated to pick up where so many before me left off. When I joined, I was under the impression that we, as a nation, were already committed to helping Vietnam. This would not be the first time in my young life I fought for someone that could not defend themselves. At the same time, I thought I would be helping to keep the Communists away from our shores. Little did I know that these Commies were within our borders already and would soon rear their ugly heads!

I was only nineteen when I started out. Although I was young and wet behind the ears, I had no illusions as to what I was doing or where I was going. I had taken an oath to defend a nation of people whom I thought believed in the same things that I believed in. Boy, was I wrong there!

Although it was at an early stage of my life, I was not joining because I liked to fight. It is my belief that very few people like to fight. We, who wear the uniform of the United States military, are not the hawks most people make us out to be. I believe that we join because we deeply love what we are defending, and what we are defending is where our loved ones live. And for those two reasons alone, I would gladly put my life on the line.

One day, not to long ago, I was watching a documentary on the 1980 Olympic hockey game, us against the Soviets in Lake Placid, New York. A lot of Americans were in attendance. I found myself being very envious of that team. The Americans in attendance were cheering and waving American flags at them. According to the team captain, one lady wrote him saying, "Beat those Commie bastards." With that statement, I just shook my head and remembered that when I was a member of America's ultimate team, the United States military, and I was standing on the field of battle, there was no flag over our heads because it was against the law to fly one. And when we looked to the stands, there were no flags or cheers of support. As a matter of fact, I saw a whole lot of rooting for the other side.

However, during this documentary there was one statement that sent me over the edge. The commentator said, "This was during the Cold War. There were a lot of hot spots during the Cold War, and this was just another one." I put my head down and thought, *Jesus Christ, they were playing for points on a scoreboard and they were calling it a hot spot, and besides, they were playing on fucking ice.* I stopped watching and immediately wrote this poem, and believe me, I am not a poem type of guy.

CHAPTER 1

WOUNDS OF THE HEART

Here is a scoreboard that has come
to be,
The points are not numbers that
You normally see,
They are faces and names from
Sea to shining Sea,
with neighbors and friends
and family,
What is not seen here are the
Wounds of all degrees,
The Blind,
The Insane,
The Amputees,
Or the men and women,
Who took the Oath?
Like Me,
With wounds of the heart That no one can see.

THERE HAVE BEEN TIMES SINCE the building of the Vietnam wall that I thought the names listed there were the lucky ones, and there have been times that I wished I were listed there with them. I do not think I ever really came home. I know I have been here in body, but I find my spirit and soul now and then drifting somewhere else. Each day that goes by, I cannot help thinking that I do not belong here; it is like I'm living in an alternate reality. It has been that way on and off for all these years.

All I know is that since I have left that place, I have never been able to forget it or the events that took place surrounding it. Not from that day to this. It was about twenty years ago when I thought that maybe there was something wrong with me because I could not stop thinking about it. I spoke with a friend of mine, Joe McConville, a former Marine veteran of World War II who helped mop up Guadalcanal and made the landings at Guam and Okinawa. This is one of the guys I grew up hearing about, and although I didn't know him at the time, he is one of the many reasons I chose to join the Marine Corps. These events in his life all took place before he became a citizen of the United States, for he was an Irish immigrant. I asked him, "Do you ever give thought to the days you spent in your war?" He said, "Every day of my life. It's too big an event in your life to forget." I felt a little better.

Over the years' conversations with people usually bring them to asking questions about the Nam and my feelings about it. One day, I was having a discussion with this lady I know. We were discussing Nam and our views on this country. In the middle of the conversation, I saw her eyes shift from me, and she looked at the top of the table. It was almost as if I was no longer sitting across the table from her when she had a thought which she happened to express aloud. She said, "Oh! He's an idealist." I remember being a little pissed, not because she said that about me but by the way she said it like it was a dirty word. After giving it some thought, I shrugged and said to myself, *She's right. After all, is it not what America is, an ideal? This is nothing more than a principle or standard to which people aspire to become.* Aren't these standards and principles set forth in the Declaration of Independence and the Constitution? The very documents that define us as a nation. Well, I guess that only applies to some people.

The love that I have for my country, disregard the ideal of my country, is strong. It was strong long before I reached my late teens. I do not know when or how it became so strong. From an exceedingly early age, I knew I was going to grow up and join the corps. Why the corps? I cannot answer that either. Maybe it was from watching all the war movies and hearing people talk about the men who have defended our land long before I came on board, like my friend, Joe McConville. Whatever the reason, I even remember feeling good about registering for the draft. Not that it mattered, I was going to join any way.

Living here is what I consider to be a gift. I am not what one would consider to be a fortunate son. I was not born with a silver spoon in my mouth. I did not have the best materialistic life—better than some, worse than most. Growing up was hard, but what I remember most is growing up free. All I know is that I am and always have been in love with the lore the history of this gift that has been bestowed upon me. This gift given to me by my parents, Pat and Agnes Keely, both of whom were Irish immigrants, and that makes me what is known as a narrowback (a first-generation American). The first time I learned that living in this country was a gift was when I was sixteen years old. It was at the height of the Cuban missile crises, and I wanted to quit school and join the Marines to go and stop the Communists from delivering nuclear missiles ninety miles off our coast. Aah, youth! Yes, even at that early age, I did not like the Communists for reasons that will become clearer later.

When my father got home from work one day, I informed him of this plan, which was quickly stepped on with the words "Over my dead body" and "You are going to finish school first. After you finish school, you can do what you want." I was really pissed, which led me to calling him a name which I regret to this day. I will not repeat it. All I know is that he didn't deserve it. However, that name engendered an immediate response that I remember to this day! It was his big Irish fist connecting to my lower jaw, causing me to go into immediate flight over the coffee table and landing on the couch. The onslaught did not stop with that one punch; however, it continued for what seemed to me like an hour, resulting with him pinning me against the back of the couch and the wall. He then uttered these words, "I gave you this country, you little bastard. It is mine by choice, and I gave it to you." Not wanting to test the waters any further on the off chance he might want to lay another one on me,

I simply apologized. He taught me a lesson; however, do not to take for granted the people that neither give you such gifts nor take for granted the gift itself.

Nevertheless, it is my belief that there are many Americans that do just that, taking for granted the freedoms and liberties that they enjoy without giving one thought as to why or how these gifts have been bestowed upon them, nor do they care. I believe that they love living here but, for reasons known only to them, will not defend here.

I do not want to be as presumptuous as I was back then and think that my fellow veterans may believe the same way I do. These people with whom I share a common bond can draw their own conclusions as to what occurred back in the sixties and early seventies and in the years since. Although I am not speaking for them, I am speaking about them. This story is their story, apart from those veterans who betrayed our oath, and they know who they are.

As a Vietnam vet, I used to feel that it was the American people who lost us the war. However, I now believe it is the American people whom we lost the war too. You may be thinking, not all Americans were guilty of these things during the Vietnam War. And you would be right! So I will use an old cliché: "If the shoe fits, wear it," and that shoe fits an awful lot of Americans. Or are they Americans? I feel it was the constant bombardment of protest rallies, marches, and demonstrations, as well as the draft evasion, which became known as the anti-war movement. It was this movement that aided the enemy from the very beginning, which prolonged the war and gave the enemy the illusion that they were winning. I have never heard, in the history of warfare, a nation or military entity winning every battle and then losing the war. That is, except this war.

The anti-war movement back then outwardly showed the enemy that there were large numbers of people in the United States that were in allegiance with them. They were mostly college students, and many of them were members of my generation. However, there were high-ranking members of the government, actors, singers, rock stars, and newspaper and media people. I feel that these people who participated in this movement were committing treason.

Some of those politicians were Ramsey Clark, US attorney general, and Ted Kennedy, to name a couple of many. These are politicians that would set their own fathers on fire for a vote. That is, if they knew who they were. Some of the entertainers were Fonda. Notice that I referred to her only by her last name. To give her a first name would lead you to believe that I think her to be something of a human being when I really think that something went drastically wrong at the abortion (*it's alive, it's alive*), but then that is just me.

Some other entertainers were Joan Baez, John Lennon, and Credence Clearwater Revival, just to name a few. These people wrote and sang anti-war songs. There were also future politicians who openly participated in the anti-war movement, such as Bill Clinton and John Kerry, who eventually became a leader of the Vietnam Veterans against the War. However, a young college student from the University of Michigan by the name of Tom Hayden, founder and leader of a left-wing organization known as Students for a Democratic Society, kicked the whole thing off way back in 1964, following the example of a couple Communist organizations in 1962, long before the escalation of the war in '65.

I have heard it argued that these kids who were involved with the movement were young and impressionable and maybe it was their ideals that they were expressing. Well, these people were no younger or any more impressionable than I or most of my fellow veterans were. However, what ideals are we talking about? We were fighting for and at the request of a nation that wanted to live free and maintain a lifestyle of freedom. However, it was most of my generation that was carrying Vietcong and North Vietnam's National Colors, the flags of Communism, making up slogans and chants supporting the side of the enemy we were fighting. So I guess that argument would be that their lofty ideals were to help spread Communism throughout the world while doing away with our republic. Gee! What a concept. Why didn't I think of that? Many of these people were college educated or in the process of getting a degree. So much for higher education.

Treason is defined as violation of the allegiance owed by a person to his or her own country, for example, by aiding an enemy.

Betrayal is defined as the act or an instance of betraying somebody or something.

This is exactly what I believe those who participated in the anti-war movement were doing.

[A] Article III, Section 3, Paragraph 1, of the Constitution of the United States: *"Treason against the United States shall consist only in levying War against them, or, in adhering to their Enemies, giving them aid and comfort." No person shall be convicted of treason unless on the testimony of two witnesses to the same overt act, or on confession in open court. The Congress shall have the power to declare the punishment of treason, but no attainder of treason shall work corruption of blood, or forfeiture except during the life of the person attainted.*

It was shortly after World War II when eight people were charged, indicted, and tried for the crime of treason. All eight were convicted, and all eight convictions were appealed, some all the way up to the Supreme Court. All convictions were upheld, and as a result, the Supreme Court issued the following opinion:

[B] *The "aid and comfort" prong of treason has been interpreted by the Supreme Court of the United States to require proof of four elements: (1) an intent to betray the United States (which can be inferred from) (2) an overt act, (3) witnessed by two people, (4) that it provides aid and comfort to an enemy of the United States.*

The way the Constitution was written by our Founding Fathers and interpreted by the Supreme Court leads me to the conclusion that treason is a non-preventable crime. And in the United States, apparently it has become an unpunishable crime because I do not think that treason charges have been brought against anyone in the United States since World War II.

[C] The eight treason indictments and convictions of the Americans that came out of World War II are broken down as follows: One resulted from mistreatment of prisoners of war held in

Japan, two arose from spying activities in the United States, four, including a case against the infamous Axis Sally, were for making propaganda broadcasts on behalf of the Nazis. The fifth was for similar broadcasts by the equally infamous Tokyo Rose, who was later pardoned by President Ford because she may have been wrongly accused. However, she did serve a ten-year prison term. The ruling of the Supreme Court regarding aid and comfort resulted from these cases.

Unless we are lucky and given information by an informant or we are lucky enough to intercept a communiqué (such as in the case of Benedict Arnold), these two events are non-preventable. In case you forgot who Benedict Arnold was, or in case you never heard of him, he is America's first and most infamous traitor. [D] Benedict Arnold was born on January 14, 1741, in Norwich, Connecticut. Arnold was one of a few *Benedict Arnolds*, including an early governor of Rhode Island who happened to be his father. Prior to the official outbreak of the revolution, Arnold became a captain in the governor's Second Company of Guards.

When the word spread of the Battles of Lexington and Concord, Arnold was in the ranks of his company. He had proved himself many times over in battle.

According to history, however, by May of 1779, Arnold had begun bargaining with the British. Why would a man commit treason against his country, especially one who had fought so valiantly? We can only speculate. It is said that he was angry and hurt over the many slights he received over the years. It is believed that he probably felt unappreciated by his country and those he fought with. Plus, he even sacrificed his own leg for the cause. Money, of course, played a big part. Somewhere along the line, he was offered more than ten thousand pounds and a commission in the British military.

I am sure that in his mind his motivation was valid. However, in my mind, no matter what the motive, treason is unacceptable, especially in this country. The bounty Arnold offered the British was West Point. Again, history shows he began correspondence with Major John Andre, who had been friends with Peggy Shippen Arnold during the Philadelphia occupation. Andre was an adjutant general and intelligence chief of Sir Henry Clinton. In the meantime, Washington supposedly offered Arnold the position of left wing of the army. However, for some reason, he was given West Point instead.

Again, according to history, Andre was the courier between Arnold and Clinton regarding the closing of the deal. With his ship forced back by American troops, Andre was sent on foot back to British lines with a pass from Arnold as well as documents for Clinton in his sock. He was captured and placed into American custody where the documents were found. Arnold heard of his capture and was able to make his escape to the same ship, the *Vulture*, in which Andre had arrived. Andre was put on trial and met his death as a spy. Arnold defected to the British and received substantial remuneration for his defection. This included pay, land in Canada, pensions for himself, his wife and his children (five surviving from Peggy and three from his first marriage to Margaret), and a military commission as a British provincial brigadier general.

The British provided handsomely for Arnold, but never completely trusted him. He was never given an important military command. (Guess what! The British do not like traitors either.) As I said, we got lucky.

This brings us back to the Constitution and the Supreme Court, two entities that materialized from the revolution, the first of many wars we would have to fight as a nation. Waging war is immediate and in your face, and if this prong of the constitution is violated, it will evoke an immediate response from the government and is, therefore, punishable.

However, the adhering to the enemy prong of the Constitution is entirely different. It is sneaky and covert in nature and may not be discovered for years. This is the prong that requires the elements of proof demanded by the Supreme Court.

There is another word that I believe goes hand and hand with the word treason, and that word is *apathy*.

> *Apathy* is defined as lack of interest in anything or the absence of any wish to do anything; it is the inability to feel normal or passionate human

> feelings or to respond emotionally, indifference,
> lack of concern, or lack of interest.

In the case of Vietnam, apathy, in my opinion, contributed to the anti-war movement just by the sheer nature of the definition of the word. People who are apathetic will kiss the ass of anyone who walks in the door. They don't care who's in charge or what is happening around them as long as they are not affected by it. Not everyone in America protested the Vietnam War, but there were as many, if not more, that sat in apathy.

Three or four people do not elect presidents, who are aspiring to serve a second term or presidents that want to give up that aspiration, nor do three or four people get governments to abandon their troops, nor do they decide the end of a war. This takes many people besides those people I mentioned. So regarding Vietnam, it was the protesters as well as all those who sat in apathy that decided the outcome of that war.

During my tours of duty in Vietnam, I was assigned to a tank battalion and to a wire platoon. However, when I went outside the perimeter to what we called the bush, I would hump a radio.

Yankee White, Yankee White, this is Sassy, over.

This is Yankee White, over.

Yankee White, this is Sassy Six Actual, be advised. Watch, your six, over.

Roger that, Sassy. Out.

Watch your six is military for "watch your rear." As a communicator, that is one radio transmission I never heard. It was always understood that you watch your rear as well as the area to the front and flanks. However, we never saw the long-distance attack from the rear—an attack that came from our far distant rear, an attack that we never expected, nor did we pay enough attention to see it coming. It came from home, from the people that we swore to protect, and it also came from our comrades in arms, people from our own ranks. This came as quite a shock to most of us. Well, anyway, at least to me it did.

A total of ten years of my life was given to the corps, four years' active duty, six years' reserves. Along with that service came three honorable discharges. I am also a former New Jersey State Trooper with twenty-six years of honorable service to them and the citizens of the state of New Jersey. I think that this more than qualifies me to write about this subject because, unlike the previous wars, I did not just hear or read about it. I lived it.

I have made some strong allegations about many people. However, no stronger than the allegations made against me or my fellow Nam vets so many years ago, and that have continued right up to this very day.

There have been allegations about us that have never been sworn to or proven, simply believed by large numbers of Americans for reasons unknown to me. However, for me to do the same thing without trying to prove it or at least to substantiate my beliefs, I would be remiss and, at the very least, ignorant, and, at the very most, as stupid as those people who participated in that anti-war movement.

For me to do this, I must bring you back to the beginning when the world was dark and void of light. Okay, I won't go back that far, but I do have to go back to when it was dark for me and the rest of my generation because we were not yet born. I think the rest of this story should move forward into two phases: the laying out of historical fact because *history is relevant* and also by investigating the allegations and accusations made against the American government and the military at that time by those who would lead and participate in the anti-war movement.

CHAPTER 2

POLICY MAKERS

IF I AM GOING ON the premise that history is relevant, and I do believe that it is, I also believe it dictates the future. One might argue that the allegations I previously made about many people who claim to be Americans were made by some malcontent who cannot let go of the past. That statement may very well be true; however, my discontent and my inability to let go of the past has only been fueled by the fact those so-called Americans, who have been constantly shoving their version of what occurred during those years in my face.

Allegations are nothing more than statements without proof. I would now like to change those allegations into accusations, which require proof, and I intend to do so during the investigation stage of this story. Vietnam did not just pop up out of the ground like a volcano. However, like a volcano, it was hot. It was the plans and calculated actions of some, which was being reacted to by others, that eventually brought us to that Southeast Asian war. It was part and parcel of a war of political ideologies known as the Cold War, which started shortly after World War II.

However, the ideological clash between Communism and the Free World began long before that in 1917. This was just after the Russian Revolution and just before we were about to enter World War I. It was the first event that would make Russian-American relations a matter of major concern to leaders in both countries (note the year). This is twenty-eight years prior to my generation's arrival and thirty years prior to the start of the Cold War.

Although there were many hot spots during the Cold War, Nam became the longest lasting. I can tell you from experience that it was not like a hockey game or like any other sport as we know them.

To see if my gut feelings of discontent are correct and the anger that I feel is justified, I have decided to investigate these accusations that I have made. However, it is important for us to travel back in time and explore the whole story—to explore the historical facts that led us on our journey of involvement in Vietnam.

History shows French Indochina was formed in October 1887 when France annexed Tonkin and Cochin China which, together, form modern Vietnam. Christ! My parents were not even born yet! It was not until 1893 after the Franco-Siamese War that the kingdom of Cambodia and Laos was added to French Indochina. This federation lasted until 1954 when the French lost the war with the Vietnamese Communist Party. However, to talk about the year 1954 is getting a little bit ahead of the story.

French rule was interrupted with the arrival of World War II and the invasion by the Japanese, who used the Vichy French as a puppet regime. Long before I, or the rest of my generation, ever saw the light of day, the Vietnam War was being shaped by the actions of individuals that arrived on this planet long before we did. So for the lack of a better word, let us call these people the policy makers.

It is the actions of these people that had direct or indirect involvement in shaping the Vietnam War, and they were doing it long before they became policy makers. I like to compare the actions of these policy makers to science, such as Sir Isaac Newton's law of motion, which states [E], "Force equals mass multiplied by acceleration, an object in motion will remain in motion unless acted upon by a net force, to every action there is an equal and opposite reaction."

Although he is talking about objects and energy, I think that this law, in a lot of respects, could also pertain to the actions and reactions of people. The actions of one person engenders a reaction of others. Regarding Vietnam, I think, over a long period of time, that is exactly what happened—action and chain reaction.

I believe from the time we are born, we are taught by parents, by teachers, and by our surroundings. But it all boils down to one thing: we, as individuals, have choices. The good thing is that we only have two. Do it or don't do it. Say it or don't say it. Believe it or don't believe it. Fight or don't fight. Or choose one side or the other, or simply do the right thing or don't! From my investigation, I have come to believe that a lot of Americans have a problem with deciding to do the right thing or are easily persuaded not to.

According to a Gallup poll during the '60s and '70s, it showed that most Americans chose *not* to support our fight against Communism. Since I was a United States Marine fighting in Vietnam, I have come to believe that they made the wrong choice, and it left me with only one question: why? The following is a result of that Gallup poll. Regarding the question why, I believe I can answer that question.

Support for the war as measured by no responses to this question asked: *"In view of the developments since we entered the fighting in Vietnam, do you think the US made a mistake sending troops to fight in Vietnam?"* (Gallup)

The Gallup poll shows the answers by date and percent number:

August 1965—61%
March 1966—59%
May 1966—49%
September 1966—48%
November 1966—51%
February 1967—52%
May 1967—50%
July 1967—48%
October 1967—44%
December 1967—46%
February 1968—42%
March 1968—41%
April 1968—40%
August 1968—35%
October 1968—37%
February 1969—39%
October 1969—32%
January 1970—33%

April 1970—34%
May 1970—36%
January 1971—31%
May 1971—28%

At this point, Gallup stopped asking this question.[1]

Within two years of sending troops to Vietnam, support of the war gradually decreased to where 72% of those polled were against the war. It is my contention that that gradual decline was due to the actions of those who participated in the anti-war movement and the apathy of others.

On the Communist side of this issue, there were two policy makers that were a constant throughout most of the war. Ho Chi Minh became president of North Vietnam and Võ Nguyên Giáp became the leader of his army. These two people remained in the forefront of that war for most of its entirety. Another Communist in the mix was Pham Van Dong; he will become important halfway through this war and, to my investigation, when he replaces Ho Chi Minh upon his death.

Then there was Joseph Stalin Leader of the Soviet Union who put himself in direct support of Ho Chi Minh, along with two Chinese Communist leaders at the time, Mao Tse-tung and Zhou Enlai.

However, on the American side, you could count on the policy makers constantly changing. The American presidency would change hands five times. Starting with President Harry S. Truman and continuing through Dwight D. Eisenhower, John F. Kennedy, Lyndon B. Johnson, and Richard M. Nixon, each would serve a term or terms before that war would start and end. However, that is just the nature of our political system.

---

[1] William L. Lunch and Peter W. Sperlich, "American Public Opinion and the War in Vietnam," Western Political Quarterly, 32 (March 1979), p. 25. All figures presented are from Hazel Erskine, "The Polls: Is War a Mistake?" Public Opinion Quarterly 34 (Spring 1970): 141—21, and Gallup Opinion Index, numbers 56, 59, 61, 69, and 73.

Communism is defined as the Marxist-Leninist version of a classless society in which capitalism is overthrown by a working-class revolution that gives ownership and control of wealth and property to the state. Any system of government in which a single, usually a totalitarian, party holds power and the state controls' the economy.

Totalitarian means "relating to or operating a centralized government system in which a single party without opposition, rules over political, economic, social, and cultural life."

I have learned as I was growing up that the system set up by our Founding Fathers, at significant risk to themselves and hard-fought for, in the American Revolution, and quite different from the one described above, is a constitutional republic, "which is a government created and controlled, at least, by the law of a Constitution, such as the Constitution of the United States. This is a law document foundationally based on the Magna Carta and the Declaration of Independence. That document recognizes the sovereignty, and the divine nature of man's creation, and commands the divine right to life, liberty, property, and the pursuit of happiness."

This system has been defended, time and time again, by millions of the noble men and women of this nation. So I have come to ask myself repeatedly since my time spent in Vietnam, why did so many people in this country who claim to be American side with the communist? That is a question I do not know will ever be answered!

Conjecture is defined as, the formation of judgments or opinions on the basis of incomplete or inconclusive information.

It is conjecture that was used by those people protesting the Vietnam War to justify, at the very least, what I believe to be their illegal and unethical activities; whether those activities were treasonous or not remains to be seen. However, I believe I have gathered enough evidence to show that it has. I believe conjecture was also used to justify why we should not be fighting that war. A lot of it was also used about the policy makers themselves. So let us look at those people.

The Communists

Ho Chi Minh. Ho is most famous for leading the Vietminh independence movement from 1941 onward, establishing the Communist-governed Democratic Republic of Vietnam in 1945 and defeating the French Empire in 1954 at Dien Bien Phu.

Ho was born Nguyễn Sinh Cung in 1890; this is three years after France annexed his country. He was born in Hoàng Trù Village, which was his mother's hometown. However, he grew up in his paternal hometown of Kim Lien Village. It is said Ho received a strong Confucian upbringing by his parents, but he supposedly had a rebellious personality. He also received a modern secondary education at a French-style Lycee in Hué. This French School would turn out to be alma mater of his future disciples, Pham Van Dong and the general of his Army Vo Nguyen Giap. *(Note: Pham Van Dong later becomes an important subject to this investigation.)*

In 1911, Ho supposedly left Vietnam on a French steamer, the *Admiral Latouche-Tréville*, working as a kitchen helper. It is said that he traveled to the United States, where, from 1912 to 1913, he lived in New York and Boston. He claimed to have arrived in Paris from London in 1917, but French police only had documents of his arrival in June 1919. To familiarize himself with Western society and politics, he was also reported to be spending most of his free time in public libraries, reading history books and newspapers.

From 1919–1923, while living in France, it is here, that he embraced communism. Following World War I, he changed his name to Nguyên Ái Quốc (Nguyen the Patriot) and he petitioned for equal rights in French Indochina on behalf of the Group of Vietnamese Patriots to the Western powers at the Versailles peace talks but was ignored. He also asked a sitting president of the United States Woodrow Wilson for help to remove the French from Vietnam and replace it with a new nationalist government. Again, he was ignored. Considering these historical facts, I have a couple questions.

The above italicized historical events, many years after the Vietnam War, would become a narrative used by the anti-war movement to show if Wilson listened to Ho Chi Minh, we probably would not have had to go to war in Vietnam.

I would like to point out this time, some historical facts that may have influenced President Wilson's decision to ignore the man known as Nguyên Ái Quốc (Nguyen the Patriot). The facts that I am about to disclose, I believe, have been overlooked by the American public when they are deciding how they feel about this narrative.

No matter what the individual opinions of the American public is about the different nationalities of the world, as a nation, we cannot ignore the following simple facts. An incredibly young Frenchman by the name of the Marquis De Lafayette traveled to the colonies and offered his assistance with the American Revolution. Not only did he fight many of our battles, he also returned to France and petitioned his government to give us aid in our quest. That aid not only came in his return to the fight but also brought monitory assistance and the French fleet. This gave us the advantage at Yorktown, which was the last battle of the American Revolution.

It should also be noted in 1865, Edouard de Laboulaye (a French political thinker, US Constitution expert, and abolitionist) proposed that a monument be built as a gift from France to the United States in order to commemorate the perseverance of freedom and democracy in the United States and to honor the work of the late president Abraham Lincoln. That monument is none other than the Statue of Liberty, which arrived in the United States in 1886 from the French government.

In addition to the significant events, we had just come out of the First World War with France and England as our ally. It is unknown to me if, at that time in history, it was the policy of the United States to be telling other nations what to do. That, along with the man that would become known as Ho Chi Minh and his associates not representing an established government of any kind, I do not think would be paid attention to by anyone at that time.

However, for those who think that Woodrow Wilson should have done something, do they think that France would have given up Vietnam, Laos, and Cambodia, the area known as French Indochina without a fight? I think not. It is a well-known fact that France was not willing to give it up to the Vietnamese in 1946. The Indochina War began in Vietnam between the French and the CPV communist party Vietnam on December 19, 1946, and lasted until July 20, 1954—a grand total of eight years.

If President Wilson did listen to Ho Chi Minh, not only would we have been fighting an ally in 1919 but we would also have been fighting a nation that helped us tremendously in our own independence from colonialism.

In researching this individual, it has left me with a number of questions.

Why does a guy who is opposed to France move to France? Why does he adopt the communist ideology while living in a country that he is opposed to? Why does he ask the president of the United States to help him rid Vietnam of the French? Unless he views Wilson as a little pink? Maybe he saw something the Americans didn't? I only ask these questions because I do not see the logic to it.

While he was in France, he helped to form the French Communist Party; after completing this task, he spent much of his time in Moscow. It is here that he became the Com Interns Asia hand and the principal theorist on colonial warfare. In case you were wondering The Com Interns is short for Communist International, an organization of Communist parties set up by Lenin in 1919. It was an international organization that was supposedly abolished in 1943. Or was it?

So here it is only two years after the Russian Revolution, twenty-seven years prior to my generation's arrival and America's involvement in Vietnam. The Communists are sending out their tentacles to engulf the world, and Ho Chi Minh is at the head of one of those tentacles. It should be noted that Ho Chi Minh is not even in his own country.

It was just after he approached President Wilson that Nguyễn Ái Quốc took the name of Ho Chi Minh—a Vietnamese name combining a common surname (Hồ), this name meaning "enlightened" (*Chi* meaning "will" and *Minh* meaning "light"). In other words, Uncle Ho became known as the one who is enlightened. Christ, this guy has more aliases than some of the criminals that I locked up.

In 1923, it was reported that he moved to Guangzhou, China. In 1925–26, he organized Youth Education Classes and occasionally gave lectures at the Whampoa Military Academy on the revolutionary movement in Indochina. Also, during this period, he stayed in Hong Kong as a representative of the Communist international (Com Interns). In June 1931, he is arrested in Hong Kong by the British police during a crackdown on political revolutionaries; they held him until his release in 1933. When he was released from prison, he fled Hong Kong and then traveled to Moscow, where he will spend much of the next seven years studying and teaching at the Lenin Institute. He also attends the Institute for National and Colonial Questions. During this period, several of those years were spent recovering from tuberculosis. In 1938, he returned to China and served as an adviser with Chinese Communist armed forces.

In 1941, Ho returned to Vietnam to lead the Vietminh independence movement. *(Ho is now fifty-one years old and a Communist for twenty-two years. I and my generation are still missing from the picture.)* During World War II, he oversaw many successful military actions against the Vichy French who were put in place by the Japanese during their occupation of Vietnam. During the war, he was supported closely but clandestinely by the United States office of strategic services. When Ho finally arrived in Hanoi, immediately following the surrender of the Japanese on September 2, 1945, the first American to greet him was an OSS agent who shook his hand and thanked him for collaborating effectively and loyally.

(It should be noted that this information would be used by the leadership of the anti-war movement during the '60s and '70s to accuse our administration of betraying him for his assistance during World War II.) When the war ended in 1945, a power struggle ensued between the members of rival groups, such as the leader of the Constitutional

Party, the head of the Party for Independence, and Ngo Dinh Khoi. These people were all killed by the Vietminh, [3] whose leader was none other than Ho Chi Minh.

Ngo Dinh Diem who would eventually become president of South Vietnam was the brother of Ngo Dinh Khoi. There were also Purges and killings of Trotskyites and it has been documented[4] that rival anti-Stalinist communists were killed as well. In 1946, when Ho traveled outside the country, his subordinates imprisoned twenty-five thousand non-communist nationalists and forced six thousand others to flee.[5] Hundreds of political opponents were also killed in July that same year.[6] All rival political parties were banned and local governments purged. It appears to me that Ho is making it impossible to be opposed. Of course, I didn't know it at this point in time because I am only one year old and eighteen years away from becoming one of many that would oppose him.

(Note: Eventually, Ngo Dinh Diem would become the first president of South Vietnam; this is the brother of one of the many people that Ho had killed during Ho's purges. So it is quite evident to me that there would be no love lost between Diem and Uncle Ho, as he eventually became known by his followers.)

Maybe it was unknown to uncle Ho and the Vietminh that President Truman, Prime Minister Churchill, and Premier Stalin had already decided the future of postwar Vietnam. At the summit meeting in Potsdam, they agreed that the country would be divided temporarily at the seventeenth parallel, with the British troops occupying south of the parallel and the nationalist Chinese occupying north of the parallel for the purpose of repatriating the Japanese soldiers back to Japan.

It was during this repatriation process that Gen. Sir Douglas Gracey, the British commander in charge of repatriating the Japanese, declared martial law amid spiraling violence between rival Vietnamese factions and French forces.

I can't remember at what point in my life since my return from the Nam that I have heard it argued that we (the United States) betrayed him because he helped us in the fight against the Japanese during World War II. This is a prime example of a conjectural state-ment. I will concede that he helped us fight the Japanese.

As a matter of fact, this was confirmed by John F. Cady, research analyst at the Office of Strategic Services, 1943–45; US Department of State officer, 1945–49, as chief of the South Asian section, Office of Near Eastern and African Affairs; and assigned as foreign service reservist to Consul General Rangoon, 1945–46.

Mr. Cady, in a 1974 interview, said that "Ho Chi Minh and his Vietnam group were actually recruited by the US OSS and intro-duced into the area of Northern Tonkin. This is because the Vichy French in Indochina refused to respond to American requests for information having to do with the numbers and location of Japanese troops in that area. This Paris refusal to cooperate angered Franklin Roosevelt very much. *(Our early connection with Ho Chi Minh was distinctly military and not political).*"

Love and war make for strange bedfellows. World War II was a catastrophic event; people were fighting all over the globe. We and the Communist, as well as every other political ideology on the planet, were sharing a common enemy. It was in everyone's best interest to defeat the Germans and the Japanese. The world leaders of the time and everyone that was not considered a world leader at the time knew this. It should be noted that the fact of the matter is the communist are the ones that joined in with us to fight Germany because Germany stuck it up their ass when the Germans imple-mented a little sneak attack against the Russians known as Operation Barbarossa. This little operation is where Hitler betrayed Stalin and invaded Russia.

There was a lot more to this guy Ho Chi Minh than the conjec-ture that was being spouted out by the people in the Vietnam anti-war movement showed. That conjecture continues to this very day.

The Next Communist

General Võ Nguyên Giáp, a disciple of Uncle Ho. He became Ho's commander of the army. Although I have not seen too much conjec-ture about him, he is a major player and policy maker of the Vietnam

War. History will show the following [G] General Võ Nguyên Giáp (was born 1912 [1]). He was a general and statesman. He fought in both the first Indochina war (1946–1954) and second Indochina war (1960–1975).

His principal battles in both wars were Lang Son (1950), Hoa Binh (1951–1952), Dien Bien Phu (1954), Tet Offensive Dien Bien Phu (1968), the Nguyen Hue Offensive (known in the West as the Easter offensive) (1972), and the final Ho Chi Minh campaign (1975). He was also a journalist; he served as interior minister in President Ho Chi Minh's Vietminh government. He was military commander of the Vietminh, commander of the People's Army of Vietnam (PAVN), defense minister and politburo member of the Lao Dong Party.

Born in the village of An-Xa, Quang Bình, his father and mother, Vo Quang Nghiem and Nguyen Thi Kien, worked the land, rented some to neighbors, and lived a relatively comfortable life-style. At fourteen, he became a messenger for the Haiphong Power Company and, shortly thereafter, joined the Tân Việt Cách Mạng Đảng, a romantically styled revolutionary youth group. This would start his journey to becoming a revolutionary. Two years later, he entered Quốc Học, a French-run Lycee in Hue, the same one Ho Chi Minh attended; however, he was expelled for organizing a student strikes in 1933. According to his own account, he said that he enrolled in Hanoi University at the age of twenty-one.

Here he earned a bachelor's degree in political economy and a law degree. After graduation, he taught history for one year at the Thang Long School in Hanoi. During most of 1930s, he remained a schoolteacher and journalist, writing articles for *Tien Dang* while actively participating in various revolutionary movements. In 1931, he took part in several demonstrations against French rule in Indochina, as well as assisting in founding the Democratic Front in 1933. All the while, he was a dedicated reader of military history and philosophy, revering Napoleon I and son.

He was arrested in 1930 for actively participating in various revolutionary movements and served thirteen months of a two-year sentence at Lao Bao Prison. During the popular front years while he was in France, he founded *Hon Tre Tap Moi*, an underground socialist newspaper. He also founded the French language paper *Le Travail* (on which Pham Van Dong, future leader of communist Vietnam, also worked).

He married Nguyen Thi Quang Thi, another socialist, in 1939. When France outlawed communism during the same year, he fled to China together with Phạm Văn Đồng, where he joined up with Ho Chi Minh, the leader of the Vietnam Independence League (Vietminh). While he was in exile, his wife, sister, father, and sister-in-law were captured and executed.

He returned to Vietnam in 1944, and between then and 1945, he helped organize resistance to the Japanese occupation forces. When the Japanese surrendered to the United States in August 1945, the Japanese decided to allow nationalist groups to take over public buildings while keeping the French in prison as a way of causing additional trouble to the Allies in the postwar period. The Vietminh and other groups took over various towns and formed a provisional government in which he was named minister of the interior. This point in time, it appears to me that the communist leadership of Vietnam is now in place.

The Next Communist

Joseph Stalin, who will play an important part, is the leader of the Soviet Union and the country where Ho Chi Minh spent approximately seven to eight years of his life studying, teaching, and working toward the communist cause.

[H] Josef Vissarionovich Dzhugashvili, better known by his adopted name, Joseph Stalin, became the general secretary of the Communist party of the Soviet Union's Central committee from 1922 until his death in 1953. Although he lacked significant influence and his office was nothing more than one of several Central Committee Secretariats, his increasing control of the party from 1928 onward led to his becoming the de facto party leader and the dictator [2] of his country; this position enabled him to take full control of the Soviet Union and its people. (*De facto: acting or existing in fact but without legal sanction.*)

His crash programs of industrialization and collectivization in the 1930s, along with his ongoing campaigns of political repression, are estimated to have cost the lives of up to twenty million people by his hand or at least by his order.[3 In the 1930s, he initiated the great purge, a campaign of political repression, persecution, and executions that reached its peak in 1937.

My generation and I have not arrived yet, but these are some of the things that we were going to hear about as we are growing up.

Confiscations of grain and other food by the Soviet authorities under his orders contributed to a famine. This occurred especially in the key agricultural regions of the Soviet Union, Ukraine, Kazakhstan Stan, and North Caucasus. This resulted in millions of deaths. Many peasants resisted collectivization and grain confiscations but were repressed.

After the failure of Soviet and Franco-British talks on a mutual defense pact in Moscow, he began to negotiate a nonaggression pact with Hitler's Nazi Germany. In his speech on August 19, 1939, he prepared his comrades for the great turn in Soviet policy—the Molotov Ribbentrop pact with Nazi Germany. (*This also included Japan. Note the date; most of the people who will be fighting in Vietnam are not even born yet.*)

Although it is officially a nonaggression treaty only, the Molotov Ribbentrop pact had a *secret* annex in which Central Europe would be divided where two powers would have respective spheres of influence. Stalin was promised an eastern part of Poland, primarily populated with Ukrainians and Belorussians in case of its dissolution, if Lithuania, Latvia, Estonia, and Finland were recognized as parts of the Soviet sphere of influence. Another clause of the treaty was that Bessarabia, then part of Romania, was to be joined to the Moldovan ASSR and become the Moldovan SSR under control of Moscow.

Not to long after this treaty was signed on September 1, 1939, Germany would invade Poland, starting World War II. This is where Stalin decided to get involved, and on September 17, the Red Army entered eastern Poland and occupied the territory assigned to it by the Molotov-Ribbentrop Pact.

On March 5, 1940, the Soviet leadership under Stalin approved an order of execution of more than 25,700 Polish nationalist, educators, and counter revolutionary activists in the parts of the Ukraine and Belarus republics that had been annexed from Poland. This event has become known as the Katlyn Massacre.[21]

In June 1941, Hitler broke that pact with Stalin and invaded the Soviet Union in Operation Barbarossa. Although he was expecting war with Germany, he may not have expected an invasion to come so soon, and the Soviet Union was relatively unprepared for this invasion.

It is this little act of dishonor among thieves that brings Mrs. Stalin's little boy, Joey, looking for help in his newly found fight. That help comes in the form of the United States and Great Britain.

We were now in bed with the communist militarily, not politically. As I said before, love and war make strange bedfellows. The Allies, and now Stalin, shared a common enemy. Bearing the brunt of the Nazis' attacks (around 75 percent of the Wehrmacht's forces), the Soviet Union under his command made the largest and most decisive contribution to the defeat of Nazi Germany during World War II. (This is known in the USSR as the great patriotic war, 1941–45.)

After the war, he established the USSR. A position maintained for nearly four decades following his death in 1953. After the war, internationally, Stalin viewed Soviet consolidation of power as a necessary step to protect Russia by surrounding it with countries with friendly governments like the variety seen in Finland, to act as a *buffer* against possible invaders. *(The West sought a similar buffer against alleged Communist expansion. He had hoped that American withdrawal and demobilization would lead to increased communist influence, especially in Europe.)*

I don't know what it was that frayed relations between the Soviet Union and its former allies, but whatever it was, it led to a prolonged period of tension and distrust between East and West, and it is this distrust and tension that became known as the Cold War. The Red

Army ended World War II, occupying much of the territory that had been formerly held by the Axis countries.

In Asia, the Red Army had overrun Manchuria in the last month of the war and then also occupied Korea North of the thirty-eighth parallel. The Communist Party of China though receptive to minimal Soviet support, defeated the pro-Western and heavily American-assisted Chinese Nationalist Party in the Chinese Civil War.

I could be wrong, but I do not believe Stalin had any intention of being our ally politically or otherwise, and I believe the leaders of the Free World saw this also. The tentacles of Communism that disappeared in 1943 were now reaching out worldwide once again, and Ho Chi Minh, an ally to Stalin, is still at the head of one of those tentacles.

The people, who would become policy makers on the American side, were continually reacting to the Communists who were trying to spread their ideology throughout the world, much like Hitler tried to do with his master race. Although some had less involvement in the decision-making process than others, those decisions, bit by bit, would have something to do with leading us in and out of that war. Make no mistake; it was Ho Chi Minh that was initiating the actions. Our leadership was reacting to those actions. Not because uncle Ho was Vietnamese but rather that he was a Communist.

The Americans

[I]*Harry S. Truman* (May 8, 1884–December 26, 1972) was the thirty-third president of the United States (1945–1953); he was Franklin D. Roosevelt's vice president and he inherited the presidency after Roosevelt's death. During his terms in office, he used executive orders to begin desegregation of the US armed forces [4] and to launch a system of loyalty checks to remove thousands of Communist sympathizers from government office. It is because of this action that, I believe, he was not very fond of Communism, and because he wasn't, it would have something to do with the way he reacted to Ho Chi Minh.

[5] He did, however, strongly oppose mandatory loyalty oaths for governmental employees, [6] and this stance led to charges that his administration was soft on Communism. Here are two different actions surrounding communism that engendered two different opinions about this man.

Supposedly, corruption in his administration ran rampant; it is supposed to have reached as far as cabinet and senior White House levels; 166 of his appointees resigned or were fired in the aftermath of revelations of financial misbehavior in the Internal Revenue Service. [7] This allowed the Republicans to make corruption a central issue in the 1952 campaign.[8] His presidency is noted for being eventful in foreign affairs; however, starting with victory over Germany, the atomic bombing of Hiroshima and Nagasaki, the surrender of Japan at the end of World War II, the founding of the United Nations, the Marshall Plan to rebuild Europe, the Truman doctrine to contain Communism, the beginning of the Cold War, and the creation of NATO, the Korean War. This war became a frustrating stalemate, with over 30,000 Americans killed.[9]

Truman never claimed to have a personal expertise on foreign matters, and although the Republicans controlled Congress, he was able to win bipartisan support for both the Truman doctrine, which formalized a policy on Communism, and the Marshall Plan, which aimed to help rebuild postwar Europe.

To get Congress to spend the vast sums necessary to restart the moribund European economy, Truman used an ideological argument, arguing forcefully that Communism flourishes in deprived areas. His goal was to "scare the hell out of Congress."[45] To strengthen the US during the Cold War against Communism, Truman signed the National Security Act of 1947 and reorganized military forces by creating the Department of Defense, the CIA, the US Air Force (separate from the United States Army air forces, which was the Air Force under the US Army during World War II), and the National Security Council.

United States' involvement in Vietnam began during the Truman administration. On V-J Day 1945, Vietnamese Communist

Leader Ho Chi Minh declared independence from France, but the US announced its support of restoring French power.

It is 1945, and Truman is the last of the presidents that Ho Chi Minh will approach prior to the war with France. As mentioned earlier, charges of being soft on Communism were made because of his stand on loyalty oaths. I believe what a man says and what a man does are two different things. I may be cynical, but during my years on this planet, I have come to feel that most people never say what they mean or mean what they say, and the only way you can know what they say is true is by their actions. To coin an old phrase, "Put your money where your mouth is."

In his inaugural address (exhibit 3), which will be discussed at length later, Truman says a lot about his discontent with Communism. However, after South Korea is attacked by North Korean communist, Truman commits troops and money along with fifteen other nations from United Nations to the South Korean peninsula to fight Communism. At the same time, he also gives mutual aid to the French in their fight with the North Vietnamese communist. Whether you like the man or not, regarding this one issue, I would say that he "put his money where his mouth was."

Dwight David "Ike" Eisenhower, born David Dwight Eisenhower (October 14, 1890–March 28, 1969) was an American soldier and politician, who served as the thirty-fourth president of the United States (1953–1961). During World War II, he served as supreme commander of the Allied forces in Europe, with responsibility for planning and supervising the successful invasion of France and Germany in 1944–45. In 1951, he became the first supreme commander of North Atlantic Treaty Organization.[1] As a Republican, he was elected the thirty-fourth US president, serving for two terms. As president, he ended the Korean War, kept up the pressure on the Soviet Union during the Cold War, made nuclear weapons a higher defense priority, launched the space race, enlarged the Social Security program, and began the interstate highway system. Eisenhower, upon receiving a request from the South Vietnamese government to assist with the flow refugees heading south from North Vietnam, is the second president to assist that country with some form of aid.

[K] *John Fitzgerald Kennedy* (May 29, 1917-November 22, 1963), also referred to as John F. Kennedy, Jack Kennedy, or JFK, was the thirty-fifth president of the United States. In 1960, he became the youngest person ever to be elected president of the United States; he served from 1961 until his assassination in 1963. The Bay of Pigs invasion, the Cuban missile crisis, the building of the Berlin Wall, the space race, the American civil rights movement all took place during his presidency.

He was noted for his leadership as commander of US PT 109. During the Second World War in the South Pacific, he swam with an injured shipmate to a nearby island after his ship had been split in two by a Japanese gunboat attack. After the war, he turned his sights toward public service. He represented the state of Massachusetts as a member of the US House of Representatives from 1947 to 1953 and in the US Senate from 1953 until his inauguration in 1961.

In 1962, he would assign an intelligence gathering duty to the United States Navy known as the DESOTO patrols. He would also send sixteen thousand troops as advisers to South Vietnam to teach them military fighting tactics.

[L] *Lyndon Baines Johnson* (August 27, 1908-January 22, 1973), often referred to as LBJ, was the thirty-sixth president of the United States (1963-1969). After serving a lengthy career in the US Congress, in 1963, he succeeded President Kennedy after his assassination. He became the thirty-sixth president, and he was a major leader of the Democratic Party and, as president, was responsible for the designing of his Great Society, comprising of liberal legislation including civil rights laws, Medicare, Medicaid, aid to education, and a major war on poverty. Simultaneously, he escalated the American involvement in Vietnam, from sixteen thousand American soldiers in 1963 to five hundred fifty thousand in early 1968.

[M] *Richard Milhous Nixon* (January 9, 1913 to April 22, 1994) became the thirty-seventh president of the United States, serving from 1969 to 1974 and thirty-sixth vice president of the United States in the administration of Dwight D. Eisenhower (1953-1961). During the Second World War, he served as a Navy lieutenant commander in the Pacific before being elected to the Congress and later served as vice president. After an unsuccessful presidential campaign in 1960, Nixon was elected in 1968. In January 1973, he announced an accord with North Vietnam to end American involvement in Indochina. *(I have come to view this as a betrayal by our commander-in-chief of the time which I will explain later.)*

Here you have the major policy makers of the Vietnam War, making decisions based on actions and reactions. If we were not forced by circumstance to put ourselves onto the world stage due to global conflict, maybe we would not have had to fight in Vietnam. However, that did not occur.

Prior to World War I, we were an isolationist nation. That ended with our entering into that war. After the war, we became a member of the League of Nations. These actions, I would say, pretty much put us on the world stage. The League of Nations eventually fell apart. And once again, we became an isolationist nation. The start of World War II found many Americans wanting to continue in this way, whose minds were changed with the bombing of Pearl Harbor.

Once again, we would find ourselves engulfed in a fight to protect our freedoms as quoted in the Constitution, as well as helping our friends and allies defend their freedoms. This war catapulted us onto the world stage once again. However, those were times when our people and elected officials worked together as one and believed in the preservation of our freedoms, as well as the freedoms of our friends.

Ho Chi Minh had a quest that started when he was twenty-two years of age, and that quest was the only thing he had on his mind. That was to unify Vietnam under Communist rule and his command. One could argue that Ho Chi Minh had right since he was Vietnamese. This is true. However, there were plenty of Vietnamese who did not want to live under Communism, and I do not care how you look at it. Those Vietnamese had just as much right to oppose his form of political ideology.

This can only be clarified through investigation; it is important to show that the lies and propaganda, as well as the actions perpetrated by the leadership of the anti-war movement and their supporters, led to the betrayal of the troops, the loss of the Vietnam War, and, eventually, what I believe to be treason against the Constitution of the United States of America.

However, it is important to separate the facts from the lies. By doing this, it will show how the leadership of the anti-war movement and all their supporters could have been charged with treason.

Now that you have had a brief introduction to the people who would become the policy makers, let us put it into perspective. Let us examine how five presidents of the United States and those of us who served in Nam will come together in conflict with the Communists of which Ho Chi Minh is one. I intend to show through investigation and historical fact how the American people, the American media, the entertainment industry, and self-centered politicians hindered our effort in defending the Constitution—the very document that lists the rights that they so proudly claim and yet were so unwilling to defend. I intend to show that these people could have been charged with treason back as far as 1969 and where these charges could have been brought before a grand jury for possible indictment and brought to trial for successful prosecution.

I also intend to show how they betrayed the other six million veterans who served their country with honor during that period.

CHAPTER 3

EARLY COLD WAR

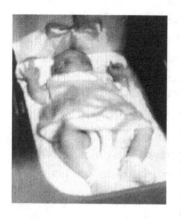

IT IS 1945 AND SOME of my generation has already arrived, with more yet to come. The month is June and I just arrived. President Truman is in office. The war in Europe just ended, and the war with Japan is about to end. The Cold War has started, but it will be two years before they officially call it the Cold War. In case you were wondering, that is me in the carriage. As you can see, I am not too concerned about world events yet. I am sure that the rest of my generation is not either. It is also my guess that we will not be for a while. However, as I said, history is relevant and many world events will take place in the next nineteen years that will lead some of us toward war and others toward what I believe to committing the unforgivable crime of treason.

These are my parents, Patrick and Agnes, and the benefactors who provided me with the gift of this nation that I live in. As I stated before, they were both Irish immigrants, and they were not here awfully long when this photo was taken. They were not rich, just a couple of hardworking people in a new land, trying to raise a family. I do not know what year my father became citizen. However, it was a decision that would make him an American by choice and my sister and I Americans by birth. The oath to become a citizen is remarkably interesting. It is not exceedingly long but says a lot about what an immigrant must give up and the responsibilities he or she agrees to accept upon making the choice to stay here and become a citizen. You do not get a lot, you don't get any promises, and you don't get any money (well, he didn't when he came on board). However, he did get one thing that I believe is more valuable than all those things put together. That thing is freedom to do with what he wanted. This is received by all who arrive on these shores. Or at least it used to be! It is entirely up to you as to where you take it. Therefore, it is entirely your responsibility whether it works out for you or not. However, there is a ton of people in this country and I can't really recollect at what point in my life where a good majority of them have come to blame you someone else or the government for everything bad that happens to them. Here is that oath. Naturalization Oath of Allegiance to the United States of America:

> I hereby declare, on oath, that I absolutely and entirely renounce and abjure all allegiance and fidelity to any foreign prince, potentate, state or sovereignty, of whom or which I have heretofore been a subject or citizen; that I will support and defend the Constitution and laws of the United States of America against all enemies, foreign and domestic; that I will bear true faith and allegiance to the same; that I will bear arms on behalf of the United States when required by the law; that I will perform noncombatant service in the armed forces of the United States when required by the law; that I will perform work of national importance under civilian direction when required by the law; and that I take this obligation freely without any mental reservation or purpose of evasion; so help me God.

I wonder how many people, when they take that oath, really pay attention to what they are saying. I wonder how many utterly understand what those words mean, what they are giving up, and what they are accepting. I believe my father did, especially by the way he reacted that day I called him that name. *("I gave you this country, you little bastard. It is mine by choice and I gave it to you.")* Although he never told me about his experience of becoming a citizen, somehow in a nonverbal and unobtrusive way, he passed the words of that oath he took down to me. I believe the same thing of most of the grandparents and parents of the guys and gals that I went to the Nam with. I hope you noticed that a considerable portion of that oath pertains to the defense of this country and its Constitution. They are asking those things from people who, for all intents and purposes, just recently arrived in this country, and I believe that the same thing was and is expected of those of us that are born here.

Did I mention that I had a sister? Her name is Maureen. She was the only child and six years my senior when I arrived. She and I are close; even back then, she was always looking after me. She told me that during the war years, she could remember my father serving as an air raid warden in New York. Although she was incredibly young, she could remember the air raid warnings, the blackouts, and the searchlights that scanned the night skies for enemy aircraft. She could also remember the rationing that went on to support the war during that period. Holy cow! American people, for the most part, united, supporting the government and the war effort. Wow, what a novelty. It makes me wish that I were born sooner so that I could have witnessed that. I only remember hearing and reading about those things. Before I get too far off the beaten path, let us get back to the journey my generation is about to embark upon.

History will show that June, July, and August of 1945 that the Soviet Union (Joseph Stalin), Great Britain (Winston Churchill), and the United States (Harry Truman) at the Potsdam Conference where they decided what would happen to the postwar world. This also included what would happen in Vietnam. It was decided by these three individuals that Chinese and British troops should be sent to Indochina, specifically Vietnam, to disarm the Japanese. The Chinese would be north of the sixteenth parallel and the British south of it.

[N] On August 14, 1945, the Japanese surrendered to the Allies. In Indochina, the Japanese officials took advantage of the situation to cause additional problems for the Allies. Violating the surrender agreements, they helped Vietnamese nationalist groups, including the Việt Minh (led by Ho Chi Minh), to take over public buildings in various cities.

[M] Bảo Đại (October 22, 1913-July 30, 1997) was the thirteenth and last ruler of the Nguyen Dynasty. He served as king of Annam from 1926 until 1945 and as emperor of Vietnam and, until 1945, as a puppet ruler for the Japanese. On August 25, 1945, he was forced to abdicate in favor of Ho Chi Minh.

Seven days after Ho Chi Minh would force Bao Dai to abdicate his throne, he would try something different in his quest to gain power in Vietnam and take over as the leader of that country. I believe this is where the investigation should begin because it is at this point in history regarding Vietnam where those laws of Sir Isaac Newton mentioned earlier come into effect, which is action versus reaction. This is where those actions and reactions can be backed up with proof and documentation, such as uncle Ho's formal declaration of independence and his written telegram (exhibit 00 and exhibit 1) to Harry S. Truman as mentioned earlier.

[N] Ho Chi Minh's new government only lasted a few days. At the Potsdam Conference, the Allies, which included Russia, decided that Vietnam would be occupied jointly by China and Britain, which would supervise the disarmament and repatriation of Japanese forces. [14] The Chinese army arrived a few days after Hồ's declaration of independence. Ho Chi Minh's government effectively ceased to exist. The Chinese took control of the area north of the sixteenth parallel. British forces arrived in the south in October. In the same month that Ho Chi Minh proclaimed himself in charge of Vietnam, the French would return on September 22, 1945, to reclaim what they thought belonged to them since 1887. It is been three months since my arrival, and the events in Vietnam will slow down pretty much for the rest of the year.

However, with the coming of 1946, things will start to heat up in Vietnam. February of 1946, Ho Chi Minh sends the telegram mentioned earlier to President Truman, requesting assistance with getting rid of the French government from Vietnam. However, Truman did not recognize Ho Chi Minh's government, and that, coupled with the fact that Ho Chi Minh is a Communist, Truman ignored him. Keep in mind that Communism and capitalism have been at odds since 1917 right after the Russian Revolution, twenty-nine years prior to this telegram.

Historical fact has it that French officials immediately sought to reassert control. They negotiated with the Chinese. By agreeing to give up its concessions in China, the French persuaded the Chinese to allow them to return to the north and negotiate with the Vietminh. Ho Chi Minh negotiated with the French to get the Chinese out of North Vietnam. He also signed a written agreement (exhibit 2) with France which, as you will see, he apparently had no intention of keeping.

[N] Nine months after this accord was signed, the First Indochina War would begin. On December 19, 1946, the Vietminh, under Ho Chi Minh's leadership, launched a rebellion against the French authority governing the colonies of French Indochina. The first few years of the war were a low-level rural insurgency against French authority. However, after the Chinese communists reached the northern border of Vietnam in 1949, the conflict became a conventional war between two armies equipped with modern weapons. These were supplied by the Chinese communist and Russian communist.

This war would keep Ho Chi Minh and the Vietnam Communist Party busy for the next eight years. [N] At the beginning of the war, the US was neutral in the conflict because of our opposition to imperialism and colonialism that we avoided helping colonial empires regain their power and influence, and because the Vietminh had recently been our allies, and because most of our attention was focused on Europe where Winston Churchill argued that an iron curtain had fallen. This was the beginning of the Cold War.

 While Uncle Ho and the French were settling in for a nice long war, the rest of the world was continuing. This year would find nine countries that would fall to Communism. There were seven in January. *(Yugoslavia modeled their new constitution after the Soviet Union's, which also established six constituent republics: Bosnia Herzegovina, Croatia, Macedonia, Montenegro, Serbia, and Slovenia.)* There was the one in March *(a Communist-dominated government under Petru Groza assumed power in Romania).* The last one was in October *(a Communist takeover in Bulgaria)*, making it a total of nine. Although Vietnam is not quite there, it is en route to the same location. At this stage of the game, I'm sixteen months old and just starting to get to know the guy standing next to me, my father; at this point, I'm not even thinking of becoming a Marine, let alone going to Vietnam.

 This is my sister and I at this point in history. The year 1947 would find that two more countries would succumb to Communism. January 31, Communists take power in Poland. August 31, Communists take power in Hungary. In retrospect, even though I do not remember these years, I can see why Harry Truman, being an American president, would be concerned about the Communist aggression that was starting to spread throughout the world, causing him to implement the Truman Doctrine, which deals with Communist containment. This is where an American president is looking to protect the interests of this country outlined in the top secret document NSC 68.

While the war raged on in Vietnam, 1948 would find that on February 25, the Communist party would seize control of Czechoslovakia. This makes number twelve since I was born. I will be three years old in June. President Harry Truman will sign the Marshall Plan, which authorizes $5 billion in aid for sixteen countries. June 24, the Soviets will begin the Berlin blockade. [M] Because of the city's location, the French, American, and British sectors of Berlin were surrounded by the Soviet occupation zone.

The three Western-held sectors of Berlin quickly became a focal point of tensions corresponding to the breakdown of the US-Soviet wartime alliance. At this point in history, Truman issues the second peacetime military draft in the United States because of increasing tensions with the Soviet Union (the first peacetime draft occurred in 1940 under President Roosevelt).

In October 1949, the mainland of China will fall to Communism. This makes the thirteenth country since I was born that will become a Communist country. I am still three years old. On May 12, the Soviets will lift the Berlin Blockade. And in June, when I turn four years old, the last US troops will leave South Korea. The reason our troops were there was to gather up the remaining Japanese troops that were still there. We were south of the thirty-eighth parallel, and the Soviets were north. American and Soviet negotiators hastily agreed to this administrative division in August 1945. However, as tensions between the two superpowers intensified, these tensions grew into a political division of the country. In the north, Soviet-educated Kim Il Sung was installed as the leader of a provisional government while, in the south, American-educated Syngman Rhee was elected president of the Republic of Korea. By 1948, the nation was divided between two opposing political systems, each claiming to represent all the Korean people. In 1949, American combat forces were withdrawn, leaving behind little more than a poorly equipped Korean defense force. In comparison, the north had a well-trained Army, which was supplied and trained by the Soviet Union. In mid-1949, Kim Il Sung of North Korea conferred with Joseph Stalin who, at the time, had come to discuss a reunification of Korea. Sung needed Soviet support to successfully execute an offensive. However, Stalin, as leader of the communist bloc, refused permission because he was concerned with the preparedness of the North Korean armed forces and with possible US involvement. The North Korean military was equipped with outdated Soviet weaponry, yet it was way better equipped than the southern forces in every category of equipment.

With the arrival of 1950, Kim Il Sung visited Stalin in March and April to plead his case once again; this time, Stalin approved. So shortly after my fifth birthday, the North Korean Army struck in the predawn hours of Sunday, June 25, 1950; they crossed the thirty-eighth parallel behind a firestorm of artillery. [15]. I think that it is important to note that World War II ended only five years prior to this attack.

Regarding the Vietnam issue, in February 1950, Ho met with Mao Tse-tung in Moscow after he recognized his government. They all agreed that now Communist China would be responsible for backing the Vietminh [9]. Mao's emissary to Moscow advised that China planned to train sixty thousand to seventy thousand Vietminh.[10] China's support enabled Ho to escalate the fight against France.

In May 1950, Chinese communist forces captured Hainan Island; President Harry Truman began covertly authorizing direct financial assistance to the French. After the outbreak of the Korean War, Truman announced to the American public that he was doing so. At the time, it was a consensus of the United States government that if Ho Chi Minh were to win the war, with his ties to the Soviet Union, he would establish a puppet state with Moscow and the Soviets would ultimately control Vietnamese affairs. The prospect of a communist-dominated Southeast Asia was enough to spur the US to support France so that the spread of Soviet communism could be contained.

[N] On June 30, 1950, the first US supplies for Indochina were delivered. In September, Truman sent the Military Assistance Advisory Group (MAAG-1) to Indochina to assist the French. The US government gradually began supporting the French in their war effort using the Mutual Defense Assistance Act; by doing this, they were trying to stabilize the French Fourth Republic in which the French Communist Party created by Ho Chi Minh himself was a significant political force.

The Mutual Defense Assistance Act, commonly known as the Battle Act, was a 1949 law passed by the United States (exhibit 3A). This act was created after Mao Tse-tung's Communist Party of China defeated the nationalist Chinese in the Chinese Civil War. The act was part of the American Cold War strategy of containment. The act had several sections. Most importantly, it promised defense assistance to any ally that might be attacked by the Soviet Union or one of its allies. It also cut off all aid and economic assistance to any country that traded in strategic materials with the Soviet Union or its allies. The act covered a wide range of materials needed to produce weapons and was especially focused on anything that could aid atomic weapons research and construction (see exhibit 3A).

History shows massive support was negotiated with France between 1950 and 1954. Support included massive financial aid, material supply from the US Army, US Navy, and the CIA. This pretty much takes care of the events that took place in Southeast Asia for the year 1950.

The United States, as well as our allies in Europe, were very much concerned about the communist aggression that was taking place throughout the world. Besides the war in Vietnam, sixteen countries from United Nations, along with the United States, were engaged in the Korean War.

[M] Anti-Communist countries were Republic of Korea, Belgium, Australia, Canada, Colombia, Ethiopia, France, Greece, Luxembourg, Netherlands, New Zealand, Philippines, South Africa, Thailand, Turkey, United Kingdom, and the United States. Communist countries include North Korea, China, supported by United Soviet Socialist Republics.

Based on these well-known facts, it is important at this time to point out that there were quite a few people in this world that were opposed to communism. It is five years since I've been born, and in the five years since the end of the Second World War, a good portion of the world powers finds itself once again engaged in a major conflict in what they apparently felt was an evil aggressor. The ideology behind that aggression is communism. At this point of my life, I am not paying attention to world affairs and only beginning to become aware of my home life.

However, since my birth, thirteen countries have already fallen to communism, including China, one of the combatants in the Korean War. The communists are trying to acquire two more through violence. At the head of one of those two communist tentacles is a guy by the name of Ho Chi Minh.

In the early part of 1951, February 1 to be exact, the United Nations General Assembly declares that North Korea is the aggressor in the Korean War. Another major event that will take place occurs on September 1. The United States, Australia, and New Zealand all sign a mutual defense pact called the ANZUS Treaty (for "Australia, New Zealand, United States") (exhibit 4).

The treaty came about following the close cooperation of the United States, Australia, and New Zealand during World War II, during which time Australia had come remarkably close to being invaded by Japan. Following the end of World War II, the United States was eager to normalize relations with Japan since the Korean War was still raging a short distance from Japan.

With the involvement of China and, possibly, the Soviet Union in Korea, the Cold War was threatening to become a full-scale war. However, Australia and New Zealand were extremely reluctant to finalize a peace treaty with Japan, which would allow for Japanese rearmament.

Both countries relented only when an Australian and New Zealand proposal for a three-way security treaty was accepted by the United States. The resulting treaty was concluded at San Francisco on September 1, 1951, and entered into force on April 29, 1952. The treaty bound the signatories to recognize that an armed attack in the Pacific area on any of them would endanger the peace and safety of the others. It stated, "The Parties will consult together whenever in the opinion of any of them the territorial integrity, political independence, or security of any of the Parties is threatened in the Pacific."

I will have turned six years old by the end of 1951, and in that six-year period, the world will lose thirteen countries to communism. President Truman will introduce the Truman Doctrine, which deals with communist containment. He will also implement the Marshall Plan which gives aid to sixteen countries. The Soviets will begin and end the Berlin Blockade. Truman will issue the second peacetime military draft in the United States amid increasing tensions with the Soviet Union. Ho Chi Minh will meet with Stalin and Mao in

Moscow after the Soviet Union recognized his government. They all agreed that China would be responsible for backing the Vietminh. After the outbreak of the Korean War, Truman will announce publicly that the US is backing the French in the Vietnam War.

In this six-year period of my life, two more major events will take place. The United States will have signed a mutual defense act with the governments of Cambodia, France, Laos, and Vietnam and will also have signed a security treaty with Australia and New Zealand known as the ANZUS Treaty (see exhibit 4).

All this since World War II, and I am not aware of any of it. I believe that I can safely say that the rest of my generation is not either. In retrospect, I can look back at these historical events and determine that the American government that just came out of a vicious war with the Nazi and Fascist and the Japanese were now trying to protect us and our friends from another aggressor—Communism. Believe me, it will not end here, and history is relevant.

CHAPTER 4

BECOMING AWARE

YEAR 1952 WAS A YEAR that would come up and hit me in the face like a bucket of freezing water. On May 29, my sister and I were at my aunt and uncle's apartment. We were sitting at the kitchen table. Well, my sister was sitting, and I was standing on the chair at the other end of the table. It was afternoon when my father, aunt, and uncle walked in the door from visiting my mother in the hospital. I am not sure, but I think it was my uncle who went over to my sister and whispered in her ear. I saw the expression on her face change and what I think is the first of two times that I ever heard my sister swear in her life. She said, "You're a goddamn liar." He smacked her face, and she started crying. I did to because I knew my mother was gone. She had been in and out of the hospital for years.

They would not let me go to the wake, which I think occurred the day before my birthday, or the funeral, which occurred on my seventh birthday. For years, I always thought, or hoped I guess, I would walk around a corner and my mother would be there. She never showed. I think I was into my early manhood before I gave up that notion of her ever coming back. I think it was this event in my life that made me more aware of my surroundings. It has allowed my memory to be more acute. I cannot get everything right, but it is like looking in an album. I have a lot of clear pictures of my life back to that time.

With my sister in school, my father working, and me getting sick all the time, it dictated me, staying at my aunt Mary's; she was my mother's sister. This necessitated me completing kindergarten and attending first grade at St. Frances Roman Catholic School.

History tells us that some of the world events that were occurring at that point in time were that President Truman announced that he would not seek another term as president. The Marshall Plan, the Korean War, and the First Indochina War (Vietnam) were still going strong. In November of that year, Dwight D. Eisenhower became the president-elect, and he traveled to Korea find out what could be done to end that conflict.

This is my sister and I a year later in 1953 when she graduated from eighth grade. I was still staying with my aunt. I would spend the weekends with her and my father. I remember that I was always anxious for the weekends to arrive so that I could be with them, not that I wasn't treated well at my aunt's; it was just that I needed to be with my sister and father. I remember that the place they were renting had an old icebox rather than a refrigerator. Every weekend, my father would give me paint and I would paint that icebox. By the time we left New York, it must have had forty coats of paint on it. This was when I was most happy, being there with them. It is the little things in life, I guess. I think it was right about this time in our lives when my sister took on the added responsibility of playing a mothers' role when it came to my well-being, but I think that she always felt a need to look after me; she still does. I tease her all the time that I do not think that she ever had a childhood because she was always looking after me.

This is a photograph of my first-grade class at St. Frances in 1953. I, for one, cannot ever remember standing in the playground or in the halls of the school, discussing the war in Indochina or the war in Korea. I think it is safe for me to say that any of the other guys depicted here were not discussing these things either in school or at home. However, I do remember having air-raid drills. The bell would ring, and everyone would be ushered into the hall where we would kneel on the floor with our hands over our heads. We were told that we were doing this because of a possible conflict with the communists. I think that this was where I started to develop a dislike for those guys. It would not be too long before the schools stopped these air-raid drills. With the development of nuclear weapons, I guess they figured that it would be just as easy for us to melt at our desks working as it would be bent over in the halls. I kind of missed the drills myself; it gave us an extra break from the classroom, but then I was not a particularly good student. I have heard it said that those of us that went to the Nam represented 12 percent of our generation; if that is the case, at least four people from this photograph would make that journey. I know for a fact that one would, but that story will come a little later.

[D] On February 11, 1953, President Eisenhower would refuse a clemency appeal for Ethel and Julius Rosenberg. Julius Rosenberg (May 12, 1918-1919 53) and Ethel Greenglass Rosenberg (September 28, 1915–June 19, 1953). They were communists who received international attention when they were executed for passing nuclear weapons secrets to the Soviet Union [1]. I believe many people in this country are under the impression that these two people were convicted and executed for treason. However, that would not be a true statement. They were charged with espionage and convicted and executed for that.

The very next month, March 1953, Joseph Stalin would die after twenty-six years of ruling the Soviet Union. Nikita Khrushchev would be selected general secretary of the Soviet communist party. In July, Castro and his brother lead a disastrous assault on the Moncada barracks, which becomes the preliminary event to the Cuban Revolution. On July 27, the Korean War ends. The United States, the People's Republic of China, North Korea, and South Korea sign an armistice agreement.

Out of that war, twenty-one American soldiers that were prisoners of war will fail to repatriate to America, and they will move to China.

Was this along with the betrayal of this country by the Rosenberg's an indication of the direction that this country was heading?

I think it was. However, this would not become apparent to me until it was too late. I do remember asking my father why the soldiers did not return to America. I remember him saying it was probably because they were brainwashed during captivity as prisoners of war, but he did not understand either. I have recently heard that twenty of the twenty-one soldiers have returned to the United States for one reason or another, mostly for health reasons. It is also my belief that it shouldn't have been allowed.

On October 30, President Eisenhower formally approved the top secret document to National Security Council paper number 162/2 wherein nuclear weapons must be maintained and expanded to counter the communist threat. On November 29, French paratroopers take Dien Bien Phu. This will be the beginning of the end of the French in Indochina. These events bring 1953 to a close.

I had just turned eight years old when the war in Korea ended. The television, which became commercially available during the late 1930s, had improved quite a bit by the 1950s. I remember my aunt owned one, but my father, sister, and I did not. However, we had a radio; both these inventions would play a big part in my becoming aware. I do not believe we got a TV until we moved to New Jersey. I can remember asking my father about things that I would hear on the radio or TV, especially things that would worry me. Things like war and Hitler and communists. I also remember the teachers in school mentioning these things from time to time. However, although I was not totally grasping the whole picture, I knew these things were happening, but I wasn't grasping the why and how of it.

Looking back in history, it seems to me that World War II created a much larger part for us to play in the world. We had proven ourselves to be a world power, and because of our efforts during World War II, people around the globe were looking to us for assistance and, in some cases, guidance.

Year 1954 would be witness to many events, but one specific event would be the war in Vietnam. Things were looking bad for the French, so on February 10, President Eisenhower, after authorizing

$385 million over the $400 million already budgeted for military aid to Vietnam, then warned against United States intervention in Vietnam. This contradiction between his actions and his words is a good indication that, at this point in his life, he may have transformed from a soldier mode to a politician mode; at least to me that is what the indication appeared to be. I believe the warning against intervention was because this country had just come out of two major wars with in thirteen years, and he did not think the American people were ready for another war. However, that is just speculation on my part. It would be two months later, April 7, that he would give his "domino theory" speech during a news conference, where he says, [D] "Finally, you have broader considerations that might follow what you would call the 'falling domino' principle. You have a row of dominoes set up, you knock over the first one, and what will happen to the last one is the certainty that it will go over very quickly. So you could have a beginning of a disintegration that would have the most profound influences."

My understanding of that quote would be, if Vietnam falls, all Southeast Asia falls.

There were and are people in this country that argue against this theory. [D] The primary evidence against the domino theory has been the failure of communism to take hold in Thailand, Indonesia, and several other large Southeast Asian countries after the end of the Vietnam War, as Eisenhower's speech warned it could.

[D] The critics of this theory charged that the Indochinese wars were largely indigenous or nationalist in nature (such as the Vietnamese driving out the French). I will concede the fight against France was indigenous. However, I believe there were more nationalists Vietnamese who did not want to live under communism. Critics who say that it was nationalist in nature fail to mention that the CPV (Communist Party Vietnam) was being aided by other communist countries, like Communist China and the USSR. As far as the statement that no such monolithic force as world communism existed is a total bullshit statement. Fourteen countries had already fallen to communism since World War II had ended.

When I am listening to these critics, I am not quite sure of what odor I am detecting, but I believe these opponents and critics have a distinct odor of Commie. It is my opinion the people who would believe this are (1) either communists, (2) dupes for the communists, or (3) simply people who should consider giving some immediate thought to leaving the arduous task of examining their colons to their proctologist and pull their collective heads out of their collective asses and look around.

I think that this would be an appropriate time to introduce an individual who has played a key role in the war against France and us.

[P] His name is Bui Tin. He was born 1927 near Hanoi. At the age of eighteen, Colonel Bui Tin joined Ho Chi Minh's revolution at the end of World War II in 1945. In 1965, he became a commentator for the daily *Quan Doi Nhan Dan* and the theoretical *Journal of Communism*.

After the Paris agreements of 1973, he was made part of the Quadripartite Military Commission to supervise the cease-fire and withdrawal of the American troops. Two years later, he was present in Saigon, being the highest-ranking officer in the CVP, he was ordered to accept the unconditional surrender of the South Vietnamese government. Since that time, he has written a book, *From Enemy to Friend*. The book is written in a question-and-answer format. I intend to use this book as written testimony from an individual who not only played a major part in both wars but, more specifically, was also on the other side.

Statement of Col. Bui Tin from his book *From Enemy to Friend*:

Page 4:

> [P] When I was a young soldier and a junior officer, I took it for granted that ours was a sacred and righteous cause, that what we did was correct because it was a national salvation effort. We were fighting against foreign aggression and occupation of our national territory by foreign troops. Nothing could be clearer or simpler. At a later stage, when I had been further educated and

indoctrinated by the Communist Party to become a faithful communist, I saw the struggle as a war waged to protect the whole socialist camp—consisting of the Soviet Union, Communist China, and the Eastern European people's democracies, plus North Korea and Cuba, and later Ethiopia, Nicaragua, and Angola—against U.S. led imperialist aggression.

Page 11:

Let me add that the CPV leaders have always considered Indochina as one geographical entity and single battlefield, relegating the Pathit Lao (Laotian's) and the Khmer People's Party (Cambodians) to subordinate positions under a single leader, Ho Chi Minh. The internationalist duty that the CPV arrogates to itself has always been to communize first the whole Indochinese Peninsula and then the rest of Southeast Asia.

The critics of the domino theory also argued that there was no monolithic force known as world communism. This makes me wonder what these anal probers would call Col. Bui Tin's statement from page 4. Oh! Wait! Wait! Maybe they were thinking that it was a friendly gathering of the hammer and sickle society. Could I be mistaken? Or did Colonel Tin mention four other countries that would eventually be added to the Communist fold besides the fourteen countries that have already fallen to Communism by the year 1954, making it a grand total of eighteen.

[D] Some critics have charged that the theory was used as a propaganda scare tactic to try to justify unwarranted intervention policies.

Theory is defined as a set of circumstances or principles that are hypothetical, a set of facts, propositions, or principles analyzed in their relation to one another and used, especially in science, to explain phenomena.

In other words, a theory is a guess. However, Col. Bui Tins' statement from page 11, I believe, changes Eisenhower's domino theory from a guess to a fact because that was their intent all along.

Enough said about the domino theory because 1954 would see a lot of activity regarding the Southeast Asian Hemisphere. On March 13, French troops engage the Vietminh at Dien Bien Phu, and on March 23, Vietminh captures the main airstrip of Dien Bien Phu and the French forces are partially isolated. On April 16, Vice President Richard Nixon announced that the United States may be "putting our own boys in Indochina regardless of Allied support." However, on May 7, Dien Bien Phu ends in a French defeat, and this will end the First Indochina War.

When both countries decided that the war would end, the Geneva conference which was held on July 20, 1954, between France and North Vietnam and known as the (Agreement on the Cessation of Hostilities in Vietnam) (exhibit 6). Part of this agreement partitioned Vietnam into North Vietnam and pro-Western South Vietnam. It was decided that Hanoi and Saigon would be the respective capitals. I think that this is an appropriate time to point out that it was an agreement between the French and the communists that split Vietnam into two countries. This split also occurred at the urging of one of the Chinese communist leaders, Zhou Enlai. This is reiterated in Col. Bui Tin's book *From Enemy to Friend*. As soon as that action occurred, I would say that Vietnam's and Ho Chi Minh's fight for independence was complete.

Statement of Col. Bui Tin from his book *From Enemy to Friend*:

Chronology, page 174:
> [P] On July 4, Chinese premier Zhou Enlai met with Ho Chi Minh and General Vo Nguyen Giap in Liao Zhou, Guangxi to persuade them to accept the division of Vietnam at the seventeenth parallel.

Chronology, page 174:
> [P] July 20 The Geneva agreements split Vietnam
> at the 17th parallel into North Vietnam, with
> Hanoi and Saigon as the respective capitals.

Regarding Col. Bui Tin's statement of July 4, 1954, I guess I would only have one question. Why would communist Chinese leader Zhou Enlai request Ho Chi Minh to accept the split of North and South Vietnam? At this point, I guess we will never know. However, I believe this set the wheels in motion toward our further involvement there.

The reason I show this photo of my buddy Tom and me as representation of the general age of my generation, we were nine years old and North Vietnam had just fallen to the communists, making that the fifteenth country to do so. However, I can tell you from recollection that we had no idea that this event had just occurred, and as I recall, I don't think we cared. Another little-known event also occurred that year.

Following the partition of Vietnam, there was a mass exodus of North Vietnamese to the South. [D] It has long been claimed that during the early years of Ho's government, 900,000 to 1 million Vietnamese, mostly Catholic, left for South Vietnam while 130,000, mostly Vietminh personnel, went from South to North. [15] [16] However, more recent research has indicated that the number of civilian refugees involved was much smaller than originally claimed, with some 450,000 moving from North to South and 52,000 moving in the opposite direction. [17]

Although this migration was allowed under the Geneva Agreement for 300 days, Canadian observers claimed that some were forced by North Vietnamese authorities to remain against their will. *(Naaaa! Come on! Do you really think the Commies would do that?)* Although there is a disparity in the number of people who were moving across the border, it does not really matter. The ratio is still 9 to 1 moving south. Regardless of the reason, the action should tell you something, like more people wanted to be free than not.

Because of this migration, a request of the American government was made by the government of South Vietnam to assist with the transportation of these refugees from the north to the south. This is indicated in a note from the government of South Vietnam to the American Embassy on August 6, 1954 (exhibit 5). This is also further reiterated in a letter from President Eisenhower to President Diệm on October 23, 1954 (exhibit 5A).

A few more major events would take place before 1954 would end. On September 8, the Southeast Asia Treaty Organization (SEATO) was established in Bangkok, Thailand (exhibit 7).

SEATO was organized that year under the Southeast Asia Collective Defense Treaty by representatives of Australia, France, Great Britain, New Zealand, Pakistan, the Philippines, Thailand, and the United States. It was established under Western auspices after the French withdrawal from Indochina.

SEATO was created to oppose further Communist gains in Southeast Asia. The treaty was supplemented by a Pacific charter, affirming the rights of Asian and Pacific peoples to equality and self-determination and setting forth goals of economic, social, and cultural cooperation between the member countries.

The civil and military organizations established under the treaty had their headquarters in Bangkok, Thailand. SEATO relied on the military forces of member nations and joint maneuvers were held annually. SEATO's principal role was to sanction the US presence in Vietnam although France and Pakistan withheld support, unable to intervene in Laos or Vietnam due to its rule of unanimity.

Again, history will show, in the first few years after the war with the French, the North, with an underdeveloped industrial economy and cut off from the agricultural areas of the South, became repressive and totalitarian.

Between 1953 and 1956, agrarian reforms were attempted due to Chinese pressure. In the process, tens of thousands of landowners were publicly denounced as landlords (địa chủ), and their lands were distributed to those considered loyal to the party. Of the 44,444 landlords, 3,939 were tried and 1,175 were executed.[2] A literary movement called *Nhân văn-Giai phẩm* (from the names of the two magazines which started the movement) attempted to encourage the democratization of the country and the free expression of thought. This resulted in a purge in which many intellectuals and writers were sent to reeducation camps because they did not agree with the government. *(This is what much of my generation in America would soon come to support!)*

On October 11, the Vietminh took control of North Vietnam, and major events in Vietnam for the year 1954 came to an end.

On February 12, 1955, President Eisenhower sent the first US advisers to South Vietnam, which is believed to be eight hundred men, establishing Military Assistance Advisory Group 5 (MAAG-V) in Saigon.

In 1956, because of the Geneva conference, Vietnam was supposed to have elections to reunify the country as agreed to between the French and Ho Chi Minh. Let me reiterate this, the French and Ho Chi Minh. Let me also reiterate, the South Vietnamese government and the United States were not involved in that decision-making process. This means that the South Vietnamese government was not obligated to abide by that agreement. When the South Vietnamese refused to have the elections, the Vietminh cadres, who were directed to stay behind in the south after the split by Ho Chi Minh, were activated and started to fight the government. The Vietminh, also known as the NLF (National Liberation Front), would eventually become known as the Vietcong, or affectionately known to us as Charlie.

This was also addressed by then Sen. John F. Kennedy at the friends of Vietnam luncheon conference in Washington, DC, on June 1, 1956 (exhibit 8). It is here that then Senator Kennedy asked of the South Vietnamese to hold out against the Communists. It is also around this time North Vietnam also invaded and occupied portions of Laos to assist in supplying the National Liberation Front in South Vietnam (Vietminh/Vietcong). This supply line became known as the Ho Chi Minh Trail. The Vietcong acted as a guerilla force.

Let us examine that. Ho Chi Minh, with the urging of the Chinese Communists, splits Vietnam in two. He has won his independence from France; he oversees his own nation. He has accomplished what he had set out to do thirty-seven years earlier in 1919. However, he is not satisfied with that. He now activates guerilla insurgents in South Vietnam and invades the neutrality of another nation (Laos) to help supply his mission. I do not see much difference between him doing that and Kim Il Sung launching a full-scale invasion of South Korea in 1950.

It was a bold-faced act of aggression by Ho Chi Minh to force the people of South Vietnam to live the way he wanted them to live against their will. I guess the way Ho Chi Minh did it made it more latent in appearance to the world in general. Or maybe it was that the world just did not care anymore? However, America had its eyes on it. America, by multiple treaties with Vietnam and other nations of the Southeast Asian region, was obligated by treaty to help protect that region of the world.

However, Vietnam was not the only place in the world that Communism was thrusting its authority on people by force and violence. At the same time Vietnam was starting to boil, another communist aggression was occurring in Europe. On October 23, 1956, the Hungarian revolution would begin against the pro-Soviet government. Hungary would attempt to leave the Warsaw Pact. This caused the Soviet Union to intervene. On October 26, the Red Army troops would invade Hungary. On November 4, more Soviet troops would invade Hungary to crush the revolt in which thousands are killed, more are wounded, and nearly a quarter million leave the country.

By November 14, fighting ends in Hungary. I only mention this because I remember watching news footage about this on TV. I remember asking myself why we, America, did not go over there and help the Hungarians. That question was never answered, but this was one of the world events, I believe, helped develop the direction that I was heading in life. I was paying attention to this. Did not the rest of my generation see these things occurring? If they did, didn't they care, or did they think that the communists were right?

I was eleven years old; I think it was now that I developed a fear, but more than that, I developed a real hate of the communists. In my midtwenties, while serving with the New Jersey State Police, I would meet one of the individuals that would leave or rather escape that country. His name is Frank Nemith; he was a brother trooper.

He was the same age as me when he and his family escaped; the difference is, I was playing ball while he was trying to escape Tierney. I could only imagine at age eleven how frightening that was. He told me stories of escaping over the mountains at night on foot into refugee camps in Austria. He also told me that he saw his mother beaten by government officials because she had a few ears of corn hidden in the attic to feed her family.

He also said that he remembered that the Hungarian people indicated that they wanted the Americans to come and help them. He also had a great disdain for these people known as communists. I always knew that fighting in Vietnam against communist aggression was the right thing to do, but the stories that Frank told me just confirmed it. This would be the most notarized communist event of 1956.

On January 5, 1957, President Eisenhower, in an address to Congress, proposed offering military assistance to Middle Eastern countries so they could resist Communist aggression; this became known as the Eisenhower Doctrine. Here was the second president since World War II whose major concern would be communist aggression.

Years 1958 and 1959 did not give much notoriety to events developing in Vietnam. However, communists were active in other parts of the world. One of those places happened to be ninety miles off the coast of Florida.

On April 3, 1958, Castro's revolutionary army began its attack on Havana. On August 23 of the same year, in the Chinese Civil War, the second Taiwan Strait crisis began with the Chinese communists' bombardment of Quemoy. On January 4, 1959, in Cuba, rebel troops led by Che Guevara and Camilo Cienfuegos enter the city of Havana. And on January 6, Fidel Castro arrives in Havana.

Just to show you how fooled we were by Fidel Castro, On January 7, the United States recognizes the new Cuban government of Fidel Castro, and on February 16, Fidel Castro becomes premier of Cuba. However, history shows that Fidel Castro apparently had our government hoodwinked. The United States would not find this out until 1960 when Castro shows his face as a communist.

Year 1960 will arrive on the scene with US Senator John F. Kennedy (D-MA) announcing on January 3 that he is a candidate for the Democratic nomination for president. On March 6, the United States advised 3,500 American soldiers will be sent to Vietnam. This is under President Eisenhower. Another Cold War event took place on May 1 when a Soviet missile shoots down an American Lockheed U2 spy plane. The pilot, Francis Gary Powers, was captured.

On June 6, US Senator John F. Kennedy won the California Democratic primary. On August 19, in Moscow, Francis Gary Powers is sentenced to ten years' imprisonment by the Soviet Union for espionage. On November 8, the United States presidential election is a close race. However, John F. Kennedy is elected over Richard M. Nixon, becoming the youngest man elected as president of the United States.

Year 1960 would end, and yet another president is elected to take over the task of running the country, which makes him number three since the end of World War II. However, there remains that constant in Vietnam (Ho Chi Minh) who is continuing his efforts to spread Communism to the rest of Vietnam even though it was made quite clear by President Diem in 1956 that he did not want Communism in South Vietnam, and another year would pass, bringing me a little closer to spending some time in that danger zone.

World events for the year 1961 will force the outgoing and incoming presidents to make some crucial decisions regarding us and Communism. By the time this year rolled around, America found that Castro had no intention of making his new country a democracy. On January 3, 1961, President Dwight Eisenhower announced that the United States had severed diplomatic and consular relations with Cuba. This now puts a Communist country just ninety miles off the southern coast of the United States. *(There are people in America saying that there was no monolithic force known as world Communism.)* The next time I get a colonoscopy, I think I will stay awake to see what those people find so interesting up there!

On January 20, John F. Kennedy became the thirty-fifth president of the United States. By all indication, of his inaugural address, he does not appear to be too fond of Communism and is committed to helping other nations be free (exhibit 9). On March 1, he established the peace corps. On April 17, the Bay of Pigs invasion of Cuba began; it failed by April 19. and by April 20, Fidel Castro announced that the Bay of Pigs invasion has been defeated. John F. Kennedy's presidency would take a lot of criticism regarding this issue.

On August 13, 1961, construction began on the Berlin Wall. Movement between East Berlin and West Berlin would remain restricted for the next twenty-eight years. On October 27, 1961, a standoff between Soviet and American tanks in Berlin heightened Cold War tensions. The wall would remain in place until November 9, 1989. I listed this tidbit of information because I believe that this structure holds an important similarity with certain events surrounding the Vietnam War, which I will make clearer later.

As the year 1961 draws to a close, our newly elected President John F. Kennedy sends eighteen thousand military advisers to South Vietnam on November 18. On December 2, in a nationally broadcast speech, Cuban leader Fidel Castro declares he is a Marxist-Leninist and that Cuba will adopt Communism *(Naaaa! Get out of town!)*

On December 11, the first American helicopters arrived in Saigon along with four hundred US personnel. Here, the youngest president in American history, in office for one year, including a transition period that every president goes through, has made several decisions regarding the spread of world Communism. It is quite apparent to me that this man had great concerns about that issue.

On the very last day of the year, December 31, the Marshall Plan expired after having distributed more than $12 billion in foreign aid to rebuild Europe. Was that our responsibility? I don't know. However, I do believe it was the right thing to do.

Although eighteen thousand troops were sent to Vietnam in 1961, I do not remember that being the major media event of the time.

However, I do remember the media coverage of the events unfolding in Cuba being very intensive. I was sixteen years old when the year 1962 rolled around, and midway through it, I will turn seventeen. Besides captured American spy pilot Francis Gary Powers being exchanged for captured Soviet spy Rudolf Abel, First Lady Jacqueline Kennedy was taking television viewers on a tour of the White House, and John Glenn was becoming the first American to orbit the Earth for three times in four hours fifty-five minutes aboard *Friendship 7*.

The rest of the year was pretty much engulfed in heavy saber rattling between us and the Soviets regarding that little island off the southern coast of Florida. This event, I believe, brought us the closest to nuclear war.

The events surrounding this standoff unfolded in the following sequence: On January 9, Cuba and the Soviet Union signed a trade pact. On January 22, the organization of American states suspended Cuba's membership, and on February 3, the US announced its trade embargo against Cuba. On February 7, the United States government banned all US-related Cuban imports and exports, and on April 14, a Cuban military tribunal convicted 1,179 Bay of Pigs attackers. These are the Cuban exiles that wanted to take their country back from Castro.

On September 2, the Soviet Union agreed to send arms to Cuba, and on October 14, the Cuban missile crisis began. A U-2 flight over Cuba took photos of Soviet nuclear weapons being installed. A standoff then ensued the next day between the United States and the Soviet Union, threatening the world with nuclear war.

On October 22, in a televised address, US President John F. Kennedy announced to the nation the existence of Soviet missiles in Cuba. On October 28, Soviet Union leader Nikita Khrushchev announced that he had ordered the removal of Soviet missile bases in Cuba, and on November 1, the Soviets began dismantling those missiles.

I remember watching the events unfold on television with images of our naval ships blockading the coast of Cuba and Russian ships steaming toward that location with what appeared to be missiles lashed to their decks. Heavy troop movements heading along our southern roadways prompted me to devise the plan of wanting to quit school and join the Marines to go and stop the Communists from delivering those missiles off our coast. This was the time I told you about earlier, the day I learned the hard way about the gift I received from my parents (America).

I remember that I equated the Communists with the likes of Hitler, Mussolini, and the Japanese. People that I considered evil were people with whom we were engaged in heavy fighting just prior to this event. These were people whom I believe were trying to take over the world for their own selfish gain. To this very day, I still do not count them out.

Although it was a scary time, I remember being enormously proud that our president made the Communists back down. It just strengthened my resolve to play a part in protecting this nation that my parents gave to me. In my ignorance, it was my belief that the rest of America felt the same way. However, in retrospect, I know there were many people like me. Not as many as there should have been, but there were many.

When 1963 rolled around, I was seventeen years old, and I will be eighteen before it ends. It was at the end of the year that my quest for joining the Marines will begin. Events surrounding Communism for 1963 will continue as it had for the past eighteen years. On February 8, travel and financial and commercial transactions by United States citizens to Cuba were made illegal by the John F. Kennedy administration. On May 23, Fidel Castro visited the Soviet Union, and on August 5, the United States, United Kingdom, and Soviet Union signed a nuclear test ban treaty.

The civil rights movement was stepping up when, on April 12, Martin Luther King Jr., Ralph Abernathy, Fred Shuttlesworth, and others are arrested in a Birmingham protest for "parading without a permit." On August 28, Martin Luther King Jr. delivered his "I have a dream" speech on the steps of the Lincoln Memorial to an audience of at least 250,000 during the March on Washington for jobs and freedom.

The space race was also continuing when, on May 15, the last mission of Mercury program launched Gordon Cooper on Mercury 9.

In Vietnam, on August 21, the army of the Republic of Vietnam special forces loyal to Ngo Dinh Nhu, brother of President Ngo Dinh Diem, vandalizes Buddhist pagodas across the country, arresting thousands and leaving an estimation in hundreds of dead. On November 2, 1963, South Vietnamese President Ngo Dinh Diem is assassinated following a military coup. The coup was sanctioned and approved by President Kennedy. However, Kennedy didn't anticipate the Diem assassination and was quite upset when he heard the news. On November 6, coup leader, General Duong Van Minh, took over as the leader.

On November 22, I, Pete Graham, Chuck Ketterman, Jack Heffernan, Alan Herre, and Stan Zegarski, all of us seniors and high school buddies, decided to skip a class and go see the Marine recruiter at the Newark library. We all took our first step at joining the Marine Corps on a 121-day program, which guaranteed that all of us would go through boot camp in the same platoon. I remember we all were in Jack's black Ford. We were all excited and carrying on like a bunch of kids. Well, I guess that's because we were. We did not have the radio on and didn't know what was going outside our own little world of excitement. However, when we got back to school, we found everyone upset and in a state of shock. That is when we found out that John F. Kennedy was assassinated in Dallas, Texas, and Governor John B. Connally was seriously wounded. As I walked through the halls of the school, I noticed some of the kids were crying while others were in small groups, talking; others, like me, were just not saying anything. The rumors were going wild, for example, it was the Russians, or maybe Castro. No one really knew at that point.

When I got home, I turned on the TV, I would assume, just like everyone else. I watched as VP Lyndon B. Johnson was sworn in as the thirty-sixth president. All television coverage for the next three days is devoted to the assassination, its aftermath, the procession of the horse-drawn casket to the Capitol rotunda, and the funeral of

President Kennedy. Stores and businesses shut down for the entire weekend and Monday in tribute. On November 25, President Kennedy was buried at Arlington National Cemetery. Schools around the nation did not have class on that day; millions watched the funeral on live international television.

Amid this tragic event, the new president Lyndon B. Johnson found himself neck-deep in presidential duties and confirmed to everyone that the United States intended to continue supporting South Vietnam militarily and economically, as did the previous three presidents. On November 29, he established the Warren Commission to investigate the assassination of President Kennedy.

In a short seven months, my buddies and I would find ourselves on our way to boot camp, which would eventually lead some of us to that place that President Johnson just pledged our support, that place that would be referred to by those of us who fought there simply as the Nam. It will also lead many of our generation and so-called fellow Americans to betray us for reasons that I can only speculate on. High school is finished, and a new era begins.

Chapter 5

Journeys to War

THE JOURNEY THAT MY HIGH school buddies and I were about to embark upon did not occur until mid-1964.

[T]However, several events would take place in that time that I think are worth mentioning. On January 18, plans to build the New York World Trade Center was announced.

On February 6, Cuba cut off the normal water supply to the United States Guantánamo Bay Naval Base in reprisal for the US's seizure four days earlier of four Cuban fishing boats off the coast of Florida. March 26 of that year, Defense Secretary Robert McNamara delivers an address that reiterates our determination to give South Vietnam increased military and economic aid in its war against the Communist insurgency. As you can see, there was no lack of effort on our part to hold Communism at bay, and there was nothing to indicate that the Communist had any intension in giving up their quest.

Another important event that would occur would take place [T] on May 2, 1964. Students from what many believe to be American institutions of higher learning, what I have come to view as nothing more than brothels providing thirty-thousand-dollars-a-year drink and fuck fests to morons, were taking to the streets to protest a war that didn't even start yet.

Some four hundred to one thousand students would march through Times Square in New York and another seven hundred in San Francisco. This would be the first major student demonstration against the Vietnam War. Smaller marches also occurred in Boston,

Seattle, and Madison, Wisconsin. They were protesting a war that, at the time, we were only providing military advisers to.

Even at this early stage of the conflict, they were taking the side of the Communists. However, I think it is important to point out now that the people who organized these demonstrations were members of the following organizations: the Progressive Labor Party and the Young Socialist Alliance, which was the Progressive Labor Party's youth affiliate.

Let us examine what these organizations are. The Progressive Labor Party was founded in 1961, with its headquarters in Brooklyn, New York. Their leadership was a central committee and the leaders of local collectives. Their ideology was militant Communism, Marxist-Leninist, anti-revisionism, and anti-electoral. Their political position was radical left. Their international affiliations, besides USA, were various countries in Central and South America, Greece, Pakistan, and the West Bank, as well as others.

This organization was an offshoot of the Communist Party USA. This group made it clear that it wanted to advocate communist revolution openly and aggressively among the working class. Supposedly this organization intensified its recruitment during the civil rights movement.

(*As a little side note to this, once the students for a Democratic Society came to the political forefront in 1965 as the US leftist activist group, the Progressive Labor Party dissolved its M2M and entered the SDS. Within a few years, this group became the largest Communist faction within the SDS.*) Their youth affiliate, Young Socialist Alliance, was a Trotskyist youth group of the Socialist Workers Party.

This group achieved substantial influence in the anti-Vietnam War movement. Between 1965 and the early '70s, they had gained almost complete control of the Student Mobilization Committee to end the war in Vietnam. This group was a national campus organization that had a peak membership of over one hundred thousand people. They were citizens of this country.

At any rate, while these homegrown Communists were gearing up to aid their Vietnamese counterparts, my buddies and I were starting our journey.

Joseph P. Keely, staff sergeant, United States Marine Corps
Enlisted 1964
Served in the Republic of Vietnam (1965, 1966, 1967)
Location: first tour Da Nang, second tour Gia Lea, north of Phu Bai and south of Hue City

Approximately five days after graduating high school in June 1964, I met up with the other guys I signed up with, and we reported to the induction station in Newark. We were placed on a bus and brought to Newark airport. While we were being guided to the aircraft departure gate, I remember seeing my father, my sister, my brother-in-law, and his mom standing there to see me off. That trip would turn out to be quite long.

Delivering us by bus to Parris Island, South Carolina, at approximately 3:00 AM, or as I would soon come to learn 0300 hours. They kept us busy until approximately 0800 hours when we were picked up by our drill instructors. Just prior to that event, we were told by the corporal that oversaw us up until that point that it would benefit us to be sitting at the position of attention with our hands folded on the desk and our eyes on the wall in front of us. He then departed the room.

What seemed like a half hour, the library-type silence was broken with the two oversized doors on the left side of the room swinging open and slamming against the tiled walls. I could see through the corner of my eyes three individuals I knew to be drill instructors moving in and out of the rows of chairs that housed my fellow recruits. Suddenly, the silence was broken with one of the drill instructors inquiring of a recruit in a loud tone of voice, "Who are you looking at, you fucking maggot? I catch you eyeballing me one more time, and I will punch your mother fucking eyeballs out."

With those words, my brain went into overdrive and my immediate thoughts were, *What in the fuck was I thinking?* and that maybe this wasn't such a bright idea. However, they did not give us too much time to think after that. Commands and orders were being bellowed out in rapid succession, and we were on the move.

In the first month of our training, a few major events were occurring—events that we were unaware of but soon would affect some of us personally. Events such as on [T] July 8, US military personnel announce that US casualties in Vietnam have risen to 1,387, including 399 dead and 17 MIA.

On July 19, at a rally in Saigon, South Vietnamese Prime Minister Nguyen Khanh calls for expanding the war into North Vietnam (which did not occur). On July 20, Vietcong forces attack a provincial capital, killing 11 South Vietnamese military personnel and 40 civilians (30 of which were children). No one in the States said anything about that. On July 27, the US sends 5,000 more military advisers to South Vietnam, bringing the total number of United States forces in Vietnam to 21,000.

However, regarding our training, days turned into weeks and weeks into months with the training breaking us down and a systematic rebuilding by the drill instructors from the ground up of both our bodies and spirits. Each day that went by, I could feel myself getting stronger. By the time graduation day arrived, we were in top shape; I was in the best shape of my life, and I was more confident than I have ever been in my life. We were in as good shape as any well-trained athlete, even better. We had to be as the game we were training for was war.

However, it would not be too long before many us would find out that war is not actually a game.

In the beginning of the last month of our training, an incident would take place that started rumors flowing through the platoon, such as cutting our boot training short. [T] On August 2, a United States destroyer, the USS *Maddox*, was attacked in the Gulf of Tonkin. On the fourth, crew members of both the *Maddox* and another destroyer, *Turner Joy*, reported that they were under attack. However, this second event, like others in our nation's history, has become the center of considerable controversy and debate. Opponents of the war accused Johnson of falsely creating this second event to justify our involvement in Vietnam and to plunge us deeper into war. This issue will be discussed in depth later.

[T]Because of those attacks, on August 5, Operation Pierce Arrow was implemented. Aircraft from carriers USS *Ticonderoga* and USS *Constellation* bombed that naval facility in North Vietnam in retaliation for those naval attacks. President Johnson sent a written request to Congress on the same date to request a resolution. On August 7, the United States Congress passed Resolution No. 1145, giving President Johnson broad war powers to deal with North Vietnamese attacks on US forces. I repeat, US forces.

Despite those events, boot camp was not cut short and our training continued. On September 16, we graduated, and the very next morning, we all boarded the buses and were delivered to a training base that is part of Camp LeJeune, North Carolina, known as Camp Geiger. It was a regimental infantry training base (ITR), where the training would last a month. Parris Island is a place that I was never so happy to leave. However, it is a place that I have never forgotten and a place that I never tire of revisiting.

We were pretty much separated from the outside world while at infantry training due to its intensity, so the following event was unknown to us. [T]On October 1, 1964, three thousand student activists (from Commie central of the western United States) at the University of California, Berkeley, surround and block a police car from taking a core volunteer arrested for not showing his ID when he violated a ban on outdoor activist card tables. This protest eventually exploded into what has become known as the Berkeley free speech movement.

The Free Speech Movement (FSM) was a student protest which began in 1964. It was under the informal leadership of students Mario Savio, David Goines, Suzanne Goldberg, Bettina Aptheker, and others. Most outsiders, however, identified the Free Speech Movement as a movement of the Left. Students and others opposed to US foreign policy did indeed increase their visibility on campus following the FSM's initial victory.

October would end, and November would find me on leave after ITR. Several incidents involving Vietnam would occur. [T]On

November 1, mortar fire from North Vietnamese forces rains on the USAF base at Bien Hoa, South Vietnam, killing four US servicemen, wounding seventy-two, and destroying five B-57 jet bombers and other planes. This would be the second attack on US forces besides the Gulf of Tonkin. President Johnson did not retaliate or send combat troops in.

[T] On November 3, 1964, Johnson defeated Republican challenger Barry Goldwater for the presidency with over 60 percent of the popular vote. After serving a year completing Kennedy's term, this would be his own. *(It should be noted that I and most of my generation were too young to vote.)*

[T]On November 10, Australia partially reintroduces compulsory military service due to the Indonesian confrontation. *(Our friends were lining up to support us.)*

By December, I was assigned to my first duty station—Eighth Communication Battalion, Second Marine Division, Camp LeJeune, North Carolina. I was detailed to a month of guard duty prior to being assigned to my company. [T]On December 1, President Johnson and his top-ranking advisers meet to discuss plans to bomb North Vietnam (after some debate, they agree to enact a two-phase bombing plan).

On December 24, 1964, Vietcong terrorists set off a car bomb explosion at the Brinks Hotel, an American officers' residence in downtown Saigon. The bomb is timed to detonate at 5:45 p.m., during happy hour in the bar. Two Americans are killed and fifty-eight wounded. President Johnson dismisses all recommendations for a retaliatory air strike against North Vietnam once again.

After guard duty, I was assigned to Radio Relay and Construction Company. Here is where I would complete my training as a communicator in wire communications. Here is where I would also obtain a military driver's license and I would become the company driver and mail orderly. My task as the company driver and mail orderly consisted of being on call for the commanding officer and driving him anywhere; he needed to go, also to pick up, sort, and deliver the mail to the men in the company.

While I was being trained and performing my duties as a young Marine, the following events were taking place in Vietnam and on the streets of the United States:

On February 6, 1965, Vietcong guerrillas attack the US military compound at Pleiku in the Central Highlands, killing 8 Americans, wounding 126, and destroying 10 aircraft. This would be the fourth and last attack including the Gulf of Tonkin perpetrated on American troops. This would be the proverbial straw that broke the camel's back which sparked the following event.

On March 8, 3,500 United States Marines arrived in South Vietnam, becoming the first American combat troops in Vietnam.

Four direct attacks on our troops within a seven-month period from the issuance of Resolution No. 1145, killing 14 and wounding 256, I would not consider an act of plunging us into war. It is a reaction by the commander in chief, protecting his troops as outlined in the resolution, as well as the United States Constitution.

Meanwhile back home, our homegrown Commies would be on the move again. On March 24 and March 25, 1965, the SDS organizes the first teach-in against the Vietnam War, with 2,500 participants, at the University of Michigan. In the spring of 1965, the FSM was followed by the Vietnam Day committee, a major starting point for the anti-Vietnam War movement. Amid the Vietnam War and the anti-war escalation, on April 28, US troops are sent to the Dominican Republic by President Johnson "for the stated purpose of protecting US citizens and preventing an alleged Communist takeover of the country," thus thwarting the possibility of "another Cuba." Some of these troops were from my company, Radio Relay and Construction.

Our friends were also busy. On April 29, Australia announced that it is sending an infantry battalion to support the South Vietnam government.

On May 5, the first draft card burnings took place at *(where else?)* the university in Berkeley, and a coffin was marched to the Berkeley draft board. On May 21, the largest teach-in to date began at Berkeley, California, attended by 30,000. The next day, several hundred participants again march to the draft board and burn more cards and Lyndon Johnson in effigy. On June 16, a planned anti-war protest at the Pentagon becomes a teach-in, with demonstrators distributing 50,000 leaflets in and around the building.

On June 2, the first contingent of Australian combat troops arrived in South Vietnam.

On July 28, 1965, President Johnson announced his order to increase the number of United States troops in South Vietnam from 75,000 to 125,000. I would become part of that number. He also said that he would double the number of men drafted per month from 17,000 to 35,000.

On July 29, the first 4,000 101st Airborne Division paratroopers arrive in Vietnam, landing at Cam Ranh Bay.

On August 18, Operation Starlite began as 5,500 United States Marines destroy a Vietcong stronghold on the Van Tuong peninsula in Quang Ngai Province in the first major American ground battle of the war. The Marines were tipped off by a Vietcong deserter who said that there was an attack planned against the US base at Chu Lai.

On September 7, in a follow-up to August's Operation Starlite, United States Marines and South Vietnamese forces initiate Operation Piranha on the Batangan Peninsula, twenty-three miles south of the Chu Lai Marine base.

I believe it was also sometime in early September 1965 that I was driving the major, my CO (commanding officer), to a meeting when, out of the clear blue sky, he said, "Hey, Keely, guess where I'm going!"

Of course, my response was, "I have no idea, sir."

"I'm going to Vietnam" he said.

I replied, "No shit, sir, that's where I want to go."

His response was, "I didn't know that."

"Well, that's what I'm trained for, sir."

"You're right there, Keely. I'll make sure that you get the next draft for a wireman to the Nam before I leave."

"Thank you, sir."

By this time, we had reached our destination, and nothing further was said on the subject between the major and me.

Approximately two weeks later, there was a change of command ceremony. The old CO is gone and a new one takes his place. Besides the first introduction to let the new major know who his driver was, I had no contact with the new CO. I suppose he was acclimating himself to his new position.

However, it was approximately two weeks after that the day was coming to an end. I returned the jeep to the motor pool and walked back to the company area. Liberty call had already sounded by the time I got back, but I had some paperwork to do, so I returned to the company office. The only other Marine in the office with me was the company clerk. Soon the silence was broken when I heard the first sergeant say my name. "Keely, the major told me to give you the next draft for a wireman to Vietnam. Do you want it?"

"Yeah, top. I'll take it."

He immediately turned to the company clerk and said, "Type his orders." He turned back to me and said, "Pack your shit."

"Now?"

"Yes. Just turn everything into the duty NCO (noncommissioned officer). Make sure your squared away before you report back here."

I answered, "Okay, top."

I obeyed his orders and returned to the company office with two seabags and dressed in my greens, the uniform of the day. The first sergeant was standing in the doorway. I put my seabags on the ground. He handed me my record book and orders. After looking at them, I placed them in one of my seabags. After looking up, the first sergeant shook my hand and said, "Keep your head down, kid."

I replied, "Aye, aye, top." I turned and started for home where I would spend thirty days of leave prior to departing for the Nam.

Not everyone who entered the service, by enlistment or draft, would have to go to Vietnam. However, here are just a few of the guys I know personally who did the honorable thing and served their country regardless in what capacity or location. Here in their own words is what they remember:

Charles Ketterman, sergeant, United States Marine Corps
Enlisted June 1964
Served in the Republic of Vietnam (February 1967 to February 1968)

If you remember, this is one of the guys I joined the Marine Corps with.

Chuck told me that when he was young, he remembers that the threat of Communist expansion had put the United States on its guard. He remembers that his school, like mine, not only had fire drills but also air-raid drills, preparing for possible nuclear attacks. As the alarm went off in his school, he remembers being directed to walk quickly and orderly down to the basement of the school and line up against the walls and then sit quietly as the teachers took the roster to be accountable for each child.

Even on Saturdays, he remembers the town where he lived would test the air-raid siren at twelve o'clock sharp.

He also remembers the arrival of the television set. It is from this that he recollects that what used to be read in papers was now coming into his living room with just the flick of a switch. He remembers seeing reports about the Korean War.

But what he remembers most about the TV was a program called *Victory at Sea*, a program series about the events of the Second World War. Chuck and his uncle would stay up until midnight when programming would sign off for the night, and he would remember that he would stand at attention and salute the flag while the "Star Spangle Banner" played in its entirety. Since his uncle had served in the Marines and his mother had been in the WACS during World War II, he said he felt destined to serve his country.

He also said he recalls in 1962 that John F. Kennedy had motivated the nation for tough times ahead with his words, "Ask not what your country can do for you. Ask what you can do for your country."

As he spoke those words, Chuck felt more compelled to do his share in the military.

Chuck conveyed to me that when we worked in the Shop Rite food store after school as kids that the highlight of those days would be when we got a chance to speak with former Marines who had the esprit de corps. He feels that it was speaking with them that one day would lead us in the direction of becoming Marines also.

He also said that he remembers by the time we entered Columbia High School in Maplewood New Jersey, the Korean War had long since reached a stalemate. However, he recalls the troops being poised at the ready on the thirty-eighth parallel. Also, that there were other trouble spots beginning to make the headlines.

Although young, he too was paying attention and knew that the Eisenhower administration had forewarned President Kennedy of the Communist expansion in Southeast Asia. He also remembered the Cuban Missile Crisis.

Chuck also recalls skipping class that day in November 1963 when President Kennedy had been assassinated. He remembers that we, along with Jack, Stan, Pete, and Allan, went to see the recruiter to begin our journey to Parris Island.

He was glad that we all committed ourselves to the buddy system offered by the Marine Corps to be in the same training platoon. He said it was weird that we all stopped singing the Marine Corps hymn when we got to the main gate in Parris Island. It was early-morning hours when we got there, and we were quickly ushered into the receiving barracks.

His recollection of boot training is, "Once inside, we sat at individual desks, filling out paperwork to register us as Platoon 357. It was now that we were picked up by our drill instructors. From there, our heads were shaved, and we were ordered to go through a series of holding up one toothbrush, toothpaste, and other toiletries for our small ditty bags. Now we all had the necessities for shaving and proper hygiene.

"Our next stop was to pick up our seabags, and we were issued our utilities, chrome dome, and PT gear. All this time we were being constantly yelled at to hurry and move in an orderly manner. From there, we were forced marched to our barracks in Third Battalion, which some called Disneyland because it was the newest of the barracks. This would be just the beginning of learning how to be a Marine."

After boot camp, Chuck was assigned to a naval ammunition depot. He said, "As the tours of duty were complete, the returning Marine Vietnam vets took our places at the ammunition depot. I was a noncommissioned officer by then, and my next duty assignment would be as a rifleman in an infantry unit in Vietnam."

He also said, "We talked with the vets about their experiences and what we could get from them about the war. With great anticipation, we watched the board for our names and assignment dates to report to Camp Pendleton. The reality of going to war had not quite hit us yet. Nevertheless, we found ourselves training in the hot California sun for further infantry training and exhaustive marches in the desert."

Chuck also wrote a book about his experience in Vietnam. The title of the book is *Nature of the Beast*.

John J. Heffernan, Jr. (Jack), sergeant, United States Marine Corps
Enlisted June 1964
Served overseas: sea duty for two years
Jack served on the USS Springfield *CLG 7 flagship, the Sixth Fleet, Homeport Villafranche, France. FMF 031*

Jack is another one of the guys I joined with. When I asked him why he joined, he said, "It was a long story," but mainly he remembers seeing his dad's Marine Dress Blues hanging in the closet. He also knew the path that he was on was not good, not good at all, and that he figured the best way to grow up and prove to himself that he could make it "was to join the best of the best, the US Marines and let the chips fall where they may." He said, "All through high school, the Marines were always on my mind!" I know that to be true from that day that Jack approached me in school, wanting to hook up and join along with him.

He remembers that although the path he chose was completely uncharted, he knew he was in shape and ready to face what was ahead of him at Parris Island but never dreamed of what was ahead of that.

What Jack remembers of boot camp is that "there was not much time to think, just react to the harsh treatment of the drill instructors, crazy thoughts of why did I do this, how can I get the hell outta here, but shortly thereafter, I was snapped into the drill of long days and short nights, actually looking forward to the next day of what the DIs could dish out." *(Being with my buddies was helpful although extraordinarily little contact, except visual with one or more of us getting our ass kicked.)* "We were in much better shape than most of our platoon and needed much less discipline, but just for general principle, we got smacked around anyway."

After boot camp, Jack said that he went to sea school. Being tall and thin and looking the part, he was picked out from boot camp by the senior DI. *(He was not given a choice of duty stations.)*

After the training, he was assigned to the USS *Springfield* CLG 7 homeported in Villafranche, France. He was part of the ship's company, guarding the hatch to the nuke warheads. He then was promoted to flag allowance and assigned to the commander of the Sixth Fleet's two vice admirals for two tours.

Jack did not go to the Nam. Each time his name and number came up, he was still assigned to the flagship. Because he spent twenty-nine months overseas, by the time he got Stateside, he was not here long enough to be redeployed. When he picked up E-5 sergeant, he got orders to Westpac, but his orders were rescinded due to his brother Danny already being deployed to the Nam and his other younger brother Glenn was in training.

Jack's job with the fleet in the Mediterranean consisted of being on station and stranding at the ready to be deployed anywhere in the NATO area of operations against possible Communist aggression in that area. Every time Jack volunteered for the Nam, his requests were denied by the admiral. Communism was a threat all over the world, not just in the Nam.

Brian W. Robinson, ATR E5 Navy
Enlisted 1966
Tours of duty dates:
October 19, 1966–May 29, 1967
December 28, 1967–August 17, 1968
April 16, 1969–October 17, 1969
Location: Western Pacific, Gulf of Tonkin, Vietnam
(Beach Detachment)

Brian told me he enlisted in the Navy because it sounded like an adventure and cleaner than the other branches, but mostly because his brother, an ex-Navy man, made it sound like great fun.

That brother that he is talking about is my brother-in-law John, married to my sister. I should say that he is more like the brother I never had. I met Brian and his other brother Roy right around the time John and my sister started dating. So basically, I inherited three other brothers. At any rate, Brian told me that two months before checking in, he quit working at his cushy job as a lab tech and went to work for a local farmer. The idea was to get in shape for the upcoming ordeal. He said he worked hard. He did about one hundred push-ups every day and over two hundred sit-ups. "I was rough and ready when I headed to New York City," where he was to sign in. ("Golly Bill"!) As he often says, he was surprised. He said he never saw a more derelict, ragtag group of guys. It seemed to him that the NYC police had pulled a rake through every slum in town and corralled those hoods into the induction center. He said those guys looked like the dregs of all the longhaired, rowdy, carjacking, mean, scary, gangsters in NYC.

They put them in lines, cut off their hair, made them strip down to their skivvies, (underwear) and then started shooting them in the arms with these newly developed air shots that none of the medics knew how to use. They had them cranked up too high, and the shots would go right through your arm. If anyone complained, like "Hey, look what you did," pointing to a jagged rip in their side where the shot had moved along the rib cage, the medic would grab their arm and shoot again since the last one obviously did not enter as it should have.

Recalling that day, he said, "Whoa! After a few hours, the group of rowdies had been turned into a tame group of bald-headed, naked guys that were not giving much lip to anyone."

Brian also told me, "I joined because I did not want to be drafted." Being facetious, he said, "Smart move. My younger brother and his buddy Tom were drafted and spent two years visiting Europe. I volunteered and did three tours in Nam."

After the induction center, they sent the whole crew of misfits, as he referred to the group he was part of, from New York City to the Great Lakes Training Center, except for one gentleman who found the sight of all those naked guys at the induction center too exciting.

At Great Lakes, they were assigned to companies under a chief petty officer who was their company commander. He remembers they were put in barracks where they were supposed to sleep. However, he does not remember getting too much of that. Mostly he remembers being marched around the base in the freezing snow with mattresses on their backs because some Jerky McGerk screwed up.

He says, in the Navy, the objective of basic training is to weed out the non-hackers so that they will not cause a problem under combat conditions. They spent most of the time crowding them into tight spaces, forcing them to live every minute with some wacko to the left, right in front, and behind you (assholes to belly buttons), a common term used in the military.

This kind of guidance, he believes, "honed them into a bunch of folks who might just survive living together while packed like sardines inside a ship at sea with no escape." He said they learned how to work together, to solve problems so that their packed tiny home would stay afloat.

His first assignment was with Heavy Reconnaissance Attack Squadron One, the Smoking Tigers. The idea was to get his tenderfeet acclimated to the work of the Navy before sending him off to school. He was stationed down in Sanford, Florida. His job was "to do all the crap work" as he calls it "that real salts did not want to do." Clean the barracks, cook, clean the PX, stand watch, clean the aircraft, mow the grass—crap work. When the squadron went off to Vietnam, they left him in Sanford with Heavy 11, the Checkertails, until he was sent to Memphis for electronics training.

His job as a Checkertail was to put a checker design on everything. On the aircraft, on the tables, on the side of the hangers, the coffee cups, forklifts. He said he cut, pasted, and painted so many checkers he started seeing them in his sleep. He was never sure how putting checkerboards on everything was helping the cause of freedom, but he is sure in some way it was.

He remembers that, aside from the grunt work, it was great duty in Sanford. It was one long vacation. He had most weekends off and went to Daytona Beach in an old Ford woodie. They chased girls, played in the sun, and drank more than they should have. He still dreams of making checkerboard designs even today. As you will see, that will soon change.

Tom Martin, sergeant, United States Army
Drafted June 1968
Served in the Republic of Vietnam (1969)
(wounded in May)
Camp Evans in Thua Thien Province

Tom told me that in his senior year in college when he was drafted, he was supposed to go in November of 1967. However, that induction was deferred until after his graduation in June of that year. He was not drafted that summer.

As a sixth-grade teacher in Byram Township, New Jersey, he was drafted again in November 1967, and this too was deferred until the end of the school year in June 1968. On July 1, 1968, he answered his last draft notice; he boarded a bus in front of the Hill Memorial Building at 6:00 AM. By 10:00 AM, he was sworn into the United States Army at the federal building in Newark. He told his mother that he would call her from Fort Dix as soon as he arrived there. However, he never got there instead; he was put on a plane heading for Fort Benning, Georgia. This is the home of the Army airborne. He remembers that the base was extremely hot that summer and sandy and that they put them in old World War II wooden barracks. Tom also told me that two teachers were drafted from Byram School that summer. One teacher served, one teacher refused to go. Tom would serve, the other would betray. Prior to leaving, Tom and Sue, his fiancée at the time, had decided to get engaged by Christmas of 1968.

However, they speeded things up when he got drafted and they were married on November 16, 1968, two days after he turned twenty-six years of age.

John (Ron) R. Nash, Spec 5 US Army
Enlisted/signed up for one more year
Served in the Republic of Vietnam (December 1968–December 1969)
Location: Hue, Phu Bai, A-Shau Valley, DMZ

Ron said that he wanted to serve like his father and wanted to be in the food service being that was already his profession.

When he entered the military, his parents took him to the bus station. From the bus station, it was on to Fort Holibird at Baltimore where he raised his hand and he was in. However, they did not know where to send him, so they sent him home for three days. When they called him back, they sent him to Fort Knox for basic training. He told me he was assigned to basic with a bunch of guys from Detroit who complained about being drafted and that they should not be there.

Ron said that after basic, he was sent to cooking school. He thought that to be a joke, and then he was sent to Picatinny Arsenal in NJ where Army life did not exist. He was a cook at the NCO Club, which was also the mess hall. He said this was the good life, civilian food, and a bar. Great-looking girls came to the club also. Most important, he met his wife there.

Ron told me he did not volunteer to go to Vietnam. However, in 1968, he got his orders and accepted the fact that he was going.

Chester Waleski, captain, US Army
Entered the Army through ROTC 1968
Served in the Republic of Vietnam (1969–1970)
Location: Cuchi

After graduating high school, Chet applied for and was accepted to Seaton Hall University in South Orange, New Jersey. This is where he joined the ROTC program for four years from 1964 to 1968.

Besides viewing anti-war protestors on television and reading about them in the paper, he witnessed firsthand the heckling from demonstrators as he marched with the Army ROTC on the drill field at Seaton Hall. This was all prior to his volunteering and leaving for Vietnam. Chet told me that he got married a month and eighteen days prior to leaving for the Nam.

He said that he graduated from college and the ROTC program in August of 1968; this is where he received his second lieutenant bars. From there, he was sent to Fort Lee Virginia for infantry training and officer quartermaster training. Chet volunteered for it and figured it wouldn't be long before he was sent to the Nam. Concerned, he decided that he would take five days' leave and marry the love of his life, now his wife of forty years. He returned to base and completed training. He was given an additional thirty days' leave prior to departing for Vietnam.

He remembers that it was on the day of President Nixon's inauguration that he flew out for the Nam. His destination was Tansannut Air Base, which served as a staging area before they sent him to his unit based in Cu Chi.

*Scott Meyer, sergeant, United States Air Force
Enlisted 1968
Served in Germany (1971, 1972, 1973)*

Scott served in a small village in the heart of Bavaria about a kilometer from the Czech border. Scott said that he never made it to Vietnam. However, Scott served with as much honor and distinction as any of us who did. His duty station may not have been a hot spot, but it contained the same enemy that we were fighting in Vietnam— the Communists.

He told me he was a senior at John J. Pershing College in Nebraska and incredibly involved in student activities. He was student body president that year and involved in everything related to the college. While there, he also became interested in the presidential election that year when Senator Eugene McCarthy opened a store-front campaign headquarters downtown. McCarthy asked young people to get involved, make a difference. He said that he had that kind of patter that appealed to students down perfectly. "Get clean with Gene" was the slogan.

Eventually he was asked by the McCarthy campaign staff to join them, and he took a short leave of absence from his senior year to become an advance man for McCarthy. One day, he would be setting up the Cow Palace in San Francisco for a McCarthy appearance, next week in Portland, etc. At the time, he thought it was a lot of responsibility for a young guy, and he was right.

The campaign rolled on through a difficult year in America and hit its nadir when Bob Kennedy was murdered on the night of the California primary election. He and a couple of the staffers went to Senator McCarthy's room to inform him of the awful event.

Scott said that the campaign ended for him at the historic Democratic convention in Chicago in the summer of 1968. By that time, Secret Service protection had been extended to the candidates and his job at the convention was liaison between McCarthy and the Secret Service detail. Most his time in Chicago was watching the street action between the protestors and the Chicago police from the windows of the Hilton with the Secret Service detail.

He returned to college, finished his coursework, and graduated. The Vietnam War was in the news every day, and he had lived through the protests and political speeches regarding the war for the past months.

Scott said that he knew that it was just a matter of time before he would receive his draft notice, so he accepted a job with the college as an admissions representative, knowing that the draft notice would be forthcoming.

He worked for about eight months and one day, on a whim, stopped in an Air Force recruiter's office just to see what the Air Force had to offer.

By this time, it was 1969. Less than a week after visiting the Air Force office, he got a letter from my draft board: "You are classified 1-A and ordered to report."

He went back to the Air Force recruiter, and he told Scott that he could enlist now (he thinks this would be about April of 1969) and he would not have to report to basic training until July. Also, the recruiter said that since he was a college graduate, he would be guaranteed one of three choices for his assignment in the Air Force. What is better than that? He selected languages first, then something he thought would be interesting, like radio and TV production, and he cannot remember what else. So he took that option and finally entered Lackland AFB in San Antonio in July 1969.

He remembers basic training was uneventful, except he remembers, like most of us that entered the service in the summer, it being hot in San Antonio. On the last day of basic training, his platoon was marched somewhere to receive their initial orders. He opened his orders and it said, "Air traffic controller." A sergeant asked if anyone had a problem with their orders. He raised his hand and was off to a new line to wait for another meeting. Finally, he got to sit with a personnel guy. He explained that he was guaranteed a choice of assignments. The sergeant said, "Airman, that's the recruiter talking. And the guarantees are only if there is actually an opening in the field you requested. Obviously, there were no openings in his fields."

The sergeant looked through his records and said that he could not be an air traffic controller anyway since Scott is color-blind. He said, "We have some openings in languages. How would that be?" (Scott's first choice had been languages anyway.) He was put on hold until new orders for a language school came in.

In the interim, he was put in charge of the medical hold barracks, essentially a holding tank for guys that were hurt during basic training or were head cases or faking head cases. He said he spent half of his time there fighting with guys who were trying to prove they were crazy enough to be released from the service.

Every day, friends were getting their orders. Virtually 100 percent of those who were going into languages were getting orders to study Vietnamese. He was sure that he would receive the same orders. After about four weeks, he got the call to report for his orders. A sergeant in the front of the room shouted, "Who's Meyer?" He stood up, and the sergeant said, "What the hell is Czech?" He did not know what it was either, but he had just received orders to study the Czech language as a member of the 6910th Security Squadron. He thought that was unbelievable.

At any rate, he was sent to Monterey, California, to the Defense Language Institute to study Czech from native Czech professors for almost a year. From language school, he was transferred to San Angelo, Texas, to electronic school, and from there, to Darmstadt, Germany, where he would stay for a few months.

Charlie Alexander, SP 4 Army
Drafted 1965
Served in the Republic of Vietnam
(1966–1967)
Location: Pleiku

Charlie was born and raised in Georgetown, Georgia, and relocated to Newark, New Jersey, when local draft board 122 of Georgetown summoned him for military service. Charlie notified the draft board that he had relocated to New Jersey and could not report to Fort Benning, Georgia, at the specified date and time.

The board granted him a ninety-day deferment. Approximately a month later, he received another notice at the Jersey address this time. It directed him to report to 1060 Broad St. at 0830 hours on November 16, 1965, for induction.

Charlie told me his first thoughts were, why me? and that he did not want to go into the military. However, Charlie said he was not raised to think like that. He was raised to believe it was one's obligation to serve if called. Therefore, when the call came, he felt he could do little else, but do as he was raised to do and answer the call.

Charlie remembers the induction and swearing-in process took somewhere around six to seven hours. He said he remembers a lot of waiting around. He said he was excited and, at the same time, frightened. He could tell that most of the other guys were as frightened as well, but none of them would admit to that. He said that he took comfort in that knowledge that someone else was as scared as he was.

He said after a full day at the induction center, they were all put on a bus and transported to Fort Dix Reception Center, where he immediately realized that he wasted an awful lot of fear at the Newark induction station. I have often wondered myself why they call it a reception center; they make it sound so friendly!

He remembers his first week was filled with a lot of "hurry up and wait," and it was during that time they were given their GI issue, haircuts, shaves, and duty assignments. He and about fifty other guys were assigned to take their basic training at Fort Hood, Texas, at the First Army Training Brigade.

They were bussed in the middle of the night to Philadelphia, Pennsylvania. From there, they were put on a transport plane and were flown to Fort Hood—a place, Charlie said, he never wanted to revisit.

When the eight weeks of training was complete, he said they were sent to Fort Lewis, Washington, for advanced infantry training. They were told early on in that training that they were being groomed for service in Vietnam.

They went through jungle training, along with the infantry training. By the end of the training cycle, they had been broken down and rebuilt into lean, mean fighting machines, confident soldiers, as Charlie put it.

Charlie remembers thinking, *I don't want to really go to Vietnam. Christ, I don't even know where Vietnam is.* However, Charlie was ordered to go, and remaining true to his upbringing, Charlie did the honorable thing and went without complaint.

I always admired people like Charlie. People who really did not want to do a thing, especially if it was dangerous, but did it anyway because, deep down, they knew it was the right thing to do.

Fredrick Goger, sergeant, United States Marine Corps
Enlisted 1964
Served in the Republic of Vietnam (1965, 1966, 1967)
Location: first tour Da Nang, second tour Gia Lea, north of Phu Bai and south of Hue City

Fred and I met on a dark early morning on Hill 34 just south of Da Nang. Like me, he joined the Marine Corps in June 1964. He told me that he had always wanted to be a Marine as long as he could remember. His sister married a Marine (grunt) who landed in Lebanon in a show of force. The stories that his brother-in-law brought back only reinforced his desire to join. After boot camp, he went to radio school. He was still an E-1 after a year. He said that he was kind of like a shitbird. He had told his DIs in boot camp that he had Russian cousins, and that meant he would have to wait a year in Florida to get a top secret clearance. Of course, he joined to play in the mud, so he got himself thrown out of Pensacola to field radio school with only a secret clearance.

He was assigned to Shore Party Battalion Second Marine Division. He immediately got involved in the deployment to Santo Domingo to evacuate Americans. That was the first time he experienced what it was really like to live and play the role of a field Marine.

He said, "The dirt, the sweat, the vigilance, the sounds of gunfire, the bullshit sessions sitting in a sandbag fort, just like I used to build with boxes and shit as a kid. But this was for real. I was hooked."

He said, "It was like I belonged in this shit." That took him through his first year. When they got back to LeJeune, he went right to S-4 and asked for transfer to Vietnam. "Wherever the fuck that was." He only knew that the Marines had landed there in Chu Lai and conducted a combat operation known as Operation Starlite. He remembers that on the way back from the Dominican Republic that Operation Starlite was the topic of all our bull sessions aboard ship. After thirty days' leave, he reported to Pendleton for training.

Little did I know that it would not be long before our paths would cross, forming a fifty-plus year friendship.

Leroy Terry Smith, sergeant, US Army Airborne
Enlisted September 15, 1965
Served in the Republic of Vietnam (1966–1967)
First Cavalry Division, 1968 82nd Airborne Division
Location: An Khe in the central highlands first tour and Phu Bai in the north on the second tour

Terry, after leaving the service, also joined the New Jersey State Police. This is where I first met Terry as his classmate in the academy. This is where we developed a lifelong friendship. When I asked him why he joined, he said that his father and all his uncles were in the army in Europe during World War II. Another uncle on his mother's side of the family enlisted in the Navy during the Korean War. He felt that it was now his turn to serve his country as they had.

Many of his friends in high school had enlisted in 1964. His friend, Jack Kopeski, and he decided that upon graduation in 1965 that they would enlist on the buddy program.

On September 15, 1965, Jack and he boarded a train in Netcong, New Jersey, en route to the recruitment center in Newark, New Jersey, to be sworn in.

When they arrived in Newark, they were given the oath which would begin their military service. Shortly after receiving the oath, they were all taken outside, formed into alphabetical platoons, and told to board the buses which would take them to Fort Dix for recruit training.

Upon arrival at Fort Dix, a group of drill instructors boarded the buses and began yelling at them to get off the buses and form up into the platoons that they were assigned. They were then introduced to their drill instructors. Terry's platoon got Staff Sergeant McAndrews, and this is what Terry told me of his first encounter with McAndrews.

"I have a bad habit of grinning or smirking when people start yelling at me. I found out immediately the sergeant did not like grinning or smirking. He personally took offense and got in my face screaming at me to wipe the smile off my face. At this point, I was wondering what the hell I had gotten myself into."

Once the sergeant calmed down, they were assigned to their barracks. He said he was assigned to the old wooden World War II buildings. And his buddy Jack was assigned to the newer brick buildings, about two blocks away. "So much for joining on the buddy system."

The next morning, at about 5:00 a.m., Sergeant McAndrews and his cadre, as Terry put it, woke the guys up by screaming, yelling, and beating on garbage cans. From that point on, he kept wondering why he had done this to himself. He said that Sergeant McAndrews then began tearing them down and building them back up, both physically and mentally.

After ten weeks of indoctrination and training, they graduated. He was then sent to Fort Ord, California, for advanced airborne infantry training. When those drill instructors finished with them after eight weeks, he said that he thought the worst was over. But then, they were sent to Fort Benning, Georgia, for Airborne Jump School. The drill instructors, or Black Hats as they are called, made the previous drill instructors look nice in comparison. Four weeks later, upon completion of jump school, they were asked if they would like to go to Vietnam, and since they were now believers that they were the toughest soldiers in the world, they all volunteered.

These are just a few of the people that I met over the years that made the journey toward war. I found that most of us who did so did it willingly and felt okay with the fact that it was a dangerous place to be. Most of all, we were proud that we were part of group that was defending our way of life and, at the same time, helping someone else that was trying to obtain the same thing.

However, that feeling of pride would be short-lived, crushed out like a cigarette butt by people whom I have come to view as selfish, self-centered, uncaring people who claim to be Americans, people whom I have come to view as nothing short of traitors.

CHAPTER 6

1965, 1966, 1967

LIKE THE JOURNEYS THAT STARTED at various times for each of us, our arrivals at our destination would also be different. That arrival that would become known as a tour of duty would span over the next eight years. Here are some of those memories.

Joseph P. Keely, staff sergeant, United States Marine Corps
Enlisted 1964
Location: first tour Da Nang, second tour Gia Lea, located north of Phu Bi and south of Hue City (1965, 1966, 1967)

On October 15, 1965, the student-run National Coordinating Committee to end the War in Vietnam staged the first public burning of a draft card in the United States to result in arrest under the new law. On October 16, anti-war protests drew one hundred thousand in eighty US cities and around the world. I was too busy to pay attention to these things that were happening as I was putting my affairs in order prior to leaving.

After spending thirty days at home, on October 25, 1965, I caught a commercial flight to Los Angeles heading to Marine Corps Base Camp Pendleton for further processing prior to heading for Okinawa.

After nine days of processing at Pendleton, on November 6, we were transported to El Toro Naval Air Station where we boarded a MATS (Military Air Transport Service) jet. We would hit Wake Island for refueling prior to landing at Okinawa. We were transported to Camp Butler arriving on the ninth of November. The next day, November 10, was the 190th birthday of the Marine Corps. The Marines always celebrate the birthday of the corps. Dinner was turned in to a mandatory celebration for the occasion. Midway through the evening pretty much everyone on camp, Butler was half hit in the ass. Whiskey muscles took the place of common sense. Fistfights were breaking out all over the camp. What was supposed to be a happy birthday party turned into a band of Marine Corps brothers kicking the shit out of one another for no apparent reason. I remember thinking how lucky I was growing up in a household with one older and sober sister and not having to worry about waking up with a bloody nose or a black eye after a birthday party. Not feeling to steady on my own feet, I went to bed.

The next few days were busy with stowing gear, orientation on what to expect, and medical. All the guys in the barracks that I was in were all part of a draft, guys with different MOS (military occupations) going to different units but having no idea which one. Because we were part of a draft and not part of a unit, no one was developing any real friendships; we were more like a bunch of strangers standing in a line waiting to get tickets to a ball game.

One day, right after we finished stowing our seabags in a warehouse, we were all standing around, smoking and shooting the shit. We were near an open garage or carport that contained a jeep. Suddenly, a handful of Navy corpsmen showed up with medical bags and needles. They advised us that we were about to get hemoglobin shots for our trip to the Nam. This shot thins out the blood, so it is easier to adjust to the intense heat. The docs just had us drop our trousers, lean over the jeep fender, and get a shot. I have never been skittish of shots, but Christ, this one hurt, not the needle but the medicine going in hurt for hours.

Right after we received those shots, we were brought into a building and told to sit on the floor. Everyone thought that felt good on our sore asses. I felt like I was back in high school health class because they started giving us a lecture on venereal disease. We were being told about the many reasons to stay away from certain indigenous female personnel that inhabit Vietnam. We were being told about the many and various disgusting venereal diseases that could be caught with such fraternization. We were shown movies about things that could make your dick fall off. All this and no one has even fired a shot at me yet. I remember thinking, *Christ, I am already going to an extremely dangerous and scary place, and I have to worry about what is supposed to be a pleasurable experience.* These people were really starting to scare me. No, not really! Everyone forgot about that lecture as soon as we left the building.

Our draft left Okinawa by ship on November 12, 1965. I was aboard the USS *Magoffin*. This was an old World War II troop ship. There were six decks below the main deck. Our draft shared the ship with a formed battalion of Marines from Okinawa (I cannot remember the unit).

However, we lucked out; our sleeping deck was the first deck down from the main deck. Sleeping sucked. The racks were stacked six high one on top of each other, and there was just enough room to slide in on your back, leaving no room to sleep on your side. A lot of guys just slept on the main deck. We left port with four other ships, one of which was the USS *Skagit*; this ship was one of the ships that participated in Operation Freedom Passage, transporting Vietnamese refugees from the north to the south after the First Indochina War at the request to South Vietnam in 1954.

Now eleven years later, she was part of a convoy bringing me to Vietnam. We arrived at Da Nang early morning on November 18. It was just starting to break dawn. However, everyone was up. A Marine, unknown to me, came halfway down the mid-ship's ladder, saying, "I think we're there."

Everyone within earshot said, "What makes you say that?"

"I see land," was his response.

Everyone bounded up the ladder after him. As I exited the hatch onto the main deck, I saw mountains jutting out of the South China Sea. They were silhouetted against the gray sky. Just as I reached the starboard side of the ship, I saw an F-4 Phantom come bounding off the land *(he was smokin')*. I could see his afterburners. He was almost vertical in flight. As he passed the mountain, I saw tracer rounds following his assent. I watched both until they disappeared. Nobody said a word; we knew we were there.

We had other tasks to perform prior to being assigned to our units. The Marines aboard the ship were divided into working parties to clean up our mess and make sure the ship was clean before we disembarked. It wouldn't be until the next morning before we left the USS *Magoffin*. Our draft was told that we were transferring to the *Skagit*. The crane on one her cargo holds was inoperable and had to be unloaded by hand. We disembarked the *Magoffin* by way of cargo nets and boarded the *Skagit* the same way. After grabbing a quick bite in the *Skagit* mess deck, we were put to work, unloading the hold. Everyone was sick of ship life by this time, so we busted our asses, unloading the cargo. We disembarked the *Skagit* at 1600 hours (4:00 PM). It wouldn't be until the next morning that I would arrive at my unit on the twentieth of November. Once I arrived at Third Tanks, I was issued my 782 gear (combat gear rifle and packs, etc.), and for the next twenty months, a good night sleep became a thing of the past.

You learn all by yourself that the overwrought worry and fear that you have when you first arrive in such a place isn't going to change the situation that you're in or is going to help you cope. Therefore, you just stop worrying about the things you can't control, and you get on with the task at hand.

Besides the newscast I heard earlier in December about Americans protesting the troops as they returned from the Nam, I would notice something else that would anger me. As I came out of the communications bunker one morning, I was stretching, and as I leaned back, I noticed that something was missing. It was the American flag. I was on a US military base and there was no flag? I noticed a fellow Marine passing by. I stopped him and asked him where the flag was. I was advised that it was against the law to fly our flag; it could only be flown over division headquarters. I thought, *What kind of shit that is. I am fighting in a country that is across the international date line from my home and I am not allowed to carry my flag into the fight?*

Here I am, in country one month, and I receive two wounds of the heart, and neither one came from a bullet. One came from the people I swore to protect, and to this day, I do not know who is responsible for the other. On the twenty-first of December, I wrote home, requesting that my family buy me a flag that I could hang over my rack in the tent. My sister whom I have mentioned earlier and who has always championed my causes took it one step further. She wrote to Congressman Frelinghuysen, requesting a flag that is flown over the Capitol. I received that flag seven days later, free of charge. That flag remained with me for the rest of my time in country. Fifty-plus years later, I still have that flag in my possession, safe and sound.

As I mentioned before, I had no illusions as to where I was going or what I was doing. However, being young, I was adventurous and thought I knew what to expect. Once again, I was proven wrong. I was on mess duty; it was early morning hours, and I was in my tent sound asleep.

Suddenly, I was awoken by an enormous explosion. My eyes shot wide-open to see red-hot metal flying through the air. The explosions were coming in rapid succession and moving through the command like they had legs and knew where they were going. The bunkers on both sides of the perimeter were firing their weapons. This turned out to be more than just a mortar attack; it was what we called a zapper raid. This is where the VC (Vietcong) would follow the attack into the compound. In this case, they were trying to blow up the fuel bladders we had just inside the perimeter.

I was scrambling to get my rifle, my trousers, and my boots, in that order. I immediately got older, and I believe my very first thought was, *What the fuck was I thinking?* That was the second time I had that thought since I joined the Marines.

My next thought was, *God, you get me out of this, and I'll be good.* After gathering the rifle trousers and boots, I crawled to a trench located behind the tent. After I got my clothes on, I felt a lot better. By that time, the mortars had stopped. However, I heard sporadic gunfire throughout the compound. I started making my way to the communication bunker to assist with restoring wire communications.

We lost six guys that night; I do not know how many were wounded. I remember the CO (commanding officer) roaming around, checking on the men. He was in his skivvies (underwear). He was wearing a shoulder holster. Although it was dark, it stood out against his white T-shirt. Besides, illumination flares were popping all over the place. I saw blood flowing from his left hip; he was being followed by the corpsman who was begging him to get on the chopper to be dusted off (helicopter medical evacuation), but the CO wasn't hearing it. He was more concerned about the men. He yelled at us wiremen who were gathered, repairing the main phone cable that was cut by shrapnel produced by the mortars. He made us stop what we were doing. He was afraid that another mortar attack would kill us all. It wasn't until dawn that he finally decided to let them medevac him.

Shortly after dawn, the communications officer told me to return to the mess hall to resume my duties there. As I started up the hill, I saw dead VC (Vietcong) being removed from the barbed wires that surrounded the command post and served as a fence. They were tangled in it. This was part of the zapper contingent that did not make it. I found out later that one of them was one of the indigenous personnel that our unit employed as a barber. This guy had cut my hair the day before the attack. He probably got himself employed so he could pace off the compound for the mortar attack.

There was another event which took place while I was on mess duty during the noon meal, which I think is worth mentioning. Occasionally, I would be assigned to the officers' tent where they ate. It was separate from the enlisted. I would serve as a waiter and as a busboy. There was an older Vietnamese woman who was employed as a dishwasher by us. Although we did not speak the same language, we communicated with each other just fine. I called her mama-san. I teased her a lot; she would laugh and call me boo-koo dinkey-dow (meaning, "you very crazy").

One day, I had just brought some dishes over to her. I no sooner got the words *here you go, mama-san* out of my mouth than I heard the report of gunfire crack. *Crack, crack, crack!* I dropped the dishes in the wash pan and grabbed my rifle and cartridge belt and helmet. I reached the exit to the tent at the same time the officers did. We all headed up the hill on a dead run, in the direction where the shots came from. I looked to my left, and it appeared that every Marine in the compound was heading in the same direction. We all jumped into the trench line at the top of the hill. I didn't see anything except the top of the trees that canopied Phong Bac hamlet. Nothing appeared to be happening, but I saw the react squad (reactionary squad) going through the gate that was incorporated into the fence where we would exit the compound to conduct patrols. Approximately an hour passed before we were secured to return to work.

The next morning, I was reassigned to the officers' mess. Mamasan didn't show up for work. When I asked why she didn't show, I was advised that her husband was the man who was shot and killed by the VC the day before. I was told that her husband was the police chief of the hamlet and, because he was friendly to us, Charlie (short for Vietcong), decided that constituted the death penalty. I remember I felt bad for mama-san. However, it was not like in the States where you go to a wake and pay your respects. I never saw mama-san after that, but I think about her often.

It was right after that I was released from mess duty to return to my platoon. We were part of a large operation. We were looking for VC in the area. I remember it was a bright sunny day. We were crossing the rice paddies that belonged to the hamlet of Phong Bac using the series of dikes that separate the paddies from one another. We weren't into the paddies for very long when our radio operator yelled that he just received a radio transmission from the tank on top of the hill, advising that an individual wearing red shorts and a white shirt just hid something in the bushes and was heading in our direction. All at once, it seemed that everyone started yelling, "Dung-lie, dung-lie, halt, halt" at a person fitting the description. However, he just kept walking like he did not hear us. It so happened that the dike that he was on intersected with the one I was on. We were about seventy-five feet away from each other when I raised my rifle, took off the safety, and took aim. I took the slack off the trigger; this man was about a half a pound of pressure away from dying. When he saw me, he raised his hands and started yelling something in Vietnamese. At that time, I did not see a threat, so I gave him quarter. I raised the muzzle of the rifle and motioned him toward me. When we got within arm's length, I said, "Can Couc, Can Couc" (ID card, ID card). He reached into his back pocket and pulled out a black wallet wrapped in clear plastic. Everyone wrapped their important things in plastic due to the climate; between the humidity and rain, it was always wet over there. By the time, he got his ID out, the ARVN (Army of the Republic of Vietnam) interpreter was by my side. I handed the card to him, and he said, "Him good, him good," meaning the card was good.

I then handed it to a gunnery sergeant who was standing behind the interpreter. He smiled, returned the card to me, and said, "He's your prisoner." For the next two hours, I kept this man in front of me until I turned him over to the Vietnamese interrogators at a midway drop-off point.

There is a reason I relayed that story. If I had continued to apply that half pound of pressure that was required to fire the weapon, I would have been accredited with one VC kill. However, at the youthful age of twenty years and my adrenaline pumping at breakneck speed through my body in that danger zone, I made a judgment that allowed another human being to live. I would find out later that the assessment I made of the situation that was presented to me that day was a good one. It turned out that he was hiding his granddaughter under the bushes. He was taking her out to work in the paddies with him when he saw the patrol and did not want to put her in any danger.

The point being, contrary to the stories that was starting to be circulated about us back home, depicting us as murderers and baby bombers, was total horse shit. The entire time that man was in my custody, I did not beat him, kick him, shove him, stick him with my bayonet, cut him with my Ka-Bar, nor did I verbally abuse him. It is my belief that if I did any of those things, that gunnery sergeant I told you about would have put his boot up my ass. The whole time I was in country, I shot when I had to shoot and held my fire when I had to do that. The whole time I was in country, I never saw any of my fellow Marines or any of my comrades in arms from any branch of service do any of those things we were accused of doing. Okay? If you want, so help me, God.

Sometimes during battle, we would find humor even when the pucker factor was high. One night, just after the beginning of my second tour, the company clerk approached me and asked if I was doing anything this particular evening. I replied, "I don't have a hot date, if that's what you mean." He smiled and said, "No, they're looking for a radio operator for an ambush patrol. Charlie has been harassing the South Vietnamese troops located at the schoolhouse the last few nights." I advised him that I would take it. That made his night; he didn't have to continue looking for someone to go.

After attending the briefing with the squad leader and the rest of the squad, I proceed to the communication bunker to pick out a radio that I would use for the patrol. When I got inside the bunker, I saw that the guys on radio watch prepared all the field radios with new batteries and plastic wrap. It was the beginning of the monsoon season there, so it was not a question of when do you think it will rain, but when do you think it will stop.

I asked the operators on duty which was the best radio; in unison, they both said, "Take any one. They're all good." I grabbed a radio and went outside the bunker to conduct a radio check.

"Sassy, Sassy, this is Yankee White, radio check, over?

"Yankee White, this is Sassy. You're five by, over."

"Roger that, out."

I returned the radio to the bunker and asked the guys not to let anyone else take that radio. They said okay, and then they both said, "If you get hit out there tonight, give us three flashes on the net." I gave them a quizzical look because that is not proper radio procedure. Then one said, "Rather than going through all the Sassy, Sassy crap in the middle of a firefight, just say flash, flash, flash, and we will know you are getting hit!" I thought that was an innovative idea, and they told me they would pass that on to the relieving radio watch.

The patrol was scheduled for midnight. I proceeded to the bunker at 2330 hours to pick up my radio. I saw my buddy Fred on watch. I said, "I'll see you in the morning." He said, "Keep your head down." I departed the bunker. As I was approaching the squad leader, the heavens opened and the monsoons that I had come to hate had officially began.

As everyone in the squad exited the gate in the wire, you could hear the bolts on the rifles going home chambering a round. As we entered deeper into the bush, visibility became zero. Because of darkness, each man in the squad was about ten feet apart. This, coupled with the rain, made it so you could hardly see the guy in front of you. This always gave me the feeling that I was out there all alone when I was out there with thirteen other guys armed to the teeth.

There was no smokin' and jokin' out there. You had to pay attention and be alert. The only connection between us and the rest of the company was that radio on my back; it was a PRC-25 (pronounced "prick 25"). When I reached checkpoint one, I squelched on once; that means I keyed the handset one time to let the company know that we reached the checkpoint with no problems.

As soon as I squelched on, I heard in the handset receiver, my buddy Fred, say, "Be advised it's raining out, over," busting my balls because he is sitting in a dry bunker. Of course, I can't answer back because of where I am at. I smiled and I'm thinking to myself, *You prick.* The patrol continued in the rain, we reached checkpoint two. I squelched on twice and I hear, "Be advised it's still raining out, over." Another smile and I'm thinking, *What a ball buster.*

We finally reach the ambush site and set up. Two fire teams to the front, one fire team to the rear watching the trail. I and the squad leader were in the middle for control; we weren't in position for more than ten minutes when the fire team to the right front opens fire on something they saw. The squad leader said to me, "I'm going to see what those guys are shooting at." He got up and disappeared from my sight into the dark rainy night.

He was not gone for more than a minute when I heard the M-79 grenade launcher he was carrying fire. That no sooner happened, and whoever they spotted returned fire, including with heavy machine guns. Both fire teams to my front engaged in the firefight.

I heard a voice out of the dark yell, "Jesus Christ, they're all over the place." I can't see nor can the fire team behind me due to the darkness, rain, and distance between us and the other fire teams, so we can't engage for fear of hitting our own people.

I immediately pick up the handset and say, "Flash, flash, flash." I get an immediate response of, "Be advised it's still raining out, over." I'm trying to climb in my helmet, and he is giving me weather reports. I don't know exactly what happened, but evidently, Charlie decided to disengage. They went their way, and after getting a head count and checking for any possible wounded, so did we.

I found out later that the previous watch did not pass on the code to Fred like they said they were going to. It wasn't funny at the time, but the next morning, when I was talking to Fred, it all seemed better. We had a good laugh, and it has become our private joke for the last fifty years. Consequently, Charlie stopped harassing the South Vietnamese troops located at the school after that.

While I was traveling to and arriving at my unit to begin my tour of duty in November and December of sixty-five, there were other events occurring both in the Nam and back home. Events which I was not aware of not to mention being slightly overwhelmed.

Events such as on November 9 in New York City, a twenty-two-year-old Catholic worker movement member Roger Allen Laporte sets himself on fire in front of the White House in protest of the war in Vietnam (this was the second such incident in a week; on November 2, a thirty-two-year-old Quaker member did the same thing in front of the Pentagon). (Wow! That showed Them? I do not know about the Quaker, but I know the Catholic committed a mortal sin. You know where he went after committing that act, don't you? That's right! Hell). I think these guys were just looking for an excuse to commit suicide anyway. Well, congratulations! Mission accomplished.

1965

On November 8, the 173rd Airborne is ambushed by over 1,200 Vietcong in operation hump.

On November 14, the Battle of Ia Drang in the Ia Drang Valley of the Central Highlands began. This was the first major engagement of the war between regular United States and North Vietnamese forces. This battle would become famous in a later book and movie *We Were Soldiers Once…and Young* by Harold G. Moore and Joseph L Galloway (authors).

On November 27, the Pentagon tells President Johnson that if planned major sweep operations to neutralize Vietcong forces during the next year are to succeed, the number of American troops in Vietnam will have to be increased from 120,000 to 400,000.

On the same date, while we were slugging it out in the bush and the paddies of Nam, tens of thousands of Vietnam War protesters picket the White House and then march on the Washington Monument.

The next day, November 28, in response to President Johnson's call for *more flags* in Vietnam, Philippine President-elect Ferdinand Marcos announced he will send troops to help fight in South Vietnam.

On December 21, the Soviet Union announced that it has shipped rockets to North Vietnam.

Brian W. Robinson, ATR E5
Navy Enlisted 1966
Tours of duty dates:
October 19, 1966May 29, 1967
December 28, 1967–August 17,1968
April 16, 1969–October 17, 1969
Location: Western Pacific, Gulf of Tonkin, Vietnam (Beach Detachment)

I was in the country for twelve months when Brian pulled into the Gulf of Tonkin for his first tour. I asked him if he volunteered for the Nam. He told me he did not have to volunteer. They just sent him where the squadron went. His squadron went to Nam three times. However, he did volunteer for beach detachment and flight duty to fly with the Cods from the ships to the bases in Da Nang, the Philippines, etc. He told me they earned $50 to $100 more a month for flight pay, but he told me he had an alternative motive. It got him off the ship and into some air base with a bar and some gals. He said, "It probably sounds crazy, but most of the time, it was safer on the tarmac of a base in Vietnam than it was performing daily flight operations on a flight deck in the Tonkin gulf."

I believe that seeing how the aircraft carrier is the most dangerous man-made work environment in the world.

All he knows when he joined up was that he did not think about anything, except that he had to do what he had to do. He told me after seeing how the rest of the world was living after being on liberty and while on beach detachment that he was glad to be an American and felt that fighting to keep our way of life was the price we have to pay. He always hoped that nothing bad would happen but felt that if it did, it would be okay, even worth it, for the great life that he had lived so far. When things got a little dicey, as they often did, like when some of his team were killed in plane crashes, when some accident, like a cable snapping a couple of sailors in half or fires and smoke took the lives of his shipmates, he thought about how they were once so alive and healthy and now they were no more. He always hoped that someone, somewhere, would know and understand that these *good guys* were gone now because they were okay with taking on the work of war. They were okay with dying, if they had to, to keep their loved ones free to vote themselves into Kerry and Jane Fonda's slavery if they choose.

After the stint of scullery duty in Florida, he was sent to NAS Memphis where he went to school for electronics, radar, radio, TACAN, IFF, ECM and gave Elvis some ideas on how to revive his career with a comeback tour in '68. He joined up with VF-191, Satan's Kittens, out of Miramar, California. VF-191 was were the original Blue Angels were from. He was scheduled for West Pac on the *Ticonderoga* (*Tyco Tigers*). He did two more tours with VF-191, one on the *Ticonderoga* and a third on the *Oriskany* (the *Big O*, but after the fires, affectionately known as the *Zippo*).

He told me he was proud of the way he and his shipmates handled themselves when the *Oriskany* caught fire on October 26, 1966 and left fourteen of them crawling around in a pitch-black, smoke-filled compartment. He remembers hacking on smoke in a small compartment in the dark is a piece of cake compared to the idea that you cannot escape because you are at general quarters, locked down in that position to keep the ship from sinking. Even if you could get away, the nearest land is a mile away, straight down. Good training!

Brian said he would like to say to any of his boot camp pals that might read this that "I am sorry about all the fights I had with you, mutton-headed scallywags, for your lousy marching. It made you better sailors. That is my story, and I am sticking with it."

BCharles Ketterman
Sergeant, United States Marine Corps
Enlisted June 1964
Served in the Republic of Vietnam (February 1967 to February 1968)

Chuck advised me they were flown over to the Nam by a civilian airliner from Los Angeles to Okinawa with a stopover at Wake Island. Once at Okinawa, they were given no liberty but were flown out the next day to Da Nang air base where they got their assignments and directions to our units.

He fell in with a group of Marines assigned to Ninth MAB, a Marine Amphibious Brigade known as special landing force Bravo.

He said he joined up with them at the DMZ where they had been fighting on Hills 881 and 861.

The May 1967 issue of *Life* magazine dedicated an article to the Second Battalion Third Marines which he had been assigned to as a replacement. For him, the war had just begun. He quickly realized about death and prayed that God would help him through that. He does not remember how many times he repeated the Psalm 23 continuously with each time he walked point or was under fire. Each day brought another nightmare. Their supplies were depleted, and he remembers how their clothes were basically all ripped and their boots fell apart. He felt that justice had abandoned them and that killing to stay alive was their only hope.

Chuck and the guys had been hearing about a peace movement in the United States and felt like they were betrayed by our country. He said he even remembers hearing that returning Vietnam vets were joining the peace movement. He also said, "Our sentiments were to invade the north and finish it all." Their feelings were that they did not need a country that had turned their backs on them after getting them to the position they were in. The way Chuck sees it is that wars are not won by cowards and draft dodgers or by the protests of college students who have no experience at all.

Chuck was wounded; he was shot in the hip on February 6, 1968, during the Tet Offensive, defending the southern perimeters of Da Nang. His company (approximately one hundred men) were ordered to stop the second NVA division of approximately five thousand men. They were outnumbered, defending their position, killing as many as they could. When morning came, the enemy had moved on, and Chuck was being medevaced back to a MASH unit in Da Nang with other dead and wounded—a day, he said, he will never forget! All he knows is they held on and did the impossible. He wishes some of those college kids and cowards were there to see what it was like to be a man who loves his country and is willing to die for it.

Charlie Alexander, SP 4
Army drafted 1965
Served in the Republic of Vietnam (1966 to 1967)
Location: Pleiku

After they completed training, Charlie said his company was assigned as a unit to the Fourth Infantry Division and designated Bravo Company, Third Battalion, First Brigade, Fourth Infantry Division. They were given thirty days' furlough and orders to report back to Fort Lewis on July 21, 1966, for embarkation preparations.

After returning from leave, they boarded a converted cargo ship for the trip to the Nam. The trip took them twenty-one days with a three-day stopover in Okinawa. He thought that they may receive liberty on Okinawa; however, only ranks higher than E-7 received liberty. But he does recall a couple of soldiers jumping ship, never to be heard from again.

After the three-day layover in Okinawa, they landed in Da Nang around August 27, 1966. Before disembarking, they were issued a full complement of ammunition and were told to load as many magazines as possible. They were issued one bandolier of clips and two bandoliers of cartridges. They spent the rest of that day loading magazines. Cleaning their M16 rifles and other issued equipment. The next day, they were off-loaded from the ship. They were told to lock and load and to keep their weapons at the ready; Charlie said this was a very frightening moment for him in his life.

After securing a perimeter along the shoreline, the supplies from the ship were off-loaded. He said they were transported by C-130 cargo planes to Pleiku airfield from there they were transported to their fire base which consisted of a secure perimeter at the base of a hill affectionately called Titie Mountain by the GIs.

The mountain is located on the outskirts of Pleiku City, Gia Lai Province, in the central highlands. The perimeter at the time was secured by member of the Twenty-Fifth Infantry Division, who immediately loaded on to the trucks that brought Charlie's unit in and departed the area. Another scary moment in time. He remembers thinking that the Twenty-Fifth's tour was over.

Charlie said that the next few weeks were full of uncertainty and sleepless nights. It was not too long before they started patrols. In his first firefight, he was hit in the chest. He was told that the wound wasn't serious. However, he thought that it was the most serious event of his life.

He returned to his unit on November 20, 1966. On November 22, he was wounded again, this time by fragmentation in the right hand. At first it was thought to be the million-dollar wound. However, that would not be his fate. He returned to the field and completed his tour.

Charlie returned to the States on July 21, 1967. His assignment Stateside was Fort Jackson, South Carolina. He was discharged from active duty on November 15, 1967. Charlie said he returned home without much fanfare, except for the greeting of immediate family. He said it seemed that nobody cared most believed that we should not have been over there in the first place. He recalls that when he first heard the negative stuff that some people were saying, he would get angry. He says that he soon learned that his anger only affected him, and nobody else gave a shit.

From then on, he just stayed out of conversation that involved Vietnam. He just chalked it up to a thankless effort and tried to move on with his life.

However, I know different. The rejection and the ridicule that we Nam vets received is something you cannot forget.

Fredrick Goger, sergeant, United States Marine Corps
Enlisted: 1964
Served in the Republic of Vietnam (1965, 1966, 1967)
Location: first tour Da Nang, second tour Gia Lea, located north of Phu Bai and south of Hue City

After Pendleton, the next trip for Fred would be an eighteen-day journey to the Nam, landing him in Da Nang. He told me it was as if he was starting a whole new life. Getting assigned to Third Tanks was like being adopted by a new family. He said, "I had family at home, sure, but who the fuck cares? Cold thoughts, but I think that not worrying about *their* problems helped me adapt to my new home." He also said, "I figured I was a dead man, so every day here would be extra, so I was gonna try and suck it all up.

"So here I am in the mud, with big fucking tracked vehicles and numb nuts just like me playing Marine. Life was good." Fred went from E-1 to E-5 in the twenty months he spent there. However, he said he feels "that don't mean shit anyway." He said he does know that the constant vigilance, carrying a weapon twenty-four hours a day and going to sleep, hoping he would not get blown up, set the tone for the rest of his life. He says, "I now can't sleep without a weapon nearby. I don't trust anyone, and I wish I never came home. What the fuck is that about?"

Fred told me that the VA has him as 80 percent disabled (60 percent diabetes and 100 percent PTSD), service connected. He has been going to group therapy once a week for the past three years. He also sees a shrink once a week. He also told me that his oldest daughter has not spoken to him for about five years. She said it was his attitude and his overprotective nature. Fred said that means he has two granddaughters he doesn't know. He also said that his other kids say they grew up in a paranoid environment due to his vigilance. His wife knows it does not take much to get him from 0–10 on the anger meter quick, so they have been carefully going through the past forty years together.

I will end Freddy's input to this project with his last quote to me. I think a lot of guys feel this way.

"The fact that we gave South Vietnam back to the North has had me wondering all this time if my *baggage* from that tour was worth it, reinforcing the idea that I should have stayed there one way or the other. But here I am, waiting for the mailman. What the fuck. Semper fi."

*Leroy Terry Smith, sergeant, US Army Airborne
Enlisted September 15, 1965
Served in the Republic of Vietnam (1966, 1967)
First Cavalry Division, 1968 Eighty-Second
Airborne Division
Location: An Khe in the central highlands first
tour and Phu Bai in the north on the second tour*

Smitty, as I like to call him, told me he was given a thirty-day leave. Prior to going to Vietnam, he said that he boarded a commercial jet at JFK and was told to report to Oakland, California. He departed Oakland on Brannif Airlines with stewardesses and everything.

They landed at Tan Son Nhut Air Base in Saigon; when he got off the plane, he said he could not believe how hot it was. From Saigon, they were loaded on a small aircraft and flown to An Khe, First Cavalry Division Headquarters. They were taken to a reception center and issued weapons, and they were assigned to their units as replacements the next morning.

He remembers his first night in the country. Hong Kong Mountain was attacked by the VC; the guys he was with were located at the base of the mountain with no weapons and not a clue as to what was happening, other than hearing the fight going on. He said, "Believe me when I say it was a long night." That next morning, he was assigned to Bravo Company, First/Fifth Cavalry on a machine gun crew. Smitty did not say too much about his tour, except that near the end of his tour, he was wounded by a hand grenade and medevaced out.

With that wound, he was on his way back home after recovering from his wound in the 106th General Hospital, Japan. He was sent back to the States on leave and assigned Bravo Company 1st/501 101st Airborne Division, at which time he was sent to the Detroit riots of 1967. A month or two in the States and not completely healed, his CO told him that the outfit was being sent to Nam and asked if he wanted to go back with them. At that time, he said, "I declined and was reassigned to Alpha Company 1st /508th 82nd Airborne."

It would not be too long before events in Vietnam were about to heat up. These events would send Smitty back for another tour.

While Smitty, Brian, Chuck Ketterman, Chuck Alexander, Goger, and I were serving our country in this hot spot in 1966 and '67, the loyal, true-blooded Americans back home were continuing with the anti-war movement—events that were taking place which we were totally unaware of because, as you can see, we were a tad bit busy.

1966

May 15. Tens of thousands of anti-war demonstrators again picketed the White House and then rallied at the Washington Monument.

May 16. In New York City, Dr. Martin Luther King Jr. made his first public speech on the Vietnam War.

August 16. The House Un-American Activities Committee starts investigating Americans who have aided the Vietcong, with the intent to make these activities illegal. Anti-war demonstrators disrupt the meeting and fifty are arrested.

1967

April 29. US troops in Vietnam total 250,000.

July 7. A Warsaw Pact conference ends with a promise to support North Vietnam. *(Well, why not? the American people were.)*

October. Bobby Seale and Huey P. Newton found the militant group the Black Panther Party.

April 4. Martin Luther King Jr. denounces the Vietnam War during a religious service in New York City.

April 28. In Houston, Texas, boxer Muhammad Ali refuses military service.

May 6. Four hundred students seize the administration building at Chaney State College, Pennsylvania.

August 7. The People's Republic of China agrees to give North Vietnam an undisclosed amount of aid in the form of a grant. *("All the while, the American people gave aid in the form of protests.")*

October 21. Tens of thousands of Vietnam War protesters march in Washington, DC. Allen Ginsberg symbolically chants to levitate the Pentagon. *(I wonder if Ginsburg was oxygen deprived at birth.)*

It is now November 1967, and here is where the abandonment of the troops begins. Starting with McNamara, top members of the

Johnson administration are starting to jump ship like they were standing on the deck of the *Titanic*, whom I liken to the pursers, crew members, and other men that were leaping into the lifeboats, taking seats from the women and children.

November 29. US Secretary of Defense Robert McNamara announced his resignation to become president of the World Bank. This action is due to President Johnson's outright rejection of McNamara's early November recommendations to freeze troop levels, stop bombing North Vietnam, and hand over ground fighting to South Vietnam.

November 21. On the Vietnam War, United States General William Westmoreland tells news reporters, "I am absolutely certain that whereas in 1965 the enemy was winning, today he is certainly losing." *(Hmm, but why listen to him? He is only the commanding general in the field.)*

November 30. US Senator Eugene McCarthy (D-Minnesota) announced his candidacy for the Democratic Party presidential nomination, challenging incumbent President Lyndon B. Johnson over the Vietnam War.

December 5. In New York City, Benjamin Spock and Allen Ginsberg are arrested while protesting the Vietnam War.

CHAPTER 7

1968, 1969, 1970

Brian W. Robinson, ATR E5
Navy Enlisted 1966
Tours of duty dates:
10/19/1966–5/29/1967
12/28/1967–8/17/1968
4/16/1969–10/17/1969
Location: Western Pacific, Gulf of Tonkin, Vietnam
(Beach Detachment)

MEANWHILE ABOARD THE *TICONDEROGA*, AFTER months of dangerous operations and sending out sorties into North Vietnam that put their pilots' lives at risk, they were sent on to North Korea, where Brian felt they were not allowed to save our ship that was taken by North Korea. They were part of the response team that went to Korea to bring back the *Pueblo*.

The USS *Pueblo* was a US Navy vessel sent on an intelligence mission off the coast of North Korea. On January 23, 1968, the USS *Pueblo* was attacked by North Korean naval vessels and MiG jets. One man was killed, and several were wounded. The eighty-two surviving crew members were captured and held prisoner for eleven months.

Brian felt it was just one more case where the politicians placating to the traitors put them in harm's way but would not let them do anything except play like a carnival bear target while they watched they're shipmates suffer. He said, "The men really hated Johnson and his whining Democrats after that tour."

The *Pueblo* was taken in January of 1968; Johnson's resolve to continue was starting to wane after four years of continual abuse by the American public, which was beginning to include members of his own Cabinet jumping on board with the traitors.

At the same time, the Tet Offensive was occurring in Vietnam, and the American media was claiming we were losing the war. This will be discussed more in depth later.

I asked Brian if he had been wounded. His reply was, "If you count the kinds of wounds that Kerry received, there were three also. Once, I stubbed my finger while replacing a radio pack in an F8 Crusader in the Tonkin gulf. Once, I jabbed my hand with a screwdriver while in nuclear weapons loading training aboard the *Oriskany*. The third time was when I cut my leg with a butterfly knife during a drunken brawl in Dog Patch. This last one was earned saving my chief from certain death at the hands of a short-changed mama-san."

I feel that the drunken brawl that Brian was involved in is more action than Kerry saw, so Brian should get three Purple Hearts and at least a Navy Cross.

In all seriousness, Brian said, "The biggest wound was seeing that mutt, Kerry, sitting with Barbarella, lying about what we were doing while in harm's way. It was the sick phonies like him who were looking for political power and acceptance from the lowest dregs of society that caused the war we had to fight. These same villains left us there defenseless, forced us into rules of nonengagement, and then maligned us as baby killers when we came home. The hatred spewed out by the collectivist is so vile in its desire to wipe out individual freedom that it somehow changed a Hollywood hottie, Barbarella, into Hanoi Jane. Where is the justice?"

Brian told me that the one site he saw when returning from the gulf that let him and his shipmates know that they were home was the Golden Gate Bridge coming into California. This has been a welcome sight to many a sailor and military man returning from war by ship for many years. That is, right up until the Vietnam War. Brian told me they came back to have the beautiful people of San Francisco dump garbage on them as they sailed under the bridge into the bay. These are sights that are never forgotten and cause wounds to be inflicted to the heart which never heals.

Leroy Terry Smith, sergeant, US Army Airborne
Enlisted September 15, 1965
Served in the Republic of Vietnam 1966, 1967 First Cavalry Division, 1968 Eighty-Second Airborne Division
Location: An Khe in the central highlands first tour and Phu Bai in the north on the second tour

Thinking that his time in the Nam was a thing of the past, Smitty was settling down, seeing that he did not have too much time before he was discharged. However, a few months later the Tet Offensive started and the outfit that he was reassigned to was deployed back to Nam TDY, a dollar a day extra for returnees, they needed experienced guys because 1,500 guys were brand-new. He remarked to me, "I was always lucky." Partway through this tour, while going to the aid of a sister company, he was blown up in the air by an RPG. He only received minor wounds this time around, not bad enough to send him home. However, it was just a couple of months later when he was sent back to the States and discharged from the service.

However, with the coming of 1968, it did not appear that the war in Vietnam was slowing down, nor was the war at home with the Communists and Communist sympathizers stepping up their activities.

For example, on January 19, at a White House conference on crime, singer and actress Eartha Kitt denounced the Vietnam War directly to President Lyndon Johnson.

On January 21, the Battle of Khe Sanh began; it became one of the most publicized and controversial battles of the war, ending on April 8. However, here is a bit of information that was not known to the military at the time or to anyone at home because they were too busy denouncing our government: Our military are taking the side of the very people we were fighting in this battle. Khe San was a diversion attack to keep everyone busy while the Communist North Vietnamese prepared for the upcoming Tet Offensive.

You probably remember the gentleman I mentioned earlier in the book, Colonel Bui Tin, the officer who took the unconditional surrender from the South Vietnam government at the end of the war. I would like to share with you now what he wrote in his book *From Enemy to Friend* regarding this battle.

1968

He said, "A few weeks before Tet, a diversion was created with the attack launched against Khe Sanh. The Khe Sanh maneuver was intended to lull the cities and municipalities in the south into a false sense of security a completely subjective security." (Subjective meaning based on somebody's opinions or feelings rather than on facts or evidence.)

Then on January 30, 1968, the Tet Offensive began as Vietcong forces launched a series of surprise attacks across South Vietnam. This is what Colonel Bui Tin says about this little event.

Statement of Col. Bui Tin
Regarding the 1968 Tet Offensive:

Nineteen sixty-eight was an election year in the United States. The CPV wanted to create a victory in Vietnam so overwhelming that it would shake up support in the rear in the United States itself—and give a big boost to the American anti-war movement.

A further rationale for the Tet attacks was Hanoi's need to reassert its influence in the south. From 1965 to 1967, the South Vietnamese army (Army of the Republic of Vietnam, or ARVN, for short) and U.S. troops went on the offensive and were very active, forcing our troops into a defensive mode. We had to pull back into remote areas in order to maintain our strength, thus losing both territory and population. Now something spectacular was needed to regain the initiative and reverse the situation if possible.

The 1968 Mau Than Tet Offensive was a shocker. It forced a worldwide reassessment of the situation in Vietnam and caused heated debates in U.S. political circles and the U.S. Media: in the printed media, on radio, and television.

After the Tet offensive, the Americans and Saigon launched an immediate counteroffensive throughout the South accompanied by quick pacification, resulting in some of the greatest losses for our side in all of 1968, 1969, and 1970. Practically all our urban hideaways, which took years to build, were uncovered in the process and wiped out.

Even rural bases were lost on a vast scale. Northern troops had to be brought south to fill the huge gaps created by the loses and on-the-spot mobilization became extremely difficult. In not a few localities, so called regional troops at provincial and district levels—even so-called village militia—were actually fresh recruits from the northern provinces of Thanh Hoa, Nghe An, and Ha Tnh.

It was during this offensive Walter Cronkite put out his famous editorial report stating that the Vietnam War was unwinnable. I would like to know! Who the fuck died and left him the commanding general of the US military? This was reported as a matter of fact before our counteroffensive took place!

February 1. A Vietcong officer is executed by Nguyn Ngoc Loan, a South Vietnamese National Police chief. The event is photographed by Eddie Adams. The photo makes headlines around the world, eventually winning the 1969 Pulitzer Prize and sways US public opinion against the war. I am pretty sure that US public opinion was pretty much swayed against the war by the time this photo was taken. To say this event was a swaying factor after five years of protest is absurd.

February 24. The Tet Offensive is halted. Hue City is recaptured. In less than a month, the Tet Offensive launched by North Vietnam was destroyed as stated above by Colonel Tin.

March 12. US President Lyndon B. Johnson edged out anti-war candidate Eugene J McCarthy in the New Hampshire Democratic primary, a vote which highlights the deep divisions in the country, as well as the Democratic Party.

March 16. My Lai Massacre. American troops kill scores of civilians. *(This wrongful deed will be discussed in length later.)*

March 17. A demonstration in London's Parliament Square against US involvement in the Vietnam War leads to violence—ninety-one people injured, two hundred demonstrators arrested.

March 19–March 23. Afrocentrism, black power. Students at Howard University in Washington, DC, signal a new era of militant student activism on college campuses in the US. Students stage rallies, protests, and a five-day sit-in, laying siege to the administration building, shutting down the university in protest over its ROTC program, and demanding a more Afrocentric curriculum.

March 21. In an ongoing campus unrest, Howard University students protesting the Vietnam War, the ROTC program on campus, and the draft confront Gen. Lewis Hershey, then head of the US Selective Service System, and, as he attempts to deliver an address, shut him down with cries of, "America is the Black man's battleground!"

March 31. US President Johnson announces he will not seek reelection. I believe that Johnson just had enough of the criticism and anti-war movement, especially when McNamara and two other Cabinet members, the newly appointed Secretary of Defense Clark Clifford and Harry McPherson, counsel to the president, were starting to jump ship and secretly conspiring to get the president to pull out of Vietnam.

My question is, where was our military intelligence or even our civilian intelligence? According to Col. Bui Tin, the Communist knew that the US military had beaten them to where we had them on their knees, again as stated above. Any military commander will tell you that when you have your enemy down, crush them.

Quagmire was the term that was given to describe the Vietnam War by the so-called American people. It is defined as a swamp, a soft marshy area of land that gives way when walked on. It is also called quag, an awkward, complicated, or dangerous situation from which it is difficult to escape.

If Vietnam was a quag or quagmire that we were in, then it was the constant crying, protesting, drug-taking, draft-evading, draft-card burning, pot-smoking, sniveling, treasonous Americans that were listened to by the same sniveling politicians that stuck our feet in it!

This is where the abandonment began; it appears that Johnson, like Pontius Pilate, washed his hands of the crucifixion that was about to be perpetrated upon the troops who fought in and were still fighting in Vietnam and would continue to do so for the next five years. And the crying at home would continue.

April 23-April 30. Student protesters at Columbia University in New York City take over administration buildings and shut down the university.

August 22-August 30. Police clash with anti-war protesters in Chicago, Illinois, outside the 1968 Democratic National Convention, which nominates Hubert Humphrey for US president and Edmund Muskie for vice president.

October 14. The United States Department of Defense announces that the United States Army and United States Marines will send about 24,000 troops back to Vietnam for involuntary second tours *(not the 206,000 that was requested by the commanders in the field).*

October 31. Citing progress in the Paris peace talks, President Johnson announces to the nation that he has ordered a complete cessation of all air, naval, and artillery bombardment of North Vietnam effective November 1. *(The abandonment continues.)*

November 5. US presidential election 1968. Republican challenger Richard M. Nixon defeats Vice President Hubert Humphrey and American Independent Party candidate George C. Wallace.

Nine months after Johnson gives up the presidency, troops like my friends Ron, Tom, and Chet are still being sent to Nam, only with less support then we had before the Tet.

John (Ron) R. Nash, Spec 5
A Battery 2/11 Artillery 101st Airborne, US Army
Enlisted/signed up for one more year
Served in the Republic of Vietnam (December 1968–December 1969)
Location: Hue, Phu Bai, A-Shau Valley, DMZ

Ron said he left from Seattle on a Continental Charter flight fully loaded with people who did not know what to expect. As they approached Nam, they saw two fighter jets come up on their wing as an escort. In the distance, he saw pillars of black smoke. Little did he know that it was shit burning. Landing at Long Bin, he said they exited from the rear of the plane while guys leaving entered in front. It was here that he realized for the first time that he was entering a part of the world at war and death.

He remembers that the in-country process took all day, and he was given orders to the 321st Artillery up north with the 101st Airborne. He and the rest of the guys were loaded on a C-130, which he thought was noisy, hot, and crowded. They flew to Da Nang, then Camp Eagle.

At the 321st Headquarters, they told him that he was needed at another artillery group, the 2/11 A Battery near Hue. He was sent to Tomahawk Firebase on Route 1. When he arrived there, he said, "I was scared and nervous and didn't know what to expect." He was sent to see the mess sergeant, who showed him around and he got into the daily routine. "Guard duty at 4:00 a.m., start the coffee, and then feed the one hundred guys." He was only in the country one week when they were overrun by the Cong. He remembered that they came from everywhere, but with the help of air support and the grunts (infantry), they did little damage.

A cook in the Nam was always a hot and dirty job in the field. If a field kitchen was set up, it got extremely hot in that tent. They started in early morning, cooking with the flaps closed, making it hotter. The flaps had to be closed because when they started cooking, it was dark and they did not want to light up the camp.

Ron told me, "The best part of being a cook was the expression and smiles on the guys face when they were able to eat *real food* not Cs."

He also said, "The best was when a patrol came in from the bush and they could have hot coffee and a good meal or two. They really appreciated us Spoons," as they were called by the guys. During his tour, he said he was at Camp Eagle or in the field; wherever they wanted him, he went. He drove the mess jeep or the Deuce and a Half to deliver the chow or supplies when they left base camp. He remembers it was scary driving the roads, not knowing what was around the next corner. He said, "Thank God for the infantry who cleared the roads and area."

The A Battery 2/11 Artillery was a Bastard Battery and was sent all over with their 155 Toads. He doesn't remember much of where he went or what happened, but as time goes on, his memory is jarred and little bits of his time in Nam come back to him. He does remember, however, that a group of South Vietnam Infantry came to his firebase, and the captain of the unit didn't like what one of his men did in a firefight, so he shot him dead. He told our CO that the man was no good to him.

Another incident that had come back to him was, while they were on a stand down at Camp Eagle, they were mortared, and everyone headed for the bunkers. He remembers a round landed in one of the holes and blew up everyone in it. I was assigned to graves registration because of that attack. I had to pick up pieces of bodies and put them in a body bag. He found a Black arm and he knew it belong to their first sergeant. He believes that these incidents are why his memory is sometimes blocked.

He said it took him many years to talk about Nam. I know this is true. I have known Ron since 1972, and he and I have never really spoken of Nam until now. He says only recently he has remembered those days, good and bad.

He works with many young people, and sometimes they ask him about the war. He said he tells them what he can remember. He deals with the public, and many of the customers that go into his restaurant see all the patriotic things he has up. If they happen to be a Nam vet, they look at him and say, "Welcome home." *(We say that to one another because our country never did.)*

When Vietnam is mentioned where he works, the kids say, "That is in our history books." However, Ron says, "I'm not history. George Washington is."

Ron also said, "I am immensely proud to say I was in the Nam and that I am an American and that I proudly served my country." He said he tells everyone that, and he stands tall when he says it. He also said, "Even though we did not get the attention that the guys coming home now do, I still to this day say that I am *proud that I served.*"

Tom Martin, sergeant, United States Army
Drafted June 1968
January 1969 to January 1970
Camp Evans in Thua Thien Province

On Friday, December 13, 1968, Tom said he flew out of Travis Air Force Base in California wearing a summer khaki uniform, PFC (private first class) stripes, National Defense ribbon, and his expert rifleman's badge. He remembers that they stopped over in Anchorage,

Alaska, and that summer khaki uniforms are not very conducive to December Alaskan weather.

By the time Tom arrived in country, January of '69, Johnson leaves office as Richard Milhouse Nixon is sworn in as the thirty-seventh president of the United States of America. Two months later, a decision made by the new administration would occur.

On March 18, Operation Breakfast, the secret bombing of Cambodia, would begin.

Back home in America, the anti-war movement would continue. On April 9, the Harvard University Administration Building was seized by close to 300 students, mostly members of the students for a democratic society. Before the takeover ended, 45 would be injured and 184 arrested. This would be the first of many anti-war movement activities for the year 1969.

Meanwhile, somewhere in that time, Tom was promoted to sergeant E-5 and assigned to 3rd Battalion, 187th Infantry Regiment, of the 101st Airborne Division. In May of 1969, Tom's unit was sent on an operation designated Apache Snow. It was part of the spring offensive reentering the A Shau Valley. The previous year the Marines were the last ones in the valley. Tom would not get to complete his tour in the Nam.

Shortly after entering the A Shau, on May 10, Tom's unit was starting up a hill designated by the military as 937, named like all the other hills in Vietnam for its elevation above sea level; it was also known as Dong Ap Bia. Ten days later, on May 20, after that many days of fighting for possession of that hill, Tom's outfit would win it. However, those who fought there would rename 937 Hamburger Hill. This battle would be made famous many years later in a movie of the same name.

Tom told me that another sergeant and friend of his, Bill Ricci, were hit by the same rocket on the second day of the battle, May 11, 1969. This rocket came from one of our Huey gunships (friendly fire). I never understood why they called it that. However, I always knew it could happen; it is the unfortunate part of being a warrior. He said Bill always lamented, "Wouldn't you know it, the year with

'69 in it, we would not be in the world." *(The world is what we said when referring to the States.)*

Even amid chaos, there is comedy. It is probably a defense mechanism to help you get through such things. Tom always told the story that Bill saved his life; he said that when he was wounded in action, he fell on top of Bill in the foxhole. If Bill hadn't been there to break the fall, he would have really been hurt.

Bill was medevacked first because of his head wound. He promised Tom before he left that he would check the TV guide so something good would be on when he got to the field hospital later. He said Bill made him laugh every day.

He also told me another story about him and Bill. This occurred sometime earlier. One day, the first sergeant approached them, asking if a wounded GI could share their foxhole. Tom was feeling a little pissy that day, a case of the ass, so to speak. He decided that he was going to interview the GI to see if he was worthy of sharing the same foxhole with them. When he first found the GI in the bushes, Tom didn't see any wound. "Where the hell are you hit?" Tom asked. The kid pointed down at the top of his boot, where a piece of shrapnel penetrated. "How long have you been in country?" The wounded guy said, "Two weeks." At this point in time, the medic advised Tom that the wound would send the young GI back to the world. Tom said, "Two weeks in country and he is going home with that wound?"

At any rate, Tom and Bill let him use the foxhole. Within the hour, their position started taking some small arms fire from the front. He and Bill returned fire from the prone position. Bill and Tom looked at each other, and at the same time, they both raised a foot in the air to get the million-dollar wound. He said they both burst out laughing like hell.

Tom remembers what's not to like about his friend Bill Ricci!

Chester Waleski, captain, Army
Army through ROTC 1968
Served in the Republic of Vietnam
(January 1969 to January 1970)
Location: Cu Chi

Upon arrival at Cu Chi, he would take on the duties of quartermaster; he was assigned as the grave's registration officer. He took care of the ARVN, civilian, Army, Navy, and Marines.

By that I mean that he would spend the next year of his life recovering the bodies of the people who died in his area of operation and making sure they were properly cared for. This included making sure that the bodies of our men were sent home.

That had to be one tough job. He was a second lieutenant promoted to first lieutenant while in country. He served with CO A S&T Battalion, Twenty-Fifth Infantry. He told me that his first child was born while he was serving there. It was a boy.

After completing his tour of duty, he was returning home, anxious to see his wife and his now three-month-old son. Although he was subject to anti-war demonstrations prior to leaving for Vietnam, he was unprepared for the reception that he and his fellow veterans received when they stepped off the plane at La Guardia Airport, New York, after returning home. What he was about to encounter would be the first noticeable wound to the heart that he would receive that he would carry all these years.

He told me that all he wanted to do is get home to see his family. He could not understand why Americans were calling him names and spitting at him for wearing the uniform of the United States Army. He just kept thinking, *Are you kidding me? What a bunch of ingrates.* He believes to this day that those people who protested were moral cowards, protesting only because they were afraid to go to Vietnam.

In the years since Vietnam, Chet told me that the following would continually hurt him deep inside. Whenever he tried to bring anything up about Vietnam to friends or family, they would listen, but he always had the feeling that they did not want to discuss "that war!"

He also remembers that when he first came home, he thought that his parents would put up a Welcome Home sign. However, that sign never materialized. According to Chet, it would not be until years later that he found out that the house his parents were renting belonged to Chet's uncle. It was Chet's uncle that requested that Chet's parents refrain from putting up a sign due to the fear that protesters may demonstrate in front of the house.

These are just a few things that Chet would live with through all these years.

Tom, Chet, and Ron were all serving the Nam at the same time, and while these guys were there doing the honorable thing, Americans back home were cooking up more treasonous activity to perform.

These are just a few of the guys that I am honored to call my friends—no, my brothers. While we served, the treason back home continued.

1969

For example, between *May 26-June 2*, John Lennon and Yoko Ono conduct their bed in at the Queen Elizabeth Hotel in Montréal, Québec. This is in protest to the Vietnam War. On June 1, in Montréal, Canada, "Give Peace a Chance" is recorded in the famous bedding for peace by John Lennon. The song is the first single recorded solo by a Beatle and released under the name Plastic Ono Band; it is still a strong anthem for peace. Lennon was not an American, but he had a lot of them in his back pocket.

On *June 8*, President Richard Nixon and South Vietnamese President Nguyen Van Thieu met at Midway Island. Nixon announced that twenty-five thousand US troops will be withdrawn by September. *(This is one year four months after we won Tet Offensive.)*

On *July 8*, the very first US troop withdrawals are made. *(The abandonment continues.)*

On *July 18*, Edward M Kennedy drove off a bridge on his way home from a party on Chappaquiddick Island, Massachusetts. Mary Jo Kopechne, a former campaign aide to his brother, was in the car with him; she dies in the incident. What a brave soul! No wonder he was against the Vietnam War; he did not even have the courage to save the young lady he was driving with. He and his brother Robert Kennedy will come to betray their own brother's memory.

July 25. President Nixon declares the Nixon Doctrine stating that the United States expects its Asian allies to take care of their own military defense. This starts the "Vietnamization" of the war. *(And the abandonment continues.)*

September 5. They found responsible for the My Lai Massacre. Lieutenant William Calley, United States Army, is charged with six counts of premeditated murder for the deaths of 109 Vietnamese civilians in My Lai.

September 24. The Chicago eight trial begins in Chicago, Illinois.

October 9-October 12. Days of rage: In Chicago, the United States National Guard is called in to control demonstrations involving the radical weatherman. The leader of this event is a guy by the name of Bill Ayers, in connection with the "Chicago eight" trial.

October 15. Hundreds of thousands of people take part in national moratorium anti-war demonstrations across the United States.

November 12. My Lai Massacre: independent investigative journalist Seymour Hersh breaks the My Lai story.

November 15. In Washington, DC, 250,000–500,000 protesters stage a peaceful demonstration against the war, including a symbolic March against Death.

November 20. The *Cleveland Plain Dealer* publishes explicit photographs of dead villagers from the My Lai Massacre in Vietnam.

November 25. John Lennon returns his MBE medal to protest the British government's support of the US war in Vietnam.

1970

December 1. The first draft lottery in the United States is held since World War II. (On January 4, 1970, the *New York Times* will run a long article, "Statisticians Charge Draft Lottery Was Not Random.")

Thus ends another year of nonsupport. However, that did not stop the forward motion of the American anti-war movement. All through 1970, the treason would continue.

February 18. A jury finds the Chicago seven defendants not guilty of conspiring to incite a riot, in charges stemming from the violence at the 1968 Democratic national convention. Five of the defendants are found guilty on the lesser charge of crossing state lines to incite a riot.

On the same day. My Lai Massacre: the United States Army charges fourteen officers with suppressing information related to the incident.

April 29. The US invades Cambodia to hunt out the Vietcong; massive anti-war protests occur in the US. *(Of course, they did not protest the North Vietnamese for being there for the entire length of the war.)*

May 1. Demonstrations against the trial of the New Haven nine, Bobby Seale, and Ericka Huggins draw twelve thousand for protesting President Richard Nixon's orders for US forces to cross into neutral Cambodia, threatening to widen the Vietnam War, sparking nationwide riots, and leading to the Kent State shootings.

May 4. Kent State shootings: four students at Kent State University in Ohio are killed and nine wounded by Ohio State National Guardsmen at a protest the incursion into Cambodia.

May 8. Unionized construction workers attack about one thousand students and others protesting the Kent State shootings near the intersection of Wall Street and Broad Street and at New York City Hall, leading to the hard-hat riot. *(How about that? Finally, a few Americans.)*

May 9. In Washington, DC, one hundred thousand people demonstrate against the Vietnam War.

June 24. The United States Senate repeals the Gulf of Tonkin resolution. This too will be discussed in more detail later.

June 28. US ground troops withdraw from Cambodia due to the pressure and demonstrations back home.

I agreed with the tactic, I disagreed with the timing. Looking at it from a tactical standpoint, the United States should have entered Laos and Cambodia back in '65 when we first entered the war to cut off the enemy's supply lines to South Vietnam. To enter Cambodia this late in the game is like throwing a punch backing up. Any boxer will tell you throwing a punch going backward doesn't have the same effect as throwing one going forward. Nixon had already started the Vietnamization program, which means he was backing up or out whichever way you want to look at. However, he is throwing punches to make it look good.

September 7. Anti-war rally is held at Valley Forge, Pennsylvania, attended by John Kerry Jane Fonda and Donald Sutherland.

October 12. Vietnam War: US President Richard Nixon announces that the United States will withdraw forty thousand more troops before Christmas. *(Backing up.)*

November 9. The Supreme Court of the United States votes 6-3 not to hear a case by the State of Massachusetts about the constitutionality of a state law granting Massachusetts residents the right to refuse military service in an undeclared war. *(The home state of the battles of Lexington and Concord. Where did all the patriots go?)*

November 10. Vietnamization for the first time in five years, an entire week ends with no reports of United States combat fatalities in Southeast Asia. *(And the treason went on year after year after year after year.)*

CHAPTER 8

1971, 1972, 1973

Name: Scott Meyer
Rank: sergeant
Branch: United States Air Force
Enlisted: yes
Tour/tours of duty dates: 1971, 1972, 1973
Location: a small village in the heart of Bavaria about a kilometer from the Czech border

THE STORY OF THE REMAINDER of Scott's four years in the Air Force is almost anticlimactic according to him. While almost everyone he had gone to basic training with was going to Vietnam, by some odd luck of the draw, he would study Czech.

His final destination was in a small village in the heart of Bavaria about a kilometer from the Czech border. The closest military base was about fifty miles away. He spent his last two years there. He became proficient in German, made a lot of friends, drank a lot of local beer, and did his job, but always with a little guilt that he had not shared the fate of so many of his friends.

Regarding him feeling guilty about not receiving orders to Vietnam, that is not his fault! Back then, the military was different. They did not have contracts and you didn't dictate to them where you wanted to be. They made the final decision. The point being, when people in America were running to the Canadian border to avoid being drafted, and as he witnessed firsthand the Chicago riots and the anti-war movement in full swing, he walked into a United States Air Force recruiting station and served his country for four years. He remained loyal to his oath then and now.

At the end of his four years, he was an Air Force sergeant (that is an E-4 in the Air Force) and considered signing on for another tour but ultimately decided not to. He said that it was a special experience in his life, and he never, even for a moment, regretted the chance to serve his country.

I did not know anyone personally that served in the Vietnam between 1971 and 1973, nor did I know any of the nurses or women who served in other capacities or our friends from other nations that served while I was there or after I left. They remained with us in that fight to the very end, which came in 1973. I would like to take this time to record some of the things I learned about all those people that I did not know; however, we share a common bond. The first group I would like to talk about are the ladies that took care of us.

Will Ye Go?

Forty-plus years ago
The winds whispered of war.
It whispered for help
Real hard at our door.

Will Ye Go lassie,
Will Ye Go?

The country would ask
Of the women in white to
Put on a Green Uniform
And enter the fight.

Will Ye Go lassie,
Will Ye Go?

A few young men
Have answered the gun
And now they are falling
One by one.

Will Ye Go lassie,
Will Ye Go?

When the battles are over
And the war is no more
We will bring you back home
To your country's door.

Will Ye Go lassie,
Will Ye Go?

And it is here that we hope,
You will find peace of mind
Walking among the Heather,
And the green mountain Thyme.

Will Ye Go lassie,
Will Ye Go?

I wrote this poem in tribute to the woman of the United States military that served beside us in Vietnam. But more than that, took care of us.

This gender of human being has been referred to as being the weaker sex. However, I am not sure that I would agree with that statement. Besides seeing them bear the burden of childbirth, I have seen them bear a lot of other burdens, equal to and surpassing those endured by men.

This includes the burden of war. Women have played a major part in both the acquisition and the defense of this nation since its beginning. They stood by our side in the fight, they nursed us, and they supported us. That includes from the revolution right up the present-day war on terror.

In the one year eight months and four days I spent in the Nam, I never had to be dusted off (medical evacuation). I consider myself incredibly lucky. But I always knew that these ladies were there to take care of me if necessary, and I would be remiss if I did not use a small portion of this project to pay them the homage they so rightly deserve.

Over five hundred WACs were stationed in Vietnam. Women Marines were in Vietnam. Over six hundred women in the Air Force were there.

Army, Navy, and Air Force nurses and medical specialists numbered over six thousand. Untold numbers of Red Cross, Special Services, Civil Service, and countless other women were there. It is estimated that almost ten thousand women served in Vietnam. A lot of them receive the same combat citations as the men. They were awarded the Purple Heart, the Bronze Star, commendation medals, and unit citations. Here are the casualties:

US Army:
2nd Lt. Carol Ann Elizabeth Drazba

2nd Lt. Elizabeth Ann Jones

Capt. Eleanor Grace Alexander

1st Lt. Hedwig Diane Orlowski

2nd Lt. Pamela Dorothy Donovan

1st Lt. Sharon Ann Lane

Lt. Col. Annie Ruth Graham

US Air Force:
Capt. Mary Therese Klinker

Civilian Women also Served

As you can see, they were there. The names of the ladies listed above are also listed on that black granite wall in the middle of Washington, DC. I have heard horror stories about what these ladies had to do. It is all too often that when the wars are over that woman are pushed to the rear and given extraordinarily little praise and recognition for the sacrifices they too have made.

The nurses who were taking care of the wounded, as well as the dying, all too often would have to play the role of a mother, a sweetheart, or a wife to a soldier as he died in their arms. I could only imagine how difficult a thing that was to do, and to have it etched in your memory forever? Never mind the constant trauma and blood they would see daily or the screams of pain that they would have to listen to.

The Red Cross doughnut dollies of Vietnam used to bring entertainment and treats to the men at the line companies and firebases. They would put themselves in danger so the guys could have a little bit of home.

The doughnut dollies and other women who served in Vietnam as civilians do not hold veteran status from an official standpoint. However, I feel that these women are as much a veteran as the men who served there, and I think that most of my fellow Nam vets would agree. And these ladies did this unarmed.

To these ladies that took care of us, I thank you from the bottom of my heart.

I think I can speak for all of us, male veterans, when I say that it would have been a lot worse without you being there, so as all of us Nam Vets say to one another, welcome home although, personally, I am not quite sure where that is yet. Maybe one day I will once again find a place I can truly call home because up until now, in my heart, I do not feel that I have arrived there yet. Maybe someday.

Besides the women that served side by side with us, there were a few countries previously mentioned that served there with us also.

During 1961 and 1962, Ngo Dinh Diem, president of the Republic of Vietnam requested assistance from us and our allies to improve South Vietnam's security.

At the same time, the United States was trying to build a coalition of forces. The Australian government's response was to send 30 military advisers, also known as the Team. The Australian military assistance was to be in jungle warfare training, and the Team comprised of highly qualified and experienced officers and NCOs, led by Col. Ted Sarong. [4] Their arrival in South Vietnam in July and August 1962 was the beginning of Australia's involvement in the war in Vietnam. [5]

The president of the United States at that time was John F. Kennedy. It was just around this time that he sent 18,000 troops to Vietnam and initiated the DESOTO patrols to the South China Sea, which were eventually expanded to the Tonkin gulf.

By the end of 1964, there were almost 200 Australian military personnel in Vietnam.

In April 1965, Australian Prime Minister Sir Robert Menzies announced that the government had received from South Vietnam a request for further military assistance. After consulting with the United States, he decided to send an infantry battalion to Vietnam. He argued that a Communist victory in South Vietnam would be a direct military threat to Australia. "It must be seen as part of a thrust by Communist China between the Indian and Pacific Oceans," he added.[12][13]

D) In total, some 50,000 Australians, ground troops, Air Force, and naval personnel served in Vietnam between 1962 and 1972. Some 520 died as a result of the war and almost 2,400 were wounded.[10] Female members of the Army and Air Force nursing services served in Vietnam at the First Australian Field Hospital and on medevacs (medical evacuation flights).

In Australia, resistance to the war was, at first, extremely limited although the Australian Labor Party (in opposition for most of the period) steadfastly opposed conscription. However, anti-war sentiment escalated rapidly in the late 1960s as more and more Australian soldiers were killed in battle. The introduction of conscription by the Australian government during the war also enraged some, and groups of people resisted the call to military service (which was punishable by imprisonment) by burning the letters notifying them of their conscription. Growing public uneasiness about the death toll was fueled by a series of highly publicized arrests of conscientious objectors and exacerbated by shocking revelations of atrocities committed against Vietnamese civilians, leading to a rapid increase in domestic opposition to the war between 1967 and 1970.

On May 8, 1970, moratorium marches were held in major Australian cities to coincide with the marches in the USA. The demonstration in Melbourne, led by future deputy prime minister Jim Cairns, was supported by an estimated 100,000 people.[30] Across Australia, it was estimated that 200,000 people were involved.

As you can see, it was not till the waning years of the war that the anti-war movement in Australia brought it up a few notches. There is no doubt in my mind that they were probably walking in the footsteps of their American counterparts. I am not even going to pretend to know anything about the laws in Australia. I do not know what their laws are pertaining to treason, or if they have any at all. However, I do know that the demonstrations were a betrayal of the men and woman of that country who were fighting in Vietnam. If it was not treason in the legal sense of the word, then definitely it was treason in the emotional sense of the word. *(It was a wounding of the heart, so to speak.)*

These men and women from that country were defending their nation and military that they joined. They were also honoring their nation's commitment to a treaty that they were signatories to.

The treaty I am talking about is the SATO Treaty (Southeast Asia Collective Defense Treaty) (exhibit 7). Thailand, Australia, New Zealand, Pakistan, the Philippines are the nations that reside in the Southeast Asian quadrant. The other signatories of that treaty were United States, United Kingdom, and France.

Sir Robert Menzies argued that a Communist victory in South Vietnam would be a direct military threat to Australia. "It must be seen as part of a thrust by Communist China between the Indian and Pacific Oceans," he added.

One might argue that Sir Robert Menzies was just speculating at the time, just like President Eisenhower's domino theory. Let me reiterate, as I did earlier, from Col. Bui Tin's book *From Enemy to Friend* regarding Sir Robert Menzies's worries.

The Communists' position on Southeast Asia:

Let me add that the communist party of Vietnam leaders always considered Indochina as one geographical entity and single battlefield, relegating the Pathet Lao and the Khmer People's Party to subordinate positions under a single leader, Ho Chi Minh. The internationalist duty that the CPV arrogates to itself has always been to communize first the whole Indochinese peninsula and then the rest of Southeast Asia.

If it were speculation on the part of Sir Robert Menzies, I would think that was a rather good guess also.

New Zealand

New Zealand's involvement in the Vietnam War was highly controversial, sparking widespread protest at home from anti-Vietnam War movements modeled on their American counterparts. This conflict was also the first in which New Zealand did not fight alongside the United Kingdom, instead following the loyalties of the ANZUS pact

From 1961, New Zealand came under pressure from the United States of America to contribute military and economic assistance to South Vietnam but refused. However, at that time, aircrafts were tasked to deliver supplies to Tourane on the way from RAF Changi to Hong Kong from time to time.

In November 1968, New Zealand's contribution to the First Australian Task Force was increased by the deployment of additional troops, New Zealand Special Air Services, comprising of an officer and 25 other ranks. The arrival of this troop raised New Zealand's deployment to Vietnam to its peak of 543 men.

Although New Zealand's involvement in the war was limited compared to the contributions of some of its allies, it still triggered a large anti-Vietnam War movement at home. New Zealand protests were similar to those in the United States, criticizing the policies of the United States government and challenging seriously for the first time New Zealand's alliance-based security, calling for a more *independent* foreign policy which was not submissive to that of the United States and denying that Communism posed any real threat to New Zealand.

Campaigns were also waged on moral grounds ranging from pacifist convictions to objections to the weapons being used to fight the war. In the early 1970s, anti-Vietnam War groups organized mobilizations when thousands marched in protest against the war in all of the country's major centers. While Prime Minister Holyoake and his government had their own misgivings about the viability of the war, they were consistent in their public belief that they were maintaining both New Zealand's foreign policy principles and treaty-bound obligations. Despite popular sentiment apparently against the conflict, especially in its final years, Holyoake's national party was reelected into government twice during the course of the war.

The next troops I would like to discuss were from the Republic of South Korea. It was just a few years prior that this country had to defend itself from Communist aggression, which was being perpetrated upon them by their own countrymen, like what was going on in Vietnam.

Korea

Korean troops participated in the Vietnam War from 1964–1973. Total number of soldiers figured approximately 300,000.

Following statistics originated from the Ministry of Defense, Republic of Korea:
Total troops: 266,363+
Total casualties: 15,172+ (KIA: 4,891+, WIA: 10,281+)

Korean Marine Corps
Total troops: 37,340
Total casualties: 4,106 (KIA: 1,202, WIA: 2,904)

D) The Republic of Korea Army Units' area of responsibility (AOR) was the southern half of the I Corps. The ROK Marine Corps units were deployed in the I Corps. The three main units deployed to Vietnam were the ROK Army Capital (Yellow Tiger) Division, the ROK Marine Corps' Second (Blue Dragon) Brigade, and the ROK Army Ninth (White Stallion) Division. Various ROK Special Forces units were also deployed.

One of the most notable operations during the Vietnam War was the Battle of Tra Binh Dong in which just fewer than 300 Marines successfully defended their base against over 2,400 Vietcong. Another notable operation is Operation Flying Tiger in early January of 1966; here, the Koreans accounted for 192 Vietcong killed as against only eleven Koreans.[3]

A total of 320,000 Koreans served in Vietnam, with peak strength (of any given time) at around 48,000.[5] About 4,000 were killed.

The official US military record on South Korean participation in the Vietnam war reads, "In summary, it appears that Korean operations in Vietnam were highly professional, well planned, and thoroughly executed."

While sitting switchboard watch on Hill 34, I believe it was early 1966. The commanding officer from third tanks brought a Korean Marine colonel to check out our landline communications. This is the only contact with ROK troops that I had the entire time I spent in Vietnam. However, I knew they were there with us, and they remained there the entire time we were there.

Besides the South Vietnamese forces, these were the major combatant forces in Vietnam. As the years went by, the commitments of these nations to preserve freedom for themselves and their neighbors with whom they shared the same treaty (SEATO) (exhibit 7) were constantly hindered by their respective civilian populaces.

I can't say for certain, but if these soldiers felt about their countries the way I felt about mine, I can only assume that the actions of their fellow countrymen also wounded their hearts which only comes with betrayal, and I am ashamed that it was the people in my country that led the way.

There were number of other nations that served, and for the life of me, I do not know why. They were the Native Americans. People like the Navajo, the Lakota, the Cherokee, and many others.

Time and time again, these Native Americans have left the sovereignty of their own nations and joined with us to fight in our wars. During World War II, many men from the Navajo Nation joined the United States Marine Corps and became the code talkers. They were part of the communications command; they would call out missions and report enemy activity. They would speak their native tongue which was never broken by the Japanese.

It was no different in the Nam. This is a friend of Sgt. Tom Martin mentioned earlier. His name was Sgt. Lenard M. Hickson of the Navajo Nation who lost his life on Hamburger Hill a couple of days after Tom was dusted off with his wounds.

Mr. and Mrs. Albert Hickson Sr. received posthumously medals presented by CWO-2 Andrews of the Navajo Army Depot, Flagstaff Arizona, at ceremonies on Monday, October 13 in the Hickson residence, Window Rock. Medals awarded were the Bronze Star Medal, Purple Heart, Good Conduct Medal, Combat Infantryman Badge, Army Commendation Medal, National Defense Service Medal, Vietnam Service Medal, Vietnam Campaign Ribbon, Parachutist Badge, and Sharpshooter and Marksman Badges with automatic rifle bars. Sgt. Lenard M. Hickson was killed in action May 18 in Vietnam.

Since I have returned from Nam, I have on occasion gone to some native powwows (native gatherings). Right after they conduct their flag ceremony, they perform a dance dedicated to the veterans. They invite all the veterans from the audience to participate in it, stating that "we are all warriors." The point of this story is that since my return from Nam some forty-plus years ago, it is among these people who are the only ones that can claim a birthright to this land that have truly made me feel that I was welcomed as a Vietnam veteran.

All the while, all these people and other nations that joined in a commitment to keep a nation free would constantly have their mission thwarted even through these years.

1971

History shows the following:

March 29. US Army Lieutenant William Calley was found guilty of twenty-two murders in the My Lai Massacre and sentenced to life in prison (later pardoned).

[D] Daniel Ellsberg (born April 7, 1931) is a former American military analyst employed by the RAND Corp. who precipitated a national uproar in 1971 when he released the Pentagon Papers, the US military's account of activities during the Vietnam War to the *New York Times.*

[D] The papers revealed, among other things, that the government had deliberately expanded its role in the war by conducting air strikes over Laos, raids along the coast of North Vietnam, and offensive actions taken by US Marines well before the American public was told about the actions. All while, President Lyndon Johnson had been promising not to expand the war. (*Why would the military tell the public about tactical missions in Vietnam? It was none of their business, especially since they were unwilling to fight there.*)

The document increased the credibility gap for the US government and was hurting the efforts by the Nixon administration to fight the war.

[D] *June 13, 1971.* The *New York Times* begins to publish the Pentagon Papers [1]. In the Pentagon Papers, a top secret United States Department of Defense history of the United States' political and military involvement in the Vietnam War from 1945 to 1971 were given (leaked) to Neil Sheehan of the *New York Times* by Daniel Ellsberg, with his friend Anthony Russo assisting in copying them. The *Times* began publishing excerpts as a series of articles on June 13. Controversy and lawsuits followed.

[D] Ellsberg served as a company commander in the Marine Corps for two years and then became an analyst at the RAND Corp. A committed cold warrior, he served in the Pentagon in 1964 under Secretary of Defense Robert McNamara. He then served for two years in Vietnam as a civilian in the State Department and became convinced that the Vietnam War was unwinnable. *(Who died and left him general.)*

[D] In one of Nixon's actions against Ellsberg, G. Gordon Liddy and E. Howard Hunt, members of the White House special investigation unit (also called the White House Plumbers), broke into Ellsberg's psychiatrist's office in September 1971, hoping to find information they could use to discredit him. *(Bad move.)*

The revelation of the break-in became part of the Watergate scandal. Due to gross governmental misconduct, all charges against Ellsberg were eventually dropped. White House Counsel Charles Colson was later prosecuted and pled no contest for obstruction of justice in the burglary of Ellsberg's psychiatrist's office.

May 3, 1971. The Harris Poll claimed that 60 percent of Americans were against the Vietnam War. Anti-war militants attempted to disrupt government business in Washington, DC; police and military units arrest as many as twelve thousand, most of whom are later released. *(Why?)*

June 30, 1971. New York Times versus United States: the Supreme Court rules that the Pentagon Papers may be published, rejecting government injunctions as unconstitutional prior restraint.

Prior restraint was a Supreme Court ruling from a court case *Near v. Minnesota*, 283 US 697(1931), where basically it said that every man shall have a right to speak, right, and print his opinions upon any subject whatsoever without any prior restraint.

It also went on to say, "So always that he does not injure any other person in his rights, person, property, or reputation, and so always said he does not thereby disturb the public peace or attempt to subvert the government."

Note: I do not know? But I see a contradiction here. Regarding the Vietnam War, yes, the government was trying to stop these papers from being published prior to them being published, which is in violation of the prior restraint ruling. However, why was the fact that the top secret Pentagon Papers were stolen ignored. What other reason would Daniel Ellsberg, Charles Colson, and the *New York Times* have to release these papers on events that already took place if it were not to, first, embarrass the government or subvert the government, thereby disturbing the public peace, which is also part of the 1938 Supreme Court ruling?

It is my opinion that the 1971 Supreme Court ruling was a bad ruling. *(Oh well! Spilled milk.)*

Note:

In 1962, in Geneva, fourteen nations, including the United States and North Vietnam, signed an agreement declaring Laos a neutral country. However, Ho Chi Minh never removed the 10,000 troops that he had there. Ignoring the agreement, as he had done with so many other treaties and agreements, he continued the buildup of troops and continued south into the sovereignty of Cambodia. He used these troops to build what would become known as the Ho Chi Minh Trail. This trail would be used to insert guerrilla and NVA troops into South Vietnam as well as supplies. I often wonder why there was never any demonstrations or complaints anywhere in the world concerning his actions. However, as stated above, so many so-called Americans objected to our tactics, trying to strategically protect our troops in South Vietnam by attacking the supply line. Once again, they handcuffed the American troops.

August 18. Australia and New Zealand decide to withdraw their troops from Vietnam. *(This is Nixon's doing.)*

October 29. Vietnamization: the total number of American troops still in Vietnam drops to a record-low of 196,700 (the lowest since January 1966). *(This too is Nixon's doing.)*

1972

June 17. Watergate scandal: five White House operatives are arrested for burglarizing the offices of the Democratic National Committee.

June 28. US President Richard Nixon announced that no new draftees would be sent to Vietnam.

Also, in July, US actress Jane Fonda tours North Vietnam, during which she is photographed sitting on a North Vietnamese antiaircraft gun. *(Syphilitic cunt.)*

August 12. The last US ground troops are withdrawn from Vietnam.

August 22. Jane Fonda makes an anti-war broadcast from a hotel room in Hanoi.

November 11. The United States Army turns over the massive Long Binh military base to South Vietnam.

November 22. The United States lost its first B-52 Stradofortress of the war.

November 30. White House Press Secretary Ron Ziegler tells the press that there will be no more public announcements concerning United States troop withdrawals from Vietnam since troop levels are now down to 27,000.

December 2. A peace delegation that includes activist Joan Baez and human rights attorney Telford Taylor visit Hanoi to deliver Christmas mail to American prisoners of war; they will be caught in the Christmas bombing of North Vietnam. *(We missed these scumbags?)*

December 25. The Christmas bombing of North Vietnam caused widespread criticism of the US and President Richard Nixon.

1973

January 15. Vietnam War: citing progress in peace negotiations, US President Richard Nixon announces the suspension of offensive action in North Vietnam.

January 23. US President Richard Nixon announces that a peace accord has been reached in Vietnam.

January 27. Paris peace accords are signed. Allies officially wins Vietnam War. *(Horse shit.)*

February 11. The first release of American prisoners of war from Vietnam took place.

August 15. The US bombing of Cambodia ends, marking the official halt to twelve years of combat activity in Southeast Asia.

Quote the Congress of the United States overrides President Richard M. Nixon's veto of the war powers resolution, which limits presidential power to wage war without congressional approval. *(These people should have been passed tested before they were elected.)*

By 1973, we were out of Vietnam, Nixon said with honor. I do not agree. We the Vietnam veterans were accredited with losing the war we did not lose. And till this very day, I have yet to find my way home.

CHAPTER 9

CONGRESSIONAL TESTIMONY

TO THIS VERY DAY, I have no idea why the American public, politicians, news media, or members of entertainment industries took such a vehement role in betraying their own country.

However, an unfortunate event took place in Vietnam that escalated the anti-war movement to a higher frenzy than it already was. This event was mentioned earlier; it was reported on March 16, 1968. American troops killed scores of civilians in South Vietnam, which became known as the My Lai Massacre. This is a despicable act that cannot or should not be condoned for any reason. It was not condoned by anyone, including the United States Army.

Due to this unfortunate act, the United States is officially accredited with this *one* war crime in the fourteen years we fought there. It was investigated, charges were brought, and convictions were upheld. This investigation was conducted by the United States Army.

History reads on September 5, 1969, that Lieutenant William Calley was charged with six counts of premeditated murder for the deaths of 109 Vietnamese civilians in My Lai. This was because of an investigation conducted by the US Army.

However, history also reads on November 12 that independent investigative journalists Seymour Hersh breaks the My Lai story. Hersh broke the story of the My Lai Massacre in which hundreds of unarmed Vietnamese civilians were killed by US soldiers in March 1968. The report prompted widespread condemnation around the world and reduced public support for the Vietnam War in the United States.

The explosive news of the massacre fueled the outrage of the American Peace Movement, which demanded the withdrawal of American troops from Vietnam. It also led more potential draftees to file for Conscientious Objector Status.

Hersh wrote about the massacre and its cover-up in My Lai titled "A Report on the Massacre and Its Aftermath and Cover-up: The Army's Secret Investigation of the Massacre at My Lai."

Let us look at this last paragraph regarding the American media, Hanoi's most important friend and ally at the time. Two months prior to Hersh's so-called breaking of the story, the Army was well into the investigation as reported by members of Calley's unit, and he had already been charged as the key suspect in the case on September 5.

But it is Mrs. Hersh's little boy, Seymour, who, two months later, takes credit for breaking the story. The only people he broke it to was an already disgruntled and treasonous American public and their allies in Hanoi. Then he calls it the "Army's Secret Investigation of the Massacre at My Lai." I bet if Hersh was old enough in 1944, he probably would have reported the date, time, and exact location of the D-Day invasion, and we would probably all be speaking German now!

Let me make something perfectly clear. If the press reported incidents back in World War II like they did in Vietnam, they would have been brought out on the street and shot. Secondly, if the authorities are investigating something and acting upon that investigation without telling anyone about it, it is not a cover-up. Nowhere in the Constitution does it say we have to talk to the press or tell the press anything. They are not officers of the court. There have been many a time when I had been approached by the press and I simply said, "No comment."

The only reason anyone speaks to the press is because they are a free mouthpiece for the politicians, and since the politicians spend their time licking the wrinkles out of the nut sacks of these demigods of the news, they instituted policies that everyone underneath them must talk to these shit heels.

This reminds me of a time when I was a trooper investigating a homicide. The phone rang and an irate female reporter from one of these media rags was on the other end of the line, asking why she was not notified about information that was found out about an investigation I was working on. My response to her was, "Because I don't fucking work for you." It is not my job to supply free stories to the press so that they can turn around and sell it to the public and draw a profit.

The First Amendment says not to abridge the freedom of the press. (*Abridge* is defined as "to deprive somebody of rights or privileges.") Nowhere in the Constitution does it say that anyone must give the press the story! They can print what they want, and they usually do, and they spin it to whatever direction they want to spin it to.

For example, *He was driving down the road at twenty-five miles an hour when he struck the child.*

Now their version: *He was careening down the road at twenty-five miles an hour when he struck the child.* Same speed, it just sounds faster, and that is the kind of shit these mutants usually pull.

These self-righteous demigods of the airways and printed word think that it is okay to commit treason if there is a possibility of a Pulitzer Prize waiting at the other end of the article.

I think this attitude of the media was adopted right after World War II and deteriorated to the irresponsible level of today's communistic journalism, so revered by a large portion of the American public who have apparently come to hate America as much as the rest of the world has. *They know who they are.*

There was so much crying and carrying on by the so-called American public back then; a group known as VVAW (Vietnam Veterans Against the War) emerged. John Kerry (do you know this presidential candidate and US senator?) was one of the founding fathers of this group in the early stages of its inception (as indicated in his book *The New Soldier* authored by him) as well as his name on the minutes of a meeting attended by him with the rest of his VVAW followers (exhibit 24).

So during the waning years of the war when more and more politicians were placating to the traitors, instead of doing the right thing as elected officials of the United States government and providing support for the very people who guaranteed their existence, certain members of the Ninety-Second Congress were assisting with the anti-war movement. They used this group known as the VVAW as a tool to discredit the United States military and undermine the government's war effort. To name a couple, Bobby and Ted Kennedy.

From February 26 to March 8, 1971, the proceedings and debates regarding alleged war crimes in addition to the My Lai incident in Vietnam were held in Washington, DC. This ad hoc meeting was the brainchild of Congressman Dellums of California. These proceedings lasted for a few months. The amount of people testifying were too many to add to this publication. However, a cross section of three testimonies were pulled to show what kind of bullshit these people were doling out.

[S] Ronald Vernie Dellums was a representative from California; born in Oakland, Alameda County, California, on November 24, 1935; attended the Oakland public schools; AA, Oakland City College, 1958; BA, San Francisco State College, 1960; MSW, University of California, 1962; served two years in United States Marine Corps, active duty, 1954–1956; he served in Congress from January 3, 1971, until his resignation on February 6, 1998.

He opened these hearing with the following statement (exhibit 19):

> Mr. Speaker, as the war spreads, so does the possibility and danger of additional war atrocities committed by American soldiers.
>
> Yet, the Military Establishment continues to ignore or downplay not only the factual existence of these ghastly horrors, but it also refuses to question the issue of ultimate responsibility for war crimes past and present.
>
> Today, along with 21 of my colleagues, I am reintroducing a joint resolution proposing a full-scale congressional inquiry of American war crimes and war crime responsibility.
>
> Joining with me in backing this resolution are Mr. Diggs, Mr. Rangel, Mrs. Abzug, Mr. Collins of Illinois, Mr. Roncallo, Mr.

Mitchell, Mr. Rosenthal, Mr. Hawkins, Mr. Ryan, Mr. Scheuer, Mr. Edwards of California, Mr. Eckhardt, Mr. Conyers, Mr. Kastenmeier, Mr. Mikva, Mr. Seiberling, Mr. Burton, Mr. Koch, Mr. Helstoski, Mr. Dow, and Mr. Badillo {4238c2}.

Mr. Speaker, the Defense Department blatantly ignores its responsibility to deal with war crimes. Instead, the Military Establishment attempts to pin the blame on lower echelon personnel—men such as Calley, Henderson, and soon, I presume, Medina—while refusing to acknowledge that the prime responsibility lies at the highest levels of civilian and military command.

Indeed, to all intent and purpose, the Military Establishment acts as if war crimes are minute aberrations, the deranged acts of men temporarily enraged by the horrors of combat. Of course, in some cases, that is true. But there have been far too many instances of premeditated atrocities for this excuse to be accepted anymore.

Mr. Speaker, the material I shall now insert into the Record is for the most part some of the most gruesome and beastly testimony that I have ever read.

The transcript which follows is that of the National Veterans Inquiry on U.S. War Crimes in Vietnam held last December here in Washington.

The inquiry was undertaken by the Citizens Commission of Inquiry in order that the American public and Government realize the terrible realities of war atrocities as an integral component of our illegal, insane, and immoral adventurism in Southeast Asia.

The testimony contained in the transcript is blunt.

But blunt also has been the Government's ridiculous efforts to bypass or soft-pedal the responsibility for these actions.

Congress represents the people of America, and I believe the people are sick of the war, sick of the war crimes, and sick of way the Military Establishment are handling these problems.

Dellums called for a joint resolution proposing a full-scale congressional inquiry of American war crimes and war crime responsibility. His biography stated that he spent two years in the Marine Corps from 1954–1956, which means he served during peacetime and probably did not see combat. However, I think that, as a Marine, he should have remembered that sometime during his training, he was told that as a Marine, he did not have to obey any unlawful orders or orders that he would find in conflict with his conscience and that, as a Marine, he was obligated to report any wrongdoing. I sure as hell remember these things being told to me as an enlisted man during my boot training.

He said, "The prime responsibility lies at the highest levels of civilian and military command." If this statement by him is correct, is he not part of the civilian command? Then I would think that he and everyone sitting in on this ad hoc meeting should have been locked up since he was part of the prime responsibility of My Lai Massacre. *(Is this meeting to draw attention away from his responsibility?)*

The first testimony I chose was by Daniel K. Amigone (exhibit 19A):

Moderator: Danny Amigone will be speaking to the problem, the area of mistreatment of civilians in ground combat. Dan?
Amigone: *Thank you, Chuck. Good afternoon. My name is Daniel K. Amigone. I'm from Buffalo, New York, the queen city of the Great Lakes.* (Oh! A tour guide.)

I enlisted in the United States Army after I received my master's degree from Arizona State. As you know Arizona State, or Arizona, is a big, conservative hotbed of American politics, and at the time I really thought that what all we were doing in Vietnam was the right thing to do. So, I enlisted in the United States Army and—for a three-year hitch by the way—and to this day I regret that."

At any rate, I went through basic and AIT because I had plans of going into OCS, but just before, just before my actual departure for OCS at Fort Benning, they had a review board in my behalf and they decided I was not officer material because of various views that I had had during basic and AIT.

There are a couple things I would like to point out in the first two paragraphs of this testimony. He received a master's degree and enlisted rather than go through officer candidate training? He claims he came from the hotbed of conservative thinking. When he decides to apply for officer training, they deny him because of what he said in boot camp; however, he doesn't expand upon what he said, nor do they ask.

But anyway, after they refused my application to OCS, they sent me to Germany and I was over in Germany for three months and I volunteered for Vietnam, not like a lot of these people who have testified here before. I actually volunteered.

At any rate, I went to Vietnam in March of 1968, March of 1968 I arrived at Bien Hoa and Bien Hoa just had been cleared of the Viet Cong. It was just right after Tet. I didn't have too much in-country training because we were really badly needed, and I was assigned to {4240} Company D, 3rd Battalion, 7th Infantry, 199th Infantry Brigade and we were called the Red Catchers. And this began my career in Vietnam, I was assigned to an infantry unit as 11 Bravo, which is an infantryman because all the training I had during basic and AIT.

And this training I think is very important to the whole philosophy that goes into the mind of a man that goes into the front lines over in Vietnam. Basic is just, as they say, basic, you know. They teach you how to fire usually a—in my case it was an M-14. They teach you the basic fundamentals of drill, and, etc. Once you get into advanced infantry training, the process gets stepped up and the process gets more involved.

And I heard a question before about racism. Well, racism starts in AIT, Advanced Infantry Training. It's not a racism designated against the Blacks and Puerto Ricans; its racism designed toward the Vietnamese people. On the ranges when you are firing for record score to qualify, you're taught by your platoon sergeant and the man who is the instructor to holler kill every time you squeeze that trigger, and you're killing a gook, as they call them.

I did not see anything thus far in the transcript, where anyone asked a question about racism.

And this is really where racism goes. They're not people anymore, they're gooks. They're not Vietnamese, they're gooks. So, on the bayonet range, your drill sergeant would holler, "What's the spirit of the bayonet?" And the people would as they lunged into their targets, would say, "kill, kill, kill." So that's it's the spirit of killing that these infantrymen have when they go over to Vietnam. It's really imbedded into them. And they get over to Vietnam and we practice what they have taught us. (No shit?)

There's one especially—topic I want to get into, and that's the question of McNamara's Brigade. In 1967, because of the drainage of manpower in the United States, Secretary of, I believe, Defense McNamara needed more manpower to fill the ranks over in Vietnam, in the infantry. So, what he did was: lowered the mentality, mentality standards for acceptance, accepting men into the armed forces, especially the Army. What happens to these men—in particular, I remember one man was in my company. He was a platoon sergeant in basic, acting platoon sergeant. I remember this one man who came up to me. He was only eighteen years old, a black boy from Newark, New Jersey, and he was married and had four kids, and he couldn't even read the letters that his wife wrote home to him. The Army had accepted him for combat duty. The Army was going to send him to paratrooper school and eventually to Vietnam. The man asked me to read his letter to him, and I read his letter to him and I said, "Well, what are you going—are you going to write to her?" And he said, "I don't know how to write."

What had happened was that the Army had drafted this man, and then put him through a three-week course so that he could learn how to write his name and sign his pay voucher. And what happens? These men go through this killing process. They learn to kill and they go to Vietnam and they do kill, and they do get killed, because given the fact that their reactions are a lot slower than a man with a normal intelligence, they haven't been told that when you hear a bullet fly you're supposed to duct. All they've been told how to do is to kill. So, they kill, and they get killed.

I think this guy was sniffing glue prior to testifying.

And if you look at Morning Reports—Morning Reports is a document, a document that registers your KIAs which are people killed in action, or your wounded people—you will find a disproportionately high number of people were these '67s. I say were because the Army had gotten a little grief about this, and they changed their system from using US or RA to social security numbers. That way they could hide anybody they wanted to {4240c2}.

At any rate, these people go to Vietnam and they die. And these people, I'd like to point out, they come from the ghettos. They come from the squalid areas of this country. They come from Appalachia, they're blacks, they're Puerto Ricans, they're poor whites. And I personally believe it's a sort of genocide, a genocide in both ways, a genocide in the effect that they're using the poor to fight the poor over in Vietnam.

Mister, I received a master's degree from Arizona State, more likely from the University of Crackerjack, was supposed to address the issue of mistreatment of civilians in ground combat. From what I have read from his testimony, that issue was never addressed. The closest he comes is the following:

So, what happens when we get over there? Well, as I say I arrived in the country just after Tet, and about the first week in the country I witnessed my first atrocity. We were in the middle of a firefight, in the middle of a firefight, and this GI to the left of me, ahead, captured a peasant girl. And he raped her, raped her. In the middle of the firefight, raped her and then when she tried to get away, she killed—he killed her. And it was written off as a KIA, enemy casualty killed in combat.

If this occurred, then the GI in question is the calmest or craziest son of a bitch I ever heard of. I can tell you from experience that during combat pussy was the furthest thing from my mind. Getting laid was not even on the agenda. Besides, one GI committing a criminal offence does not constitute a war crime. It constitutes a criminal offense by an individual, which he was obligated to report! Between 1969 and the end of the Cold War, as a New Jersey State trooper, I investigated many rapes and homicides and a combination of both. These were committed by civilians, does that mean because they were committed during the Cold War, they were war crimes?

And one more incident I'd like to bring up. I did not actually see it, but it happened when we were out on a patrol. We had captured three enemy prisoners and because of the lateness of the evening, we decided to hold them in our camp. And we held them and the next morning all three of them were dead, and they were shot in the back. And the—one of the platoon sergeants who were on duty at the time claimed the victory for killing them in the back saying that—he said that they tried to escape but what actually came out later, that he really just killed them. He loosened their binds and just killed them. And we both times went to the CO, both times, and he said," Well, that's war.

Moderator: *Excuse me, Dan. How did it come out that he had killed them? Did anyone see him?*
Amigone: *Well, nobody really saw him kill them but he—one night he got drunk and it came out through his spirits.*

This kangaroo court allowed him to testify to something he didn't even see.

Moderator: *Are there any questions to be addressed to Mr. Amigone from the press?*

Floor: *You support that a disproportionate number of the poor were killed because I think you said their responses were slower. Would it be—would that be the case, or would it be the case that a disproportionate number of them are sent up to the front lines?*

Amigone: *Well—a very high rate of this 1967's that I'm talking about, that's where they go. The Army cannot use them anywhere else. And the real sad part of it is, after they have used them for two years and if they're still alive after their two-year period, they cannot re-enlist in the army because the Army's standards are too high for reenlistment. And yet they have fought their war for two years.*

I think if bullshit were electricity, this guy would be a fucking powerhouse.

One of the other testimonies I chose to show was that of a Mr. McCusker; he describes himself as an ex-Marine. Thank God because I am a Marine, and I would not want to be associated with this man.

My name is Mike McCusker (exhibit 19B).

I am an ex-Marine. I was discharged as a sergeant. I enlisted in the reserves in 1959 in July; served six years in the reserves; and then in 1965 went active duty for two years, which means I had eight years of service. While in the reserves, I was trained in Recon {4238c3}, which meant that I became a jumper, a parachutist, scuba, and all the other John Wayne varieties.

In the two years that I was active I was what was called a combat correspondent for the First Marine Division in Vietnam, generally out of Chu Lai. In that position, I saw damn near everything from command to the field.

I find that a little hard to swallow. It seems strange to me that the Marine Corps would take a Marine trained for six years in recon and send him into Vietnam as a combat correspondent. It could be true, but I find it hard to believe.

At one point in his testimony, he spoke about what he believed to be an atrocity, regarding unit garbage. He said,

Perhaps that was the most degrading atrocity: the garbage cans of the different battalions and companies, they would allow one or two Vietnamese to empty these garbage cans into their buckets—which also let the Marines think, after these farmers were reduced to nothing else, that these people must be inferior if they lived out of garbage cans.

Are you kidding me? How does he turn that into an atrocity? I was serving in the Nam at the same time as him. Our battalion's policy was to take the garbage cans from where the mess tents were and transport them to the dump at red beach. These cans were filled with the food scraps from the Marines' mess kits when they were finished eating, where we dumped them was a large treeless open area full of sand; I could not see hamlets or huts, but as soon as we stopped the truck, I could see large crowds of people running toward the truck. By the time they got to the truck, most of the cans were dumped. The people appeared to be taking the larger meat products and bones from what was dumped from the mess cans. My first thought was that they were taking it for their livestock. I did not think ill of these people, nor did I look down upon them. Maybe he did, but I did not. Who the hell gave him permission to speak for me anyway! Evidently, Dellums and that herd of politicians who were undermining our mission.

I also remember these people to be very resourceful. They took a lot of our trash that we threw out, made things out of it (such as shower shoes and tin mirrors), and sold it back to us. I do not or did not look down on that. However, Charlie (the Vietcong) were also resourceful; they would take a lot of our trash and use it as booby traps.

Furthermore, I gather from his testimony that the battalion commanders that he is referring to were being nice. Evidently, the Vietnamese living in that area must have advised the battalion commanders of their needs, and instead of dumping the garbage, the battalion commanders allowed them to take it.

He mentioned two other incidents that he described as atrocities.

There are two incidents, perhaps, that are of particular value as far as atrocity is concerned. They were SOP and they're examples of general procedure. One happened on my mother's birthday, October 27, 1966, northwest of the Chu Lai perimeter, at a village called Duc Pho. It was a large village complex. A sniper killed a staff sergeant, so the skipper pulled us back and then ordered nape [Napalm] on the village itself. "Just napalm the hell out of it." When we went in later, after the fires burned down, there were many, many bodies of old women and men. But I think the worst was thirty dead children who had been laid out for us to see by the survivors, who got the hell out of there before we got in. They laid these children out for us to see in one courtyard, and from being completely—just their bodies mutilated, to some of these kids looking like they'd just been sunburned, all of them were dead, all of them were very young—boys and girls both {4239}.

Another time we destroyed two entire villages—which was a month earlier than that. One of our old men, a man who had been around for six months, got hit by a sniper. The battalion went into frenzy and destroyed these two villages in the Pineapple Forest, which was southwest of Tam Ky about ten miles. Everything living died. It was just—it was mad, it was insane. Everything died and burned, and there was nothing left, nothing left of those two villages. The general trend in Vietnam at that time that I was there, for the entire year, if you received incoming rounds, sniper rounds from a village, one or two or three, you called in artillery strikes on that village, you napalmed that village; whether it was artillery or air, whichever was the closest. And this was indiscriminate, and this was usual.

In this main body of his testimony, McCusker says, "The battalion went into frenzy and destroyed these two villages in the Pineapple Forest, which was southwest of Tam-Ky, about ten miles."

Later, in his testimony, McCusker was questioned from the floor as was everyone who testified that day.

Floor: *Mr. McCusker, could you give us the names of the villages and the dates that this happened—pinpoint this just as close as you possibly can?*

McCusker: *The two villages that were destroyed.*
Floor: *Yes.*

It was, as I said, ten miles northwest—well, about ten miles due west of Tam Ky. It was down from Hill 488 where Howard got his medal of honor, and it was in the same area where the same battalion had gotten into a firefight the month before.

Now there is one thing that I am almost positive about! That as a Marine trained for six years in recon, he knows how to do one thing, and that is read a map. However, based on this mutt's testimony, I don't believe that he can read a map or write a byline. You mean to tell me that he participated in the alleged destruction of two villages and he doesn't know the names or their exact location? However, he can remember the name of a village ten miles from that location.

That is like standing on the East Coast and facing west, waving your hand from the direction of Mexico to the state of Washington and saying the villages are out there someplace or referring to September 11, 2001, saying, "I saw these two tall buildings get hit by planes and collapse. There was smoke and dust and thousands of people died. It was approximately ten miles southeast, northeast, uhhh, due east of Weehawken, New Jersey." Anyway, the questions continued.

Floor: *Have you reported these incidents before?*
McCusker: *No, I'm afraid I never officially reported either of these two incidents.*
Floor: *Why haven't you, seeing as it happened four years ago and being?*
McCusker: *Oh, I have, I have, since I've been out of the Marine Corps, I've written of these incidents, I've spoken of these incidents, in the Marine Corps I've spoken of these incidents but I never did anything official.*
Floor: *What I'm driving at is why do you choose now to come here and instead of, if you feel this was an atrocity.*

Exactly!

McCusker: *All right, I wrote the Fulbright Commission about this. I received nothing but an innocuous answer. Every time I've ever written anything to the government, and I have carbons of these, you just receive an answer that says, yes, we'll check into this, and we'll call you later about it, and you hear nothing.*

I've done this many times, until you just throw up your hands in disgust; you know it's just going to be swept under the floor.

And I have, as I said, carbons of damn near every letter I've ever written, even to the prisoner of war issue—H. Ross Perrot, to which I never received an answer.

Also, the Saigon news correspondent who said the Army was lying—he was immediately made a chaplain's assistant.

I wrote to the Fulbright Commission which said it was going to begin to check into the management of news by the Pentagon, and military news, and I received nothing but a little answer saying, well, we don't have enough time to really call this commission right now. It's very interesting testimony you have, but we'll call you later.

After being pressured, he says that he had reported it earlier.

Floor: *Is it your impression that these incidents were the exception or were these, the rule?*

McCusker: *No. These were not the exception. Oh, pardon me, these are not the rule. I'm sorry, I'm getting all fuddled up—these are not exceptions; these are generally the rule.* Ahum ahumahumahuema!

Michael Paul McCusker subsequently testified twice at the Winter Soldier Investigation (Detroit, Michigan, January 31, February 1–2, 1971) and at the House ad hoc hearing for Vietnam Veterans Against the War (April 23, 1971).

Moderator: *We'd like to move to the next witness, Mr. McCusker, unless there is a really pressing other question. We've got five other guys.*

The following are excerpts from the testimony of Kenneth Barton Osborn (exhibit 19C):

My name is Kenneth Barton Osborn. I live here in Washington and I'm a student here at American University, in the International Service Division. This is my DD 214, which proves that I was honorably discharged this past, let's see, October of 1969. I entered the Army—can you all hear me—I entered the Army in 1966 and was released from active duty in October of 1969, and this is the form that proves that.

I was in Vietnam from September of 1967 until December of 1968. My MOS in the Army was 97C40, which simply is described as an area intelligence specialist. I was trained at Fort Holibird from April of 1967 until right before leaving for Vietnam in September of 1967. My job in the Army is described overtly—unclassifiedly—as that of an area intelligence specialist; that is, I'm supposedly familiar with the geographical area, culture in that area—and work to provide cross-cultural empathy facility for the Army, that is, so they can understand the culture into which they go on any operational basis.

There are two basic functions in military intelligence: that of the counter-intelligence agent, who supposedly does just that—counter the enemy's intelligence—and the classified function, which is denied by our government, of the overt, active, aggressive collection of intelligence. It was my job to perform that classified function. Of course, the starting point with the orientation at Holibird was that, all this that we were going to be trained to do was against the Geneva Accords, and if we had moral compunctions about it, we could opt out of the program if we wanted to.

Did he mean covert as opposed too overt? At any rate, I guess there were no moral compunctions when he decided to take the job.

Osborn: *That is, at one point in our training we would be released from uniform, from military {4242} structure, we would be subservient to only a few people. In other words, we would be more or less free agents.*

I traveled there under the cover of a GS-7 and later a GS-9 as I promoted myself during the year. I lived under a cover name which is not my own name—which is not necessary to go into,

These statements indicate to me that he is not taking orders but giving them. He lived under a cover name which he did not want to disclose for this hearing. He never revealed in his testimony what his military rank was. If enlisted, it would be an E rate, if an officer, an O rate. He is using a government service (GS) rating to travel. Why? How does a guy in the Army get to promote himself? Just asking.

Osborn: *When I first got there, there was no liaison with the using units, and I had to establish that and also start from the beginning and establish nets and so forth. It took me a couple of months to get into business, and also to sell my services to the American military, who were reticent to use "foreign nationals," that is, indigenous Vietnamese personnel, for information.*

Question: Let me see, an American who supposedly in the Army, dressed as a civilian, shows up in Vietnam, and must sell himself to the United States military as an intelligence specialist? That does not make sense to me. I remember when we wanted to deal with people in the village outside our compound, we would use ARVN troops and interpreters.

Osborn: *When I proved on a retrospective plausibility basis, that is, look what I report and see what happens and if you believe it then accept my reports—when I sold them this information that way and they believed it, we were in business and I served in the 1st Marine Division, and the 3rd Marine Amphibious Force primarily, because at that time the majority of the operations in the area were Marine operations.*

My liaison was with the G-2 officers of those organizations and with subordinate S-2 officers in regimental headquarters subservient to those divisions in the area.

So that was my function in Vietnam. I was there, in that function, for 16 months.

During that time, I worked with interrogations and I worked with the using units in their field operation at different times mostly to get a reading on what kind of information they needed—I needed requirements.

So according to him, the United States military was reluctant to use—how did he put it?—foreign nationals, that is, indigenous Vietnamese personnel, for information. So he would get this information *for them*? I am not sure if that is horseshit or bullshit that I smell.

Osborn: *In the course of collecting intelligence information, I would come up with what Ed Murphy referred to as VC infrastructure detail, personalities, descriptions of people working in the local committees in the villages which were VC organizations.*

Who in the fuck is Ed Murphy, and where did he come from?

There was a lieutenant, first lieutenant Marine, who was later promoted to captain during his tour there that I knew him, who would go out to the village with other Marines, Marine EM—enlisted men—and scarf up these people who were described in my reports and bring them in for interrogation.

Not arrest them as possible NLF or better known as Vietcong infiltrators, but *scarf up*. Interesting choice of words when testifying before the Communist sympathetic press and bunch of elected scumbags.

Osborn: *They had two hootches right there on that 3rd Marine Amphibious Force compound, which were devoted to interrogation and they used the following modus operandi:*

At one point, I had described a certain individual of a local village—suburban village of Danang. They went out and scarfed her up and brought her in and simply put her in one of the wire mesh cages that were inside this hootch, which was divided into four cages. She was in one of them, and they simply put her in there. There were no facilities other than a wooden bench—regular, like a picnic bench, which stood on, like, a sawhorse—on which she could sit, sleep, do whatever she wanted to. There were no toilet facilities. There was no food and there was no water.

And the idea was that she should stay there until she talked. When they had weakened her, I was on the compound one day and the—a lieutenant said to me, I want to show you what we're doing with so-and-so whom you—who we got from your report there. Come on over next door and I'll show you the process and when we went over—and they had set this hootch up within the week. And they were quite proud of the fact that they were just leaving the people there to starve. I said, well, we'll just leave her there until she talks.

So according to him, these people are scarfed up, brought in, and interrogated, all on his say-so, and badly mistreated, but it is they who are preventing her from drinking and eating and relieving herself. That does not sound right to me.

They did leave her there for about ten days until, finally, she was so weak that she couldn't respond to anything, and at that point, they just sent her back to her village and called it a loss—got no information from her.

Ten days without water, I doubt it.

At another point, I had identified one of the members of the village committees for VC logistical supply, as I remember. In any case, he was picked up and brought in as what was described earlier as a detainee, not a POW, but a detainee.

The fellow was put in the same hootch with the four cages, in another cage, and he was forced to lay on the floor with his hands tied behind his back and they would insert a bamboo peg—a wooden peg, I'm not sure if it was bamboo—a wooden peg, a dowel with a sharpened end, into the semicircular canal of the ear, which would be forced into the head little by little as he was interrogated. And eventually, did enter the brain and killed the subject, the detainee.

They never got any viable information out of him—they called that a loss but, in any case, that was one thing that was a standard operating procedure.

And I asked the lieutenant, I said, how often do you do this kind of thing? He said, whenever we can't get information by easier methods. These methods being, I won't re-describe the ringing up of the telephone sort of thing to the women's breast nipples and the men's genitals.

When these things failed, then they went further into—the, I think, worst of the torture methods that I saw was the one of the inserting the dowel into the ear.

With that same unit, the 3rd Marine Division, I went along twice when they would go up in helicopters which belonged to the Marine Division and take two detainees along.

They used one as a scare mechanism for the other. If they wanted to interrogate detainee A, they would take someone along who was either in bad health or whom they had already written off as a loss—take both these Vietnamese along in the helicopter and they would say, they would start investigating Detainee B, the one they had no interest in, and they wouldn't get any information out of him and so they would threaten to throw him out of the helicopter {4242c3}.

All the time, of course, the detainee they wanted information from was watching. And they would threaten and threaten and, finally, they would throw him out of the helicopter.

I was there when this happened twice and it was very effective, because, of course, at the time the step one was to throw the person out of the helicopter and step two was to say, "You're next."

And that quite often broke them down, demoralized them, and at that point they would give whatever information. Sometimes the information was accurate; sometimes this was considered an ineffective method of investigation. Sometimes the Vietnamese, when threatened with things like the dowel treatment or the telephone treatment or in one case, the helicopter incident, would start babbling anything at all—would say whatever you, he felt, wanted to hear, and this, again was ineffective.

But that was the modus operandi used, and those were the incidents that I actually was involved in.

Floor: *Excuse me—you did actually see these two people thrown out of the helicopters?*
Osborn: *Yes, sir, on two different occasions, yes sir.*
Floor: *Could you tell me when and—*
Osborn: *Yes, sir, that was—*
Floor: *Be as specific as you can?*
Osborn: *Yes, sir, I will. That was in the month of April 1968, and it was northwest of Danang, perhaps fifteen miles just beyond the suburban villages there. The base of operations was the 3rd Marine Amphibious Force compound adjacent to the Danang air base in I Corps, and they would go from there up in a helicopter and go through this procedure and come back down again with what was considered a successful interrogation.*

Okay, where is the specificity in that paragraph that the floor asked for?

Floor: *You went up there for that specific purpose?*
Osborn: *That's right.*
Floor: *Now, what was, what procedure did you follow, how did you do it?*
Osborn: *Simply go out to—from the Marine Wing, they called it, there, there were on the compound that were the interrogation headquarters, go out to the helicopter there in a jeep, take these people with us. They weren't badly restrained; they had their hands tied behind their backs. They walked, they were pushed and so forth onto the helicopter, and when they got up they would simply start on the subject that they didn't want to interrogate, to scare the one that they did want to interrogate, and they'd terminate—they would throw the second subject out to scare the first one into whatever they either wanted to hear or whatever was appropriate.*
Floor: *Who did the throwing?*
Osborn: *The throwing was done by Marine enlisted men.*

Floor: *On whose orders?*

Osborn: *On the lieutenant's orders.*

Floor: *Where were you when it happened?*

Osborn: *I was there in the helicopter on one of the side seats observing—*

Floor: *How far would you be from the door?*

Osborn: *Five feet.*

Floor: *What would you say? Did you ever make an attempt to stop it or—*

Osborn: *No, I did not. I was there to observe.*

Oh! He was just a crime observer?

Moderator: *Mr. Osborn has some additional testimony, sir. Could we— unless you have any objections—could we get that out before we have any additional questions.*

Osborn: *What else do you want to know?*

Moderator: *Bart, you said that you worked closely with the CIA in the Phoenix program; how closely did you work with the CIA, and what did the Phoenix program mean to you?*

Osborn: *As I had mentioned briefly earlier, sometimes the using combat units in the I Corps area, which is the area I basically {4243} served because that's where the nets were gathering information, had no use for potentially valuable information, accurate information and timely, that we would gather just in the course of getting reports in from the field, from the Vietnamese agents.*

I was frustrated to let a lot of the information on a timely basis go down the drain. If I would have a VC who was the head of a committee or a fairly high-placed individual in the VC infrastructure and I found out where he was, where he would be, how he could be picked up and so forth, and I'd take this to the Marine Division and they'd say that's nice, but we really don't have the facilities to use it.

I lived in Danang and I happened to run into a fellow in the club where I—the Stone Elephants, the Navy officers' club—ate there, and I ran into a fellow who ran the I Corps area for CIA operations and I talked to him and found out through him that they had a program that could receive that kind of information.

On a discreet basis, I called him aside after dinner one night and asked him if he knew where I could disseminate this information on an effective basis. He put me in contact with an Army major who was at a house there rented by the CIA in Danang, and I established the liaison necessary in order to disseminate whatever VCI information I got with my reports, and did that for, I guess, for the last eight months or so that I was in Vietnam.

Moderator: *Does the term exterminate, to terminate with extreme prejudice—are you familiar with that term?*

Osborn: *There are two ways—yes—there are two ways to terminate an agent. When you are through with the agent, that is, when he serves no more function to you, you can do one of two things.*

You can terminate him by paying him an amount of money, thanking him for his service, swearing him to secrecy, and simply letting him go—that's without prejudice.

There is termination with prejudice where the agent constitutes a threat either to your operations, to you personally as a case officer, to whatever has determined the threat, and you terminate him with prejudice by either killing the individual or perhaps relocating him in the—

I remember one incident of an agent up in Phu Bi who was relocated as a prisoner of war into a Chieu Hoy camp and reoriented I'm not really familiar with the details of that, but the main idea was to, of course, neutralize the individual.

I got orders a couple of times to terminate agents with prejudice because of things they had done which were considered illegal or in bad taste or threatening—bad security—while I was there.

Floor: *Did you follow those orders out, sir?*

Osborn: *I had an agent, for instance, in Danang who was an effective principal agent—ran a net in the I Corps area around Danang. And who had worked—had told me when I hired him that he had never worked for American intelligence before. That was a starting point when I hired him. He spoke English so we communicated well—he was fluent in French and English, and he told me, no, he had never worked for the American intelligence community before.*

It turned out, though, that while he had been working for us for some time, in March of 1968, a list came out from the CIA, from CSD, they're in Danang. And it was called the catalog of undesirable personalities, and we called that a blacklist. People who had done nothing and were to be left untouched by the American military intelligence community.

His name was on that list and I was shocked to find that out.

I went—I went to a captain, an Army military intelligence captain, and I asked him what he thought I ought to do in that method of termination. He said, well, you do whatever you want to do, he's your {4243c2} man, and generally that was the case, that the case officers were able to use their own discretion.

But he said, "I want the man dead," and so I said, "All right."

And I went out and he was a resident of Danang, had a family, a wife who also spoke English and a fine woman, also two children, two or three children. And so this would be eliminating the father of two children, obviously, and for no real reason, because what he had done was to have worked previously for the CIA as an interpreter and they didn't like his interpreting because he had been feeding information to agents on the side in order to corroborate their information and get them better pay. He'd sit down with two agents and say, what do you have and what do you have, and he'd cross the information.

They found this out and they fired him, on the blacklist as a result.

He was an active agent with me, he was blacklisted, so he had to go.

I took him aside; at the time he had quite a number of pieces of equipment. He had a Yamaha motorcycle that I had lent him for running around, he had a two-way radio, a little Motorola set that we communicated with on an emergency basis, he had a number of things and he owed me a lot of piasters which he's drawn on his salary—which I had done in order to get a handle on him, in order to make him work effectively.

And so, he was strung out, and he was obligated in this way, and I sat him down and said I need these things back—it was a period of about ten days.

And when I had gotten all these things back, which, of course, were compromising logistics, I then told him what I had been told to do and told him that if he did not disappear from the city, with his family or without his family but in any case disappear for at least three months, I would have to come back and kill him. That was a hollow threat, but it worked. And he left and whether it was followed up or not, I don't know, but that's an example of going beyond what the orders were in neutralizing agents.

Floor: *What about the other orders?*

Osborn: *I had an agent in Phu Bai, which was the 3rd Marine Division base, and he had been involved in some black market activities, and that came up in the course of an interview one time that I had with him one time.*

And I reported it to—in a report which was standard after every interrogation, after every what they call personal meeting with your agent.

Because he would be compromised by having his finger in the black market and was not working exclusively for me or for the American intelligence community, he was considered a threat.

I was told to terminate him.

I went up to Phu Bai and I brought him down to Danang to live with some relatives, and that's what happened.

Moderator: *Are you familiar, Bart, with any incident where a person was actually terminated, liquidated, with extreme prejudice?*

Osborn: *Yes, I'm afraid I had at one point in my employ a woman who was Chinese and who lived in Vietnam. She was a Chinese Vietnamese citizen. She was educated to the point where she spoke several languages, she spoke fluent English. And I used her as an interpreter and also as a guide to the culture that I was working in because as a Westerner, there were a lot of things there that I couldn't have been sensitive to. She was my guide in that respect.*

174

She also was my direct contact with agents, that is, I had people I didn't want to meet because I didn't want them to know me because in case they got compromised, they couldn't compromise me.

So, she was my go-between. She acted as an interpreter, guide, and support agent, that is, a courier. And at one point she had been—because we were short of people who were that well trained in Vietnamese, she was cross-exposed to operations. She was into a lot of my operations. {4243c3} She worked with—and incidentally, I ran only unilateral operations, American operations only, not in cooperation with the Vietnamese, which is against the Geneva Convention. And so, this was a sensitive area.

When it was determined by a military intelligence captain that she was too cross-exposed, he reported that to Saigon and he got the reading back that she ought to be terminated from the scene. She ought to be let go. It was not determined—it wasn't said whether she ought to be terminated with prejudice or not. He took it upon himself to terminate her by murdering her.

He murdered her with a .45 in a street in Danang, shot her in the neck and let her lay in the street there. It was said that there were Viet Cong agents, or terrorists, or sappers, or something in the area who shot her, and it was plausible because we knew that she was heavily involved in intelligence and would have been targeted by the unfriendlies—that's the Viet Cong.

Moderator: *I have one further question before I turn this over to the press. Bart, since your return to the United States have you ever worked, have you ever been in contact with the CIA since that time?*

Osborn: *Yes, I have, Mike. I had been pretty deeply involved in a number of operations in Vietnam, as I said, and as a result when you recruit agents you usually do it by recruiting their loyalty to you, and then get them to relate to the mission.*

When I left Vietnam I turned over my operation to my successor, but because a number of these things were CIA-supported, like the Phoenix program, VCI operations, and so forth, I was recontacted when I got back to the states, back a couple of months.

They recontacted me and asked if I would serve on an advisory basis, and I did for a while. I don't think that that's all that relevant to this whole thing, but it is true that these things continue. I ter-minated that whole thing this June, and I have no association with the CIA anymore.

Moderator: *Gentlemen, any questions, please.*

Floor: *When you were recruiting these agents, you were working for the CIA?*

Osborn: *Yes, sir, these were military intelligence modus operandi—you know, method of operation—nets. They were serving military combat units for combat intelligence and the Phoenix program for VC infrastructure, and they were laterally disseminated on a discretionary basis. If I had only combat information, I'd only send it to combat units. If I had only VCI I'd send it only to the Phoenix program, the Phoenix coordinator there in Danang.*

Floor: *Mr. Osborn, in that first incident you mentioned, about the termination, you said that was a hollow threat. Why did you say that?*

Osborn: *Because at the time that I said that, I didn't have any intention of killing him, but just of exercising a second threat if the first one didn't work. I may have killed him eventually if he became a viable threat. That is, he may have gotten bitter and compromised a number of things I was involved in and as a result have threatened my life. I may have. But I didn't. But as I say, at the time that was a hollow threat because I didn't intend to kill him, when I told him I did.*

Floor: *You would have killed him if necessary?*

Osborn: *Yes, I would have.*

Floor: *Why are you spilling all the beans now? Because we haven't won the war?*

Osborn: *No, ma'am, it's not.*

Floor: *Well, will you tell us why?*

Osborn: *Yes. I feel as if this standard operating procedure, which is authorized by the American military community, and by the CIA, is against the American value system.*

I don't feel that I can come back with a clear conscience from Vietnam and con- {4244} sider myself a good Christian, or I don't feel I can have a clear conscience, knowing that my government is working

176

despicable methods of operation in other parts of the world, and denying it; working against the Geneva Conference and blaming other nations for doing the same; taking action against foreign interests which are doing the same thing that we're doing, it's just that we classify it as they do—we catch them, they catch us, and it constitutes one heck of a hypocrisy. The reason I've said these things today is simply to document or add evidence to the fact that we are doing these things, and my suggestions would be that we don't have to. We should not criticize others for doing the same things that we're doing, or we ought to cut it out. One of the two. I simply want to add to what the others have said, and that's why I'm here today.

Floor*: Do you consider yourself a war criminal, under Nuremberg?*
Osborn*: Yes, for some of the things that I did in Vietnam I feel that they definitely were criminal. Then why wasn't he arrested and charged during this confession?*
Floor*: Mr. Noetzel, did you ever terminate an agent yourself?*
Osborn*: Mr. Noetzel?*
Floor*: No, I'm sorry.*
Osborn*: Mr. Osborn. I beg your pardon.*
Floor*: Did you ever terminate an agent by death yourself? Did you ever kill an agent?*
Osborn*: No, I didn't. I never killed an agent.*
Floor*: In that first case, the case of the agent with the Yamaha. Is it possible that when he was working for the CIA, he was not aware of that?*
Osborn*: No, it is not possible that he was not aware that he was working for the American military intelligence community, and that was my question to him that he had denied. So, in essence he had lied to me. And the interest in lying was simply this: the American intelligence community was hiring him, and they were the only force hiring him in the area, and if he wanted a job—and he was qualified because of his multi-language capability—he had to get on with somebody. And he had been fired by the CIA, and as a matter of fact he had not re-approached us, we had approached him.*
Floor*: With the Chinese agent who was killed, did you have any advance news that he was going to be killed?*

Osborn: *No, I had not advance news.*

Floor: *In that case, what was your reaction, if you felt it was unnecessary? Did you protest?*

Osborn: *Yes, I protested to the fellow who had murdered her and asked him why, and he simply explained that she was too cross-exposed and was too involved in operations. And I didn't feel that since she had been asked to help us, and had never done anything actively or passively that was against our interest, but had only followed through and had gotten involved in as many operations as we had asked her to get involved in, then to determine her fair bait for murder seemed wrong.*

Floor: *Sir, did you ever kill anyone other than an agent?*

Osborn: *In Vietnam?*

Floor: *In Vietnam.*

Osborn: *Not that I can tell you about. In fact, during the fifteen months that I was in Vietnam I was responsible for deaths, yes.*

Floor: *In what respect?*

Osborn: *Several respects. One of our functions in supplying combat information to the 1st Marine Division, especially their G-2 office, was to get targeting areas for B-52 strikes, and we would follow these up to see how effective we had been.*

For instance, if we had gotten an NVA unit reported in an area, and they would come in with the B-52s and they would target them as they came in and they would plough an area—that is, they'd drop bombs and plough an {4244c2} area there—and we'd follow up occasionally, and I'd find that we had killed civilians in the process.

And whether or not they were Viet Cong agents or not I don't know. There were civilian's dead as a result who were not, in fact, part of the NVA units that were targeted.

Floor: *Did you ever kill any civilians or POWs yourself?*

Osborn: *Not myself, no.*

Floor: *Did you ever make any attempts to tell anybody, any government authorities, about these things?*

Osborn: *In other words, bring charges or make an official complaint? No, never did.*

Floor: *Will you tell us why?*

Osborn: *Yes. Because it was so much the SOP, and my entire peer group had been doing the same thing, and to bring this up as a subject was old news.*

And as a matter of fact the people to whom I talked privately, private citizens, when I came back to the United States, doubted this—frankly didn't believe me, or if they believed me generally, and knew that I was not known to be a liar, knew that I wouldn't have any reason to lie about this, thought it was sad that I had been exposed to a war, but that's war.

Floor: *Have you ever told this in public before?*

Floor: *What about your peer group, what is their attitude about these cages, and throwing people out of helicopters and that sort of thing, as you say?*

Osborn: *They vary. They do vary in their attitudes. I know people who are conscience-stricken about the methods of operations that we described, I know other people who just looked on it as a dirty necessity, of being in Vietnam for a year. And you get your year over and you go home and forget about it. There were all levels of conscience about it. Generally, though, it was an accepted thing.*

Floor: *Tell us what your rank was.*

Osborn: *Yes, sir, I was in Vietnam, when I first got there, a Pfc, an E-3 in the Army, and when I left Fort Holabird an E-3. It was a long time before I was promoted to an E-4. I was an E-4 when I left Vietnam and was promoted to E-5 by administrative process just before I left the Army.*

Floor: *Did you ever get extra pay? Did you have a living allowance, or that sort of thing?*

Osborn: *Yes. We had allowance for separate rations, because we had to eat, we had to live in the status and keep up—GS-9s make a good bit of money in Vietnam. They have a 25 per cent pay increment and so forth. On Pfc salary I couldn't necessarily do that, and so there were separate rations, separate living allowance, and then a lot of our expenses were paid through a separate intelligence fund, so we didn't have to put it out of our own pockets.*

Floor: *Would you explain what you understand to be your violations of the Geneva Accords?*

Osborn: *Yes. Primarily it was this.*

I mentioned the scare lecture that we had at Holabird, and it mentioned that we would be working in an area, that is, agent operations, that is plausibly denied by the American government. If we didn't want to associate with it that was up to us, but we had to make that value judgment and do it voluntarily. In fact, out of a class of thirty-seven people only one opted out, and we were told that it would not be a mark against us if we decided not to continue with this at that point, but that we would have the rest of the day to think about it, and we were let go that day from class. And the next day we came back and a fellow had opted out, and the rest stayed because about half the class knew that that was the case, that area intelligence specialists were in fact agent handlers, and the others, who were surprised, accepted it. {4244c3}

Floor: *Sir, what were the violations, though?*

Osborn: *Oh, all right. Yes.*

And we were told, we were told at the time that our function would be to run illegal operations, that is, active collection of intelligence by utilization of spies, nets, agent nets—and this was illegal. It alludes to the thing about if you are caught or compromised, we'll deny the whole thing. And that's basically why we lived in cover status in Vietnam.

Because if John Smith, and that's a fictional name, was caught doing so and so, he would be pulled back to Saigon and perhaps sent out of country, perhaps changed back to uniform, and he would simply evaporate—and so if charges were officially ever brought against the government that said, "We know of a John Smith in the I Corps area, who was in fact recruiting agents," they'd say, well, you document that, and that's fine.

That was plausible denial, and it worked very effectively. This was illegality number one.

Another example of what we were doing illegally, I mentioned before, we were running unilateral operations only. Just unilateral. They were an American effort, no cooperation whatsoever with the Vietnamese, based on the assumption that whatever the Vietnamese did was compromising because they might be infiltrated by the Viet Cong.

In any case, it is, in fact, it is in conflict with our agreement with the government of South Vietnam to have exclusively unilateral collection of intelligence operations, which is what we had.

Floor: *Sir, do you feel in any personal danger as a result of your appearance here today?*

Osborn: *I don't feel as if, if somebody came out and reported to the press involvement with classified operations which are still classified, to which I have agreed not to speak, and I have signed agreements with the Department of Defense saying that I would not go into specific detail, which I, in fact, have not named names today—this is not a crucifying session of any kind—I have agreed not to go into this in detail.*

It was implicit in my agreement with the Department of Defense, that if anyone asked me what I did in Vietnam, I was an area intelligence specialist; "What was that?" Well, you were kind of familiar with the area and you studied geography and knew map reading and things, but I don't know map reading and things very well, so that was not very plausible.

And so I don't think that this would do me any good, if I went to apply for top-secret clearance, like I had before, I probably wouldn't make out too well, but what I plan to do is go into private industry on the basis of my education when I complete it, and so forth.

And I hope to be able to stand on my own two feet—not a precarious process like investigation. Is the "pinko" questionable? I feel as though the classification system is closed to me as a result of today, and whatever else I get into.

Floor: *You say you are at George Washington?*

Osborn: *I'm at American.*

Floor: *And what is your major?*

Osborn: *My major is languages and linguistics. I'm in a master's degree for International Services program, in the school there, and I'm Western Europe oriented—German and so forth.*

Floor: *What was your analysis of the Green Beret case in 1969, in Nha Trang? The way in which the Administration and the Department of the Army handled that?*

Osborn: *I mentioned plausible denial to you before. And I think that if you were familiar with the method of operation that went on, and it was a part of your life, you lived with it—and if that were your goal, your mission, your assignment, and so forth, if you heard of having a double agent through the 5th Special Forces, who was to {4245} be terminated, and it flapped, that is, it became known, and it was necessary for our government to deny it, to see them deny it, and go through the legal process to divert attention from it or whatever they were trying to do, was not surprising at all.*

That's the way I saw it.

Floor: *Sir, you say you saw Marines push Vietnamese out of helicopters. Could you tell me what the reaction of the Marines aboard the helicopters was when this occurred? Was there any reaction, or this sort of thing, and what was the reaction of the victims?*

Osborn: *The victims fell.*

Floor: *Before.*

Osborn: *Before they left the helicopter? That's two questions, sir.*

Floor: *I'd like to know a little about what was going on in the helicopter.*

Osborn: *Right. We'd go up, and the interrogation team chief—the lieutenant—and one, two, three EM, I'm not—there were two or three EM, I guess. And they would have these people with them, and they would have their hands tied behind their back, and they would load them on the helicopters, and the helicopter would take off and the.*

The Marines, you have to understand that wherever they were in a function like interrogation, any support function at all, they considered it less dangerous than a combat mission.

They would go out in the boonies and kill via their M-16 rifles. And so, I didn't ever see any moral compunctions about that

being done; as a matter of fact, when they were told to go ahead and push the fellow they would go ahead and push him.
    And on both occasions that happened.
Moderator: I'm sorry to interrupt this right now. We're already five minutes over the time of this session, and we have two more witnesses. Mr. Osborn will be available for additional interviews, he'll be here during the day, so I'd like to move on right now.

Kenneth Barton Osborn subsequently testified before two congressional committees: a House Government Operations Subcommittee (August 2, 1971) and the Senate Armed Services Committee (July 20, 1973). He did not reveal what rank he was, but it appears that he was enlisted man telling Marine lieutenants what to do. I am not sure if that is true. As a matter of fact, I do not believe this puke even served in the military. However, at the end of this guy's testimony, he takes questions from the press.

Floor: *Sir, did you ever kill anyone other than an agent?*
Osborn: *In Vietnam?*
Floor: *In Vietnam.*
Osborn: *Not that I can tell you about. In fact, during the fifteen months that I was in Vietnam I was responsible for deaths, yes.*
Floor: *In what respect?*
Osborn: *Several respects. One of our functions in supplying combat information to the 1st Marine Division, especially their G-2 office, was to get targeting areas for B-52 strikes, and we would follow these up to see how effective we had been.*
    For instance, if we had gotten an NVA unit reported in an area, and they would come in with the B-52s and they would target them as they came in and they would plough an area—that is, they'd drop bombs and plough an {4244c2} area there—and we'd follow up occasionally, and I'd find that we had killed civilians in the process. And whether or not they were Viet Cong agents or not I don't know. There were civilian's dead as a result who were not, in fact, part of the NVA units that were targeted.
Floor: *Do you consider yourself a war criminal, under Nuremberg?*

Osborn: *Yes, for some of the things that I did in Vietnam I feel that they definitely were criminal.*

Then based on his last statement, why wasn't this man arrested and charged during this confession? If you are not reporting it at the time it happens, or shortly after, then you are part of it. As a detective with the state police, if you came into my office and told me you were responsible for killing people, I would detain you and take a statement. After taking the statement, I would investigate it. If the confession turned out to be true, you would be arrested and charged.

When Dellums said, "The prime responsibility lies at the highest levels of civilian and military command." Did he mean himself since he was a member of Congress, and it is civilian rule that runs the military in the United States? Since he was in a position of authority, especially regarding the military, then as he said the prime responsibility lies with him and the rest of his colleagues that attended these meetings.

If what he said is true, then every individual that is elected to office, whether in the federal state or municipal governments, share the primary responsibility for every homicide, rape, holdup, and robbery, as well as every other major and minor criminal offense that occurs here instead of the individual committing it.

With that way of thinking, then I must be guilty of nonfeasance of office since I did not lock up the various mayors, councilmen and women, freeholders, and clerks in the numerous towns of the seven hundred plus homicides I investigated.

Twenty-nine veterans, including the ones listed in this chapter, testified at these hearings regarding these alleged war crimes like the excerpts from transcripts above [Q]. The other transcripts also describe alleged details of the US military's conduct in Vietnam; some tactics were described as gruesome, such as the severing of ears from corpses to verify body count. Others involved the indiscriminate killing of civilians. Soldiers claimed to have ordered artillery strikes on villages which did not appear to have any military presence. Soldiers were claimed to use racist terms, such as *gooks*, *dinks*, and *slant eyes* when referring to the Vietnamese.

(Let us see, munchkins come from the land of Oz. However, these twenty-nine mutts come from the land of ethnic slurs—America. I think I have heard every ethnic slur used by every color of rainbow and every ethnic group against all the other ethnic groups in this land, and that is before I went to Vietnam.) Never mind since they are saying calling the enemy names is an atrocity. What ever happened to "sticks and stones will break your bones, but names will never hurt you"?

These twenty-nine sanctimonious veterans confessed to being witness to and participants in war crimes in Vietnam, absolving themselves from sin, like everyone else that protested the Vietnam War by pointing the finger at the highest levels of the United States military as well as their fellow veterans. The act of pointing their finger, I equate with the actions of members of the Nazi Party testifying at the Nuremburg trials, "Sure we killed six million Jews, but Hitler said it was okay!"

Somewhere along the line, the individual who commits the act such as these assholes who testified regarding what they did should have taken responsibility for their own actions. If they did what they said they did, then shame on them, not on me or any of us Nam vets who served our country honorably. All through these testimonies, these so-called Americans are admitting to crimes and nothing happened to them; at least Calley was arrested and convicted, and he didn't admit to shit.

I would not believe these guys if they told me they had mothers. I believe them to be traitors to the oath they took as soldiers, sailors, airmen, and marines. If you were a scumbag in the military, then you were a scumbag before you got there. That is why the military has the UCMJ and the military police. Due to the sheer number of people that enter the military, a few degenerates happen to slip through the cracks like these slugs, just like in all other professions and all other walks of life.

Congress, on a whole, chose not to endorse these proceedings. As such, the hearings were ad hoc and only informational in nature. As a condition of room use, press and camera presence were not permitted, but the proceedings were transcribed. A small number of other anti-Vietnam War congressional representatives listed above took part in the hearings.

It is my belief that these hearings were used for one purpose, and that was to discredit the US military. (These people accomplished their mission.)

However, long before the VVAW and the whining sniveling treasonous public, there were elected officials, whose loyalty to the United States I would question, not to mention their loyalty to democracy and freedom. However, at least Morse and Gruening were up-front about their feelings in voting against what was called the Tonkin Resolution, but then I believe they did everything in their power to assist with the anti-war movement, whereas Fulbright and Mansfield voted for it and then spoke against it. Mansfield was against it in 1962 and voted]s for the resolution in 1964. Fulbright votes for the resolution, and then goes on a media blitzkrieg against the war.

Mansfield served as a member of the Democratic Party in the House of Representatives from 1943 until 1953 and in the Senate from 1953 until 1977. During his tenure in the Senate, he served as the majority leader from 1961 to 1977; he is the longest-serving majority leader in the history of the Senate.

An early supporter of Ngo Dinh Diem, Mansfield had a change of heart on the Vietnam issue after a visit to Vietnam in 1962. He reported to President Kennedy on December 2,1962, that US money given to Diem's government was being squandered and that the US should avoid further involvement in Vietnam. He was thus the first American official to comment adversely on the war's progress. During the Johnson presidency, he became a frequent and vocal critic of US involvement in the Vietnam War.

He hailed the new Nixon administration, especially when the Nixon Doctrine announced in Guam in 1969 that the US would honor all US treaty commitments against those who might invade the lands of allies of the United States, provide a nuclear umbrella against threats of other nuclear powers, supply weapons and technical assistance to countries where warranted but without committing American forces to local conflicts.

In turn, Nixon turned to Mansfield for advice and as his liaison with the Senate on Vietnam. However, by 1970, with Nixon still pursuing the war, he adopted the position that the Congress ought to pressure Nixon more, especially by stringent legislative limitations on the use of American forces and appropriated funds for the war. As a result, Nixon reduced American forces by 95 percent, leaving only 24,200 in late 1972; the last ones left in 1973.

The controversial Mansfield Amendment of 1973 expressly limited appropriations for defense research (through ARPA) to projects with direct military application. An earlier Mansfield Amendment, offered in 1971, called for the number of US troops stationed in Europe to be halved. On May 19, 1971, however, the Senate defeated this amendment by a vote of 61-36.

These are but a few of the politicians that jumped on the antiwar movement.

In 1964, Morse was one of only two United States senators to vote against the Gulf of Tonkin resolution (Alaska's was the other), [1] which authorized an expansion of US involvement in the Vietnam War. During the following years, Morse remained one of the country's most outspoken critics of the war. As early as 1966, he told a student union that he would like to see "protests such as these multiply by the hundreds" across the country. In 1966, he angered many in his own party for supporting Oregon's Republican Gov. Mark Hatfield over the Democratic nominee, Congressman Robert Duncan, in that year's senatorial election due to Duncan's support of the Vietnam War.

Ernest Gruening was appointed governor of Alaska, lobbied for statehood, and became one of Alaska's first US senators. A Democrat, he was an early opponent of the Vietnam War, voting with Wayne Morse of Oregon against what was called the Gulf of Tonkin Resolution in August 1964. He was defeated in the 1968 primary. His works include *The State of Alaska* (1954) and *The Battle for Alaska Statehood* (1967).

On August 7, 1964, a unanimous House of Representatives and all but two members of the Senate voted to approve what was known as the Gulf of Tonkin Resolution, which a good number of people believe led to a dramatic escalation of the Vietnam War. Fulbright, who voted for the resolution, would later write: "Many senators who accepted the Gulf of Tonkin Resolution without question might well not have done so had they foreseen that it would subsequently be interpreted as a sweeping congressional endorsement for the conduct of a large-scale war in Asia."

As chairman of the Foreign Relations Committee, Fulbright held several series of hearings on the Vietnam War. Many of the earlier hearings in 1966 were televised to the nation in their entirety.

In 1966, Fulbright published *The Arrogance of Power* in which he attacked the justification of the Vietnam War, Congress's failure to set limits on it, and the impulses which gave rise to it. Fulbright's scathing critique undermined the elite consensus that US military intervention in Indochina was necessitated by Cold War geopolitics.

April 1971, the hearings started by Dellums in February and March continued. The following is an excerpt **of** one of the more famous witnesses who testified before the hearings.

COMPLETE TESTIMONY OF LT. JOHN KERRY TO
SENATE FOREIGN RELATIONS COMMITTEE3 of
40 From the Congressional Record (92nd Congress, 1st
Session) for Thursday, April 22, 1971, pages 179-210.
LEGISLATIVE PROPOSALS RELATING TO
THE WAR IN SOUTHEAST ASIA1
THURSDAY, APRIL 22, 1971
UNITED STATES SENATE; COMMITTEE ON
FOREIGN RELATIONS, Washington, DC.

*THE COMMITTEE MET, PURSUANT TO notice, at 11:05 a.m., in Room
4221, New Senate Office Building, Senator J. W. Fulbright (Chairman)
presiding.*
Present: Senators Fulbright, Symington, Pell, Aiken, Case, and Javits.
The CHAIRMAN. The committee will come to order.

OPENING STATEMENT

The committee is continuing this morning its hearings on proposals relating to the ending of the war in Southeast Asia. This morning the committee will hear testimony from Mr. John Kerry and, if he has any associates, we will be glad to hear from them. These are men who have fought in this unfortunate war in Vietnam. I believe they deserve to be heard and listened to by the Congress and by the officials in the executive branch and by the public generally. You have a perspective that those in the Government who make our Nation's policy do not always have and I am sure that your testimony today will be helpful to the committee in its consideration of the proposals before us.

I would like to add simply on my own account that I regret very much the action of the Supreme Court in denying the veterans the right to use the Mall. [Applause.]

I regret that. It seems to me to be but another instance of an insensitivity of our Government to the tragic effects of this war upon our people.

I want also to congratulate Mr. Kerry, you, and your associates upon the restraint that you have shown, certainly in the hearing the other day when there were a great many of your people here. I think you conducted yourselves in a most commendable manner throughout this week. Whenever people gather there is always a tendency for some of the more emotional ones to do things which are even against their own interests. I think you deserve much of the credit because I understand you are one of the leaders of this group.

I have joined with some of my colleagues, specifically Senator Hart, in an effort to try to change the attitude of our Government toward your efforts in bringing to this committee and to the country your views about the war. 2. I personally don't know of any group which would have both a greater justification for doing it and also a more accurate view of the effect of the war. As you know, there has grown up in this town a feeling that it is extremely difficult to get accurate information about the war and I don't know a better source than you and your associates. So, we are very pleased to have you and your associates, Mr. Kerry.

At the beginning if you would give to the reporter your full name and a brief biography so that the record will show who you are.

*Senator JAVITS. Mr. Chairman, I was down there to the veterans'
camp yesterday and saw the New York group and I would like to say I am
very proud of the deportment and general attitude of the group. I hope it
continues. I have joined in the Hart resolution, too. As a lawyer, I hope
you will find it possible to comply with the order even though like the
chairman, I am unhappy about it. I think it is our job to see that you are
suitably set up as an alternative so that you can do what you came here to
do. I welcome the fact that you came and what you're doing.*
[Applause.]
The CHAIRMAN. You may proceed, Mr. Kerry.

STATEMENT OF JOHN KERRY, VIETNAM VETERANS AGAINST THE WAR

The reason I show this excerpt is to show the opening proceedings prior to the actual testimony given by Kerry. This testimony by Kerry was that famous televised speech. Because it was televised, I believe this entire testimony was taken as the truth. However, one thing I noted in this transcript from those hearings just before Kerry began to speak, no one administered to him the oath to tell the truth. Not that an oath guarantees the person taking it is going to be truthful (i.e., Bill Clinton during the Monica Lewinsky incident). However, by not administering the oath, the person testifying does not have to worry about committing the crime of perjury. In the case of this testimony, I remember reading in the book *Stolen Valor* by B. G. Burkett and Glenna Whitley that Kerry's testimony might have been written by then Sen. Robert Kennedy's speechwriter. I also remember reading that in a recent news article somewhere. Senator Robert Kennedy or his speechwriter never spent any time in the military nor were they ever in combat.

On April 19, 1971, over two thousand veterans from the VVAW started their encampment on the mall in Washington, DC, and they also protested all over the city. This was called Operation Dewey Canyon Three by these mutts known as the Vietnam Veterans Against the War, and on April 22, while they conducted their Dewey Canyon Operation, John Kerry, one of their fearless leaders, testified in front of Senate without an oath being uttered, promising to tell the truth.

I do not know if it is true, but I have read that Abraham Lincoln made the following statement. I guess it really does not matter who made it, I happen to agree with it.

"Congressmen who willfully take actions during war time that damage morale and undermine the military are saboteurs and should be arrested, exiled, or hanged."

CHAPTER 10

RESOLUTIONS TONKEN
AND WAR POWERS

I MENTIONED THE GULF OF Tonkin Resolution earlier; let us look at these incidents a little closer. Over the years, it seems to have become the battle cry for those involved in the anti-war movement to justify their feelings about and their actions surrounding the Vietnam War. The events of the United States Navy specifically and the people in the military and the civilians attached to the military charged with the gathering of intelligence information and reporting it through documents known as SIGINT and COMINT reports on the nights of August 2 and 4, 1964, have come under great scrutiny.

Let us examine what a SIGINT and COMINT report is. Individuals monitoring radio transmissions type the information that they are listening to. The report is called a SIGINT report, or a signal intercept. COMINT reports are transcribed documents from communiqués, faxes, teletypes, and the like. They are often cryptic (secret), or they must be deciphered by an intelligence gathering specialist.

On November 30, 2005, the National Security Agency (NSA) released the first installment of previously classified information regarding the Vietnam era, specifically the Gulf of Tonkin incident. This release includes a variety of articles, chronologies of events, oral history interviews, signals intelligence reports, and translations, and other related memoranda.

On May 30, 2006, NSA released the second and final installment of Gulf of Tonkin materials. This final release includes additional articles, chronologies of events, oral history interviews, and other related memoranda.

Because of the declassification, there were extensive investigations regarding the SIGINT reports because these were the documents that President Johnson was receiving and making most of his decisions on regarding the events that were happening in the Tonkin gulf.

Prior to the years 2005 and 2006, when all the documents pertaining to these events were still classified top secret, all the accusations regarding these incidents were based on speculation due to the fact the documents surrounding these events were still not available to the public. The accusation was that Johnson contrived the attack of the fourth to get the resolution that would plunge us deeper into war, at least that is what I was hearing. (This, I believe to be the furthest thing from the truth.)

Since the declassification and the investigations, conclusions were drawn based on the SIGINT reports that an attack more than likely did not take place. The conclusions are also saying that there is no clear evidence that there was collusion between the administration and the NSA (National Security Administration) to show that the attack of August 4 did occur. However, they are still saying that these events and the resolution were the reason that we went to war. (As I said, I disagree.)

Let us examine how the United States came to be involved in the Tonkin gulf in the first place.

John F. Kennedy was elected president in 1960. In late 1961, a military operation was implemented as part of the Cold War strategy. It was a naval operation given the code name DESOTO. The following excerpts extracted from release 00011 (Exhibit 10) declassified in 2005/2006 shows the purpose of the patrols:

In late 1961–early 1962 a series of U.S. Navy patrols off the east coast of Communist China was proposed. The purpose of these patrols was to be three-fold. In the first place, they would establish and maintain the presence of the U.S. Seventh Fleet in the international waters off the China coast; second, they would serve as a minor Cold War irritant to the Chicoms and third, they would collect as much intelligence as possible concerning the initial phasing called for one US destroyer to conduct each mission. Patrols were given the cover name DESOTO. From 14 to 20 April 1962 the first DESOTO patrol was conducted, with the destroyer USS -DE HAVEN as the participating vessel. The area of responsibility encompassed by the mission focused around the Tsingtao area of the Yellow Sea, and the ship was instructed not to approach any Chicoms-held territory, including the offshore islands, closer than 10 miles.

Major intelligence targets for this mission fell into five categories: This first DESOTO patrol was singularly effective in evoking Chicoms reaction. Such things as shadowing of the DE HAVEN by three or more Chicoms vessels at one time, jamming of the DE HAVEN communications facilities, and the use of deceptive pennant numbers on the shadowing vessels all contributed to the success of the intelligence effort on this mission. In addition, the Chicoms issued three "serious warnings" to the DE HAVEN for violation of territorial rights during the 7 days the mission was in progress.

Prelude to Violence

The fourth DESOTO patrol into the international waters of the Gulf of Tonkin was programmed in July 1964. Concerned more with the Vietnamese problem than the Chicoms problem of its predecessors, this mission was to observe the junk fleet vessels believed to be a constant source of resupply to the guerrillas in the south, obtain navigational and hydrographic information, and procure any available intelligence on the DRV navy. Since the 1954 Geneva agreements specifically prohibited the DRV from establishing a navy, the emergence of this force had been, until late 1963–early 1964, extremely covert. During late 1957 the first DRV naval communications facilities were isolated with an estimated 30 ships involved in the transmissions. Then in 1959 the first evidence of the emergence of a modern DRV navy was noted during a probable joint DRV/Chicoms naval exercise in the Pearl River estuary. Some of the vessels involved in this exercise were believed to be the same

10 motor gunboats later noted passing through the Hainan Strait and probably represented the DRV's initial acquisition of modern naval craft. Augmentation of this force was continual after 1959, and as of late 1964 the DRV navy had a total complement of nearly 100 vessels.

Armed with this background, and clear on the purpose of the mission, the USS MADDOX reached a point on the 17th parallel about 12 miles off the coast of the DRV on 31 July 1964 at 1300 hours' local time. From that point, the MADDOX turned northward on a tack that was to take her up the coast for three days in what was believed to be another routine running of a DESOTO patrol.

That is how the navy came to be in the Tonkin gulf, and what its purpose was for being there. I would like to note, that this action does not take place without the consent of the commander in chief of the Armed Forces of the United States. In this case, John F. Kennedy.

According the above excerpt no. 3 from release 00011 (exhibit 10), North Vietnam was in violation of the 1954 Geneva Treaty, prohibiting them from having a Navy. The treaty they are talking about is the Agreement on the Cessation of Hostilities in Vietnam, July 20, 1954 (exhibit 06). Here are excerpts from that treaty confirming that statement:

Article 17

(a) With effect from the date of entry into force of the present Agreement, the introduction into Viet-Nam of any reinforcements in the form of all types of arms, munitions and other war material, such as combat aircraft, naval craft, pieces of ordnance jet engines and jet weapons and armored vehicles, is prohibited.

Article 18

With effect from the date of entry into force of the present Agreement, the establishment of new military bases is prohibited throughout Viet-Nam territory.

Article 19

With effect from the date of entry into force of the present Agreement, no military base under the control of a foreign State may be established in the regrouping zone of either party; the two parties shall ensure that the zones assigned to them do not adhere to any military alliance and are not used for the resumption of hostilities or to further an aggressive policy.

It should be noted, that the Agreement on the Cessation of Hostilities in Vietnam, July 20, 1954 (exhibit 06), is a treaty signed by the North Vietnam government in Hanoi and France, not the South Vietnamese government in Saigon or the United States.

At any rate, the DESOTO intelligence patrols were in this area long before 1964. Due to the events of August 2 and 4, 1964, in the Tokin gulf, a retaliatory air strike against North Vietnam and the request by President Johnson of Congress to pass a resolution became a major point of controversy during and since the Vietnam War. Mostly it has been a focal point for the anti-war movement/anti-American dissidents whom I believe used it to defend their position of treason.

In 1998, an individual by the name of Robert J. Hanyok wrote an article "Skunks, Bogies, Silent Hounds, and the Flying Fish" for the *Cryptologic Quarterly*, Release 00012 (exhibit 25).

The article is a result of an extensive investigation conducted by Hanyok.

Due to his experience and education, for me to disagree with his findings would be ludicrous. However, he has come to some conclusions that I absolutely disagree with. Also, I do not believe his investigation was complete, so let's examine his document and conclusions:

(U/Fœ6)—Mr. Hanyok is a senior historian with the Center for Cryptologic History (E05). He worked in the NSA/CSS Archives from 1992 to 1994 and in the National SIGINT Operations Center from 1990 to 1992. Mr. Hanyok has also served as a collection officer in G Group (1976-1979). in the COMSEC Doctrine organization (1979-1982). as a Traffic Analysis intern (1982-1984).and as an analyst in A

Group (19841990). He holds the title of master in the technical track program of the Intelligence Analysis Career field.

CHSĐ The Gulf of Tonkin incidents of 2 to 4 August 1964 have come to loom over the subsequent American engagement in Indochina. The incidents, principally the second one of 4 August, led to the approval of the Gulf of Tonkin Resolution by the U.S. Congress, which handed President Johnson the carte blanche charter he had wanted for future intervention in Southeast Asia. From this point on, the American policy and programs would dominate the course of the Indochina War. At the height of the American involvement, over a half million U.S. soldiers, sailors, airmen, and marines would be stationed there. The war would spread across the border into Cambodia and escalate in Laos. Thailand assumed a Beater importance as a base for supporting the military effort, especially for the air war, but also for SIGINT purposes of intercept and direction finding.

(U) However, within the government, the events of 4 August were never that clear. Even as the last flare fizzled in the dark waters of the South China Sea on that August night, there were conflicting narratives and interpretations of what had happened. James Stockdale, then a navy pilot at the scene, who had "the best seat in the house from which to detect boats, "saw nothing. "No boats," he would later write, "no boat wakes, no ricochets off boats, no boat impacts, no torpedo wakes—nothing but black sea and American firepower."[2] The commander of the Maddox task force, Captain John J. Herrick, was not entirely certain what had trans-pired. (Captain Herrick actually was the commander of the destroyer division to which the Maddox belonged. For this mission, he was aboard as the on-site commander.) Hours after the incident, he would radio the Commander-in-Chief, Pacific (CINCPAC) telling them that he was doubtful of many aspects of the "attack."

Two startling findings emerged from the new research. First, it is not simply that there is a different story as to what happened; it is that no attack happened that night. Through a compound of analytic errors and an unwillingness to consider contrary evidence, American SIGINT elements in the region and at NSA HQs reported Hanoi's plans to attack the two ships of the Desoto patrol. Further analytic errors and an obscur-ing of other information led to publication of more "evidence." In truth,

Hanoi's navy was engaged in nothing that night but the salvage of two of the boats damaged on 2 August.

The second finding pertains to the handling of the SIGINT material related to the Gulf of Tonkin by individuals at NSA Beginning with the period of the crisis in early August, into the days of the immediate aftermath, and continuing into October 1964, SIGINT information was presented in such a manner as to preclude responsible decision makers in the Johnson administration from having the complete and objective narrative of events of 4 August 1964. Instead, only SIGINT that supported the claim that the communists had attacked the two destroyers was given to administration officials.

A few last notes before we review the attacks. It will be necessary to limit the discussion to the role SIGINT played during the incident. Other evidential sources, such as that from the American ships' own radar, sonar, and sightings, will be mentioned in passing simply because they are part of the story and cannot be altogether ignored. However, the brunt of the following discussion center on the SIGNT evidence because of its critical role in convincing the Johnson administration that the attack actually occurred.

(U) Then at 2134G (1434Z) came the most important radar contact of the entire incident. What appeared to be a single boat suddenly appeared on the Maddox's radar screen east of the two destroyers at 9,800 yards and closing at nearly 40 knots. The Turner Joy detected another object approaching, but on a different heading, distance, and speed. According to Marolda and Fitzgerald, the navy claimed that this was the same return as the Maddo£s.[87] At 2137G (1437Z) at a distance of 6,200 yards from the Desoto vessels, the return tracked by the Maddox appeared to make a sharp turn to the south. This maneuver was interpreted by the Maddox combat information center as a turn after a torpedo run. If this was a torpedo launch, then it was an extraordinarily desperate one. Hanoi's tactical specifications for its P-4s called for torpedo launches at ranges under 1,000 yards. At over 6,000 yards, it was unlikely a torpedo launched at a moving target could hit anything.[88] The sonar operator aboard the Maddox detected a noise spike on his equipment but did not report it as a torpedo. This conclusion was reached on the CIC. However,

the Turner Joy never detected any torpedoes on its sonar. Nor did it detect any torpedoes at all on its sonar that night.

(U) At 2140G (1440Z), Herrick informed CNCPACFLT that he had commenced firing on the attacking PT boat. The Turner Joy had begun firing at its return shortly before this. Both destroyers had a difficult time holding a radar on their targets. Within five minutes, the return on Maddox's radar, which was moving away from the destroyers, disappeared from its screen at a distance of about 9,000 yards. The one that the Turner Joy was kept approaching, and at a distance of about 4,000 yards, it disappeared as well.[90]

(U) For the next fifteen minutes, all surface contacts were gone from the radars of the two destroyers. Then, at 2201G (15010, more contacts were detected coming from the west. Now the thickest part of the naval action commenced. The two destroyers fired wildly in the dark waters of the Gulf of Tonkin, the Turner Joy firing over 300 rounds madly at swarms of attacking North Vietnamese boats—maybe as many as thirteen—and dodging over two dozen torpedoes. Another twenty-four-star shell had been fired to illuminate the area and four or five depth charges had been dropped to ward off the pursuing boats and the torpedoes. The Maddox vectored overhead aircraft to the surface contacts, but time and again the aircraft reached the designated point, dropped flares, and reported they could not find any boats. By the time the attack was considered over at 2335G (1635Z), Herrick reported two enemy patrol boats sunk and another damaged. (The count of the damaged boats varied; Herrick believed that the DRV boats sank one of their own accidentally. It is not understood how he arrived at this conclusion, except as a misinterpretation of the radar data which itself was of dubious quality.)

—S Within an hour of the end of the attack, Herrick relayed his doubts about the attack in an after-action report. After reviewing the number of contacts and possible sinking's, he stated, "ENTIRE ACTION LEAVES MANY DOUBTS EXCEPT FOR APPARENT ATTEMPTED AMBUSH AT BEGINNING." [96] *Herrick then suggested in the morning that there be a thorough air reconnaissance of the area for wreckage. In a follow-up message, Herrick added that the Maddox had "NEVER POSITIVELY IDENTIFIED A BOAT AS SUCH."*[97]

(light of what finally transpired with T-142 and the two P-4 torpedo boats, it seems that they were not part of a defensive plan against the raiders. That this Swatow received the message about the raiders does not seem odd in light of the fact that T-142 seems to have served as some sort of radio relay for other boats or as a communications guard vessel for all DRV naval operations: a majority of intercepted messages during the period seem to have been sent to or through T-142. From other intercepts, we know that at least another Swatow, T-379, was near Hon Matt; two others, T-130 and T-132, were near Hon Me Island; and T-165 had deployed, as well. If the DRV was planning to attack the 34A raiders on 4 August, these craft would have been the local ones to use because of their substantial deck gun armament. However, no other communications activity related to any other Swatow patrol craft was intercepted that night. So, it remains uncertain what, if anything, Hanoi was planning to do to fend off the 34A mission of 4 August.

Exhibit B: The Lack of Vietnamese Command, Control, Communications, and Intelligence (U) Unfortunately, the administration chose to hang the rationale for expanding its war-making franchise in Southeast Asia on an incident which could not stand up to any kind of objective examination of the full documentation. So, as eventually happened in 1968, when the Gulf of Tonkin Resolution came to be reviewed, the incident that it was based on also came under scrutiny. When the events of 4 August were revealed to have been based on very thin evidence, it concurrently was demonstrated that the Johnson administration had indulged in a very selective use of information. If the administration had not lied exactly, it had not been exactly honest with the public, or, for that matter, even honest within its own deliberations. The question no longer was about the appropriateness of the resolution, but the basic honesty of the administration. It would cast a pall on an already distrusted Johnson presidency. As Senator Barry Goldwater, who had run against Johnson in the 1964 presidential election, bitterly noted years later in 1972, "I had no reason to believe that Mr. Johnson's account of the gravity existing in the Gulf of Tonkin was not legitimate."196

(U) As for the Tonkin Gulf incident itself, President Johnson summed it up best just a few days later: "Hell, those damn, stupid sailors were just shooting at flying fish."

The exact "how" and "why" for this effort to provide only the SIGINT that supported the claim of an attack remain unknown. There are no "smoking gun" memoranda or notes buried in the files that outline any plan or state a justification. Instead, the paper record speaks for itself on what happened: what few product (six) were actually used, and how 90 percent of them were kept out of the Chrono low; how contradictory SIGINT evidence was answered both with speculation and fragments lifted from context; how the complete lack of Vietnamese C31 was not addressed; and, finally, how critical original Vietnamese text and subsequent product were no longer available. From this evidence, one can easily deduce the deliberate nature of these actions. And this observation makes sense, for there was a purpose to them: This was an active effort to make SIGINT fit the claim of what happened during the evening of 4 August in the Gulf of Tonkin.

The question why the NSA personnel handled the product the way they did will probably never be answered. The notion that they were under "pressure" to deliver the story that the administration wanted simply cannot be supported. If the participants are to be believed, and they were adamant in asserting this, they did not bend to the desires of administration officials. Also, such "environmental" factors as overworked crisis center personnel and lack of experienced linguists are, for the most part, not relevant when considering the entire period of the crisis and follow-up. As we have seen, the efforts to ensure that the only SIGINT publicized would be that which supported the contention that an attack had occurred continued long after the crisis had passed. While the product initially issued on the 4 August incident may be contentious, thin, and mistaken, what was issued in the Gulf of Tonkin summaries beginning late on 4 August was deliberately skewed to support the notion that there had been an attack. What was placed in the official Chrono low was even more selective. That the NSA personnel believed that the attack happened and rationalized the contradictory evidence away is probably all that is necessary to know in order to understand what was done. They walked alone in their counsels.

Here conclude the excerpts from exhibit 25. Before we continue, I would like to state that when the Token gulf events occurred, there were twenty-one thousand troops on the ground in Vietnam. They were assigned there by three presidents that were in office prior to Johnson. Johnson had only been in office since November 1963, a total of nine months prior to the Tonkin gulf events. Thus, making him the only president in a nineteen-year period that did not send any troops to Vietnam prior to these incidents and would not for another seven months.

That being said, let us examine the conjecture, speculation, and lies that surrounded these events.

In case you do not remember from the beginning, *conjecture* is defined as "the formation of judgments or opinions on the basis of incomplete or inconclusive information, or a conclusion, judgment, or statement based on incomplete or inconclusive information."

From page 1 in the Hanyok article, he states, "The Incidents principally the second one of 4 August, led to the approval of the Gulf of Tonkin Resolution by the U.S. Congress, which handed President Johnson the carte blanche charter he had wanted for future intervention in South East Asia." Now that is what I consider an arrogant conclusion. How does he know what Johnson wanted to do or what he was thinking? However, that is the kind of conjecture that permeated the anti-war movement.

Do not get me wrong. Mr. Hanyok's investigation is thorough regarding the SIGINT information, and for me to question that would be as wrong as the statement he made. He apparently based his conclusion on the SIGINT investigation only, and there is a lot more to the story which you will see as we go along.

The second excerpt from page 1 of Hanyok's article emphasized that a Navy pilot from the USS *Ticonderoga*, James Stockdale, was flying in support of both the destroyers and advised that he could not see any enemy from his location, which was above the action. However, that does not necessarily mean that they were not there. He further said that Captain Herrick the on-sight commander expressed his doubts in a SIGINT report about the attack; this will be discussed further later.

He also made a statement on page 3 of his article that the people taking the SIGINT reports made errors and had an unwillingness to consider contrary evidence. The consideration of contrary evidence is something, I believe, he failed to do also.

For example, on page 10 of his article, he makes the following statement: "It will be necessary to limit the discussion to the role SIGINT played during the incident. Other evidential sources, such as that from the American Ships own radar, sonar, and visual sightings will be mentioned in passing, simply because they are part of the story and cannot be altogether ignored."

To limit the discussion just to the role of SIGINT, I believe, is an unwillingness to consider contrary evidence as well as fitting the definition of *conjecture*. If it does not fit the definition based on inconclusive information, it most definitely fits it based on incomplete information. There were other things happening that night besides electronic communications! These things carry just as much weight as the signal intercepts.

The next two excerpts from pages 22 and 23 of Hanyok's article talk about the USS *Maddox's* and *Turner Joy's* radar and sonar picking up readings indicating that they were under attack. This would be the second attack on the *Maddox* in two days. The *Maddox* also received a SIGINT on August 3 that they may be attacked again. The excerpt from page 23 shows both ships expending rounds, flairs, and depth charges, believing that they are under attack. No one anywhere in any report that I have seen denies that both ships fired their weapons, expending rounds on the night of August 4. *(This is part of the picture and cannot be ignored, or just mentioned in passing.)*

From the excerpt on page 24, he says that Captain Herrick expressed doubts about the attack with the following statement: "Entire action leaves many doubts except for apparent attempted ambush at beginning."

I would like to discuss this statement a little more because I found a couple of things regarding this that raises a couple of questions.

Another gentleman by the name of Louis F. Giles, director of policy and records, also wrote an article regarding Mr. Hanyok's article on December 5, 2005. The following is an excerpt from Mr. Giles's article (exhibit 25A):

As noted by Mr. Hanyok, many historians now believe the supposed attack by North Vietnam naval forces on the Desoto patrol on 4 August did not occur. Mr. Hanyok provides an even more convincing argument for this position based upon previously unreleased SIGINT.

Evidence supporting the attack on 4 August is based principally upon eyewitness accounts, as well as radar and sonar data from the U.S. destroyers Maddox and Turner Joy. Additionally, analysis of communications intelligence (COMINT) intercepted immediately after the purported attack appeared to confirm that such an attack did indeed occur and this COMINT was used by Secretary of Defense McNamara and President Johnson as supporting evidence to order a U.S. retaliation strike.

While later reports questioned the intensity of the attack, Captain Herrick as well as other officers and seamen were adamant then and remain adamant to this day that the ships were attacked. From an NSA perspective, however, it is important to note that the COMINT evidence was supporting evidence to justify the U.S retaliation attacks. In testimony before the Committee on Foreign Relations in 1968, Secretary McNamara responded to a question asking if he would have proceeded with the attacks without the COMINT by stating, "Yes, it was not the deciding factor, but it justified the decision." Thus, it is clear that the U.S. retaliation was based principally on eyewitness accounts from the destroyers on the scene, not from intelligence.

This article does not dispute Mr. Hanyok's ultimate conclusion— an attack did not occur. Nevertheless, while Mr. Hanyok's analysis of the available COMINT evidence is convincing, on its own, the COMINT does not prove that an attack did or did not occur. Unlike the 2 August COMINT where an actual attack message was intercepted, circumstantial evidence and the absence of a 4 August COMINT attack message cannot conclusively prove there was not an attack.

Note in the Giles article, he states, "While later reports questioned the intensity of the attack, Capt. Herrick as well as other officers and seamen were adamant then and remain adamant to this day that he ships were attacked." These later reports that he is talking about are chronologies written about the events. Again, you must pay attention to the eyewitnesses' accounts as well as the SIGINT and COMINT reports; they go hand in hand.

So Captain Herrick's statement ("Entire action leaves many doubts except for apparent attempted ambush at beginning"), I believe, was used as a supporting statement in the Hanyok report to slant toward the idea that an attack did not occur when the fact is that Herrick believes an attack did take place.

Besides the article by Mr. Giles, in Colonel Bui Tin's book *From Enemy to Friend*, he also makes a statement regarding this issue:

> *On August 2, 1964, the* Maddox *did indeed exchange fire with the Vietnamese Navy. Two small Vietnamese patrol boats were slightly hit resulting in four dead and six wounded, and the fighting happened in Vietnamese territorial waters (within twenty nautical miles of shore). The August 4 "incident" never occurred. On that night, the sea was in an ugly mood with roaring winds, and it was very dark.*
>
> *The Vietnamese navy was ordered to keep track of the* Maddox *but did not shoot or engage in any action.*
>
> *The way we interpreted the August 4 "incident" was as follows. After the exchange of gunfire on August 2, tension was in the air with each side watching each other's moves. It thus took very little prompting for the American side to take a vague indication of hostility to be the real thing.*

At first, he says the August 4 incident never occurred. However, in the last paragraph, he says tension was in the air with each side watching each other's moves. It thus took very little, prompting for the American side to take a vague indication of hostility to be the real thing.

So the two questions regarding Bui Tin's statement is what the prompting was and what was the vague indication.

So as not to be accused of speculation as to what Bui Tin was saying, I have decided to include the definitions of prompting and indication.

Prompting: *to cause (someone) to do something; to be the cause of (something) to say (something that encourages a person to talk); to move to action: incite; to assist (one acting or reciting) by suggesting or saying the next words of something forgotten or imperfectly learned: cue to serve as the inciting cause of <evidence prompting an investigation>*

Indication: *anything serving to indicate or point out, as a sign or token;*

Medicine/Medical. a special symptom or the like that points out a suitable remedy or treatment or shows the presence of a disease; an act of indicating; the degree marked by an instrument.

The above paragraph containing these two words is the written testimony of one of the Communist leaders. As a matter of fact, the one that took the unconditional surrender from the South Vietnamese government at the end of the war in '75. With these two words, the man contradicts himself, first he says it did not occur, then he says we the Americans may have taken a little prompting as an indication of hostility. That statement says to me that they did something. Were these two things the "apparent attempted ambush at the beginning" that Captain Herrick saw according to the Giles document?

Louis F. Giles does not dispute the findings of Mr. Hanyok's investigation or his conclusion. Nor would I, giving the amount of training or knowledge of which I have about cryptologic analyzing, which is absolute zero.

However, in Mr. Giles's report, as well as Mr. Hanyok's report, they both say that there was activity aboard the two destroyers the night of August 4, and that the president considered those eyewitnesses accounts in his decision-making. Mr. Giles also states, "While Mr. Hanyok's analysis of the available COMINT evidence is convincing, on its own, the COMINT does not prove that an attack did or did not occur." Again, the issue of the attack is in question.

Hanyok also uses exhibit B from page 30 which shows a lack of any North Vietnamese communications and uses this as an indication that an attack did not take place.

I guess that you could surmise from the lack of communication on the part of the enemy that an attack did not take place. However, to hang the conclusion that was made on something that did not happen does not make sense to me. Just because the enemy does not communicate their intent to attack does not mean it is not going to happen.

Unlike Hanyok, I was in Vietnam, and I can tell you that in the one year eight months and four days that I was there, I think that we only received intelligence information once that an attack was eminent. This information put us on 100 percent alert waiting and staying awake all night long for an attack that never came.

We generally knew an attack was eminent when it occurred and when Charlie was running through the compound proceeded by a whole bunch of mortars blowing up around us or bullets whizzing past our heads or through our tents. I could pretty much tell everyone in the CP knew that an attack occurred by the way everyone was talking about it the next day or the carnage that it caused and the after-action reports that went out to division headquarters. I do not remember anyone in the compound after the attack saying, "I wonder why the enemy didn't let us know that they were attacking."

I would imagine that the same thing occurred aboard the *Turner Joy* and the *Maddox* the night of the fourth. Like us, when we were under attack, we usually returned fire. The point I am trying to make is that the people aboard the two destroyers were shooting at something that they believed to be a real threat. To dismiss that fact in passing is horseshit.

The excerpts from pages 46, 47, and 49 appear to be conclusions drawn by Hanyok based on his investigation.

The following conclusion made by Hanyok is what I believe to also be conjecture because it is based on incomplete information by his own self admission; he only conducted half an investigation.

His words: "Unfortunately, the administration chose to hang the rationale for expanding its war making franchise in South East

Asia on an incident that could not stand up to any kind of objective examination of the full documentation. So as eventually happened in 1968, when the Gulf of Tonkin Resolution came to be reviewed, the incident that it was based on came under scrutiny. When the events of 4 August were reviled to have been based on very thin evidence."

Yes, the resolution did come to be reviewed in 1968, that is true. However, it was also reviewed prior to that in 1967; it was also discussed at a Senate Foreign Relations Committee meeting.

This was shown in the video *Vietnam: An American History* made for public television.

August 21 to 23, 1967, the Senate Foreign Relations Committee held hearings headed up by Senator Fulbright, who asked the following question of Nicholas Katzenbach, undersecretary of State.

Fulbright: *Would the President if there was no resolution, be with or without constitutional authority, to send soldiers to South Vietnam in the numbers that are there today?*
If there was no resolution!
Katzenbach: *It would be my view, as I indicated Mr. Chairman, that he does have that authority.*

Then senators in attendance commented that they disagree that the president should have that authority to be able to send troops overseas without the okay of Congress. This kind of ignorant or stupid thinking on their part would have them produce another resolution in the future. However, according to this, apparently, Johnson did not need a resolution to go to Vietnam. *(He was just being a cunt and did not want to decide on his own.)*

However, that does not stop Hanyok from drawing the following conclusion: "If the resolution had been tied to the naval action of the afternoon of 2 August, or to the Communist bombing of the officers' quarters in Saigon on Christmas Eve 1964, or even to the VC sapper attack on the air base at Bien Hoa on 1November 1964, then the administration at least would have an actual incident upon which to base support for it."

Let us examine this conclusion. I do not know what in the hell he is talking about! The resolution is not tied to just the August 4 incident of the Gulf of Tonkin. It was the naval action of August 2 and August 4 that brought the request for the resolution off the table. The additional attacks that he is talking about did not occur when the resolution was being requested nor when the resolution was passed. As far as I know, Johnson did not have psychic powers allowing him to see into the future.

So I guess the question is, how is the president going to tie the request for the resolution to two attacks that did not even occur yet?

It should also be noted that after each one of those attacks that he talks about, President Johnson dismissed all recommendations for a retaliatory action against North Vietnam. The request for military action came from the ambassador to South Vietnam, Maxwell Taylor.

It was not until February 6, 1965 when Vietcong guerrillas attacked the US military compound at Pleiku in the Central Highlands, killing 8 Americans, wounding 126, and destroying 10 aircraft. That he decided to send in troops to protect the air bases. This decision did not occur until a month after this attack when the Marines were put ashore March 8, 1965.

Also, in Hanyok's article, he repeats a statement that Johnson made a few days after the events, which he apparently agrees with; however, it pisses me off. He wrote, "As for the Tonkin Gulf incident itself, President Johnson summed it up best just a few days later: 'Hell those damn, stupid sailors were just shooting at flying fish.'"

That is easy to say when you are sitting in the White House in the middle of Washington, DC, surrounded by Secret Service agents that are standing there ready to take a bullet for you. To agree with that statement is to be as ignorant as the asinine, moronic individual who made it.

Let us look at the request and the actual resolution that Johnson used to allegedly plunge us deeper into war. The following two articles and everything pertaining to the events surrounding both dates of the Gulf of Tonkin events or outlined in the president's chronology (exhibit 17). But first excerpts from the request (exhibit 17A):

Last night I announced to the American people that the North Vietnamese regime had conducted further deliberate attacks against U.S. naval vessels operating in international waters, and I had therefore directed air action against gunboats and supporting facilities used in these hostile operations. This air action has now been carried out with substantial damage to the boats and facilities. Two U.S. aircraft were lost in the action. These latest actions of the North Vietnamese regime, has given a new and grave turn to the already serious situation in Southeast Asia.

In President Johnson's request, all that was mentioned about the incidents in the Tonkin gulf is the above—a whopping seven lines. With those seven lines, what he was doing was informing Congress that he advised the American people of the attacks and that he ordered an air strike and that we lost two planes. He also advised congress that he felt that the situation was getting worse.

However, based on the twenty-two lines below, I am of the impression that Johnson made his plea for a resolution based on treaties dating back to 1954, 1955, and 1962, all of which were agreed to by previous presidents and Congresses, signed in accordance with the United States Constitution, public law, and the United Nations charter, not the incidents that occurred in the gulf.

Exhibit 17A (continuation):

Our commitments in that area are well known to the Congress. They were first made in 1954 by President Eisenhower. They were further defined in the Southeast Asia Collective Defense Treaty approved by the Senate in February 1955.

This treaty with its accompanying protocol obligates the United States and other members to act in accordance with their constitutional processes to meet Communist aggression against any of the parties or protocol states. The threat to the free nations of Southeast Asia has long been clear. The North Vietnamese regime has constantly sought to take over South Vietnam and Laos. This Communist regime has violated the Geneva accords for Vietnam. It has systematically conducted a campaign of subversion, which includes the direction, training, and supply of per-

sonnel and arms for the conduct of guerrilla warfare in South Vietnamese territory. In Laos, the North Vietnamese regime has maintained military forces, used Laotian territory for infiltration into South Vietnam, and most recently carried out combat operations—all in direct violation of the Geneva Agreements of 1962.

Note: the treaties mentioned above can be seen in the back of this manuscript under the following exhibit numbers: exhibit 7, the Saito Treaty; exhibit 17B, Geneva Agreements of 1962; the commitment made by President Eisenhower in 1954 that he referred to is the letter to Diem (exhibit 5A).

Exhibit 17A (continuation):

As President of the United States I have concluded that I should now ask the Congress, on its part, to join in affirming the national determination that all such attacks will be met, and that the United States will continue in its basic policy of assisting the free nations of the area to defend their freedom.

We must make it clear to all that the United States is united in its determination to bring about the end of Communist subversion and aggression in the area. We seek the full and effective restoration of the international agreements signed in Geneva in 1954, with respect to South Vietnam, and again in Geneva in 1962, with respect to Laos.

Inserted below is (exhibit 17C) the document that became known as the Gulf of Tokin Resolution. This document came about as a result of the above request (exhibit 17A). I do not know where that title came from because when you examine it, you will not see any reference to the Tonkin gulf, but to international waters, between August 2 and 4, 1964, not even the title of the document, which states Joint Resolution of Congress HJ RES 1145. It is dated August 7, 1964.

It says in part, "That the Congress approves and supports the determination of the President, as Commander in Chief, to take all necessary measures to repel any armed attack against the forces of the United States and to prevent further aggression," which that power has been granted him by the Constitution anyway. It also refers to our obligations dictated by treaty.

H.J. Res 1145
Joint Resolution: To promote the maintenance of international.
Peace and security in Southeast Asia.

Aug. 7, 1964

Whereas naval units of the Communist regime in Vietnam, in violation of the principles of the Charter of the United Nations and of international law, have deliberately and repeatedly attacked United States naval vessels lawfully present in international waters, and have thereby created a serious threat to international peace; and

Whereas these attacks are part of a deliberate and systematic campaign of aggression that the Communist regime in North Vietnam has been waging against its neighbors and the nations joined with them in the collective defense of their freedom; and

Whereas the United States is assisting the peoples of southeast Asia to protect their freedom and has not territorial, military or political ambitions in that area, but desires only that these peoples should be left in peace to work out their own destinies in their own way: Now, therefore, be it.

Resolved by the Senate and House of Representatives of the United States of America in Congress assembled,

Section 1. That the Congress approves and supports the determination of the President, as Commander in Chief, to take all necessary measures to repel any armed attack against the forces of the United States and to prevent further aggression.

Section 2. The United States regards as vital to its national interest and to world peace the maintenance of international peace and security in southeast Asia. Consonant with the Constitution of the United States and the Charter of the United Nations and in accordance with its obligations under the Southeast Asia Collective Defense Treaty, the United States is, therefore, prepared, as the President determines, to take all necessary steps, including the use of armed force, to assist any member or protocol state of the Southeast Asia Collective Defense Treaty requesting assistance in defense of its freedom.

Section 3. This resolution shall expire when the President shall determine that the peace and security of the area is reasonably assured by international conditions created by action of the United Nations or otherwise, except that it may be terminated earlier by concurrent resolution of the Congress. Speaker of the House of Representatives President pro tempore of the Senate.

In summary, based on the above information, this is what I see of the Gulf of Tonkin events:

1. Late 1961 early 1962, an intelligence gathering mission is assigned to the United States Navy in the South China Sea to gather intelligence regarding the Chinese Communist, which is later expanded into the Tonkin gulf. These were called DESOTO patrols.

2. On August 2, 1964, the USS *Maddox* is attacked by the North Vietnamese Navy in the Tonkin gulf, and no one disagrees.

3. The night of August 4, 1964, the USS *Maddox* and the USS *Turner Joy* are attacked by the North Vietnamese Navy in the Tonkin gulf, many doubts that an actual attack took place. Also, many believe that it is not clear weather an attack took place or not. However, this is based on an investigation of the SIGINT and COMINT data only.

4. No one disagrees that the *Maddox* and the *Turner Joy* are expending rounds.

5. Based on the information he is receiving from both ships, President Johnson orders a retaliatory air strike against North Vietnam for those actions. He conferred with his Cabinet, congressional leadership at the time, the National Security Council, and yes, he even conferred with Republican Presidential Candidate Barry Goldwater, all of whom agreed with him that a retaliatory strike should take place. This is documented in the presidential chronology that was declassified for release 2006 (exhibit 17).

6. He also advised the nation of his actions in a televised speech.

7. On August 5, 1964, President Johnson sent the request for the resolution (exhibit 17A) to Congress (excerpts from this document inserted above).

8. Joint Resolution of Congress HJ Resolution 1145 dated August 7, 1964, is the resolution that was passed by Congress, with two dissenting votes. On August 10, the president signs this resolution into law.

Two things came out of the Gulf of Tonkin incidents and two things only.

1. The retaliatory air strike.
   It was called Operation Pierce Arrow, conducted on August 5, and it involved aircraft from carriers USS *Ticonderoga* and USS *Constellation*.
2. The request for the resolution.
   The night of August 4, 1964 has been argued, rehashed, investigated, and argued over and over for fifty-plus years. Regardless of whether the attack took place or not, based on the above information, it is a moot point.
   The reason that it is a moot point is because an event did occur. It was that event that was being reported to the president, and it was that event that he was reacting to. The event was happening to the very people that were charged with the gathering of intelligence and are responsible for a lot of those SIGINT and COMINT reports.

That being said, it doesn't matter if an attack took place or not. The people aboard those ships believed that they were under attack and they were returning fire, and no one denies or disagrees with this fact.

They believed they were defending the only thing that stood between them and certain death. That was the very decks of the ships that they were standing on. If those ships are sunk, the closest land is approximately one mile down. That bit of real estate is not conducive to breathing, which is necessary for most humans.

So if they were shooting at an attacking boat, a figment of their imagination, or, as some assholes would put it, flying fish, it just doesn't matter. The event was real. The other fact of that night is that the request for the resolution was not based on this event, the retaliatory air strike was. Also, the resolution has nothing to do with the Tonkin gulf; it pertains to our commitment through treaties to Southeast Asia.

So there is no document known as the Gulf of Tonkin Resolution; it is Resolution 1145, and the request for the resolution is not based on the incidents of that night.

This brings me to another resolution. Unlike the previous resolution, this one does have a title, and it is called the War Powers Resolution (exhibit 21). It was drawn up by the Ninety-Third Congress. This leads me to believe that they had attended some of the same brothels the anti-war demonstrators were attending. It also leads me to believe that they were probably using some of the same drugs.

That may seem a little harsh to you, but let us examine one resolution to the other and the purpose for dissolving one and implementing another in its place. The War Powers Resolution:

The Purpose:

On November 7, the Congress of the United States overrides President Nixon's veto of the War Powers Resolution, which limits presidential power to wage war without congressional approval.

The purpose of this resolution, known as the War Powers Resolution, is to make sure that a president consults with them prior to sending troops into combat.

The dissolving of Joint Resolution of Congress HJ RES 1145 (exhibit 17A), replacing it with Public Law 93-148 Ninety-Third Congress, HJ Res. 542 joint resolution cited as the War Powers Resolution. Exhibit 21 would lead one to believe that Johnson was remiss in consulting with Congress regarding Vietnam when in fact that is exactly what Johnson did. Let us recap in order regarding the attack of August 2, 1964. Johnson waves his fist, goes boo-hoo, and sends a telegram to Ho Chi Minh, saying, "Do not do that." Why? I do not know.

Regarding the event on the night of August 4, 1964, he conferred with his Cabinet, congressional leadership at the time, the National Security Council, with Republican presidential candidate Barry Goldwater, all of whom agreed with him that a retaliatory strike should take place.

Then on the morning of August 5, 1964, he sends a message to the Congress, requesting a resolution, which, according to the Constitution, he did not have to do. I don't know about you or what grade you got to in school or what kind of grades you got or whether you attended any of those Ivy League brothels I spoke of earlier. This sure as hell sounds like he conferred with Congress to me.

Only after one day of discussion, Congress passes the resolution with only two dissenting votes.

Then nine years later, the brilliant minds of the Ninety-Third Congress writes the following resolution, telling the president that he must confer with them regarding sending troops into combat, especially, when the Constitution says he does not have to as they themselves point out in the resolution: section 2, letter C, which states, "or (3) a national emergency created by attack upon the United States, its territories or possessions, or its armed forces." This constitutional power was executed by Johnson after three additional attacks on United States military forces after the Tonkin gulf events.

I believe that the Ninety-Third Congress used this resolution to pacify an already-treasonous American public so that they could get themselves reelected.

EXHIBIT 21

Public Law 93-148
93rd Congress, H. J. Res. 542
November 7, 1973
Joint Resolution
Concerning the war powers of Congress and the President.
Resolved by the Senate and the House of Representatives of the United States of America in Congress assembled,

SHORT TITLE
SECTION 1. This joint resolution may be cited as the "War Powers Resolution".
PURPOSE AND POLICY

SEC. 2. (A) IT IS the purpose of this joint resolution to fulfill the intent of the framers of the Constitution of the United States and insure that the collective judgments of both the Congress and the President will apply to the introduction of United States Armed Forces into hostilities, or into situations where imminent involvement in hostilities is clearly indicate by the circumstances, and to the continued use of such forces in hostilities or in such situations.

(b) Under article I, section 8, of the Constitution, it is specifically provided that the Congress shall have the power to make all laws necessary and proper for carrying into execution, not only its own powers but also all other powers vested by the Constitution in the Government of the United States, or in any department or officer thereof.

(c) The constitutional powers of the President as Commander-in-Chief to introduce United States Armed Forces into hostilities, or into situations where imminent involvement in hostilities is clearly indicated by the circumstances, are exercised only pursuant to (1) a declaration of

218

war, (2) specific statutory authorization, or (3) a national emergency created by attack upon the United States, its territories or possessions, or its armed forces.

Note: Or its armed forces—that is exactly what happened in the Tonkin gulf on August 2 and August 4, 1964. An additional attack is exactly what happened on November 1, 1964, at Bein Hua Air Base, South Vietnam, killing 4 and wounding 72, and 5 aircraft destroyed. An additional attack happened on December 24, 1964 at the Brinks Hotel in Saigon, where the Vietcong planted a bomb, killing 2 Americans and wounding 58 who were celebrating Christmas Eve. There was an additional attack on February 6, 1965, at the air base and Pla Ku in the Central Highlands, which killed 8 Americans, wounding 126, and 10 aircraft destroyed.

To recap, 5 direct attacks targeting American military personnel over a six-month period, killing 14 and wounding 256, before the president of the United States sent any troops anywhere, especially, when, according to the Constitution, he could have sent troops after the attack on August 2, 1964.

CONSULTATION

SEC. 3. The President in every possible instance shall consult with Congress before introducing United States Armed Forces into hostilities or into situation where imminent involvement in hostilities is clearly indicated by the circumstances, and after every such introduction shall consult regularly with the Congress until United States Armed Forces are no longer engaged in hostilities or have been removed from such situations.

Duh! The Ninety-Third Congress had no idea what the hell they were talking about.

No president since the writing of this War Powers Resolution, either Democrat, Republican, independent, or otherwise, has complied with this resolution. Basically, resolutions are horseshit political documents. I have been mentioned in two local resolutions, basically you can use them as toilet paper.

CHAPTER 11

BEYOND ANY DOUBT

DURING AND SINCE MY TOURS of duty in Vietnam, I have always felt that the people who participated in the anti-war movement were guilty of treason. The first time I felt this was on Hill 34 just south of the Da Nang Air Base in Vietnam. I heard the newscast over the armed forces radio network announce that troops returning to Stateside from Vietnam were being cursed at by demonstrators and had dog shit thrown at them. Although it was not done directly to me, I looked at it as an act of treason and an act of betrayal because it was done to my fellow veterans. When they threw at them, they were throwing it at me. Well, anyway, that is the way I looked at it. I am angry and I am hurt.

However, over the years, I have learned that treason is viewed through two sets of eyes. The first set of eyes are those of the betrayed. I know that the emotional response suffered by the betrayed means nothing to anyone but them. I have also discovered that unless the act of treason meets all the elements of a crime as viewed through the other set of eyes, the eyes of the law, it is not considered treason.

But the emotional response that is felt by the betrayed, whether it meets those elements of a crime or not, is a wound to the heart that is felt forevermore.

That being said, the Anti-War Movement during the 1960s and 1970s (also known as the War at Home, the Free Speech Movement, and the Peace Movement)—these names given to it by those who participated in it permeated the American landscape from sea to shining sea. I also believe that the people who participated in the

Anti-War Movement, regardless of their stature in life or their level of participation, committed what I have come to view as an unforgivable crime.

It is a crime, not only by definition, but also as written in the Constitution of the United States and mandated by the ruling of Supreme Court of the United States.

I am no longer just looking at this through the eyes of one who was betrayed, but through what I have found to be the only set of eyes that seem to matter—in this case, the eyes of the law.

Treason is defined as "violation of the allegiance owed by a person to his or her own country, for example, by aiding an enemy."

Betrayal is defined as "the act or an instance of betraying somebody or something."

Although I am not an attorney, I was an investigator. I can read, I can think, and I can reason. Therefore, I believe that I can show, not beyond a reasonable doubt, but beyond any doubt, a large number of the American public, the press, the entertainment industry, and self-centered politicians, not only could have but also should have been charged with treason and that they carried this crime to a level unmatched anywhere on the planet or in the annals of history, either modern or ancient. Yet these people were never charged or punished for it.

Since I am not an attorney in order to prove my case, I have acquired a lot of information from a constitutional law professor by researching his work.

His name is Henry Mark Holzer, professor emeritus at Brooklyn Law School; he is a constitutional and appellate lawyer. His latest book is *Keeper of the Flame: The Supreme Court Jurisprudence of Justice Clarence Thomas.*

I have never met with or spoken with Mr. Holzer; however, I know from research that he wrote a book along with Erika Holzer where they proved conclusively that Jane Fonda's 1972 trip to Hanoi was treason. The name of their book is *Aid and Comfort: Jane Fonda in North Vietnam.*

Taken from Mr. Holzer article Treason, they proved that she was Indictable for the following activities:

Touring, in the company of North Vietnamese Communist and civilian officials and members of the international press, the War Crimes Museum, hospitals, dikes, private dwellings, countryside, and a textile center among other places.

Making anti-American, pro-communist propaganda broadcasts on Radio Hanoi, which were replayed to American prisoners of war.

Meeting with seven POWs and haranguing them with anti-American, pro-Communist propaganda.

Giving interviews too East European and other anti-American, pro-Communist journalists.

Holding press conferences before Communist and pro-Communist journalists.

Visiting with high-ranking North Vietnamese Communist officials.

Posing, in the company of Communist civilian and military officials and members of the international press, in the gunner's seat of a North Vietnamese anti-aircraft gun while taking sight on an imaginary American airplane.

In all these activities, Fonda relentlessly made anti-American, pro-Communist statements.

Regrettably, Fonda was not indicted because of political calculations made at the highest level of the Nixon Administration.

As a Vietnam veteran, this alone has gained them my deepest gratitude and respect; I am sure it has also gained the gratitude of many of my fellow Vietnam veterans as well. Although there is no chance of her ever receiving any punishment for her contemptuous acts, it is good to know that somewhere out there is truthful book revealing to the world the low-life Communist scumbag that she is.

Unlike Mr. Holzer, however, I am taking my charge of treason one step further and charging first that the leadership of the anti-war movement, then the rank and file of the movement violated the treason law listed in the constitution and that they all could have been charged with that crime.

These charges were never brought against anyone who participated in the Anti-War Movement. However, just because someone is not charged or prosecuted for a crime does not mean they did not do it. Think of it like a murder case that has been placed into the cold case file. You have the dead body, so therefore, you have a crime. You may even have a suspect. However, some of the evidence needed for a conviction is missing. That evidence may not show up until years later when the case can be reopened, allowing charges to be brought and a conviction obtained.

In the case of the Anti-War Movement, charges will never be brought and convictions will never take place. But I believe that the crime of treason did occur. So let us take this step by step, and I will show how the participants of the Anti-War Movement meet every element of committing the crime of treason.

Mr. Holzer has given examples of other traitors in America besides Arnold, who were never charged with treason.

The first was the notorious episode involving Aaron Burr, one of the most interesting characters of the post-colonial period. Thomas Jefferson and Burr were tied for election to the presidency in December 1801. The House of Representatives elected Jefferson, and Burr became Vice President. He was not a happy Vice President. Though a Republican, Burr not only later made common cause with his party's opponents, the Federalists, but he conspired against the United States government itself. The "Burr Conspiracy," born at the end of his vice presidency, consisted of a bold plan to "liberate" Mexico from Spain, and at the same time make Louisiana an independent republic, which Mississippi Territory would surely decide to join. [xiii]

During preparation of the conspiracy, a confederate betrayed Burr to President Jefferson. Even though the United States was not at war with any other nation at that time, Burr was charged with the "levying war" prong of the treason crime.

Thus, if in time of non-war, a person, like Burr, can be charged with the "levying war" prong of the treason crime, one can be surely charged with the "adhering" prong during cold war and hostilities. Indeed, no one can reasonably doubt—as "Aid and Comfort": Jane Fonda in North Vietnam proves—that Hanoi Jane could have been indicted for, and convicted of, treason for her conduct in North Vietnam even though we were not formally at war with the Asian Communists.

The second case, in the Supreme Court of the United States, as pointed out by Mr. Holzer, occurred in 1863 and arose out of the civil war.

On the fifteenth day of March, 1863, the schooner J. M. Chapman was seized in the harbor of San Francisco, by the United States revenue officers, while sailing, or about to sail, on a cruise in the service of the Confederate States, against the United States; and the leaders… [including Greathouse] were indicted…for engaging in, and giving aid and comfort, to the then existing rebellion against the government of the United States. [xiv]"

Since Greathouse, like Burr, appeared to be a "levying war" case leg, the actual question before the court was not whether in an "adhering" case a declared war was a necessary prerequisite for indictment and conviction. However, in language appearing in Justice Field's discussion of the concept "enemies," the Greathouse Court did have something to say about the concept of "war." According to Field, "The term 'enemies,' as used in the second clause [of the Constitutional treason provision], according to its settled meaning, at the time the constitution was adopted, applies only to the subjects of a foreign power in a state of open hostility with us." [xv]

The difference between Arnold, Burr, and Greathouse is, Arnold committed treason when there was no Constitution, so there was no law pertaining to treason, and accordingly, he was never charged with a crime. When Burr and Greathouse committed treason, they were charged with the crime of treason as outlined in the Constitution. This is further explained by Mr. Holzer:

Justice Field's words were written only seventy-six years after adoption of the Constitution. He knew his constitutional history, and he chose his words carefully. If, in Justice Field's discussion of the status of a "foreign power" in relation to the United States, he meant to refer to "war," he certainly would have done so. Instead, the Supreme Court justice chose the word "hostility," denoting a very different relationship: one not of war.

Accordingly, based on the background of English, colonial, constitutional, and post-constitutional decisional history, the absence of a formal declaration of war is no impediment to a charge of treason. That being so it is important to understand something else very important about the crime of treason.

Because treason is the only crime defined in the Constitution, conduct constituting that crime should be taken seriously—and other than by prosecuting, there is no other way to do that.

In 1969, under President Richard Nixon, I believe that there was ample enough evidence of treason that charges could have been brought by the administration, at least against the leadership. Under President James Carter, there was ample time to also bring charges and to prosecute the participants of the Anti-War Movement. However, the leadership of this nation, charged with the protection of the Constitution, for some reason, chose not to perform their duties as mandated by law as well as the oath they took.

However, in retrospect, I am sure that the monumental cost that would accompany the prosecution was a mitigating factor in their decision.

When an individual takes an oath of office, putting himself or herself in an authoritative position, they are obligated to perform those duties. If they fail to do so, they are in violation of one or all the following laws.

Misfeasance of office: acting improperly or illegally in performing an action that is in itself lawful.

Malfeasance of office: wrong or illegal conduct, especially in politics or the civil service.

Nonfeasance of office: failure to meet legal obligations/failure to do something that is legally obligatory.

Regarding the Vietnam Anti-War Movement, at the very least, I believe the leadership of the nation was guilty of nonfeasance of office for failing to bring charges and prosecute. They may have chosen not to do so because of the enormous volume of individuals participating. However, I feel that they could at least have prosecuted the leadership of the movement.

Mr. Holzer also stated another interesting fact regarding the "levying war" prong of the Constitution.

It is popularly, and erroneously, believed that a "levying war" charge requires that the United States actually be at war. For example, when people considered Taliban John Walker-Lindh's activities with the Taliban and al-Qaeda in Afghanistan—as a member of armed forces with which the United States was not formally at war—the question was often asked as to whether one can be convicted of treason absent a formal declaration of war.

The answer is yes.

So there you have it. According to Mr. Holzer, you do not have to be in a declared war in order to bring a charge of treason.

In researching Mr. Holzer, I found that during the year, 1945 the Supreme Court of the United States reviewed a treason conviction. Cramer v. United States[i] was the first. Seven other cases followed, two in the Supreme Court and five in United States Courts of Appeal: Haupt v. United States, [ii] Chandler v. United States, [iii] Gillars v. United States, [iv] Best v. United States, [v] Burgman v. United States, [vi] D'Aquino v. United States, [vii] Kawakita v. United States. [viii]

From what I understand, the eight people mentioned above were convicted of treason against the United States during World War II. Everyone appealed their convictions to different levels of the Supreme Courts. All eight convictions were upheld.

It is my understanding all the individuals involved were charged with (prong 2), or the "aid and comfort" prong if you prefer. This is the prong for which the ruling was issued after World War II. This is where the Supreme Court makes it extremely clear as too what is needed to bring a charge of treason under that clause.

Mr. Holzer describes the ruling of the World War II convictions of the Supreme Court as follows:

Cumulatively, in these eight decisions arising from World War II, the Supreme Court of the United States established that for a prosecutor to take an "aid and comfort" treason indictment to a jury he must prove four elements beyond a reasonable doubt:

Within the case of Vietnam, I had a look at the following three things, regarding the charge of treason. They are as follows.

1. Article 3, section 3, paragraph 1: The US Constitution
   1.1 Treason against the United States shall consist only in levying War against them,
   1.2 or in adhering to their Enemies, giving them Aid and Comfort.
   1.3 No Person shall be convicted of Treason unless on the Testimony of two Witnesses to the same overt Act, or on Confession in open Court.
   1.4 The Congress shall have Power to declare the Punishment of Treason, but no Attainder of Treason shall work Corruption of Blood, or Forfeiture except during the Life of the Person attainted (exhibit 26).

2. The Supreme Court ruling (regarding article 3):
   "(1) An overt act, (2) testified to by two witnesses, (3) manifesting an intent to betray the United States (which can be inferred from the overt act itself), (4) the act providing aid and comfort to the enemy."
3. Amendment I (1791):
   Congress shall make no law respecting an establishment of religion, or prohibiting the free exercise thereof; or abridging the freedom of speech, or of the press; or the right of the people peaceably to assemble, and to petition the government for a redress of grievances.

As you can see, the ruling by the Supreme Court differs just a little in comparison to how it is written within the Constitution. The two things added to the ruling are (1) manifesting an intent to betray the United States, which can be inferred from the overt act itself and (2) it must show that the act provided aid and comfort.

Before we continue, let us define a few of the words listed in the elements required by the Supreme Court. I feel it is important to understand the meaning of words, especially in law, because it helps me to understand and to decipher the law.

First, overt act: 1. done openly and without any attempt at concealment. 2. Done openly and intentionally, and therefore able to be taken as a sign of criminal intent.

Second, manifesting: 1. to make something evident by showing or demonstrating it very clearly.

Third, inferred:

1. *to come to a conclusion or form an opinion about something on the basis of evidence or reasoning.*
2. *To lead you necessarily to suppose or conclude something.*

I had mentioned this earlier, but I would like to reiterate one of the three things that I need to bring a charge of treason against those who participated in the Anti-War Movement. That is the first amendment. Nowhere in the First Amendment does it say that you are allowed to break any law while exercising those rights as outlined in the amendment.

Since we are dealing with the *aid and comfort prong of the treason law*, it is important that I show that I have all four elements demanded by the Supreme Court in their ruling.

First, I need an overt act. I believe that setting up a demonstration or a protest, for any reason, could be construed as an overt act. Not a crime, but an overt act. The applying for permits, the making of phone calls to gather support, the making of signs, the organizing of time and places to meet, the organizing of transportation to the demonstration or the event can be construed as an overt act. I say again, not a crime, but one of the elements required by the Supreme Court.

The second thing I would need is two witnesses to its occurrence. Regarding the Vietnam issue, I can tell you that I witnessed those demonstrations, and the ten other guys I mentioned earlier also witnessed those demonstrations. Again, that does not make it a crime, but it does make it an element required by the Supreme Court in order to bring a charge. The eleven witnesses far surpasses the two-witness requirement demanded by the Supreme Court.

The next element that I need is the overt act must manifest an intent to betray the United States, but this can be inferred from the overt act itself (inferred): (1) to come to a conclusion or form an opinion about something on the basis of evidence or reasoning, (2) to lead you necessarily to suppose or conclude something.

I am sure most of these people who participated in the movement would tell you that they had no intent to betray the United States. However, we were fighting the Communist in North Vietnam, and since most of the demonstrations between 1963 and 1973 were organized by either Communist organizations or organizations heavily infiltrated with Communist, I think it would be fair to say that the leadership of these demonstrations just by the nature of who they are had every intent to betray the United States.

I have already shown some Communist affiliation earlier, and I intend to demonstrate more organizations with Communist ties. Although I feel I have the third element required by the Supreme Court, I still do not have a crime, but I do have the element.

The next element needed is that the act must show that it gave aid and comfort to the enemy. That comes in 1969, October, to be exact. As a matter of fact, the day before the anti-war moratorium was to be held. On October 14, 1969, a letter from Pham Van Dong was intercepted and read into the congressional record (exhibit 18). On this date, the United States was still engaged in the conflict in Vietnam. Pham Van Dong was the new leader of the North Vietnamese government; he replaced Ho Chi Minh upon his death. This letter was sent to the leadership of the anti-war moratorium. I believe that this letter is prima facie evidence of the fourth element of treason required by the Supreme Court. This letter expresses the fact that the North Vietnamese Communist appreciated the aid given to them with these demonstrations, and they took comfort in it.

EXHIBIT 18

29968 Congressional Record—House October 14, 1969
(By unanimous consent Mr. Morten was allowed to speak out of order)

MR. MORTEN. MR. CHAIRMAN, A few moments ago, there was handed to me by a messenger from the White House a letter from the premiere of North Vietnam, Pham Van Dong. The letter was sent from Hanoi in Vietnamese to Paris and transmitted from Paris to the United States, 1317 Greenwich Mean Time, October 14, 1969 it says:

> *Dear American friends: up until now the U. S. Progressive people have struggled against the war of aggression against Vietnam. This fall large sectors of the US people, encouraged and supported by many peace—and justice loving American personages, are also launching a broad and powerful offensive throughout the United States to demand that the Nixon administration put an end to the Vietnam aggressive war and immediately bring all American troops home.*
>
> *Your struggle eloquently reflects the U. S. People's legitimate an urgent demand, which is to save U. S. Honor and to prevent their sons from dying uselessly in Vietnam. This is also a very appropriate and timely answer to the attitude of the U. S. Authorities who are still obdurately intensifying and prolonging the Vietnam aggressive war in defiance of protests by U. Y. And world public opinion.*

The Vietnamese and world people fully approve of and enthusiastically acclaim you're just struggle.

The Vietnamese people demand that the U. S. Government withdraw completely and unconditionally U. S. Troops and those of other foreign countries in the American camp from Vietnam, thus allowing the Vietnamese people to decide their own destiny by themselves.

The Vietnamese people deeply cherish peace, but it must be peace in independence and freedom. As long as the US government does not end its aggression against Vietnam, Vietnamese people will persevere in their struggle to defend their fundamental national rights.

Our people's patriotic struggle is precisely the struggle for peace and justice that you are carrying out.

We are firmly confident that, with the solidarity and bravery of the Peoples of our two countries and with the approval and support of peace—loving people in the world, the struggle of the Vietnamese people and U. S. Progressive people against U. S. Aggression will certainly be crowned with total victory.

May your fall offensive succeed splendidly,

Affectionately yours,
Pham Van Dong,
Premier of the DRV government.

This letter more than shows that the North Vietnamese Communist was aided by a large number of the American public by their acts of demonstrations and protests, and it clearly shows that they were pleased and that they took comfort in it.

I would like to emphasize specifically the words in this letter that coincide with the element that was demanded by the Supreme

Court. That the acts of demonstrating, protesting, sit-ins, marches, making placards and signs, and, in some cases, rioting were all considered by the enemy as giving aid to them and that they took comfort in it, which is the fourth and final element that is demanded by the Supreme Court that must be shown to bring a charge of treason.

1. *Up until now*—in the opening line of the letter, Pham Van Dong refers to all those protests and demonstrations that occurred prior to him writing this letter.
2. *US Progressive people*—with this, he describes people to whom he is talking to and the people that participated.
3. *Offensive*—he uses this word to describe the upcoming moratorium on October 15, 1969, that is about to be launched by the American personages as he refers to them and as if it were military action.
4. *The Vietnamese and world people fully approve of and enthusiastically acclaim your just struggle.*

acclaim: verb:
1. praise enthusiastically and publicly.
"The conference was acclaimed as a considerable success."
Synonyms: celebrated, admired, highly rated, lionized, revered, honored, esteemed, exalted, lauded, vaunted.

This sentence and the word *acclaim* clearly shows that the enemy approves of the action that they are pleased, and they take comfort in it.

solidarity: noun
1. unity or agreement of feeling or action, especially among individuals with a common interest; mutual support within a group.
"Factory workers voiced solidarity with the striking students."
Synonyms: unanimity, unity, like-mindedness, agreement, accord, harmony, consensus, concord, concurrence, singleness of purpose.

This element added to the previous three does constitute the crime of treason. With that, it is my belief that the attorney general of the United States at that time, with the receiving of this letter, should have pushed, and I believe could have pushed, to have the leadership of these demonstrations from 1963 to 1969 arrested and prosecuted for that crime.

It is important to know that the Vietnam War lasted for a long time. Like the war, the Anti-War Movement grew slowly. However, over time, the magnitude of the people participating in the Anti-War Movement was astronomical in size to those of us who served in Vietnam. Most importantly, the Anti-War Movement from the beginning was started by organizations that were Communistic in policy and led by people who were Communist themselves and sympathetic to the Communist cause, such as the Communist organization stated earlier, the Progressive Labor Party and the Young Socialist Alliance, which was the Progressive Labor Party's youth affiliate. These two organizations would also infiltrate the SDS and become a major influence in those demonstrations.

The SDS, known as the Students for a Democratic Society, would play a major part in the Anti-War Movement formally known as the Student League for Industrial Democracy (SLID); they were the youth branch of a socialist educational organization known as the league for industrial democracy (LID). LID descended from the intercollegiate socialist society started in 1905.

Early in 1960, SLID changed its name to SDS. SDS held its first meeting in 1960 at Ann Arbor, Michigan, where Alan Harper was elected president. Its political manifesto, known as the Port Huron statement, was adopted at the organization's first convention in 1962,[1] based on an earlier draft by staff member Tom Hayden. Within this organization, there were people who would eventually come to officially declare war against the United States. These are people who would call themselves Americans.

From the SDS, other organizations emerged on the scene spewing out its Communist propaganda lies and deceit through the Anti-War Movement, which, by the end of the war, 60 percent of the nation was participating in.

The SDS was responsible for many of the teach-ins and demonstrations against the Vietnam War from 1963 to 1969.

{D} *In June 1969, a group known as the Weatherman took control of the SDS at its national convention, where Bill Ayers was elected "Education Secretary".*[4]

{D} Later in 1969, Bill Ayers, founder of the Weatherman, participated in planting a bomb at a statue dedicated to police casualties in the 1886 Haymarket riot.[7] The blast broke almost one hundred windows and blew pieces of the statue onto the nearby Kennedy Expressway.[8] (The statue was rebuilt and unveiled on May 4, 1970, and blown up again by other Weathermen on October 6 1970.[9][8] Built yet again, the city posted a twenty-four-hour police guard to prevent another blast.)[8]

Ayers participated in the days of rage riot in Chicago in October 1969 and, in December, was at the War Council meeting in Flint, Michigan.

{D} *In 1970 the group issued a "Declaration of a State of War" against the United States government, using for the first time its new name, the "Weather Underground. Organization" (WUO), Adopting fake identities, and Pursuing Covert activities only. These initially included preparations for a bombing of a U.S. military non-commissioned officers' dance at Fort Dix, New Jersey in What Brian Flanagan said had been intended to be "the most horrific hit the United States government had ever suffered on its territory".*[13]

They also plotted to contaminate the water supply here in the United States as well. At one point, they wanted to place the drug LSD into it. However, for some reason, they never accomplished that.

But most important, these people are *self-admitted communist.* Communism is the ideology that the United States was engaged in a cold war with since 1948. It is also the ideology we fought in Korea, and at the time this declaration of war was issued by the (WUO), we had been in an open hostility with the Communist in North Vietnam for six years.

Unlike Aaron Burr, Greathouse, and the leaders of the schooner J. M. Chapman mentioned earlier, the Weather Underground, would eventually become allies with the Black Liberation Army. As the war went on, these two groups gave their alliance the title— the May 19th Communist Order. This order also became known as Armed Resistance Unit, May 19 Communist Coalitions, Red Guerrilla Resistance, Resistance Conspiracy, and Revolutionary Fighting Group.

The May 19th Communist Order was a front for the Revolutionary Armed Task Force (RATF), a coalition of Weather Underground and Black Liberation Army members who robbed banks in order to finance their radical leftist agenda. May 19th kept a network of safe houses for the RATF and forged further alliances with other leftist organizations such as FALN, the New Afrikan Freedom Fighters, and the Palestine Liberation Organization. May 19th can also be considered a cell of the RATF.

The fact that the Black Liberation Army, the FALN, the New Afrikan Freedom Fighters, and the Palestine Liberation Organization formed an alliance with the Weather Underground makes them partners in levying war against the United States. So I also believe that this alliance makes them all equal in violating the treason article of the Constitution.

The name May 19th Communist Order adopted by this alliance of morons refers to the day on which both Malcolm X and Ho Chi Minh were born. Several of the May 19th's leaders were also members of Students for a Democratic Society.

There were other groups who also advocated the violent overthrow of the United States: government, groups like the Black Panther Party and the United Freedom Front.

{D}The United Freedom Front (UFF) was a radical US-based left-wing organization which was responsible for a string of attacks in the late 1970s and 1980s. It went under several aliases including the Armed Guerrilla Resistance Movement, Revolutionary Fighting Group, Sam Melville/Jonathan Jackson group (its original name).

The group was founded in 1974 by two Vietnam War veterans, Raymond Luc Levasseur and Tom Manning. The two first met in prison, where Levasseur was serving a sentence for drug dealing and

Manning for robbery. After their release, the two incorporated other members in to the UFF, mostly family members and close friends.

Congress was given the power to punish those who commit treason as outlined in Article III. "4. The Congress shall have Power to declare the Punishment of Treason." But for the life of me, I do not understand why they didn't even charge these people with the crime. Why they did not pursue them as the enemy soldiers that these morons claimed to be, especially when it was members of the May 19 coalition who issued that formal Declaration of a State of War against the United States government?

Besides this information being well-documented facts, I know them to be true. I was heavily involved in a lot of these investigations and pursuing members of a number of these organizations as a detective with the New Jersey State Police, along with another Vietnam vet and New Jersey state trooper Leroy T. Smith mentioned earlier.

The members of these groups were pursued under violations of state statutes in the states where they were conducting their war, mainly by local authorities. *When the Japanese bombed Pearl Harbor, the president and the United States and Congress pursued them with our military for levying war against us.* So I guess my question is, besides pursuing these homegrown traitors using local authorities alone, why didn't the president and the Congress issue an order to activate our military and hunt these people down and shoot them dead in the streets, like the low-life Communist scum that they are?

When engaged in conversation with some people over the years, anytime I would say to them that the American people betrayed not only us Vietnam veterans but that they also committed treason against the United States, the response is usually, "Not all Americans" or "They had a right to do what they did."

One thing is true with those responses; it was not all the Americans, but according to the polls, it appeared to be the majority of Americans. By the time we pulled out of Vietnam, it had been by one of the many polls' standards reported that 60 percent of this nation was against the war. As to what extent or how many participated in the anti-war movement, I am not certain, but I am certain everyone that did, regardless of their reason, could have been charged with treason.

The statement that they had a right to do what they did could not be any further from the truth. This statement comes out of ignorance. I believe that the people that say this are speaking of the rights guaranteed to them in the First Amendment of the Bill of Rights.

So I guess the question would be, when does speech become treason?

According to Mr. Holzer, while pure speech (i.e., speech not combined with action) can mutate into treason, even the worst political speech, standing alone, does not come close to constituting treason.

As Mr. Holzer pointed out in his article, "Speech becomes treason when it transcends mere words, ceasing to be communication alone, and satisfies the four requisites demanded by the Supreme Court":

{D} *The Moratorium to End the War in Vietnam*
This was just another Large Demonstration against the United States Involvement in the Vietnam War that took place across the United States on October 15th 1969. [1] *The Moratorium developed from Jerome Grossman's April 20, 1969 call for a general strike if the war had not concluded by October.* David Hawk and Sam Brown who had previously worked on *the unsuccessful 1968 presidential campaign of Eugene McCarthy, changed the concept to a less radical moratorium and began to organize the event as the Vietnam Moratorium Committee with David Mixner, Marge Sklenkar, John Gage, and others.*

By the standards of previous anti-war demonstrations, the event was a clear success, with millions participating throughout the world. Boston was the site of the largest turnout; *about 100,000 attended a speech by anti-war Sen. George McGovern.*

The first nationwide Moratorium was followed a month later, on November 15th 1969, by a massive Moratorium march on Washington DC which attracted over 500,000 demonstrators against the war, including many performers and activists on stage at a rally across from the White House.

Activists at some universities continued to hold monthly moratoria on the fifteenth of each month.[2][3]

Although the crime may have been forgotten, it did not go away, which means, to this very day, charges against those people who are still alive could still be brought. This is due to the fact that there is no statute of limitations for the crime of treason.

However, that did not stop our political leaders from helping out those who would betray the country. James Earl Carter was elected to the presidency of the United States in January 1977. That very day, January 21, his first act in office was to grant amnesty to the people who violated the draft laws by running to Canada, burning their draft cards, and protesting the Vietnam War. When he was asked why he did that, his reply was to heal the wounds of the nation. So let me see if I understand this. His thought is to heal the wounds of the nation by forgiving the people that betrayed the country, by sticking a knife into the hearts of those that defended it? He was just elected as the commander in chief of the armed forces of the United States, and with that one act, he betrayed the very people that he was elected to command.

That one action gave rise to me thinking that maybe this guy's family tree does not fork. I think that maybe there was a little hanky-panky in the peanut patch. He probably introduces himself as, "This is my mother and my wife, and I am my own grandpa!"

Later in his presidency, he will reinstate the registration for the draft that was abolished by Nixon in 1973. He did this because the Soviet Union went to war with Afghanistan, and he wanted to be prepared if we were drawn into it. What did little Jimmy think? Did he think the so-called American people would now rise up and go fight in Afghanistan for him when they wouldn't fight in Vietnam?

Then forty years later, this mutt writes a book on morality; he would not know morality if it came up and bit him on his balls. However, I believe that this action of his gave a good majority of the people in this country the idea none of these things that were done by them during that period of time was wrong.

Periodically, over the past fifty-plus years, these mutants that participated in the movement have publicly reminisced about their actions of those years wearing their coat of treason as if it were the red badge of courage.

Pham Van Dong was the first of our enemy that showed that the American anti-war movement was helpful to the war effort being perpetrated by the North Vietnamese Communist back in '69. However, twenty-two years after the last American combatant left Vietnam, the crime of treason emerged once again. It was brought forth in an interview by another individual that I introduced earlier, Colonel Bui Tin.

Thursday, August 3, 1995, taken from, the *Wall Street Journal*:

Bui Tin, a former colonel in the North Vietnamese army, was assigned to receive the unconditional surrender of South Vietnam on April 30, 1975. Stephen Young, an attorney and human-rights activist, conducted the interview.

Here is the Second question asked by Stephen Young in his interview of Bui Tin.

Q: *Was the American antiwar movement important to Hanoi's victory?*
A: *It was essential to our strategy. Support of the war from our rear was completely secure while the American rear was vulnerable. Every day our leadership would listen to world news over the radio at 9 a.m. to follow the growth of the American antiwar movement. Visits to Hanoi by people like Jane Fonda, and former Attorney General Ramsey Clark and ministers gave us confidence that we should hold on in the face of battlefield reverses.*

That one sentence, "It was essential to our strategy" provided by a member of the enemy force that we were fighting in Vietnam is written testimony and additional proof of the crime of treason, the fourth element required by the Supreme Court for treason. On August 3, 1995, the crime of treason came out of the cold case file and met all the elements of the Supreme Court required to bring a charge of treason once again. The interview went on.

Q: *Did the Politburo pay attention to these visits?*
A: *Keenly.*
Q: *Why?*
A: *America lost because of its democracy; through dissent and protest it lost the ability to mobilize a will to win.*

Although this statement alone by Bui Tin is more than enough proof to bring a charge of treason, I didn't stop there. As I said earlier, I bought his book *From Enemy to Friend.* So here are more excerpts from him regarding the American anti-war movement.

Bui Tin said, *"From 1965 to 1967, the South Vietnamese army (Army of the Republic of Vietnam, or ARVN, for short) and U.S. troops went on the offensive and were very active, forcing our troops into a defensive mode."* Now something spectacular was needed to regain the initiative and reverse the situation if possible.

The 1968 Mau Than Tet Offensive was a shocker. It forced a world-wide reassessment of the situation in Vietnam and caused heated debates in U.S. political circles and the U.S. Media: in the printed media, on radio, and television.

And the North Vietnamese Communists are watching this.

Col. Bui Tin wrote his book like he was being interviewed, first he would pose a question and then he would answer it.

During the War through what Means did you try to understand the political situation in the United States?

Primarily we used the media: The American press and radio broadcasts as well as books published in the United States. We had diplomatic missions and Vietnamese news agency representatives in Paris, New Delhi, and Havana.

We regularly received, *LeMomde, L'Humanite, Time, Newsweek,* the *Washington Post,* and the *New York Times* in Hanoi.

The Vietnam News agency had a group of language specialist whose sole function was to produce full translations of articles, or summarize them, providing excerpts that were compiled in a daily special edition that were distributed to a very restricted list of recipients (from the deputy minister and head of institute level on up).

During World War II, the Allied Forces had large rooms that were used to plot enemy troop movements, as well as aircraft and ship movements. This information was gathered by their various intelligence agencies, along with military recon and surveillance units.

However, what Col. Bui Tin described above was the North Vietnamese Communists' intelligence agency the American media. They provided everything the communists could hope for in the way of the printed documents, verbal broadcasts (not even in code), and video footage. And Uncle Ho Chi Minh, I am sure, appreciated that.

The mere fact that Communist North Vietnam was conducting this operation is proof of the fourth element required by the Supreme Court.

One might argue that nobody in the United States knew that the Communists were conducting such an operation, so therefore cannot be held accountable for committing treason.

I would say bullshit. Why? For example, you are a methamphetamine dealer. You build a meth lab; this is illegal. The mere fact that the lab exists is a violation of the law whether anyone knows about it or not.

The fact that the Communists were using the information being reported by the American media about the treason being committed in the United States is a violation of the giving aid and comfort prong of the Constitution, an element required by the Supreme Court, whether anyone knew they were monitoring us or not. They were using that information to conduct their war against us.

Colonel Bui Tin continues,

I personally participated in this translation effort. For instance, I received early copies of David Halberstam's book The Best and the Brightest and Don Oberdofer's Tet and at once proceeded to summarize them for the leaders in Hanoi. My translations were later printed in Tap Chi Cong San (Journal of communism) and Quan Doi Nhan Dan.

Memoirs by Lyndon B Johnson, Richard M. Nixon, and Henry Kissinger, and books such as Townsend Hoopes's the Limits of Intervention and Phillip Knightley's First Casualty were also extremely useful in understanding the thinking in Washington's political circles.

But material passed along in this fashion also had its drawbacks, its distortions! Unsophisticated leaders who never stepped a foot abroad, who were used to reading only material favorable to Hanoi, after a while were inclined to think that most American Politicians were of the type of Senators Wayne L. Morse, Ernest Gruening, William J. Fulbright, and Mike Mansfield; That all American artists were like Jane Fonda and Joan Baez; that all American athletes were like Muhammad Ali; and that all Western and American intellectuals were like Bertrand Russell, Gabriel Kolko, Ramsey Clark, and Bishop Thomas Gumbleton. They believed that all journalists were like Walter Cronkite, Don Luce, Tom Hayden, and John Hittinger; and that U.S. military officers were all cruel and inhuman like 1ˢᵗ Lt. William L. Calley Jr. in My Lai!

This kind of prejudiced thinking led them to believe that Western workers lived in rat holes and were constantly engaged in strikes and boycotts. That the American GIs in South Vietnam were all grumbling antiwar protesters, and that black soldiers were constantly throwing grenades at white officers. Pictures of American veterans and active duty GIs burning the American flag, tearing off medals and decorations and throwing them away, or wrapping the Statue of Liberty with flags of the NLF (National Liberation Front for South Vietnam); of GIs holding their heads and crying as in Khe Sanh; and images of captured U.S pilots with hands raised or heads hanging as they were paraded through the streets were enlarged and printed in daily newspapers and on large posters, making a deep impressions on those who saw them.

These images distortions of the truth or not, all contributed to nurturing the North Vietnamese people's will to fight and their faith in final victory during the war years.

Colonel Bui Tin was the man who received the unconditional surrender from the South Vietnamese in 1975. The excerpt from "How North Vietnam Won the War" was information that was provided unwittingly by him in an interview. The excerpts from his book *From Enemy to Friend* is just some more proof that those who were conducting the anti-war movement were committing treason. This, along with the Pham Van Dong's thank-you letter, I believe, proves my accusation of treason beyond any doubt. However, that is only up to a court to decide. However, if charges are never brought, then court is irrelevant.

If what I have shown here does not meet the four requisites demanded by the Supreme Court, then I don't know what does: "(1) an overt act, (2) testified to by two witnesses, (3) manifesting an intent to betray the United States (which can be inferred from the overt act itself), (4) the act providing aid and comfort to the enemy."

Or if it does not meet the statement by Mr. Holzer, as expressed in his article, then I don't what does. "Speech becomes treason when it transcends mere words, ceasing to be communication alone, and satisfies the four requisites demanded by the Supreme Court."

This lack of action on the part of the so-called leadership of this nation regarding the anti-war movement brought consequences, of which were second to none in the annals of American history.

One is that individuals that participated in that movement were and can hold office in the top levels of the United States government, i.e. Bill and Hillary Clinton, Ted Kennedy, John Kerry (VVAW), just to name a few.

However, in all fairness to these mutts, you are innocent until proven guilty.

Amendment XIV (1868) (exhibit 26B):

Section 3. No person shall be a Senator or Representative in Congress, or elector of President and Vice President, or hold any office, civil or military, under the United States, or under any state, who, having previously taken an oath, as a member of Congress, or as an officer of the United States, or as a member of any state legislature, or as an executive or judicial officer of any state, to support the Constitution of the United States, shall have engaged in insurrection or rebellion against the same, or given aid or comfort to the enemies thereof. But Congress may by a vote of two-thirds of each House, remove such disability.

Colonel Holms wrote a letter September 1992 (exhibit 22) as entered in Congressional record (page H5550) on July 30, 1993, providing Congress with a copy of a letter that was written to him on

December 3, 1969 (exhibit 23). Colonel Holmes was the commanding officer of the University of Arkansas ROTC Program.

If my assessment of the constitution regarding treason is correct and my assessment of the Supreme Court ruling regarding treason is correct, and I believe they are, then the author of the following paragraph admitted to committing treason. In the letter written to Colonel Holms, the author wrote, *I have written and spoken and marched against the war. One of the national organizers of the Vietnam Moratorium is a close friend of mine. After I left Arkansas last summer, I went to Washington to work in the national headquarters of the Moratorium, then to England to organize the Americans here for demonstrations October 15 and November 16.*

The author of that paragraph is none other than William Jefferson Clinton.

That, to me, is an admission of guilt. I believe if he were charged with treason back then in 1969 and possibly convicted, he would never have been able to run for president of the United States. This particular letter became an issue in his first campaign, and no one paid attention to it.

That lack of action on the part of leadership of this nation back then has carried on to this very day as expressed by a young soldier from Iraq that I had a conversation with not too long ago. His name is Sgt. Anthony Noto; he served with the US Army Tenth Mountain Division.

I spoke with this young man upon his return from his second tour in Iraq. I asked him if he has felt any sense of betrayal or apathy toward him or his fellow soldiers from this country, like us Nam veterans. Although I do not see it on the same grandiose scale as during the Vietnam War, I, for one, feel that it is occurring all over again and from the same people as before, as well as their protégés who also don't have the common sense, honor, or decency of a nat.

He says he does not see as much treason as there was during Vietnam, but he does see apathy which, in his experience, is a bigger issue regarding his feelings. He said he returned from his second tour on November 2, 2007, and he has not heard anything about Iraq.

He remembers that just a few days after his return, actor Heath Ledger had died. He said he was watching the news and there was a thirty-minute story told about Ledger, and this was only one of many stories on him. There were a multitude of questions, inquiring what could have happened to Ledger, then the newscaster announced the following.

"In other news, four more soldiers died in Iraq, and now a word from our sponsors."

He feels that there is no more support for what happens in Iraq, and it seems that nobody cares what happens in or to Iraq. He also feels that nobody cares what happens to the soldiers fighting there.

He did relay a story to me that occurred while he was in Iraq that he took as a treasonous act. Anthony said that they were detailed to escort some detainees to Camp Victory. While they were there, they had an opportunity to get some hot chow and catch up with news from home that was being broadcast on television.

He said that a Democrat politician whose name he cannot remember now was being interviewed; he was slandering the president and the war. Then something happened that he will never forget. A soldier younger than him was sitting across the table from him when he asked, "Then why should I have to be here! Fuck this country! I quit."

This is how Anthony expressed his thoughts to me regarding that incident. "Our politicians are helping America toward one huge helping of defeat. Apparently, treason is still not punishable, but still fatal."

(This is just one more incident resulting in two more hearts of America's warriors being wounded, forevermore. Not wounded by the enemy but by the very people that they protect.)

CHAPTER 12

AMERICA LOSES ITS HONOR

I GUESS I WAS NAIVE about the nation I lived in when I started my journey to war. I believed since we lived in the same country at least most of the people that lived here would feel the same way I did. However, my naivete was short-lived long before my return from the war. I believed it was the right thing to do when I joined the Marine Corps, as well as it being something I was obligated to do I believe everyone living in this country has a responsibility and an obligation to serve and defend it. This could not be made any clearer than in the oath taken by an individual when he or she chooses to take America as their own.

Naturalization Oath of Allegiance to the United States of America:

> I hereby declare, on oath, that I absolutely and entirely renounce and abjure all allegiance and fidelity to any foreign prince, potentate, state or sovereignty, of whom or which I have heretofore been a subject or citizen; that I will support and defend the Constitution and laws of the United States of America against all enemies, foreign and domestic; that I will bear true faith and allegiance to the same; that I will bear arms on behalf of the United States when required by the law; that I will perform noncombatant service in the armed forces of the United States when required by the

law; that I will perform work of national importance under civilian direction when required by
the law; and that I take this obligation freely
without any mental reservation or purpose of
evasion; so help me God.

I guess there are people in this country who feel and always
felt, for whatever reason, that it is not worth defending. During the
Vietnam War, what was once a few grew to an unprecedented number. During that period and since, I have come to believe that the
words of this oath and all the oaths taken on a daily basis in this
country by people who vow to protect the Constitution have become
nothing more than empty words to be uttered and forgotten.

The Declaration of Independence was signed in 1776 by men
who put everything they had at risk. If the revolution were lost, these
men would have been hung by the neck as the criminals and the
traitors, as they were described to be by the King of England. Yet
there are people in this country who find it necessary to belittle the
accomplishments of these men and write them off as individuals who
were out of touch with reality.

These are men who risked it all to provide freedom not only to
themselves but also to all those that would seek it. Those people who
have found it necessary to continually ridicule and demean these
men whom they never met, except in printed word, I believe to be
nothing more than Communists, or at the very least un-American.

It is not without just cause that I believe this because you see,
during the course of this investigation, I have found a bit of evidence
that the United States government was aware that the condemnation
of the Founding Fathers was one of many goals of the Communist.
I know this because of a document I found that was read into the
congressional record. On Thursday, January 10, 1963 (congressional
record, appendix, pp. A34-A35) (exhibit 27).

That particular goal of ridicule by the Communists is listed
among forty-five goals and is the thirtieth goal listed. I have seen this
little goal expressed as recently as 2008 by an actor who claims to be
an American.

30. Discredit the American Founding Fathers. Present them as selfish aristocrats who had no concern for the "common man." (Exhibit 27)

[*] A man that was unknown to me until recently, W. Cleon Skousen (1913–2006), was a popular teacher, lecturer, and author. Dr. Skousen served the FBI for sixteen years (1935–1951); in 1956, he was asked to serve as chief of police of Salt Lake City. During his four-year service to the city, he wrote a national best seller, *The Naked Communist.*

It is in this book, *The Naked Communist,* he listed what he called the goals of the Communist. Three years after its publication, these goals were read into the congressional record. This was also ten months prior to Kennedy's assassination.

Evidently, nobody in the public or the government was paying attention, or maybe they just did not care. However, it was read into the record under unanimous consent, which, I am assuming, that to have it read, required a vote. I wonder if anyone in Congress was even listening to the words that were being read.

The person who read it into the congressional record was [*] the Hon. Mr. A. S. Herlong Jr. of Florida at the request of Mrs. Patricia Nordman, who had published the *De Land Courier,* which she dedicated to the purpose of alerting the public to the dangers of Communism in America.

After witnessing firsthand the distorted and debased version of what was being force-fed to this country by its own citizens during sixties and seventies by those who participated in the anti-war movement, I believe there are a number of other goals listed in the congressional record that were achieved by the Communist leadership of that movement during that period:

12. *Resist any attempt to outlaw the Communist Party.*
16. *Use technical decisions of the courts to weaken basic American institutions by claiming their activities violate civil rights.*
17. *Get control of the schools. Use them as transmission belts for socialism and current Communist propaganda. Soften the cur-*

riculum. Get control of teachers' associations. Put the party line in textbooks.

18. *Gain control of all student newspapers.*
19. *Use student riots to foment public protests against programs or organizations which are under Communist attack.*
20. *Infiltrate the press. Get control of book-review assignments, editorial writing, and policymaking positions.*
21. *Gain control of key positions in radio, TV, and motion pictures.*
27. *Infiltrate the churches and replace revealed religion with "social" religion. Discredit the Bible and emphasize the need for intellectual maturity which does not need a "religious crutch."* (Exhibit 27)

These are just a few of the goals that were served up by the participants of the anti-war movement to undermine the defense of freedom and assist the Communists with their endeavors. These goals were fed to a large portion of America's population, and it was accepted and eaten up like it was their last meal.

I remember reading a sign one time. I do not know the author; however, I wholeheartedly agree with it: "For those who defend it, freedom has a flavor the protected will never taste."

The ungrateful protected of this nation during the Vietnam War chewed the gift of freedom as if someone fed them dog shit, then they turned around and spit it in the face of those of us who were defending it. From that day to this, all I can ask is, why?

I was asked recently, "Why can't you let the war go? After all, it was forty-five years since you were there?" I said, "That is true." Yet that part of my life experience in my mind's eye just happened this morning.

I often wonder why people think that I or anyone of us who fought there should be the ones to forget it happened. Those who participated in the anti-war movement sure as hell didn't. Over the past fifty-plus years, those pompous morons who conducted those treasonous acts and who still appear to have an unrealistically high self-image of themselves continually produce shows and books praising their actions. They continually compare today's conflicts with

Vietnam, indicating that the Vietnam War was wrong. I could not forget it happened or let go even if I wanted to.

As one who fought there, I, for one, do not want to forget that there were and are people in this country who call themselves Americans yet helped bring their own government to their knees by doing everything in their power to help the Communist in North Vietnam.

A lot has happened since I marched off to war those fifty-plus years ago. Somewhere between World War II and Vietnam, the country I swore to protect and die for, disappeared. Somewhere between the Korean War and Vietnam, a large portion of my generation, for one reason or another, decided that the way of life that was given to them was not worth defending. I think that they still feel the same way to this very day.

I have been told that the World War I generation was known as the lost generation; the World War II generation was known as the greatest generation. This leaves the generation I was born into known as the baby boomer generation. Based on my observations pertaining to the activities of the vast majority of my generation during the Vietnam War and since, I think my generation's name should be changed.

In the Marine Corps, we have a motto: semper fidelis (*semper* meaning "always" and *fidelis* meaning "faithful"). I would now like to submit to the generation naming community, whoever they may be, a new name for my generation: the "Semper I and Fuck the other guy generation." I feel that title would fit at least three quarters of my generation.

Unfortunately, I, as well as other members of the generation that remained loyal to this country, will also have to be burdened with carrying that name. However, it will not be the first or last time I have been saddled with a disparaging name.

When I was growing up, I always looked at the defenders of this nation as the honorable people and the wars that they fought as being on the side of right. I believed this mainly because we generally fought against ternary, or we stuck up for the little guy or those that could not defend themselves. When the fight was finished, we did not rule them; we helped them rebuild and gave them back their own destiny, for example Germany and Japan. The proof of that would be, after winning the World War I, the Germans came after us again in World War II. Yet again we gave them back their country.

I remember, as a young boy in school, the teacher reading us a poem. The poem was titled "Trees"; the author of that poem was Joyce Kilmer. At first, I believed the author to be a girl because of the name. However, the teacher told us a little more about the man who wrote that poem and changed the way I think of things forevermore.

His full name was Alfred Joyce Kilmer. At the age of thirty-one, during the second Battle of Marne, there was heavy fighting throughout the last days of July 1918. On July 30, 1918, he was killed in action.

I remember that it wasn't the poem that impressed me but the fact that even though he was famous, he was a soldier that sacrificed his life, protecting his country, which, in turn, allowed me an opportunity to be born free. There is a service area on the Jersey Turnpike that honors his name, and yet I wonder if most of the people passing through it in their travels know who he is or that he died serving his country.

As I grew older, there were other men who fought other wars protecting our freedoms. These are the men whose footsteps I was honored and proud to follow in. Since following in their footsteps, I have met some of these men. Men like my friend, Joe McConville, one of the men I only heard about as a young boy. He fought with the Marines in World War II. Also my friend Ken Benson, who fought in Korea along with his buddies, Hector Cafferata Jr. and Paul Tallman, also United States Marines.

Ken and Hector are pictured here with my son LCpl Joe Keely Jr., recently discharged from the Marine Corps. This is at a recent ceremony where Ken Benson was the recipient of the Silver Star for his actions in the same battle that Hector was the recipient of the Congressional Medal of Honor. Since Ken lives not too far from me, I asked him to tell me the details of that event in his life.

Ken said that he wanted to be a marine since he was a young man also. He remembers writing to a marine that was fighting in the Pacific during World War II. That marine gave his life on Okinawa.

Ken had two friends, Hector Cafferata and Paul Tallman; they joined the Twenty-First Infantry Battalion of the United States Marine Corps at Picatinny Arsenal. During this time, they were sent to two summer camps while waiting to be sent to boot camp. However, that trip to boot camp would never come. In June 1950, the North Korean Communist invaded South Korea, starting the Korean War. That little act of aggression affected the lives of the guys listed above as well as people from sixteen other nations.

Ken told me that because he, Hector, and Paul had attended two summer camps that boot camp was not an option. This little trip was going to take them straight to Korea right after some additional infantry training.

By September, they were aboard ship to Japan. After a week in Japan, they were back on ship steaming toward Korea. It took about a week. When they made a wet landing at Won-Son, they went in hot (locked and loaded). They went in unopposed. He remembers that they were loaded on to a train, all flat cars, approximately one thousand Marines. It was an eleven-mile trip to Haga-Ru at the base of the Chosen Reservoir; form there, it took approximately two hours before they were transported by truck to a hilltop above Kota-Ri. During their travels, they learned that twelve divisions of Chinese infantry approximately 150,000 men were sent into the area to eliminate the Marine Corps.

They arrived at Fox Hill approximately 1500 hours. The snow was knee-deep, and it was twenty degrees below zero. Ken said that they just dug down to ground level in the hard snow, and that served as their cover and concealment. Colonel Barber was the commanding officer and ordered the men to set up a horseshoe defense for the night.

Shortly after, Ken and Hector were sent approximately thirty yards down the hill as a listening post. Hector told ken that he would take the first watch. Ken said that he cannot remember how long he was asleep when Hector woke him, saying, "We got trouble." Ken opened his eyes and saw red tracers going down the hill and green going up. Our tracers were red, the Chinese were green.

There were Chinese all around. It was November 28, 1950, within fifteen minutes, everyone in his platoon was either dead or wounded. A grenade landed near Ken; it blew his glasses off and blinded him. Hector was wounded. For the next eight hours, these two guys protected the perimeter. Ken loaded one M-1 after another for Hector while he ran up and down the line shooting. Because of the actions of these two guys, the perimeter was never breached. For their actions, Hector received the Congressional Medal of Honor and Ken received a Silver Star.

All I know is I had and have a great admiration for the men who fought those wars. I believed them to be men of honor. *Honor.* Now there is a word I believe that is quickly disappearing from the American vocabulary.

These are just a few of the men whose example I chose to follow; I believe that when these warriors left the battlefield behind, they also left a symbolic item of their combat gear behind—the gauntlet: a medieval glove, as of mail or plate, worn by a knight in armor to protect the hand. I believe the old warrior hopes a younger warrior comes along and picks it up and carries on the fight. I and many honorable men and women who marched off to Vietnam those many years ago did just that.

The people of this country should get down on its knees and thank Christ; there are some honorable young men and woman still living here that are willing to pick up the gauntlet that we who fought in Nam left behind. I do think, however, that the number of young men and woman who are willing to do so is dwindling. It is also my belief that the Vietnam anti-war movement is a major cause for that dwindling number.

While Ken, Hector, and Paul were engaged in the war for Korea, the war between France and Ho Chi Minh's communist Vietminh was raging in Vietnam. Approximately one year after the Korean War ended, so did the war between Ho Chi Minh and the French. With the ending of Ho Chi Minh's war with France in 1954, an agreement between the French and the North Vietnamese split Vietnam at the seventeenth parallel.

Ho Chi Minh described his wars with the French and us as fights for independence. I have noticed over the years that when Communist fight wars, it is always about independence; they just fail to mention that freedom doesn't accompany that independence.

The fact of the matter is Ho Chi Minh and North Vietnam had already gained independence with the end of the French Indochina War, so did South Vietnam, but the difference is that South Vietnam chose a path toward freedom and democracy.

Yet the so-called Americans of the anti-war movement set out very early to make sure that South Vietnam would not achieve that liberty they were yearning for, and the anti-war movement accomplished that goal with a pride that they display to this very day.

The entire anti-war movement was designed to show solidarity with the North Vietnamese Communists. The people from this country chose to take the side of Ho Chi Minh, Stalin, and Mao Zedong over our own government and the troops that were defending our way of life.

Also included in the anti-war movement were Philip Berrigan and Daniel Berrigan brothers. Both Catholic priests were setting fires to building that housed draft boards along with protesting the war. I guess what I understand the least is the Catholic priests and clergy from all religions that took the side of the Communist over ours during that period.

Colonel Bui Tin mentions this in the interview with the *Wall Street Journal.* Here he tells of visits to Hanoi by the clergy pledging their support of the Communist in the Vietnam War that is a total puzzlement to me, seeing that freedom of religion was not allowed under North Vietnamese Communist rule; this is verified by Colonel Bui Tin in his book *From Enemy to Friend.*

I do not understand how religious people could have taken the side the Communist over the men and women who were safeguarding the Constitution which houses the First Amendment and freedom of religion. Were these people an infiltration to the religious sect by the Communist? My guess would be yes.

I do not know what happened to my generation between the Korean War and the Vietnam War. However, they, as well as others from previous generations that lived in this country at the time, chose the Vietnam War as an excuse to commit treason and break a whole slew of other laws in the process.

I have come to the conclusion that we have become a nation of laws to be broken and condoned. This attitude has infected every level of our society like an incurable cancer. It appears that the attitude that has emerged from the anti-war movement is, rather than punish illegal behavior, let's just whitewash it and cloak it as something that was the right thing to do. At the same time they were breaking the treason laws, they were also breaking the drug laws. They brought to this country a drug abuse problem second to none, and rather than look at it as a bad choice in behavior, they whitewash it as being a sickness.

Rhetoric has many definitions. One is "the ability to use language effectively, especially to persuade or influence people." I believe that the Communist leadership that infested the anti-war movement was highly effective at this during the Vietnam War, as well as today.

Rhetoric also conveys "speech or writing that communicates its point persuasively, fine-sounding but insincere or empty language." A good example of that is like the bumper sticker I observed while driving recently; it stated, "Peace is patriotic." I happen to believe that those words are absolutely true. However, since it was being displayed during our present-day war in Iraq and next to a Vietnam era peace symbol, when presented that way, I believe these words to be absolute rhetoric and insincere or misunderstood.

People who like to use this type of rhetoric to express their thoughts and gather support for their causes display these things and say these things as if those of us who are engaged in the fight don't want it or believe in it. They would like everyone that is watching to think that they are the only ones on the planet that believe in it.

Encarta defines *peace* as: "freedom from war or a time when a conflict ends." The mere definition of the word shows that that peace is derived from war or conflict, period. That means that before there is peace, there is conflict.

Most of these sanctimonious assholes that express their feelings of peace never knew anything else but peace. It is conflict that they don't know. The reason they don't know conflict is because there are only a few, and I mean a few, of us that continually keep stepping up and placing ourselves in harm's way between those who cry for peace and those who want to breach the peace for whatever reason.

Is it because these people like to think that anyone who fights in a war or stands up to injustice for themselves or someone else doesn't believe in peace? Allow me to expose a little secret. There is nobody on the planet that wants peace more than those of us who are listening to the bullets whizzing past our heads or when we are running for cover to avoid getting hit with the hot molten metal that is flying through the air from a mortar or artillery shell or an IED.

A good example of someone breaching the peace may be to deny someone of their freedoms. This was done by Ho Chi Minh, activating the Vietcong to deny the South Vietnamese their right to be free.

I know this much that regarding Vietnam, the Communist student organizations that emerged from the Communist-infested American brothels of higher education in this country did not believe in peace. They just did not want the United States to win it. I believe the leadership of the movement used their rhetoric to gather the support from the sanctimonious, the frightened, the apathetic, and the just plain self-centered individuals of this country to come on board with them to win their fight against America.

Peace is not a given; peace must be won. I believe in peace, and I believe *peace is patriotic*, but I believe it becomes unpatriotic when we accept it at any cost. During the Vietnam era, the American public opted for peace at an extremely high cost (an extremely high cost!).

"A symbol is something that stands for or represents something else, especially an object representing an abstraction." The participants of the anti-war movement were no different they also used a symbol to identify themselves and their treasonous activity. They called that

257

symbol the peace sign. It was not really theirs; it didn't belong to them. It belonged to a pacifist from England. Evidently, these people could not come up with their own design.

The following is an excerpt from one of the local rags I have read recently, describing just where that symbol came from. The article was written in April of 2008, thirty-five years after the last American combatant left Vietnam, and yet people are asking me why I cannot let go of the war. Gee, I wonder why.

Tuesday April 8, 2008

Local Newspaper: The Record Written by Joseph B. Frazier about a book written by Ken Kolsbun with Michael Sweeney the Biography of a Symbol The article is about the Peace Sign.

The Symbol was designed by a pacifist from Brittan by the name of Gerald Holtom in 1958 to promote nuclear disarmament.

It was designed out of the semaphore positions N and D; somewhere along the line it was adopted by the American Anti War Movement as a peace symbol the U.S. Patent Office in 1970 ruled that it was in public domain.

D-4

N

The symbol itself is a combination of the semaphore signals for the letters N and D, standing for "nuclear disarmament." In semaphore, the letter N is formed by a person holding two flags in an upside-down semaphore N, V.

The letter D is formed by holding one flag pointed straight up and the other pointed straight down. These two signals imposed over each other form the shape of the peace symbol.

It was subsequently adopted as an international emblem for the 1960's anti-war movement and was also adopted by the counterculture of the time. These symbols littered the American landscape starting in the 1960s, and they continue to litter it to this very day.

It is because of the rhetorical way in which this symbol was used in the sixties and seventies that I feel what should be viewed by everyone as a symbol meaning something good is viewed at least in my eyes as a symbol of treason, and those who display it as nothing more than traitors. The participants of the American anti-war movement, along with others that would call themselves Americans, adopted this symbol to represent their cause.

I left Vietnam in 1967; I returned to the States and finished out my last ten months in the corps at Camp LeJeune. Like many other returning vets, I entered law enforcement. Those of us who did would find ourselves right back in the fight in Vietnam. The only thing that changed was the geography and the color of the uniforms that we wore.

The jungles and the rice paddies turned into concrete sidewalks and blacked topped highways. The more brazen of Uncle Ho's buddies here in the States consisted of the Students for a Democratic Society, and Student Peace Union, the Black Liberation Army, the New African Front, the United Freedom Front, the Anti-Vietnam War Moratorium, the Black Panthers, and the various religious groups that assisted the Communists with their quest for world domination. The tactics were the same—covert and guerrilla in nature.

Those of us who became law enforcement agents from time to time would meet up with and engage usually violently with the members of these groups as they waged their war against the United States. They hid themselves among the other dregs of society who found it easier to break the laws of the country rather than conform to be a lawful and productive citizen.

The Weathermen, as previously pointed out {D}, issued a Declaration of a State of War against the United States government in 1970. In this declaration of war, Bernardine Dohrn, the now wife of Bill Ayres, made statements, such as, *Revolutionary violence is the only way. Now we are adapting the classic guerrilla strategy of the Vietcong and the urban guerrilla strategy of the Tupamaros to our own situation here in the most technically advanced country in the world. Ché taught us that 'revolutionaries move like fish in the sea.' The alienation and contempt that young people have for this country has created the ocean for this revolution. The hundreds and thousands of young people who demonstrated in the Sixties against the war and for civil rights grew to hundreds of thousands in the past few weeks actively fighting Nixon's invasion of Cambodia and the attempted genocide against black people.* This group, along with the groups they formed an alliance with, called themselves the May 19th Communist Organization.

 In May 1973, JoAnne Deborah Byron, a.k.a. Assata Olugbala Shakur (born July 16, 1947)[1] married name Chesimard, and a member of the Black Panther party (BPP) and Black Liberation Army (BLA) became involved in a shootout on the New Jersey Turnpike during which time a New Jersey State trooper Werner Forester and BLA member Zayd Malik Shakur were killed and Assata Shakur (JoAnne Chesimard) and Trooper James Harper were wounded.

Another BLA member, Marilyn Jean Buck (born 1947 in Jasper, Texas),[1] is a white woman and a so-called American. A self-described lifelong anti-racist and anti-imperialist activist, [2] a convicted felon, she was convicted of conspiracy in a number of violent crimes. She has also been convicted for her participation in the 1979 prison break of Assata Shakur.

She was also convicted of conspiracy to commit armed robbery as a participant in the Brinks robbery of 1981 in which members of the Weather Underground and Black Liberation Army used a car owned by her and apartments rented in her name. Buck played a key role in the Brinks robbery of 1981. She provided the robbers with a safe house and weapons. During the investigation into the armed robbery and attack, I was part of an investigation team that found a supply of automatic weapons, shotguns, ammunition, bomb-making material and something else, detailed blueprints of six Manhattan police precincts[6] in an apartment in East Orange, New Jersey, rented by Carol Durant, an alias of Buck's. We also found papers there that led us to an address in Mount Vernon, New York, where they found bloody clothing and ammunition: "Investigation later revealed that the bloody clothing belonged to Marilyn Buck, who had accidentally shot herself in the leg when she tried to draw her weapon during the shootout at Mountain view."[7]

[3][4] She was also convicted for her role in the 1983 US Senate bombing—conspiracy to protest and alter government policies through use of violence.[5] Buck received an eighty-year sentence for

the Capitol bombing that she is serving at FCI Dublin in California. Her federal prison register number is 00482-285.

When the last American combatant left Vietnam in 1973 and the draft became a thing of the past, the majority of the anti-war dissidents left the garbage-strewn demonstration fields of America and scurried back into their holes like the cockroaches they are. This was done only after they found out they would not have to serve their country or go to war, which the majority of them probably wouldn't have had to go anyway. The more violent scum of the earth continued their war against America.

That war lasted well past our involvement in Vietnam. It lasted well past the seventies into the nineties.

The very next year, on September 16, 1974, President Ford unveiled a conditional clemency program for Vietnam-era military deserters and draft evaders. Hmm! This guy may have also had a problem with the number of branches in his family tree. This could have been a major cause as to why he kept falling down. That many falls may have caused damage. However, in all fairness to this mutt, it never materialized during his presidency. Regardless, Mr. Peanuts sure as hell made it a reality.

On December 21, 1981, the war on the streets of the United States continued. Thomas William Manning and Richard Charles Williams, two members of the United Freedom Front who were conducting their war against America since 1972, gunned down a friend of mine, Trooper Philip Lamonaco.

Phil was a marine Vietnam veteran continuing in the defense of his state and country. He surrendered his life on a snow-covered blacktop at the western-end Route 80, attempting to bring these two mutts to justice. In the highest traditions of the Marine Corps and the New Jersey State Police, Phil did not go down without a fight.

Mine and Smitty's last battle of Vietnam ended 1992 in the second courtroom battle regarding this case in Somerville, New Jersey. This is where, after many days of testimony, a guilty verdict was received on Richard Charles Williams. So as you can see, it wasn't forty-five years since we were in that war. Our tour lasted twenty-seven years. This makes it exceedingly difficult for anyone to forget they were ever in such a place as Vietnam, especially when it was the Americans that continued the fight for Communism long after we left there.

I have heard it argued that some of the people joined in the anti-war movement because they were idealistic and joined in the demonstrations to have fun. In answer to that argument, I will respond by quoting Lee Ermey or, if you prefer, Gunny Hartman from the movie *Full Metal Jacket*. I don't care if they were there to "finger bang Mary Jane Rotten crotch through her pretty pink panties" if they joined in the demonstration. I believe they were committing treason period and should've been brought up on charges.

Regardless, the reason that they were there does not matter. The minute they joined the protest, they were showing solidarity with the traitors. Any person reaching the age of reason would have known that the anti-war movement was treasonous, and if they didn't know it was treasonous, they had to know at the very least it was disloyal. If they did not, then ignorance is no excuse. I am sure there are people who can't remember if they were disloyal or treasonous to America or not. However, all they have to do is just look in the mirror, and I'm sure it will all come back to them.

Significant decisions were made by the so-called leadership of the nation between 1970, 1973, and 1975. It made me choose the words *America loses its honor* for this chapter.

The Cooper-Church Amendment (exhibit 20) was introduced in the United States Senate during the Vietnam War. The proposal of the amendment was the first time that Congress had restricted the deployment of troops during a war against the wishes of the president.[1]

The amendment sought to

- end funding to retain US ground troops and military advisers in Cambodia and Laos.

- bar air operations in Cambodian airspace in direct support of Cambodian forces without congressional approval.
- end American support for Republic of Vietnam forces outside territorial South Vietnam.

The amendment was presented by senators John Sherman Cooper and Frank Church and attached to a major bill, the Foreign Military Sales Act (HR 15628). After a seven-week filibuster and six months of debate, the amendment was approved by the Senate by a vote of 58 to 37 on June 30, 1970. The bill failed in the House of Representatives, which opposed inclusion of the amendment by a vote of 237 to 153. President Richard M. Nixon threatened to veto the bill if it contained the Cooper-Church provisions, and the foreign assistance bill was subsequently passed without it.

A revised Cooper-Church amendment, Public Law 91-652, passed both Houses of Congress on December 22, 1970, and was enacted on January 5, 1971, although this version had limited restrictions on air operations and was attached to the Supplementary Foreign Assistance Act of 1970. By that time, US ground forces had already officially withdrawn from Cambodia while US bombing missions in Cambodia (operations freedom deal) continued until 1973. The Nixon administration denounced all versions of the amendment, claiming that they harmed the military effort and weakened the American bargaining position at the Paris peace talks *(To me, this is a perfect example of Nixon placating to both sides of the issue.)*

Author David F. Schmitz stated that the amendment was a landmark in the history of opposition to the war, congressional initiatives to bring the fighting to an end, and efforts to control executive power in foreign policy.[1]

With the passing of these bills, South Vietnam was left all alone to fend for itself, just like the American troops were back in 1968.

On May 10, 1973, the House voted (219-188) for the first time to cut off Indochina funds, and on May 31, 1973, the Senate took strong action prohibiting the use of any funds appropriated by Congress to be used for combat activities in Laos or Cambodia.

It is my opinion that these bills were passed due to pressures placed on the American government by the American public. In 1975, President Thieu requested aid from President Gerald Ford and the US Senate. However, they would not release extra money to provide aid to South Vietnam. It is my belief this sealed South Vietnams fate and cinched their disastrous defeat at the hands of the Communists.

In desperation, Thieu called back Nguyen Cao Ky from retirement as a military commander but resisted calls to name his old rival prime minister.

(So bye-bye, America). This was the day that brought shame upon America. This is where America pulled back its hand and reneged on both its written and oral word; this is the day when America lost its honor.

It was shortly after the final slap in the face to South Vietnam that peace finally came to the lower half of that country or, as John F. Kennedy referred to it in a 1956 speech (exhibit 8), "free Vietnam." However, it was that constant bombardment of the so-called American public calling for peace at any cost that snatched the freedom from those people who were fighting so valiantly for it.

Acting President Minh unconditionally surrendered the capital city of Saigon and the rest of South Vietnam to North Vietnam on April 30, 1975, and free Vietnam fell to Communism.

During the hours leading up to the surrender, the United States undertook a massive evacuation of its embassy in Saigon. The evacuees included US government personnel as well as high-ranking members of the ARVN and other South Vietnamese who had aided the US-backed administration and were seen as potential targets for persecution by the Communists.

Many of the evacuees were taken directly by helicopter to an aircraft carrier waiting off the coast. An iconic image of the evacuation is the widely seen footage of empty Huey helicopters being ditched over the side of the carrier to provide more room on the ship's deck for more evacuees to land.

It is my belief that some people in this country feel that because they wake up in the morning, look out the window, and see the

American flag that they are entitled to call themselves American. America is not a guarantee, and it never was. This country was spawned out of war; the Founding Fathers took it from what they considered a tyrant.

That war was a fight for both independence and freedom, and since that war, time and time again, there were and are people who would take that freedom from us and our friends who also live under democratic forms of government.

Adolf Hitler attempted that starting in 1939, a few short years after his gaining control of the German government. He launched a war upon the world, killing millions. However, it is here where Americans stepped up to the plate and helped to put a stop to the madness this man forced upon this world.

Shortly after Hitler's demise, a once former ally of his, Joseph Stalin of the Soviet government, proceeded with his plans for world domination. He started with East Berlin, Germany. He blockaded the free sections of Berlin, and then he built a wall to keep people from fleeing into the arms of freedom.

During the wall's existence, there were around 5,000 successful escapes into West Berlin which stood as a bastion of freedom (the American sector). Varying reports claim around 192 people were killed trying to cross [9][10] and many more injured. Guards were told by East German authorities that people attempting to cross the wall were criminals and needed to be shot.

The reason I mention this is that during the Vietnam War, approximately 50,000 people from this country crossed the border into Canada to avoid serving in the United States military, who are the defenders of freedom. During that period, I did not hear or see any of these traitors die at the Canadian border like the poor souls who died at the Berlin Wall.

As I have said continually, history is relevant. It is as pertinent to today's problems as it was back then because the players are the same. Many of the players are in the top levels of the US government. Many of them played a part in the betrayal of this nation. The shame of it is that for the past fifty years, those of us who fought there have watched the American public dish out a constant diet of innuendoes, indicating that our war and our service to our country was wrong, all the while holding themselves and their pseudo patriotism out as being loyal Americans.

Since then, I have not seen any evidence that most the people are willing to protect their own Constitution, never mind wanting to help someone else obtain freedom. Apparently, after World War II and Korea, Americans weren't willing to step up to the plate any more. Back when newspaper people had integrity, and loyalty to the United States, a renowned American newspaper editor, William Allen White, died on February 10, 1868, in Emporia, Kansas. On January 31, 1944, he wrote *Liberty is the only thing you cannot have unless you are willing to give it to others.* I look at these words as being patriotic. *Patriotic*, now there is a word that is almost invisible in this country.

During the Vietnam War, the anti-war movement was willing to use our own constitution as an apparatus to deceive. A lot happened in that fourteen-year period that the war lasted, but what I remember the most is those of us who fought there were maligned with such names as baby bomber, killers, murderers, to mention just a few. Those words wound the heart with the same severity as a bullet, and that wound was inflicted by our fellow Americans.

I think that I can speak for most of my comrades in arms when I say that we didn't or don't mind standing between the devastation of war and the protection of our loved ones and our homeland, but we did or do not expect to be betrayed for our efforts.

The biggest lesson I learned from the Vietnam War was to always watch my six, to always keep looking over my shoulder, and to never trust anyone, including those who claim to be like me.

There are 58,000-plus names etched into that black granite wall in the middle of DC. It may have been the NVA and VC bullets that put them there, but it was the American people that used that very same hallowed ground to conduct their treasonous activity which negated the sacrifice that they made, as well as the sacrifice of all of us who fought there.

From the first demonstrations in 1962 to the court battles with these treasonous groups in 1992, a lot had happened. Although those of us who fought the war were saddled with the name's murderers and killers and baby bombers, let's look at whom the real murders and killers were. The anti-war movement brought major consequences far beyond anything they accused the military of doing.

There are one hundred forty panels that make up the Vietnam wall. I hold all those who participated in the anti-war movement personally responsible for every death between panels 30 on the east wall to 70 on the west wall. This equates out to approximately 37,789 deaths. By panel 30, we had won the war. However, thanks to the actions of the American anti-war movement and the abandonment of the troops on the field of battle by the politicians, this denied us that were serving in that war the opportunity to complete our mission. These actions elongated the war. The commanders on the field of battle felt we could have ended the war by the end of 1968.

The anti-war movement was in solidarity with the North Vietnamese Communist from the time we provided advisers to South Vietnam in 1962. They gave no thought to the South Vietnamese or what they wanted out of this war, which was nothing more than wanting to live free. The participants of the anti-war Movement proved this time and time again on the demonstration fields of America.

In 1975, with the unconditional surrender of the South Vietnamese government, I hold these pseudo patriots of the anti-war movement personally responsible for killing a budding democracy. Their actions are also responsible for the 165,000 South Vietnamese who died in the reeducation camps who would not conform to Communism. They are responsible for the 250,000 South Vietnamese who became known as the boat people that died at sea, trying to escape Communism in 1978.

They are responsible for 2,410,000 South Vietnamese who were displaced worldwide escaping Communism, of which 833,000 of them came to the United States.

They are also responsible for the millions of people who had to conform to Communism to stay alive.

I also believe that they are responsible for the 1.5 million Cambodian's that died in their reeducation camps at the hands of the Communist Khmer Rouge. If we were allowed to complete our mission in Vietnam, we would have still been in the area and may have been able to prevent the killing fields of Cambodia.

I think what I have shown here is that John F. Kennedy had no intention of abandoning the South Vietnamese. I believe that this is quite apparent in his actions when he sent 18,000 troops to Vietnam to train the South Vietnamese troops, as well as his luncheon speech to friends of Vietnam in 1956 (exhibit 8), his excerpt from Honolulu conference in 1963 (exhibit 11), his US policy on Vietnam White House statement on October 2, 1963 (exhibit 12), his National Security Administration Memorandum 263 (exhibit 13), or his eyes-only telegram regarding Memorandum 263 (exhibit 14).

On September 2, 1963, in a televised interview, he said, *It is the Government itself who have to win or lose this struggle. All we can do is help, and we are making it very clear. But I don't agree with those who say we should withdraw. That would be a great mistake. That would be a great mistake. I know people don't like Americans to be engaged in this kind of an effort. Forty-seven Americans have been killed in combat with the enemy, but this is a very important struggle even though it is far away. We took all this—made this effort to defend Europe. Now Europe is quite secure. We also have to participate—we may not like it—in the defense of Asia.*

And he said in another televised interview on September 9, 1963, *We can't make the world over, but we can influence the world. The fact of the matter is that with the assistance of the United States and SEATO [Southeast Asia Treaty Organization], Southeast Asia and indeed all of Asia has been maintained independent against a powerful force the Chinese Communists. What I am concerned about is that Americans will get impatient and say, because they don't like events in Southeast Asia or they don't like the Government in Saigon, that we should withdraw. That only makes it easy for the Communists. I think we should stay we should use our influence in as effective a way as we can, but we should not withdraw.*

These two interviews, as well as Bobby Kennedy's interview (exhibit 16), I think I have also shown that Johnson did not plunge us into war using the Gulf of Tonkin events nor did he request a resolution based on those events but based on previous treaties initiated by previous presidents.

I think I have shown that the leadership of the anti-war movement could have been brought up on charges of treason according to law, as well as members of the entertainment industry, clergy, members of government, members of the media, not to mention all the participants that permeated the demonstration fields of America.

This is backed up by the US Constitution article 3, section 3, paragraph 1 pertaining to treason (exhibits 26 and 26A), the Supreme Court ruling regarding treason, as well as uncovered statements and interviews of once-enemy Col. Bui Tin, and letter from Pham Van Dong showing the aid and comfort supplied by these people (exhibits 18, exhibit 27) and Mr. W. Cleon Skousen's goals of the Communist.

The real irony of this war, however, is when I criticize those who protested the Vietnam War, the major responses to that is they we had a right to do that. When I ask them what right is that, without giving me a quote of the amendment, they say the right to free speech, free press, and free assembly under the Constitution of the United States. The American public loves to say, "I know my rights." However, here lies the irony as it is shown in Col. Bui Tin's book *From Enemy to Friend.*

Col. Bui Tin:
   When did you change your opinion about the war?
   Essentially in 1975. After April 30, 1975, I had a chance to live in South Vietnam for four consecutive years, right in Saigon (since renamed Ho Chi Minh City), I and many others who came down from the north experienced a profound conversion. We discovered South Vietnam through direct experience—as it really was and not as it had been pictured to us in the indoctrination sessions. Through the society and political regime had flaws and shortcomings, we nonetheless gradually concluded that, Before the liberation, it had also possessed many advantages over our system in the north. There was economic and entrepreneurial freedom, and for journalists like me in particular there was freedom of the press and opinion (privately owned newspapers; freedom to assemble, demonstrate,

stage sit ins and protest marches, and distribute leaflets), and freedom of religion and worship—freedoms unthinkable in the north.

There you have it, the irony. Col. Bui Tin, a Communist, in his own book, in his own words, described the very rights guaranteed to the American public, what he described was the First Amendment to the Constitution of the United States. The so-called Americans that protested the Vietnam War used those very same rights to deny the South Vietnamese people the freedom they were fighting for.

This story has a conclusion but by no means an end because it lives on in the never-ending string of wounded hearts of the men and women of the United States military, who remained loyal to their oath and fought with honor and distinction. Men and women who proudly served their country. Wounds that were inflicted by those who participated in the anti-war movement, made up of people that would call themselves American.

I have been asked on occasion if I would have done the same thing knowing the outcome. I do know that I can speak for the guys in the book. So I will answer that question with a phrase that we used in the Nam when we agreed with one another.

FUCKEN A!
THE CONCLUSION

EPILOGUE

IT WAS JUST A SIMPLE PIN

IT WAS NOVEMBER 10, 2011, the 235th birthday of the United States Marine Corps. I wore my black baseball cap with the staff sergeant chevron, showing my rank when I left the corps.

Also, on that hat were four pins, one was my unit designation, the others were replicas of the Vietnam Service Ribbon, each bearing the years I spent in that country.

The day was gray with a slight chill in the air. I was with my family shopping factory outlets. I bought some items and was at the checkout counter. I turned my head to the right and saw an Asian man. He looked at me quizzically. I turned away. I do not know why, but I turned back and looked at him one more time. This time, he approached me with a smile and asked me in broken English if I fought in Vietnam. I replied, "Yes, I did."

He shook my hand, pointed at my pins, and said, "Have to get one of them." He then said, "I served in the South Vietnamese Navy." I smiled and shook his hand. He said, "I wonder why we fought" and shook his head from side to side. I did not know what to say, so I just patted his shoulder and walked away. As I placed the items I bought in my daughters shopping cart, I said to myself, "What in the hell is the matter with you?" I thought he was probably asking for a pin but didn't know how. I turned around and approached him, this time with my hat in hand. I said, "Excuse me. When did you serve?" He told me the first year, but I didn't understand him due to his accent. He continued, "Until 1975."

I said, "Well then, you certainly deserve one of these." I gave him the pin with the year '67 on it. As he took it, he said, "Wow." Again, he shook my hand and said thank you for fighting for my country. His eyes welled up and his voice cracked as he uttered, "I don't know why we fought so hard. It is in the hands of the Communist now." I put my arm around him and patted his shoulder and said, "You're in a better place for right now." He just shook his head.

I walked away. I didn't get his name, nor did he ask me for mine. We were just a couple of old warriors sharing a moment, reminiscing about a place and time we shared so many years ago. As I looked back one last time, I saw he attached the pin to his light blue hat. Suddenly, it dawned on me that this simple pin minus the green bars on the end was the flag of his country. That flag and that country no longer exist due to the actions of so many people in this country that have the nerve to call themselves American These actions provided by these people not only gave away a democracy but also left two old warriors that shared a common bond so many years ago, standing in the middle of Pennsylvania, one wondering how and the other wondering why.

THIS IS DEDICATED TO ALL the men and woman of the United States military who served honorably and stayed loyal to their oath and their country during the Vietnam War as well as our incredibly good friends from.

- Republic of Vietnam
- Republic of Korea
- Thailand
- Australia
- New Zealand
- the Philippines

I would call these nations our allies, but that would give credence to the thought that America was in this fight on a national level, attempting to stop the spread of Communism throughout the Free World. Nothing could be further from the truth, at least as far as many Americans were concerned. So I will refer to these people from these other lands simply as our good friends that stood by our side in that fray. I thank them from the bottom of my heart, and I apologize to them for the lack of commitment on the part of my nation.

Exhibits Index

EXHIBIT 00

Ho Chi Minh's Declaration of Independence

September 2, 1945

"ALL MEN ARE CREATED EQUAL. They are endowed by their Creator with certain inalienable rights; among these are Life, Liberty, and the pursuit of Happiness."

This immortal statement was made in the Declaration of Independence of the United States of America m 1776. In a broader sense, this means: All the peoples on the earth are equal from birth, all the peoples have a right to live, to be happy and free.

The Declaration of the French Revolution made in 1791 on the Rights of Man and the Citizen also states: "All men are born free and with equal rights and must always remain free and have equal rights." Those are undeniable truths.

Nevertheless, for more than eighty years, the French imperialists, abusing the standard of Liberty, Equality, and Fraternity, have violated our Fatherland and oppressed our fellow-citizens. They have acted contrary to the ideals of humanity and justice. In the field of politics, they have deprived our people of every democratic liberty.

They have enforced inhuman laws; they have set up three distinct political regimes in the North, the Center, and the South of Vietnam in order to wreck our national unity and prevent our people from being united.

They have built more prisons than schools. They have mercilessly slain our patriots- they have drowned our uprisings in rivers of blood. They have fettered public opinion; they have practiced obscurantism against our people. To weaken our race, they have forced us to use opium and alcohol.

In the fields of economics, they have fleeced us to the backbone, impoverished our people, and devastated our land.

They have robbed us of our rice fields, our mines, our forests, and our raw materials. They have monopolized the issuing of banknotes and the export trade.

They have invented numerous unjustifiable taxes and reduced our people, especially our peasantry, to a state of extreme poverty.

They have hampered the prospering of our national bourgeoisie; they have mercilessly exploited our workers.

In the autumn of 1940, when the Japanese Fascists violated Indochina's territory to establish new bases in their fight against the Allies, the French imperialists went down on their bended knees and handed over our country to them.

Thus, from that date, our people were subjected to the double yoke of the French and the Japanese. Their sufferings and miseries increased. The result was that from the end of last year to the beginning of this year, from Quang Tri province to the North of Vietnam, more than two million of our fellow-citizens died from starvation. On March 9, the French troops were disarmed by the Japanese. The French colonialists either fled or surrendered, showing that not only were they incapable of "protecting" us, but that, in the span of five years, they had twice sold our country to the Japanese.

On several occasions before March 9, the Vietminh League urged the French to ally themselves with it against the Japanese. Instead of agreeing to this proposal, the French colonialists so intensified their terrorist activities against the Vietminh members that before fleeing they massacred a great number of our political prisoners detained at Yen Bay and Cao Bang.

Notwithstanding all this, our fellow-citizens have always manifested toward the French a tolerant and humane attitude. Even after the Japanese putsch of March 1945, the Vietminh League helped many Frenchmen to cross the frontier, rescued some of them from Japanese jails, and protected French lives and property.

From the autumn of 1940, our country had in fact ceased to be a French colony and had become a Japanese possession.

After the Japanese had surrendered to the Allies, our whole people rose to regain our national sovereignty and to find the Democratic Republic of Vietnam.

The truth is that we have wrested our independence from the Japanese and not from the French

The French have fled, the Japanese have capitulated, Emperor Bao Dai has abdicated. Our people have broken the chains which for nearly a century have fettered them and have won independence for the Fatherland. Our people at the same time have overthrown the monarchic regime that has reigned supreme for dozens of centuries. In its place has been established the present Democratic Republic.

For these reasons, we, members of the Provisional Government, representing the whole Vietnamese people, declare that from now on we break off all relations of a colonial character with France; we repeal all the international obligation that France has so far subscribed to on behalf of Vietnam and we abolish all the special rights the French have unlawfully acquired in our Fatherland.

The whole Vietnamese people, animated by a common purpose, are determined to fight to the bitter end against any attempt by the French colonialists to reconquer their country.

We are convinced that the Allied nations which at Tehran and San Francisco have acknowledged the principles of self-determination and equality of nations, will not refuse to acknowledge the independence of Vietnam.

A people who have courageously opposed French domination for more than eighty years, a people who have fought side by side with the Allies against the Fascists during these last years, such a people must be free and independent.

For these reasons, we, members of the Provisional Government of the Democratic Republic of Vietnam, solemnly declare to the world that Vietnam has the right to be a free and independent country and in fact it is so already. The entire Vietnamese people are determined to mobilize all their physical and mental strength, to sacrifice their lives and property in order to safeguard their independence and liberty.

Source: Ho Chi Minh, Selected Works (Hanoi, 1960–1962), vol. 3, pp. 17–21

EXHIBIT 1

Telegram from Ho Chi Minh to President Truman

VIỆT-NAM DÂN CHỦ CỘNG HÒA

CHÍNH PHỦ LÂM THỜI

BO NGOAI GIAO

HANOI FEBRUARY 28 1946

TELEGRAM

PRESIDENT HOCHIMINH VIETNAM DEMOCRATIC REPUBLIC HANOI

TO THE PRESIDENT OF THE UNITED STATES OF AMERICA WASHINGTON D.C.

ON BEHALF OF VIETNAM GOVERNMENT AND PEOPLE I BEG TO INFORM YOU THAT IN COURSE OF CONVERSATIONS BETWEEN VIETNAM GOVERNMENT AND FRENCH REPRESENTATIVES THE LATTER REQUIRE THE SECESSION OF COCHINCHINA AND THE RETURN OF FRENCH TROOPS IN HANOI STOP MEANWHILE FRENCH POPULATION AND TROOPS ARE MAKING ACTIVE PREPARATIONS FOR A COUP DE MAIN IN HANOI AND FOR MILITARY AGGRESSION STOP I THEREFORE MOST EARNESTLY APPEAL TO YOU PERSONALLY AND TO THE AMERICAN PEOPLE TO INTERFERE URGENTLY IN SUPPORT OF OUR INDEPENDENCE AND HELP MAKING THE NEGOTIATIONS MORE IN KEEPING WITH THE PRINCIPLES OF THE ATLANTIC AND SAN FRANCISCO CHARTERS

RESPECTFULLY

HOCHIMINH

EXHIBIT 2

Treaty between Ho Chi Minh and France

[N] ON MARCH 6, 1946, a French-DRV accord was reached in the following terms:

1. The French Government recognizes the Vietnamese Republic as a Free State having its own Government, its own Parliament, its own Army and its own Finances, forming part of the Indochinese Federation and of the French Union. In that which concerns the reuniting of the three "Anna mite Regions" [Cochin China, Annam, Tonkin] the French Government pledges itself to ratify the decisions taken by the populations consulted by referendum.

2. The Vietnamese Government declares itself ready to welcome amicably the French Army when, conforming to international agreements, it relieves the Chinese Troops. A Supplementary Accord, attached to the present Preliminary Agreement, will establish the means by which the relief operations will be carried out.

3. The stipulations formulated above will immediately enter into force. Immediately after the exchange of signatures, each of the High Contracting Parties will take all measures necessary to stop hostilities in the field, to maintain the troops in their respective positions, and to create the favorable atmosphere necessary to the immediate opening of friendly and sincere negotiations. These negotiations will deal particularly with:

    a. diplomatic relations of Viet-nam with Foreign States

b.   the future law of Indochina
c.   French interests, economic and cultural, in Viet-nam.

Hanoi, Saigon or Paris may be chosen as the seat of the conference.

DONE AT HANOI, the 6th of March 1946
Signed: Sainteny
Signed: Ho Chi Minh and Vu Hong Khanh

EXHIBIT 3

President Truman's Inaugural Address

By Harry S. Truman
January 20, 1949

Mr. Vice President, Mr. Chief Justice, and fellow citizens, I accept with humility the honor which the American people have conferred upon me. I accept it with a deep resolve to do all that I can for the welfare of this Nation and for the peace of the world.

In performing the duties of my office, I need the help and prayers of every one of you. I ask for your encouragement and your support. The tasks we face are difficult, and we can accomplish them only if we work together.

Each period of our national history has had its special challenges. Those that confront us now are as momentous as any in the past. Today marks the beginning not only of a new administration, but of a period that will be eventful, perhaps decisive, for us and for the world.

It may be our lot to experience, and in large measure to bring about, a major turning point in the long history of the human race. The first half of this century has been marked by unprecedented and brutal attacks on the rights of man, and by the two most frightful wars in history. The supreme need of our time is for men to learn to live together in peace and harmony.

The peoples of the earth face the future with grave uncertainty, composed almost equally of great hopes and great fears. In this time of doubt, they look to the United States as never before for good will, strength, and wise leadership.

It is fitting, therefore, that we take this occasion to proclaim to the world the essential principles of the faith by which we live, and to declare our aims to all peoples.

The American people stand firm in the faith which has inspired this Nation from the beginning. We believe that all men have a right to equal justice under law and equal opportunity to share in the common good. We believe that all men have the right to freedom of thought and expression. We believe that all men are created equal because they are created in the image of God. From this faith we will not be moved.

The American people desire, and are determined to work for, a world in which all nations and all peoples are free to govern themselves as they see fit, and to achieve a decent and satisfying life. Above all else, our people desire, and are determined to work for, peace on earth—a just and lasting peace—based on genuine agreement freely arrived at by equals.

In the pursuit of these aims, the United States and other like-minded nations find themselves directly opposed by a regime with contrary aims and a totally different concept of life.

That regime adheres to a false philosophy which purports to offer freedom, security, and greater opportunity to mankind. Misled by this philosophy, many peoples have sacrificed their liberties only to learn to their sorrow that deceit and mockery, poverty and tyranny, are their reward.

That false philosophy is communism.

Communism is based on the belief that man is so weak and inadequate that he is unable to govern himself, and therefore requires the rule of strong masters.

Democracy is based on the conviction that man has the moral and intellectual capacity, as well as the inalienable right, to govern himself with reason and justice.

Communism subjects the individual to arrest without lawful cause, punishment without trial, and forced labor as the chattel of the state. It decrees what information he shall receive, what art he shall produce, what leaders he shall follow, and what thoughts he shall think.

Democracy maintains that government is established for the benefit of the individual and is charged with the responsibility of protecting the rights of the individual and his freedom in the exercise of his abilities.

Communism maintains that social wrongs can be corrected only by violence. Democracy has proved that social justice can be achieved through peaceful change.

Communism holds that the world is so deeply divided into opposing classes that war is inevitable. Democracy holds that free nations can settle differences justly and maintain lasting peace.

These differences between communism and democracy do not concern the United States alone. People everywhere are coming to realize that what is involved is material well-being, human dignity, and the right to believe in and worship God.

I state these differences, not to draw issues of belief as such, but because the actions resulting from the Communist philosophy are a threat to the efforts of free nations to bring about world recovery and lasting peace.

Since the end of hostilities, the United States has invested its substance and its energy in a great constructive effort to restore peace, stability, and freedom to the world.

We have sought no territory and we have imposed our will on none. We have asked for no privileges we would not extend to others.

We have constantly and vigorously supported the United Nations and related agencies as a means of applying democratic principles to international relations. We have consistently advocated and relied upon peaceful settlement of disputes among nations.

We have made every effort to secure agreement on effective international control of our most powerful weapon, and we have worked steadily for the limitation and control of all armaments. We have encouraged, by precept and example, the expansion of world trade on a sound and fair basis.

Almost a year ago, in company with 16 free nations of Europe, we launched the greatest cooperative economic program in history. The purpose of that unprecedented effort is to invigorate and strengthen democracy in Europe, so that the free people of that continent can resume their rightful place in the forefront of civilization and can contribute once more to the security and welfare of the world.

Our efforts have brought new hope to all mankind. We have beaten back despair and defeatism. We have saved a number of countries from losing their liberty. Hundreds of millions of people all over the world now agree with us, that we need not have war—that we can have peace.

The initiative is ours.

We are moving on with other nations to build an even stronger structure of international order and justice. We shall have as our partner's countries which, no longer solely concerned with the problem of national survival, are now working to improve the standards of living of all their people. We are ready to undertake new projects to strengthen the free world. In the coming years, our program for peace and freedom will emphasize four major courses of action.

First, we will continue to give unfaltering support to the United Nations and related agencies, and we will continue to search for ways to strengthen their authority and increase their effectiveness. We believe that the United Nations will be strengthened by the new nations which are being formed in lands now advancing toward self-government under democratic principles.

Second, we will continue our programs for world economic recovery. This means, first of all, that we must keep our full weight behind the European recovery program. We are confident of the success of this major venture in world recovery. We believe that our partners in this effort will achieve the status of self-supporting nations once again.

In addition, we must carry out our plans for reducing the barriers to world trade and increasing its volume. Economic recovery and peace itself depend on increased world trade.

Third, we will strengthen freedom-loving nations against the dangers of aggression. We are now working out with a number of countries a joint agreement designed to strengthen the security of the North Atlantic area. Such an agreement would take the form of a collective defense arrangement within the terms of the United Nations Charter.

We have already established such a defense pact for the Western Hemisphere by the treaty of Rio de Janeiro. The primary purpose of these agreements is to provide unmistakable proof of the joint determination of the free countries to resist armed attack from any quarter. Each country participating in these arrangements must contribute all it can to the common defense.

If we can make it sufficiently clear, in advance, that any armed attack affecting our national security would be met with overwhelming force, the armed attack might never occur.

I hope soon to send to the Senate a treaty respecting the North Atlantic security plan.

In addition, we will provide military advice and equipment to free nations which will cooperate with us in the maintenance of peace and security.

Fourth, we must embark on a bold new program for making the benefits of our scientific advances and industrial progress available for the improvement and growth of underdeveloped areas.

More than half the people of the world are living in conditions approaching misery. Their food is inadequate. They are victims of disease. Their economic life is primitive and stagnant. Their poverty is a handicap and a threat both to them and to more prosperous areas.

For the first time in history, humanity possesses the knowledge and the skill to relieve the suffering of these people.

The United States is pre-eminent among nations in the development of industrial and scientific techniques. The material resources which we can afford to use for the assistance of other peoples are limited. But our imponderable resources in technical knowledge are constantly growing and are inexhaustible.

I believe that we should make available to peace-loving peoples the benefits of our store of technical knowledge in order to help them realize their aspirations for a better life. And, in cooperation with other nations, we should foster capital investment in areas needing development.

Our aim should be to help the free peoples of the world, through their own efforts, to produce more food, more clothing, more materials for housing, and more mechanical power to lighten their burdens.

We invite other countries to pool their technological resources in this undertaking. Their contributions will be warmly welcomed. This should be a cooperative enterprise in which all nations work together through the United Nations and its specialized agencies wherever practicable. It must be a worldwide effort for the achievement of peace, plenty, and freedom.

With the cooperation of business, private capital, agriculture, and labor in this country, this program can greatly increase the industrial activity in other nations and can raise substantially their standards of living.

Such new economic developments must be devised and controlled to benefit the peoples of the areas in which they are established. Guarantees to the investor must be balanced by guarantees in the interest of the people whose resources and whose labor go into these developments.

The old imperialism—exploitation for foreign profit—has no place in our plans. What we envisage is a program of development based on the concepts of democratic fair-dealing.

All countries, including our own, will greatly benefit from a constructive program for the better use of the world's human and natural resources. Experience shows that our commerce with other countries expands as they progress industrially and economically.

Greater production is the key to prosperity and peace. And the key to greater production is a wider and more vigorous application of modern scientific and technical knowledge.

Only by helping the least fortunate of its members to help themselves can the human family achieve the decent, satisfying life that is the right of all people.

Democracy alone can supply the vitalizing force to stir the peoples of the world into triumphant action, not only against their human oppressors, but also against their ancient enemies—hunger, misery, and despair.

On the basis of these four major courses of action we hope to help create the conditions that will lead eventually to personal freedom and happiness for all mankind.

If we are to be successful in carrying out these policies, it is clear that we must have continued prosperity in this country, and we must keep ourselves strong.

Slowly but surely, we are weaving a world fabric of international security and growing prosperity.

We are aided by all who wish to live in freedom from fear—even by those who live today in fear under their own governments.

We are aided by all who want relief from the lies of propaganda—who desire truth and sincerity.

We are aided by all who desire self-government and a voice in deciding their own affairs.

We are aided by all who long for economic security—for the security and abundance that men in free societies can enjoy.

We are aided by all who desire freedom of speech, freedom of religion, and freedom to live their own lives for useful ends.

Our allies are the millions who hunger and thirst after righteousness. In due time, as our stability becomes manifest, as more and more nations come to know the benefits of democracy and to participate in growing abundance, I believe that those countries which now oppose us will abandon their delusions and join with the free nations of the world in a just settlement of international differences.

Events have brought our American democracy to new influence and new responsibilities. They will test our courage, our devotion to duty, and our concept of liberty.

But I say to all men, what we have achieved in liberty, we will surpass in greater liberty. Steadfast in our faith in the Almighty, we will advance toward a world where man's freedom is secure. To that end we will devote our strength, our resources, and our firmness of resolve. With God's help, the future of mankind will be assured in a world of justice, harmony, and peace.

EXHIBIT 3A

Appendix I
MUTUAL DEFENSE ASSISTANCE IN INDOCHINA
AGREEMENT SIGNED AT SAIGON
DECEMBER 23, 1950; ENTERED INTO
FORCE DECEMBER 23, 1950

THE GOVERNMENT OF THE UNITED States of America, and the Governments of Cambodia, France, Laos and Vietnam:

— Recognizing the common interest of the free peoples of the world in the maintenance of the independence, peace, and security of nations devoted to the principles of freedom.

— Considering that the Governments of Cambodia, France, Laos and Vietnam are engaged in a cooperative effort toward these goals as members of the French Union.

— Considering that, in furtherance of those common principles, the Government of the United States of America has enacted Public Law 329, 81st Congress, which permits the United States of America to furnish military assistance to certain other nations dedicated to those principles:

— Desiring to set forth the understandings which shall govern the furnishings of military assistance by the United States of America under Public Law 329, 81st Congress, to the forces of the Associated States and the French Union in Indochina,

Have agreed as follows:

Article I

Any assistance furnished under this agreement will be governed by the following basic considerations:

1. All equipment, material and services, made available by the United States of America under the terms of this agreement to the States signatory to it, in accordance with their needs, will be furnished under such provisions, and subject to such terms, conditions and termination provisions of Public Law 329, 81st Congress, as amended, as affect the furnishing of such assistance, and such other applicable United States of America law as may hereafter come into effect.

2. In accordance with the principles of mutual aid, each Government receiving equipment, material, or services from the Government of the United States of America under this agreement agrees to facilitate the production, transport, within its means, and the transfer to the Government of the United States of America for such period of time, in such quantities and upon such terms and conditions of purchase as may be agreed upon, of raw and semi-processed materials required by the United States of America as a result of deficiencies or potential deficiencies in its own resources, and which may be available in their territories.

The conditions governing such transfers will be the object of particular agreements and will take into account the needs of these states and the normal requirements of the French Union with respect to internal consumption and commercial export of such materials.

Article II

The signatory powers, recognizing that the effectiveness of military assistance will be enhanced if maximum use is made of existing facilities,

Have resolved that:

1. The Governments of Cambodia, France, Laos and Vietnam shall cooperate to assure the efficient reception, distribution and maintenance of such equipment and materials as are furnished by the United States of America for use in Indochina.
2. Each Government receiving aid from the United States of America shall, unless otherwise agreed to by the Government of the United States of America, retain title to all such equipment, material or services so transferred.
3. Each Government receiving aid from the United States of America shall also retain full possession and control of the equipment, material or services to which they have such title, taking into account the accords and agreements which now exist between Cambodia, France, Laos and Vietnam.
4. With respect to aid received from the United States of America, each State shall designate a member or representative of the High Military Committee and authorize such person to receive from the Government of the United States of America the title to the materials received. Each State shall, as the need exists, provide for such extensions of that authority as may be necessary to insure the most efficient reception, distribution and maintenance of such equipment and materials as are furnished by the United States of America.
5. For aid received from the United States of America destined exclusively for forces of the French Union in Indochina, the Commander in Chief of the French Forces in the Far East or his delegates shall be the person authorized to accept title.

Article III

Taking into consideration the military conventions concluded between France and the Governments of Cambodia, Laos, and Vietnam, each Government receiving grants of equipment, material or services from the Government of the United States of America pursuant to this agreement,

Undertakes:

1. To use effectively such assistance only within the framework of the mutual defense of Indochina.
2. To take appropriate measures consistent with security to keep the public informed of operations under this agreement.
3. To take security measures which will be agreed upon with the United States of America in each case to prevent the disclosure or compromise of classified articles, services, or information received under this agreement.
4. To take appropriate action to prevent the illegal transportation into, out of, and within the area of Indochina, including the territorial waters thereof, of any equipment or materials substitutable for, or of similar category to, those being supplied by the United States of America under this agreement.
5. To provide local currency for such administrative and operating expenses of the Government of the United States of America as may arise in Indochina in connection with this agreement, taking into account ability to provide such currency. An Annex to this agreement will be agreed between the United States of America on one hand the States of Cambodia, France, Laos and Vietnam on the other, with a view to making arrangements for the provision of local currency within the limits of an overall sum to be fixed by common agreement.
6. To enter into any necessary arrangements of details with the Government of the United States of America with

respect to the patents, the use of local facilities, and all other matters relating to operations in connection with furnishings and delivering of materials in accordance with this agreement.

7. To consult with the Government of the United States of America, from time to time, to establish means for the most practicable technical utilization of the assistance furnished pursuant to this agreement.

Article IV

To facilitate operations under this agreement, each Government agrees:

1. To grant, except when otherwise agreed, duty-free treatment and exemption from taxation upon importation, exportation, or movement within Indochina, of products, material or equipment furnished by the United States in connection with this agreement.

2. To receive within its territory such personnel of the United States of America as may be required for the purposes of this agreement and to extend to such personnel facilities freely and fully to carry out their assigned responsibilities, including observation of the progress and the technical use made of the assistance granted. Such personnel will in their relations to the Government of the country to which they are assigned, operate as part of the diplomatic mission under the direction and control of the Chief of such mission of the Government which they are serving.

Article V

1. This agreement shall enter into force upon signature. Any party may withdraw from this agreement by giving written notice to all other parties three months in advance.

2. The Annexes to this agreement form an integral part hereof.

3. This agreement shall be registered with the Secretary General of the United Nations in compliance with the provisions of Article 102 of the Charter of the United Nations.

In witness thereof the respective representatives, duly authorized for this purpose, have signed the present agreement.

Done in quintuplicate in the English, Cambodian, French and Vietnamese languages at Saigon on this 23 day of December 1950.

All texts will be authentic, but in case of divergence, the English and French shall prevail.

DONALD R. HEATH

HUU   VORABONG

V. SAI   G. de LATTRE

(Seal)

Annex A

In implementation of paragraph 5 of Article III of the agreement for Mutual Defense Assistance in Indochina, the Governments of Cambodia, France, Laos and Vietnam will deposit piasters at such times as requested in accounts designated by the diplomatic missions of the United States at Phnom Penh, Vientiane, and Saigon, not to exceed in total 6,142,230$ piasters for the use of these missions on behalf of the Government of the United States of America for administrative expenses in the States of Cambodia, Laos and Vietnam in connection with carrying out that agreement for the period ending June 30, 1951.

The piasters will be furnished by each of the Governments of Cambodia, France, Laos and Vietnam in accordance with percentages agreed upon among the four Governments, taking into consideration the amount of military aid received by each Government. This Annex will be renewed with appropriate modifications for the fiscal year ending June 30, 1952 and similarly thereafter before the end of each current fiscal year, for the duration of the agreement.

Annex B

In recognition of the fact that personnel who are nationals of one country, including personnel temporarily assigned, will in their relations with the Government of the country to which they are assigned, operate as part of the Diplomatic Mission of the Government of their country under the direction and control of the Chief of that Mission, it is understood, in connection with Article IV, paragraph 2, of the Mutual Defense Assistance Agreement, that the status of such personnel, considered as part of the Diplomatic Mission of such other Government, will be the same as the status of personnel of corresponding rank of that Diplomatic Mission who are nationals of that country.

The personnel will be divided into 3 categories:

(a) Upon appropriate notification of the other, full diplomatic status will be granted to the senior military member and the senior Army, Navy and Air Force officer assigned thereto, and to their respective immediate deputies.

(b) The second category of personnel will enjoy privileges and immunities conferred by international custom, as recognized by each Government, to certain categories of personnel of the Diplomatic Mission of the other, such as the immunity from civil and criminal jurisdiction of the host country, immunity of official papers from search and seizure, right of free egress, exemption from customs duties or similar taxes or restrictions in respect of personally owned property imported into the host country by such personnel for their personal use and consumption, without prejudice to the existing regulations on foreign exchange, exemption from internal taxation by the host country upon salaries of such personnel. Privileges and courtesies incident to diplomatic status such as diplomatic automobile license plates, inclusion on the "Diplomatic List", and social courtesies may be waived by both Governments for this category of personnel.

(c)   The third category of personnel will receive the same status as the clerical personnel of the Diplomatic Mission.

It is understood among the five Governments that the number of personnel in the three categories above will be kept as low as possible.

Annex C

All the countries which are signatory to the agreement for Mutual Defense Assistance in Indochina agree that the benefits of any modification or ameliorations of this agreement in favor of any one of the contracting parties will be extended to all the countries party to the agreement.

Ch. 1, Directive Number 27-1, HQ MACV   30 September 1965

SOP FOR LITIGATION ACTIONS UNDER THE PENTALATERAL AGREEMENT.

I.   General.

A.   Background.

During 1949 France approved self-government for Vietnam within the French Union. On 23 December 1950 the newly created self-governing nation entered into a multi-lateral mutual defense assistance agreement with the US, France, Cambodia, and Laos. This agreement is known as the Penta lateral Agreement. The agreement is still in effect and is so regarded by both the US and the Republic of Vietnam.

B.   Grant of Immunity from Jurisdiction.

Under Article 4 and Annex B of the Agreement, immunity from criminal and civil jurisdiction is granted to US military personnel in Vietnam along with certain categories of civilians (Para 10, MACV Directive 27-1).

C. *Responsibility of US Personnel.*

This grant of immunity, however, imposes upon US personnel the responsibility, under appropriate US instructions, of complying with Vietnamese law and law enforcement authorities insofar as it is consistent with US law and US military requirements to do so.

II. *Procedures.*
A. *Apprehension of US Military Personnel by Vietnamese Authorities.*
  1. When an American serviceman is apprehended by Vietnamese authorities, he will comply and cooperate with them (Para 11, MACV Directive 27-1).
  2. If the serviceman is requested to accompany the Vietnamese law enforcement authorities to their booking station, he will comply with their requests. The serviceman will inform US military police or his unit CO as soon as possible.
  3. If the serviceman has a military obligation requiring him to proceed elsewhere, he will attempt to persuade the law enforcement officials to allow him to proceed with his mission, after fully identifying himself. If the situation permits, he will attempt to telephone the US military police for assistance. If the serviceman is required by the law enforcement officials to remain at the scene or accompany the policeman, he will do so if he is unable to persuade the police to allow him to proceed. In no case will he resist the Vietnamese police by using force. If he is allowed to leave, or call, he will notify his CO or the US MI's as soon as practicable. In situations such as this, the serviceman must use mature judgment, weighing the importance of his mission as compared with creating an incident which might be detrimental to US-Vietnamese relations.

Annex A to MACV Directive 27-1, Dated 16 April 1965

EXHIBIT 4

ANZUS Treaty

DEPARTMENT OF EXTERNAL AFFAIRS CANBERRA
Security Treaty between Australia, New Zealand
and the United States of America [ANZUS]
(San Francisco, 1 September 1951)
Entry into force generally: 29 April 1952
AUSTRALIAN TREATY SERIES
1952 No. 2
Australian Government Publishing Service
Canberra
(c) Commonwealth of Australia 1997

SECURITY TREATY BETWEEN AUSTRALIA, NEW ZEALAND, AND THE UNITED STATES OF AMERICA

THE PARTIES TO THIS TREATY, REAFFIRMING their faith in the purposes and principles of the Charter of the United Nations and their desire to live in peace with all peoples and all Governments, and desiring to strengthen the fabric of peace in the Pacific Area,

NOTING that the United States already has arrangements pursuant to which its armed forces are stationed in the Philippines, and has armed forces and administrative responsibilities in the Ryukyus, and upon the coming into force of the Japanese Peace Treaty may also station armed forces in and about Japan to assist in the preservation of peace and security in the Japan Area,

RECOGNIZING that Australia and New Zealand as members of the British Commonwealth of Nations have military obligations outside as well as within the Pacific Area,

DESIRING to declare publicly and formally their sense of unity, so that no potential aggressor could be under the illusion that any of them stand alone in the Pacific Area, and

DESIRING further to coordinate their efforts for collective defense for the preservation of peace and security pending the development of a more comprehensive system of regional security in the Pacific Area,

THEREFORE, DECLARE AND AGREE as follows:

Article I

The Parties undertake, as set forth in the Charter of the United Nations, to settle any international disputes in which they may be involved by peaceful means in such a manner that international peace and security and justice are not endangered and to refrain in their international relations from the threat or use of force in any manner inconsistent with the purposes of the United Nations.

Article II

In order more effectively to achieve the objective of this Treaty the Parties separately and jointly by means of continuous and effective self-help and mutual aid will maintain and develop their individual and collective capacity to resist armed attack.

Article III

The Parties will consult together whenever in the opinion of any of them the territorial integrity, political independence or security of any of the Parties is threatened in the Pacific.

Article IV

Each Party recognizes that an armed attack in the Pacific Area on any of the Parties would be dangerous to its own peace and safety and declares that it would act to meet the common danger in accordance with its constitutional processes.

Any such armed attack and all measures taken as a result thereof shall be immediately reported to the Security Council of the United Nations. Such measures shall be terminated when the Security Council has taken the measures necessary to restore and maintain international peace and security.

Article V

For the purpose of Article IV, an armed attack on any of the Parties is deemed to include an armed attack on the metropolitan territory of any of the Parties, or on the island territories under its jurisdiction in the Pacific or on its armed forces, public vessels or aircraft in the Pacific.

Article VI

This Treaty does not affect and shall not be interpreted as affecting in any way the rights and obligations of the Parties under the Charter of the United Nations or the responsibility of the United Nations for the maintenance of international peace and security.

Article VII

The Parties hereby establish a Council, consisting of their Foreign Ministers or their Deputies, to consider matters concerning the implementation of this Treaty. The Council should be so organized as to be able to meet at any time.

Article VIII

Pending the development of a more comprehensive system of regional security in the Pacific Area and the development by the United Nations of more effective means to maintain international peace and security, the Council, established by Article VII, is authorized to maintain a consultative relationship with States, Regional Organizations, Associations of States or other authorities in the Pacific Area in a position to further the purposes of this Treaty and to contribute to the security of that Area.

Article IX

This Treaty shall be ratified by the Parties in accordance with their respective constitutional processes. The instruments of ratification shall be deposited as soon as possible with the Government of Australia, which will notify each of the other signatories of such deposit. The Treaty shall enter into force as soon as the ratifications of the signatories have been deposited.[1]

Article X

This Treaty shall remain in force indefinitely. Any Party may cease to be a member of the Council established by Article VII one year after notice has been given to the Government of Australia, which will inform the Governments of the other Parties of the deposit of such notice.

Article XI

This Treaty in the English language shall be deposited in the archives of the Government of Australia. Duly certified copies thereof will be transmitted by that Government to the Governments of each of the other signatories.

IN WITNESS WHEREOF the undersigned
Plenipotentiaries have signed this Treaty.

DONE at the city of San Francisco this
first day of September 1951.

FOR AUSTRALIA:

[Signed:]

PERCY C SPENDER
FOR NEW ZEALAND:

[Signed:]

C A BERENDSEN
FOR THE UNITED STATES OF AMERICA:

[Signed:]

DEAN ACHESON
JOHN FOSTER DULLES
ALEXANDER WILEY
JOHN J SPARKMAN

[1] Instruments of ratification were deposited for Australia, New Zealand and the United States of America 29 April 1952, on which date the Treaty entered into force.

EXHIBIT 5

Avalon Project: Prime Minister Diem's Request for Assistance

The Avalon Project at Yale Law School
Indochina—Assistance to Refugees from North Viet-Nam: Note from the American Embassy at Saigon to the Vietnamese Foreign Ministry, August 8, 1954(1)

ON AUGUST 6 THE U.S. Government received from the Government of Viet-Nam a request that the United States provide assistance in moving over 100,000 refugees from North Viet-Nam, the area which is being turned over to the Viet Minh, to South Viet-Nam areas under control of the anti-Communist government of Viet-Nam. The United States on August 8 replied as follows [Note in Department of State Bulletin]:

The United States Government desires to extend to the Government of Viet-Nam all reasonable assistance to evacuate from areas defined in the cease-fire agreement its nationals who understandably are unwilling to face the grim certainties of life under the Communists. The United States is well aware that mere removal does not solve the problem for such people or for the Government of Viet-Nam. The United States is also prepared to provide as far as possible material help needed to enable refugees from Viet Minh domination to resume existence under their chosen government with maximum opportunity to add to the strength of that government through their own efforts.

The American Embassy will continue close cooperation with the Government of Viet-Nam to ensure that United States assistance is made effective in meeting the needs of the Government of Viet-

Nam and its people. The United States will expect the maximum cooperation of the Government of Viet-Nam in working to this mutual end.

(1) Department of State Bulletin, Aug. 16, 1954, p. 241, see also statement by Harold Stassen, Director of Foreign Operations Administration (ibid., Aug. 23, 1954, pp. 265-266) and White House statement of Aug. 22, 1954 (infra).

Exhibit 5A

Eisenhower's Letter of Support to Ngo Dinh Diem, October 23, 1954

Dear Mr. President:

I HAVE BEEN FOLLOWING WITH great interest the course of developments in Viet-Nam, particularly since the conclusion of the conference at Geneva. The implications of the agreement concerning Viet-Nam have caused grave concern regarding the future of a country temporarily divided by an artificial military grouping, weakened by a long and exhausting war and faced with enemies without and by their subversive collaborations within.

Your recent requests for aid to assist in the formidable project of the movement of several hundred thousand loyal Vietnamese citizens away from areas which are passing under a *de facto* rule and political ideology which they abhor are being fulfilled. I am glad that the United States is able to assist in this humanitarian effort. We have been exploring ways and means to permit our aid to Viet-Nam to be more effective and to make a greater contribution to the welfare and stability of the government of Viet-Nam.

I am, accordingly, instructing the American Ambassador to Viet-Nam to examine with you in your capacity as Chief of Government, how an intelligent program of American aid given directly to your government can serve to assist Viet-Nam in its present hour of trial, provided that your Government is prepared to give assurances as to the standards of performance it would be able to maintain in the event such aid were supplied.

The purpose of this offer is to assist the Government of Viet-Nam in developing and maintaining a strong, viable state, capable of resisting attempted subversion or aggression through military means.

The Government of the United States expects that this aid will be met by performance on the part of the Government of Viet-Nam in undertaking needed reforms. It hopes that such aid, combined with your own continuing efforts, will contribute effectively toward an independent Viet-Nam endowed with a strong government. Such a government would, I hope, six I be so responsive to the nationalist aspirations of its people, so enlightened in purpose and effective in performance, that it will be respected both at home and abroad and discourage any who might wish to impose a foreign ideology on your free people.

Sincerely,

Dwight D. Eisenhower

Source: *Department of State Bulletin*. November 15, 1954, pp.735–736

EXHIBIT 6

AGREEMENT ON THE CESSATION OF HOSTILITIES IN VIET-NAM, JULY 20, 1954

(The Genera Agreements theoretically ended the war between French Union forces and the Vietminh in Laos, Cambodia, and Vietnam. These states were to become fully independent countries, with the last-named partitioned near the 17th parallel into two states pending reunification through "free elections" to be held by July 20, 1956. The United States and Vietnam are not signatories to these agreements.)

CHAPTER I-PROVISIONAL MILITARY DEMARCATION LINE AND DEMILITARIZED ZONE

Article 1

A PROVISIONAL MILITARY DEMARCATION LINE shall be fixed, on either side of which the forces of the two parties shall be regrouped after their withdrawal, the forces of the People's Army of Viet-Nam to the north of the line and the forces of the French Union to the south.

The provisional military demarcation line is fixed as shown on the map attached (omitted).

It is also agreed that a demilitarized zone shall be established on either side of the demarcation line, to a width of not more than 5 kms. from it, to act. as a buffer zone and avoid any incidents which might result in the resumption of hostilities.

Article 2

The period within which the movement of all the forces of either party into its regrouping zone on either side of the provisional military demarcation line shall be completed shall not exceed three hundred (300) days from the date of the present Agreement's entry into force.

Article 3

When the provisional military demarcation line coincides with a waterway, the waters of such waterway shall be open to civil navigation by both parties wherever one bank is controlled by one party and the other bank by the other party. The joint Commission shall establish rules of navigation for the stretch of waterway in question. The merchant shipping and other civilian craft of each party shall have unrestricted access to the land under its military control.

Article 4

The provisional military demarcation line between the two final regrouping zones is extended into the territorial waters by a line perpendicular to the general line of the coast.

All coastal islands north of this boundary shall be evacuated by the armed forces of the French union, and all islands south of it shall he evacuated by the forces of the People's Army of Viet-Nam.

Article 5

To avoid any incidents which might result in the resumption of hostilities, all military forces, supplies and equipment shall be withdrawn from the demilitarized zone within twenty-five (25) days of the present Agreement's entry into force.

Article 6

No person, military or civilian, shall be permitted to cross the provisional military demarcation line unless specifically authorized to do so by the Joint Commission.

Article 7

No person, military or civilian, shall be permitted to enter the demilitarized zone except persons concerned with the conduct of civil administration and relief and persons specifically authorized to enter by the Joint Commission.

Article 8

Civil administration and relief in the demilitarized zone on either side of the provisional military demarcation line shall be the responsibility of the Commanders-in-Chief of the two parties in their respective zones. The number of persons, military or civilian, from each side who are permitted to enter the demilitarized zone for the conduct of civil administration and relief shall be determined by the respective Commanders, but in no case shall the total number authorized by either side exceed at any one time a figure to be determined by the Trung Gia Military Commission or by the Joint Commission. The number of civil police and the arms to be carried by them shall be determined by the Joint Commission. No one else shall carry arms unless specifically authorized to do so by the joint Commission.

Article 9

Nothing contained in this chapter shall be construed as limiting the complete freedom of movement, into, out of or within the demilitarized zone of the Joint Commission, its joint groups, the International Commission to be set up as indicated below, its inspection teams and any other persons, supplies or equipment specifically authorized to enter the demilitarized zone by the Joint Commission.

Freedom of movement shall be permitted across the territory under the military control of either side over any road or waterway which has to be taken between points within the demilitarized zone when such points are not connected by roads or waterways lying completely within the demilitarized zone.

CHAPTER II-PRINCIPLES AND PROCEDURE GOVERNING IMPLEMENTATION OF THE PRESENT AGREEMENT

Article 10

The Commanders of the Forces on each side, on the one side the Commander-in-Chief of the French Union forces in Indo-China and on the other side the Commander-in-Chief of the People's Army of Viet-Nam, shall order and enforce the complete cessation of all hostilities in Viet-Nam by all armed forces under their control, including all units and personnel of the ground, naval and air forces.

Article 11

In accordance with the principle of a simultaneous cease-fire throughout Indochina, the cessation of hostilities shall be simultaneous throughout all parts of Viet-Nam, in all areas of hostilities and for all the forces of the two parties.

Taking into account the time effectively required to transmit the cease-fire order down to the lowest echelons of the combatant forces on both sides, the two parties are agreed that the cease-fire shall take effect completely and simultaneously for the different sectors of the country as follows:

Northern Viet-Nam at 8:00 a. m. (local time) on 27 July 1954

Central Viet-Nam at 8:00 a. m. (local time) on 1 August 1954

Southern Viet-Nam at 8:00 a. m. (local time) on 11 August 1954

It is agreed that Pekin mean time shall be taken as local time.

From such time as the cease-fire becomes effective in Northern Viet-Nam, both parties undertake not to engage in any large-scale offensive action in any part of the Indo-Chinese theatre of operations and not to commit the air forces based on Northern Viet-Nam outside that sector. The two parties also undertake to inform each other of their plans for movement from one regrouping zone to another within twenty-five (05) days of the present Agreement's entry into force.

Article 12

All the operations and movements entailed in the cessation of hostilities and regrouping must proceed in a safe and orderly fashion

(a) Within a certain number of days after the cease-fire Agreement shall have become effective, the number to be determined on the spot by the Trung Gia Military Commission, each party shall be responsible for removing and neutralizing mines (including river- and sea-mines), booby traps, explosives and any other dangerous substances placed by it. In the event of its being impossible to complete the work of removal and neutralization in time, the party concerned shall mark the spot by placing visible signs there. All demolitions, mine fields, wire entanglements and other hazards to the free movement of the personnel of the Joint Commission and its joint groups, known to be present after the withdrawal of the military forces, shall be reported to the Joint Commission by the Commanders of the opposing forces;

(b) From the time of the cease-fire until regrouping is completed on either side of the demarcation line:

(1) The forces of either party shall be provisionally withdrawn from the provisional assembly areas assigned to the other party.

Where (2) When one party's forces withdraw by a route (road, rail, waterway, sea route) which passes through the territory of the other party (see Article 24), the latter party's forces must provisionally withdraw three kilometers on each side of such route, but in such a manner as to avoid interfering with the movements of the civil population.

Article 13

From the time of the cease-fire until the completion of the movements from one regrouping zone into the other, civil and military transport aircraft shall follow air-corridors between the provisional assembly areas assigned to the French Union forces north of the demarcation line on the one hand and the Laotian frontier and the regrouping zone assigned to the French Union forces on the other hand.

The position of the air-corridors, their width, the safety route for single-engine military aircraft transferred to the south and the search and rescue procedure for aircraft in distress shall he determined on the spot by the Trung Gia Military Commission.

Article 14

Political and administrative measures in the two regrouping zones, on either side of the provisional military demarcation line:

(a) Pending the general elections which will bring about the unification of Viet-Nam, the conduct of civil administration in each regrouping zone shall be in the hands of the party whose forces are to be regrouped there in virtue of the present Agreement

(b) Any territory controlled by one party which is transferred to the other party by the regrouping plan shall continue to be administered by the former party until such date as all the troops who are to be transferred have completely left that territory so as to free the zone assigned to the party in question. From then on, such territory shall be regarded as transferred to the other party, who shall assume responsibility for it.

Steps shall be taken to ensure that there is no break in the transfer of responsibilities. For this purpose, adequate notices shall be given by the withdrawing party to the other party, which shall make the necessary arrangements, in particular by sending administrative and police detachments to prepare for the assumption of administrative responsibility. The length of such notice shall he determined by the Trung Gia Military Commission. The transfer shall he effected in successive stages for the various territorial sectors.

The transfer of the civil administration of Hanoi and Haiphong to the authorities of the Democratic Republic of Viet-Nam shall be completed within the respective time-limits laid down in Article 15 for military movements.

(c) Each party undertakes to refrain from any reprisals or discrimination against persons or organizations on account of their activities during the hostilities and to guarantee their democratic liberties.

(d) From the date of entry into force of the present agreement until the movement of troops is completed, any civilians residing in a district controlled by one party who wish to go and live in the zone assigned to the other party shall be permitted and helped to do so by the authorities in that district.

Article 16

The disengagement of the combatants, and the withdrawals and transfers of military forces, equipment and supplies shall take place in accordance with the following principles:

(a) The withdrawals and transfers of the military forces equipment and supplies of the two parties shall be completed within three hundred (300) days, as laid down in Article 2 of the present Agreement.

(b) Within either territory successive withdrawals shall be made by sectors, portions of sectors or provinces. Transfers from one regrouping zone to another shall be made in successive monthly installments proportionate to the number of troops to be transferred.

(c) The two parties shall undertake to carry out all troop withdrawals and transfers in accordance with the aims of the present Agreement, shall permit no hostile act and shall take no step whatsoever which might hamper such withdrawals and transfers. They shall assist one another as far as this is possible

(d) The two parties shall permit no destruction or sabotage of any public property and no injury to the life and property of the civil population. They shall permit no interference in local civil administration.

(e) The Joint Commission and the International Commission shall ensure that steps are taken to safeguard the forces in the course of withdrawal and transfer:

(f) The Trung Gia Military Commission, and later the Joint Commission, shall determine by common agreement the exact procedure for the disengagement of the combatants and for troop withdrawals and transfers, on the basis of the principles mentioned above and within the framework laid down below:

    1. The disengagement of the combatants, including the concentration of the armed forces of all kinds and also each party's movements into the provisional assembly areas assigned to it and the other party's provisional withdrawal from it, shall be completed within a period not exceeding fifteen (15) days after the date when the cease-fire becomes effective.

The general delineation of the provisional assembly areas is set out in the maps annexed to the present Agreement.

In order to avoid any incidents, no troops shall be stationed less than 1,500 meters from the lines delimiting the provisional assembly areas.

During the period until the transfers are concluded, all the coastal islands west of the following lines shall be included in the Haiphong perimeter:

— meridian of the southern point of Kebao Island
— northern coast of the Ile Rousse (excluding the island), extended as far as the meridian of Campha-Mines
— meridian of Champha-Mines.

2. The withdrawals and transfers shall be affected in the following order and within the following periods (from the date of the entry into force of the present Agreement)

Forces of the French Union........ Days
Hanoi perimeter....... 80
Haiduong perimeter....... 100
Haipbong perimeter....... 300
Forces of the People's Army of Viet-Nam.......Days
Ham Tan and Xuyeninec provisional assembly area....... 80
Central Viet-Nam provisional assembly area-first instalment..... 80
Plaine des Jones provisional assembly area....... 100
Point Camau provisional assembly area........ 200
Central Viet-Nam Provisional assembly area-last installment. 300

CHAPTER III-BAN ON INTRODUCTION OF FRESH TROOPS, MILITARY PERSONNEL, ARMS AND MUNITIONS, MILITARY BASES

Article 16

With effect from the date of entry into force of the present Agreement, the introduction into Viet-Nam of any troop reinforcements and additional military personnel is prohibited.

It is understood however, that the rotation of units and groups of personnel, the arrival in Viet-Nam of individual personnel on a temporary duty basis and the return to Viet-Nam of individual personnel after short periods of leave or temporary duty outside Viet-Nam shall be permitted under the conditions laid down below:

(a) Rotation of units (defined in paragraph (c) of this Article) and groups of personnel shall not be permitted for French Union troops stationed north of the provisional military demarcation line laid down in Article 1 of the present Agreement, during the withdrawal period provided for in Article 2.

However, under the heading of individual personnel not more than fifty (50) men, including officers, shall during any one month be permitted to enter that part of the country north of the provisional military demarcation line on a temporary duty basis or to return there after short periods of leave or temporary duty outside Viet-Nam.

(b) "Rotation" is defined as the replacement of units or groups of personnel by other units of the same echelon or by personnel who are arriving in Viet-Nam territory to do their overseas service there.

(c) The units rotated shall never be larger than a battalion-or the corresponding echelon for air and naval forces.

(d) Rotation shall be conducted on a man-for-man basis, provided, however, that in any one quarter neither party shall introduce more than fifteen thousand five hundred (15,500) members of its armed forces into Viet-Nam under the rotation policy.

(e) Rotation units (defined in paragraph (c) of this Article) and groups of personnel, and the individual personnel mentioned in this Article, shall enter and leave Viet-Nam only through the entry points enumerated in Article 20 below:

(f) Each p arty shall notify the Joint Commission and the International Commission at least two days in advance of any arrivals or departures of units, groups of personnel and individual personnel in or from Viet-Nam. Reports on the arrivals or departures of units, groups of personnel and individual personnel in or from Viet-Nam shall be submitted daily to the Joint Commission and the International Commission.

All the above-mentioned notifications and reports shall indicate the places and dates of arrival or departure and the number of persons arriving or departing.

(g) The International Commission, through its Inspection Teams, shall supervise and inspect the rotation of units and groups of personnel and the arrival and departure of individual personnel as authorized above, at the points of entry enumerated in Article 20 below.

Article 17

(a) With effect from the date of entry into force of the present Agreement, the introduction into Viet-Nam of any reinforcements in the form of all types of arms, munitions and other war material, such as combat aircraft, naval craft, pieces of ordnance jet engines and jet weapons and armored vehicles, is prohibited.

(b) It is understood, however, that war material, arms and munitions which have been destroyed, damaged worn out or used up after the cessation of hostilities may be replaced on the basis of piece-for-piece of the same type and with similar characteristics. Such replacements of war material, arms and munitions shall not be permitted for French Union troops stationed north of the provisional military demarcation line laid down in Article 1 of the present Agreement during the withdrawal period provided for in Article 2.

Naval craft may perform transport operations between the regrouping zones.

(c) The war material, arms and munitions for replacement purposes provided for in paragraph (b) of this Article, shall be introduced into Viet-Nam only through the points of entry enumerated in Article 20 below. War material, arms and munitions to be replaced shall be shipped from Viet-Nam only through the points of entry enumerated in Article 20 below.

(d) Apart from the replacements permitted within the limits laid down in paragraph of this Article, the introduction of war material, arms and munitions of all types in the form of unassembled parts for subsequent assembly is prohibited.

(e) Each party shall notify the Joint Commission and the International Commission at least two days in advance of any arrivals or departures which may take place of war material, arms and munitions of all types.

In order to justify the requests for the introduction into Viet-Nam of arms, munitions and other war material (as defined in paragraph (a) of this Article) for replacement purposes, a report concerning each incoming shipment shall be submitted to the Joint Commission and the International Commission. Such reports shall indicate the use made of the items so replaced.

(f) The International Commission, through its Inspection Teams, shall supervise and inspect the replacements permitted in the circumstances laid down in this Article, at the points of entry enumerated in Article 20 below.

Article 18

With effect from the date of entry into force of the present Agreement, the establishment of new military bases is prohibited throughout Viet-Nam territory.

Article 19

With effect from the date of entry into force of the present Agreement, no military base under the control of a foreign State may be established in the regrouping zone of either party; the two parties shall ensure that the zones assigned to them do not adhere to any military alliance and are not used for the resumption of hostilities or to further an aggressive policy.

Article 20

The points of entry into Viet-Nam for rotation personnel and replacements of material are fixed as follows:

— Zones to the north of the provisional military demarcation line: Laokay, Langson, Tien-Yen, Haiphong, Vinh, Dong-Hoi, Muong- Sen.

— Zone to the south of the provisional military demarcation line: Tourane, Quinhon, Nhatrang, Bangoi, Saigon, Cap St. Jacques, Tanchan.

CHAPTER IV-PRISONERS OF WAR AND CIVILIAN INTERNEES

Article 21

The liberation and repatriation of all prisoners of war and civilian internees detained by each of the two parties at the coming into force of the present Agreement shall be carried out under the following conditions:

(a) All prisoners of war and civilian internees of Viet-Nam, French and other nationalities captured since the beginning of hostilities in Viet-Nam during military operations or in any other circumstances of war and in any part of the territory of Viet-Nam shall be liberated within a period of

322

thirty (30) days after the date when the cease-fire becomes effective in each theatre.

(b) The term "civilian internees" is understood to mean all persons who, having in any way contributed to the political and armed struggle between the two parties, have been arrested for that reason and have been kept in detention by either party during the period of hostilities.

(c) All prisoners of war and civilian internees held by either party shall be surrendered to the appropriate authorities of the other party, who shall give them all possible assistance in proceeding to their country of origin, place of habitual residence or the zone of their choice.

CHAPTER V-MISCELLANEOUS

Article 22

The commanders of the Forces of the two parties shall ensure that persons under their respective commands who violate any of the provisions of the present Agreement are suitably punished.

Article 23

In cases in which the place of burial is known and the existence of graves has been established, the Commander of the Forces of either party shall, within a specific period after the entry into force of the Armistice Agreement, permit. the graves service personnel of the other party to enter the part of Viet-Nam territory under their military control for the purpose of finding and removing the bodies of deceased military personnel of that party, including the bodies of deceased prisoners of war. The Joint Commission shall determine the procedures and the time limit for the performance of this task. The Commanders of the Forces of the two parties shall communicate to each other all information in their possession as to the place of burial of military personnel of the other party.

Article 24

The present Agreement shall apply to all the armed forces of either party. The armed forces of each party shall respect the demilitarized zone and the territory under the military control of the other party, and shall commit no act and undertake no operation against the other party and shall not engage in blockade of any kind in Viet-Nam.

For the purposes of the present Article, the word "territory" includes territorial waters and air space.

Article 25

The Commanders of the Forces of the two parties shall afford full protection and all possible assistance and co-operation to the Joint Commission and its joint groups and to the international Commission and its inspection teams in the performance of the functions and tasks assigned to them by the present Agreement.

Article 26

The costs involved in the operations of the Joint Commission and joint groups and of the International Commission and its inspection Teams shall be shared equally between the two parties.

Article 27

The signatories of the present Agreement and their successors in their functions shall be responsible for ensuring and observance and enforcement of the terms and provisions thereof. The Commanders of the Forces of the two parties shall, within their respective commands, take all steps and make all arrangements necessary to ensure full compliance with all the provisions of the present Agreement by all elements and military personnel under their command.

The procedures laid down in the present Agreement shall, whenever necessary, he studied by the Commanders of the two parties and, if necessary, defined more specifically by the Joint Commission.

CHAPTER VI—JOINT COMMISSION AND INTERNATIONAL COMMISSION FOR SUPERVISION AND CONTROL IN VIET-NAM

28. Responsibility for the execution of the agreement on the cessation of hostilities shall rest with the parties.
29. An International Commission shall ensure the control and supervision of this execution.
30. In order to facilitate, under the conditions shown below, the execution of provisions concerning joint actions by the two parties, a Joint Commission shall be set up in Viet-Nam.
31. The Joint Commission shall be composed of an equal number of representatives of the Commanders of the two parties.
32. The Presidents of the delegations to the Joint Commission shall hold the rank of General.
    The Joint Commission shall set up joint groups the number of which shall be determined by mutual agreement between the parties. The groups shall be composed of an equal number of officers from both parties. Their location on the demarcation line between the regrouping zones shall he determined by the parties whilst taking into account the powers of the Joint Commission.
33. The Joint Commission shall ensure the execution of the following provisions of the Agreement on the cessation of hostilities:
    (a) A simultaneous and general cease-tire in Viet-Nam for all regular and irregular armed forces of the two parties.
    (b) A re-groupment of the armed forces of the two parties.
    (c) Observance of the demarcation lines between the regrouping zones and of the demilitarized sectors.

Within the limits of its competence it shall help the parties to execute the said provisions, shall ensure liaison between them for the purpose of preparing and carrying out plans for the application of these provisions, and shall endeavor to solve such disputed questions as may arise between the parties in the course of executing these provisions.

34. An International Commission shall be set up for the control and supervision over the application of the provisions of the agreement on the cessation of hostilities in Viet-Nam. It shall be composed of representatives of the following States: Canada, India and Poland.
It shall be presided over by the Representative of India.

35. The International Commission shall set up fixed and mobile inspection teams, composed of an equal number of officers appointed by each of the above-mentioned States. The fixed teams shall be located at the following points: Laokay, Langson, Tien-Yen, Haiphong, Vinh, Dong-Hoi, Muong-Sen, Tourane, Quinhon, Nhatrang, Bangoi, Saigon, Cap St. Jacques, Tranchau. These points of location may, at a later date, he altered at the request of the Joint Commission, or of one of the parties, or of the International Commission itself, by agreement between the International Commission and the command of the party concerned. The zones of action of the mobile teams shall be the regions bordering the land and sea frontiers of Viet-Nam, the demarcation lines between the re-grouping zones and the demilitarized zones. Within the limits of these zones they shall have the right to move freely and shall receive from the local civil and military authorities all facilities they may require for the fulfilment of their tasks (provision of personnel, placing at their disposal documents needed for supervision, summoning witnesses necessary for holding enquiries, ensuring the security and freedom of movement of the inspection teams etc...). They shall have at their disposal such modern means of trans-

port, observation and communication as they may require. Beyond the zones of action as defined above, the mobile teams may, by agreement with the command of the party concerned, carry out other movements within the limits of the tasks given them by the present agreement.

36. The International Commission shall be responsible for supervising the proper execution by the parties of the provisions of the agreement. For this purpose, it shall fulfill the tasks of control, observation, inspection and investigation connected with the application of the provisions of the agreement on the cessation of hostilities, and it shall in particular:

(a) Control the movement of the armed forces of the two parties, effected within the framework of the re-groupment plan.

(b) Supervise the demarcation lines between the re-grouping areas, and also the demilitarized zones.

(c) Control the operations of releasing prisoners of war and civilian internees.

(d) Supervise at ports and airfields as well as along all frontiers of Viet-Nam the execution of the provisions of the agreement on the cessation of hostilities, regulating the introduction into the country of armed forces, military personnel and of all kinds of arms, munitions and war material.

37. The International Commission shall, through the medium of the inspection teams mentioned above, and as soon as possible either on its own initiative, or at the request of the Joint Commission, or of one the parties, undertake the necessary investigations both documentary and on the ground.

38. The inspection teams shall submit to the International Commission the results of their supervision, their investigation and their observations, furthermore they shall draw up such special reports as they may consider necessary or

as may be requested from them by the Commission. In the case of a disagreement within the teams, the conclusions of each member shall be submitted to the Commission.

39. If anyone inspection team is unable to settle an incident or considers that there is a violation or a threat of a serious violation the international Commission shall be informed; the latter shall study the reports and the conclusions of the inspection teams and shall inform the parties of the measures which should be taken for the settlement of the incident, ending of the violation or removal of the threat of violation.

40. When the Joint Commission is unable to reach an agreement on the interpretation to be given to some provision or on the appraisal of a fact, the International Commission shall be informed of the disputed question. Its recommendations shall be sent directly to the parties and shall be notified to the Joint Commission.

41. The recommendations of the International Commission shall be adopted by majority vote, subject to the provisions contained in article 42. If the votes are divided the chairman's vote shall be decisive.

The International Commission may formulate recommendations concerning amendments and additions which should be made to the provisions of the agreement on the cessation of hostilities in Viet-Nam, in order to ensure a more effective execution of that agreement. These recommendations shall be adopted unanimously.

42. When dealing with questions concerning violations, or threats of violations, which might lead to a resumption of hostilities, namely:

(a) Refusal by the armed forces of one party to affect the movements provided for in the re-groupment plan.

    (b) Violation by the armed forces of one of the parties of the regrouping zones, territorial waters, or air space of the other party.

The decisions of the International Commission must be unanimous.

43. If one of the parties refuses to put into effect a recommendation of the International Commission, the parties concerned or the Commission itself shall inform the members of the Geneva Conference.

If the International Commission does not reach unanimity in the cases provided for in article 42, it shall submit a majority report and one or more minority reports to the members of the Conference.

The International Commission shall inform the members of the Conference in all cases where its activity is being hindered.

44. The International Commission shall be set up at the time of the cessation of hostilities in Indochina in order that it should lie able to fulfill the tasks provided for in article 36.
45. The International Commission for Supervision and Control in Viet-Nam shall act in close co-operation with the International Commissions for Supervision and Control in Cambodia and Laos.

The Secretaries-General of these three Commissions shall be responsible for coordinating their work and for relations between them.

46. The International Commission for Supervision and Control in Viet-Nam may, after consultation with the International Commissions for Supervision and Control in Cambodia and Laos and having regard to the development of the situation in Cambodia and Laos, progressively reduce its activities. Such a decision must be adopted unanimously.

47. 0All the provisions of the present Agreement, save the second sub-paragraph of Article 11, shall enter into force at
2400 hours (Geneva time) on 22 July 1954.

Done in Geneva at 2400 hours on the 20th of July 1954 in
French and in Viet-Namese, both texts being equally authentic.

For the Commander-in-Chief of the French Union Forces in
Indochina

Brigadier-General DELTEII.

For the Commander-in-Chief of the People's Army of Viet-Nam

TA-QUANG BUU, Indochina

*Vice-Minister of National Defense of the Democratic Republic of
Viet-Nam*

Source: U.S. Congress, Senate, Committee on Foreign
Relations, 90th Congress, 1st Session, *Background Information Relating
to Southeast Asia and Vietnam* (3d Revised Edition) (Washington,
DC: U.S. Government Printing Office, July 1967), pp. 50–62

EXHIBIT 7

Southeast Asia Collective Defense Treaty (Manila Pact); September 8, 1954(1)

The Parties to this Treaty,

RECOGNIZING THE SOVEREIGN EQUALITY OF all the Parties,

Reiterating their faith in the purposes and principles set forth in the Charter of the United Nations and their desire to live in peace with all peoples and all governments,

Reaffirming that, in accordance with the Charter of the United Nations, they uphold the principle of equal rights and self-determination of peoples, and declaring that they will earnestly strive by every peaceful means to promote self-government and to secure the independence of all countries whose people's desire it and are able to undertake its responsibilities,

Desiring to strengthen the fabric of peace and freedom and to uphold the principles of democracy, individual liberty and the rule of law, and to promote the economic well-being and development of all peoples in the treaty area,

Intending to declare publicly and formally their sense of unity, so that any potential aggressor will appreciate that the Parties stand together in the area, and

Desiring further to coordinate their efforts for collective defense for the preservation of peace and security,

Therefore, agree as follows:

ARTICLE I

The Parties undertake, as set forth in the charter of the United Nations, to settle any international disputes in which they may be involved by peaceful means in such a manner that international peace and security and justice are not endangered, and to refrain in their international relations from the threat or use of force in any manner inconsistent with the purposes of the United Nations.

ARTICLE II

In order, more effectively to achieve the objectives of this Treaty, the Parties, separately and jointly, by means of continuous and effective self-help and mutual aid will maintain and develop their individual and collective capacity to resist armed attack and to prevent and counter subversive activities directed from without against their territorial integrity and political stability.

ARTICLE III

The Parties undertake to strengthen their free institutions and to cooperate with one another in the further development of economic measures, including technical assistance, designed both to promote economic progress and social well-being and to further the individual and collective efforts of governments toward these ends.

ARTICLE IV

1. Each Party recognizes that aggression by means of armed attack in the treaty area against any of the Parties or against any State or territory which the Parties by unanimous agreement may hereafter designate, would endanger its own peace and safety, and agrees that it will in that event act to meet the common danger in accordance with its constitutional processes. Measures taken under this paragraph shall be immediately reported to the Security Council of the United Nations.

2. If, in the opinion of any of the Parties, the inviolability or the integrity of the territory or the sovereignty or political independence of any Party in the treaty area or of any other

State or territory to which the provisions of paragraph one of this article from time to time apply is threatened in any way other than by armed attack or is affected or threatened by any fact or situation which might endanger the peace of the area, the Parties shall consult immediately in order to agree on the measures which should be taken for the common defense.

3. It is understood that no action on the territory of any State designated by unanimous agreement under paragraph one of this article or on any territory so designated shall be taken except at the invitation or with the consent of the government concerned.

ARTICLE V

The Parties hereby establish a Council, on which each of them shall be represented, to consider matters concerning the implementation of this Treaty. The Council shall provide for consultation with regard to military and any other planning as the situation obtaining in the treaty area may from time to time require. The Council shall be so organized as to be able to meet at any time.

ARTICLE VI

This Treaty does not affect and shall not be interpreted as affecting in any way the rights and obligations of any of the Parties under the charter of the United Nations or the responsibility of the United Nations for the maintenance of international peace and security. Each Party declares that none of the international engagements now in force between it and any other of the Parties or any third party is in conflict with the provisions of this Treaty and undertakes not to enter into any international engagement in conflict with this Treaty.

ARTICLE VII

Any other State in a position to further the objectives of this Treaty and to contribute to the security of the area may, by unanimous agreement of the Parties, be invited to accede to this Treaty. Any State so invited may become a Party to the Treaty by depositing its instrument of accession with the Government of the Republic of the Philippines. The Government of the Republic of the Philippines shall inform each of the Parties of the deposit of each such instrument of accession.

ARTICLE VIII

As used in this Treaty, the "treaty area" is the general area of Southeast Asia, including also the entire territories of the Asian Parties, and the general area of the Southwest Pacific not including the Pacific area north of 21 degrees 30 minutes' north latitude. The Parties may, by unanimous agreement, amend this Article to include within the treaty area the territory of any State acceding to this Treaty in accordance with article VII or otherwise to change the treaty area.

ARTICLE IX

1. This Treaty shall be deposited in the archives of the Government of the Republic of the Philippines. Duly certified copies thereof shall be transmitted by that government to the other signatories.
2. The Treaty shall be ratified, and its provisions carried out by the Parties in accordance with their respective constitutional processes. The instruments of ratification shall be deposited as soon as possible with the Government of the Republic of the Philippines, which shall notify all of the other signatories of such deposit.(2)
3. The Treaty shall enter into force between the States which have ratified it as soon as the instruments of ratification of a majority of the signatories shall have been deposited, and

shall come into effect with respect to each other State on the date of the deposit of its instrument of ratification.

ARTICLE X

This Treaty shall remain in force indefinitely, but any Party may cease to be a Party one year after its notice of denunciation has been given to the Government of the Republic of the Philippines, which shall inform the Governments of the other Parties of the deposit of each notice of denunciation.

ARTICLE XI

The English text of this Treaty is binding on the Parties, but when the Parties have agreed to the French text thereof and have so notified the Government of the Republic of the Philippines, the French text shall be equally authentic and binding on the Parties.

UNDERSTANDING OF THE UNITED STATES OF AMERICA

The United States of America in executing the present Treaty does so with the understanding that its recognition of the effect of aggression and armed attack and its agreement with reference thereto in article IV, paragraph 1, apply only to communist aggression but affirms that in the event of other aggression or armed attack it will consult under the provisions of article IV paragraph 2.

In witness whereof, the undersigned Plenipotentiaries have signed this Treaty.

Done at Manila, this eighth day of September 1954.

(1) TIAS 3170; 6 UST 81-86. Ratification advised by the Senate Feb. 1, 1955; ratified by the President Feb. 4, 1955; entered into force Feb. 19, 1955.

(2) Thailand deposited its instrument of ratification Dec. 2, 1954; the remaining signatories (the United States,

Australia, France, New Zealand, Pakistan, the Philippines, and the United Kingdom) deposited their instruments Feb. 19, 1955.

Source: American Foreign Policy 1950–1955
Basic Documents Volumes I and II
Department of State Publication 6446
General Foreign Policy Series 117
Washington, DC: U.S. Government Printing Office, 1957

EXHIBIT 8

Remarks of Senator John F. Kennedy at the Conference on Vietnam Luncheon in the Hotel Willard, Washington, D.C., June 1, 1956

THIS IS A REDACTION OF this speech made for the convenience of readers and researchers. Two copies of the speech exist in the Senate Speech file of the John F. Kennedy Pre-Presidential Papers here at the John F. Kennedy Library. One copy is a draft with handwritten notations and the second copy is a press release. The redaction is based on the press release. Links to page images of the two copies are given at the bottom of this page.

It is a genuine pleasure to be here today at this vital Conference on the future of Vietnam, and America's stake in that new nation, sponsored by the American Friends of Vietnam, an organization of which I am proud to be a member. Your meeting today at a time when political events concerning Vietnam are approaching a climax, both in that country and in our own Congress, is most timely. Your topic and deliberations, which emphasize the promise of the future more than the failures of the past, are most constructive. I can assure you that the Congress of the United States will give considerable weight to your findings and recommendations; and I extend to all of you who have made the effort to participate in this Conference my congratulations and best wishes.

It is an ironic and tragic fact that this Conference is being held at a time when the news about Vietnam has virtually disappeared from the front pages of the American press, and the American people have all but forgotten the tiny nation for which we are in large measure responsible. This decline in public attention is due, I believe, to three factors: (1) First, it is due in part to the amazing success of President Diem in meeting firmly and with determination the major political and economic crises which had heretofore continually plagued Vietnam. (I shall say more about this point later, for it deserves more consideration from all Americans interested in the future of Asia).

(2) Secondly, it is due in part to the traditional role of American journalism, including readers as well as writers, to be more interested in crises than in accomplishments, to give more space to the threat of wars than the need for works, and to write larger headlines on the sensational omissions of the past than the creative missions of the future.

(3) Third and finally, our neglect of Vietnam is the result of one of the most serious weaknesses that has hampered the long-range effectiveness of American foreign policy over the past several years—and that is the over emphasis upon our role as "volunteer fire department" for the world. Whenever and wherever fire breaks out—in Indo-China, in the Middle East, in Guatemala, in Cyprus, in the Formosan Straits—our firemen rush in, wheeling up all their heavy equipment, and resorting to every known method of containing and extinguishing the blaze. The crowd gathers—the usually successful efforts of our able volunteers are heartily applauded—and then the firemen rush off to the next conflagration, leaving the grateful but still stunned inhabitants to clean up the rubble, pick up the pieces and rebuild their homes with whatever resources are available.

The role, to be sure, is a necessary one; but it is not the only role to be played, and the others cannot be ignored. A volunteer fire department halts, but rarely prevents, fires. It repels but rarely rebuilds; it meets the problems of the present but not of the future. And while we are devoting our attention to the Communist arson in Korea, there is smoldering in Indochina; we turn our efforts to Indochina until the alarm sounds in Algeria—and so it goes.

Of course Vietnam is not completely forgotten by our policy-makers today—I could not in honesty make such a charge and the facts would easily refute it—but the unfortunate truth of the matter is that, in my opinion, Vietnam would in all likelihood be receiving more attention from our Congress and Administration, and greater assistance under our aid programs, if it were in imminent danger of Communist invasion or revolution. Like those peoples of Latin America and Africa whom we have very nearly overlooked in the past decade, the Vietnamese may find that their devotion to the cause of democracy, and their success in reducing the strength of local Communist groups, have had the ironic effect of reducing American support. Yet the need for that support has in no way been reduced. (I hope it will not be necessary for the Diem Government—or this organization—to subsidize the growth of the South Vietnam Communist Party in order to focus American attention on that nation's critical needs!)

No one contends that we should now rush all our firefighting equipment to Vietnam, ignoring the Middle East or any other part of the world. But neither should we conclude that the cessation of hostilities in Indochina removed that area from the list of important areas of United States foreign policy. Let us briefly consider exactly what is "America's Stake in Vietnam":

(1) First, Vietnam represents the cornerstone of the Free World in Southeast Asia, the keystone to the arch, the finger in the dike. Burma, Thailand, India, Japan, the Philippines and obviously Laos and Cambodia are among those whose security would be threatened if the Red Tide of Communism overflowed into Vietnam. In the past, our policymakers have sometimes issued contradictory statements on this point—but the long history of Chinese invasions of Southeast Asia being stopped by Vietnamese warriors should have removed all doubt on this subject.

Moreover, the independence of a Free Vietnam is crucial to the free world in fields other than the military. Her economy is essential to the economy of Southeast Asia; and her political liberty is an inspiration to those seeking to obtain or maintain their liberty in all parts of Asia—and indeed the world. The fundamental tenets of this nation's foreign policy, in short, depend in considerable measure upon a strong and free Vietnamese nation.

(2) Secondly, Vietnam represents a proving ground of democracy in Asia. However, we may choose to ignore it or deprecate it, the rising prestige and influence of Communist China in Asia are unchallengeable facts. Vietnam represents the alternative to Communist dictatorship. If this democratic experiment fails, if someone million

refugees have fled the totalitarianism of the North only to find neither freedom nor security in the South, then weakness, not strength,
will characterize the meaning of democracy in the minds of still
more Asians. The United States is directly responsible for this experiment—it is playing an important role in the laboratory where it is
being conducted. We cannot afford to permit that experiment to fail.

(3) Third and in somewhat similar fashion, Vietnam represents
a test of American responsibility and determination in Asia. If we are
not the parents of little Vietnam, then surely we are the godparents.
We presided at its birth, we gave assistance to its life, we have helped
to shape its future. As French influence in the political, economic
and military spheres has declined in Vietnam, American influence
has steadily grown. This is our offspring—we cannot abandon it; we
cannot ignore its needs. And if it falls victim to any of the perils that
threaten its existence—Communism, political anarchy, poverty and
the rest—then the United States, with some justification, will be held
responsible; and our prestige in Asia will sink to a new low.

(4) Fourth and finally, America's stake in Vietnam, in her
strength and in her security, is a very selfish one—for it can be measured, in the last analysis, in terms of American lives and American
dollars. It is now well known that we were at one time on the brink of
war in Indo-china—a war which could well have been costlier, more
exhausting and less conclusive than any war we have ever known.
The threat to such war is not now altogether removed from the horizon. Military weakness, political instability or economic failure in
the new state of Vietnam could change almost overnight the apparent security which has increasingly characterized that area under the
leadership of Premier Diem. And the key position of Vietnam in
Southeast Asia, as already discussed, makes inevitable the involvement of this nation's security in any new outbreak of trouble.

It is these four points, in my opinion, that represent America's
stake in Vietnamese security. And before we look to the future, let us
stop to review what the Diem Government has already accomplished
by way of increasing that security. Most striking of all, perhaps, has
been the rehabilitation of more than ¾ of a million refugees from
the North. For these courageous people dedicated to the free way

of life, approximately 45,000 houses have been constructed, 2,500 wells dug, 100 schools established, and dozens of medical centers and maternity homes provided.

Equally impressive has been the increased solidarity and stability of the Government, the elimination of rebellious sects and the taking of the first vital steps toward true democracy. Where once colonialism and Communism struggled for supremacy, a free and independent republic has been proclaimed, recognized by over 40 countries of the free world. Where once a playboy emperor ruled from a distant shore, a constituent assembly has been elected.

Social and economic reforms have likewise been remarkable. The living conditions of the peasants have been vastly improved, the wastelands have been cultivated, and a wider ownership of the land is gradually being encouraged. Farm cooperatives and farmer loans have modernized an outmoded agricultural economy; and a tremendous dam in the center of the country has made possible the irrigation of a vast area previously uncultivated. Legislation for better labor relations, health protection, working conditions and wages has been completed under the leadership of President Diem.

Finally, the Vietnamese army—now fighting for its own homeland and not its colonial masters—has increased tremendously in both quality and quantity. General O'Daniel can tell you more about these accomplishments.

But the responsibility of the United States for Vietnam does not conclude, obviously, with a review of what has been accomplished thus far with our help. Much more needs to be done; much more, in fact, than we have been doing up to now. Military alliances in Southeast Asia are necessary but not enough. Atomic superiority and the development of new ultimate weapons are not enough. Informational and propaganda activities, warning of the evils of Communism and the blessings of the American way of life, are not enough in a country where concepts of free enterprise and capitalism are meaningless, where poverty and hunger are not enemies across the 17th parallel but enemies within their midst. As Ambassador Chuong has recently said: "People cannot be expected to fight for the Free World unless they have their own freedom to defend, their freedom from foreign domination as well as freedom from misery, oppression, corruption."

I shall not attempt to set forth the details of the type of aid program this nation should offer the Vietnamese—for it is not the details of that program that are as important as the spirit with which it is offered and the objectives it seeks to accomplish. We should not attempt to buy the friendship of the Vietnamese. Nor can we win their hearts by making them dependent upon our handouts. What we must offer them is a revolution—a political, economic and social revolution far superior to anything the Communists can offer—far more peaceful, far more democratic and far more locally controlled. Such a Revolution will require much from the United States and much from Vietnam. We must supply capital to replace that drained by the centuries of colonial exploitation; technicians to train those handicapped by deliberate policies of illiteracy; guidance to assist a nation taking those first feeble steps toward the complexities of a republican form of government. We must assist the inspiring growth of Vietnamese democracy and economy, including the complete integration of those refugees who gave up their homes and their belongings to seek freedom. We must provide military assistance to rebuild the new Vietnamese Army, which every day faces the growing peril of Vietminh Armies across the border.

And finally, in the councils of the world, we must never permit any diplomatic action averse to this, one of the youngest members of the family of nations—and I include in that injunction a plea that the United States never give its approval to the early nationwide elections called for by the Geneva Agreement of 1954. Neither the United States nor Free Vietnam was a party to that agreement—and neither the United States nor Free Vietnam is ever going to be a party to an election obviously stacked and subverted in advance, urged upon us by those who have already broken their own pledges under the Agreement they now seek to enforce.

All this and more we can offer Free Vietnam, as it passes through the present period of transition on its way to a new era—an era of pride and independence, and era of democratic and economic growth—an ear which, when contrasted with the long years of colonial oppression, will truly represent a political, social and economic revolution.

This is the revolution we can, we should, we must offer to the people of Vietnam—not as charity, not as a business proposition, not as a political maneuver, nor simply to enlist them as soldiers against Communism or as chattels of American foreign policy—but a revolution of their own making, for their own welfare, and for the security of freedom everywhere. The Communists offer them another kind of revolution, glittering and seductive in its superficial appeal. The choice between the two can be made only by the Vietnamese people themselves. But in these times of trial and burden, true friendships stand out. As Premier Diem recently wrote a great friend of Vietnam, Senator Mansfield, "It is only in winter that you can tell which trees are evergreen." And I am confident that if this nation demonstrates that it has not forgotten the people of Vietnam, the people of Vietnam will demonstrate that they have not forgotten us.

EXHIBIT 9

John F. Kennedy Inaugural Address

Friday, January 20, 1961

HEAVY SNOW FELL THE NIGHT before the inauguration, but thoughts about canceling the plans were overruled. The election of 1960 had been close, and the Democratic Senator from Massachusetts was eager to gather support for his agenda. He attended Holy Trinity Catholic Church in Georgetown that morning before joining President Eisenhower to travel to the Capitol. The Congress had extended the East Front, and the inaugural platform spanned the new addition. The oath of office was administered by Chief Justice Earl Warren. Robert Frost read one of his poems at the ceremony

Vice President Johnson, Mr. Speaker, Mr. Chief Justice, President Eisenhower, Vice President Nixon, President Truman, reverend clergy, fellow citizens, we observe today not a victory of party, but a celebration of freedom—symbolizing an end, as well as a beginning—signifying renewal, as well as change. For I have sworn before you and Almighty God the same solemn oath our forebears prescribed nearly a century and three quarters ago.

The world is very different now. For man holds in his mortal hands the power to abolish all forms of human poverty and all forms of human life. And yet the same revolutionary beliefs for which our forebears fought are still at issue around the globe—the belief that the rights of man come not from the generosity of the state, but from the hand of God.

We dare not forget today that we are the heirs of that first revolution. Let the word go forth from this time and place, to friend and foe alike, that the torch has been passed to a new generation of

Americans—born in this century, tempered by war, disciplined by a hard and bitter peace, proud of our ancient heritage—and unwilling to witness or permit the slow undoing of those human rights to which this Nation has always been committed, and to which we are committed today at home and around the world.

Let every nation know, whether it wishes us well or ill, that we shall pay any price, bear any burden, meet any hardship, support any friend, oppose any foe, in order to assure the survival and the success of liberty.

This much we pledge—and more. To those old allies whose cultural and spiritual origins we share, we pledge the loyalty of faithful friends. United, there is little we cannot do in a host of cooperative ventures.

Divided, there is little we can do—for we dare not meet a powerful challenge at odds and split asunder

To those new States whom we welcome to the ranks of the free, we pledge our word that one form of colonial control shall not have died merely to be replaced by a far more iron tyranny. We shall not always expect to find them supporting our view. But we shall always hope to find them strongly supporting their own freedom—and to remember that, in the past, those who foolishly sought power by riding the back of the tiger ended up inside.

To those peoples in the huts and villages across the globe struggling to break the bonds of mass misery, we pledge our best efforts to help them help themselves, for whatever period is required—not because the Communists may be doing it, not because we seek their votes, but because it is right. If a free society cannot help the many who are poor, it cannot save the few who are rich.

To our sister republics south of our border, we offer a special pledge—to convert our good words into good deeds—in a new alliance for progress—to assist free men and free governments in casting off the chains of poverty. But this peaceful revolution of hope cannot become the prey of hostile powers. Let all our neighbors know that we shall join with them to oppose aggression or subversion anywhere in the Americas. And let every other power know that this Hemisphere intends to remain the master of its own house

To that world assembly of sovereign states, the United Nations, our last best hope in an age where the instruments of war have far outpaced the instruments of peace, we renew our pledge of support—to prevent it from becoming merely a forum for invective—to strengthen its shield of the new and the weak—and to enlarge the area in which its writ may run

Finally, to those nations who would make themselves our adversary, we offer not a pledge but a request: that both sides begin anew the quest for peace, before the dark powers of destruction unleashed by science engulf all humanity in planned or accidental self-destruction.

We dare not tempt them with weakness. For only when our arms are sufficient beyond doubt can we be certain beyond doubt that they will never be employed.

But neither can two great and powerful groups of nations take comfort from our present course—both sides overburdened by the cost of modern weapons, both rightly alarmed by the steady spread of the deadly atom, yet both racing to alter that uncertain balance of terror that stays the hand of mankind's final war.

So, let us begin anew remembering on both sides that civility is not a sign of weakness, and sincerity is always subject to proof. Let us never negotiate out of fear. But let us never fear to negotiate

Let both sides explore what problems unite us instead of belaboring those problems which divide us.

Let both sides, for the first time, formulate serious and precise proposals for the inspection and control of arms—and bring the absolute power to destroy other nations under the absolute control of all nations

Let both sides seek to invoke the wonders of science instead of its terrors. Together let us explore the stars, conquer the deserts, eradicate disease, tap the ocean depths, and encourage the arts and commerce.

Let both sides unite to heed in all corners of the earth the command of Isaiah—to "undo the heavy burdens...and to let the oppressed go free.

And if a beachhead of cooperation may push back the jungle of suspicion, let both sides join in creating a new endeavor, not a new balance of power, but a new world of law, where the strong are just and the weak secure and the peace preserved

All this will not be finished in the first 100 days. Nor will it be finished in the first 1,000 days, nor in the life of this Administration, nor even perhaps in our lifetime on this planet. But let us begin.

In your hands, my fellow citizens, more than in mine, will rest the final success or failure of our course. Since this country was founded, each generation of Americans has been summoned to give testimony to its national loyalty. The graves of young Americans who answered the call to service surround the globe

Now the trumpet summons us again—not as a call to bear arms, though arms we need; not as a call to battle, though embattled we are—but a call to bear the burden of a long twilight struggle, year in and year out, "rejoicing in hope, patient in tribulation"—a struggle against the common enemies of man: tyranny, poverty, disease, and war itself.

Can we forge against these enemies a grand and global alliance, North and South, East and West, that can assure a more fruitful life for all mankind? Will you join in that historic effort?

In the long history of the world, only a few generations have been granted the role of defending freedom in its hour of maximum danger. I do not shrink from this responsibility—I welcome it. I do not believe that any of us would exchange places with any other people or any other generation. The energy, the faith, the devotion which we bring to this endeavor will light our country and all who serve it—and the glow from that fire can truly light the world

And so, my fellow Americans: ask not what your country can do for you—ask what you can do for your country.

My fellow citizens of the world: ask not what America will do for you, but what together we can do for the freedom of man.

Finally, whether you are citizens of America or citizens of the world, ask of us the same high standards of strength and sacrifice which we ask of you. With a good conscience our only sure reward, with history the final judge of our deeds, let us go forth to lead the land we love, asking His blessing and His help, but knowing that here on earth God's work must truly be our own.

EXHIBIT 10

THE GULF OF TONKIN INCIDENT

IN LATE 1961–EARLY 1962 A series of U.S. Navy patrols off the east coast of Communist China was proposed. The purpose of these patrols was to be three-fold. In the first place they would establish and maintain the presence of the U.S. Seventh Fleet in the international waters off the China coast; second, they would serve as a minor Cold War irritant to the "Chicoms and third, they would collect as much intelligence as possible concerning The initial phasing called for one U.S destroyer to conduct each mission.

Patrols were given the cover name DESOTO. From 14 to 20 April 1962 the first DESOTO patrol was conducted, with the destroyer USS -DE HAVEN as the participating vessel. The area of responsibility encompassed by the mission focused around the Tsingtao area of the Yellow Sea, and the ship was instructed not to approach any Chicoms-held territory, including the offshore islands, closer than 10 miles.

Major intelligence targets for this mission fell into five categories: This first DESOTO patrol was singularly effective in evoking Chicoms reaction. Such things as shadowing of the DE HAVEN by three or more Chicoms vessels at one time, jamming of the DE HAVEN communications facilities, and the use of deceptive pennant numbers on the shadowing vessels all contributed to the success of the intelligence effort on this mission. In addition, the Chicoms issued three "serious warnings" to the DE HAVEN for violation of territorial rights during the 7 days the mission was in progress.

Forth remainder of 1962, eight more DESOTO patrols were run, and prior to December of that year, these patrols were all conducted in the East and North China areas as well as up the Korean coast to the Soviet Gulf of Tartary. After the first mission, intelligence derived from the patrols was quite sparse. Shadowing of the patrol vessels was noted, and serious warnings were issued to almost all the patrols by the Chinese Government, but unique information was virtually nil.

In December 1962, with DESOTO patrol number I X, the USS AGERHOLM conducted the first probe into South China waters and the Gulf of Tonkin around Hainan Island. This pattern was repeated in April 1963 when the USS EDWARDS traversed the same path around Hainan Island and then extended its mission down the coast of the Democratic Republic of Vietnam (DRV). No DRV reflections were recorded at this time, and Chicoms reaction was again limited to shadowing and issuance of serious warnings. Since serious warnings were not reserved for DESOTO missions (at that time the U.S. had received over 350 of these warnings for both air and sea violations), no particular significance could be attached to them.

The first DRV reaction to a DESOTO patrol came in late February–early March 1964 on the third venture into the Gulf of Tonkin, this time by the USS CRAIG. DRV radar stations performed extensive tracking of the CRAIG on her first run up the coast, and DRV naval communications referred to the CRAIG by hull number on one occasion. Although intelligence collected from this mission was not voluminous, it did contribute new insight into the place-ment and capability of DRV tracking stations and equipment.

Prelude to Violence

The fourth DESOTO patrol into the international waters of the Gulf of Tonkin was programmed in July 1964. Concerned more with the Vietnamese problem than the Chicoms problem of its pre-decessors, this mission was to observe the junk fleet vessels believed to be a constant source of resupply to the guerrillas in the south, obtain navigational and hydrographic information, and procure any available intelligence on the DRV navy. Since the 1954 Geneva agreements specifically prohibited the DRV from establishing a navy, the emergence of this force had been, until late 1963–early 1964, extremely covert. During late 1957 the first DRV naval communications facilities were isolated with an estimated 30 ships involved in the transmissions. Then in 1959 the first evidence of the emergence of a modern DRV navy was noted during a probable joint DRV/ Chicoms naval exercise in the Pearl River estuary. Some of the vessels involved in this exercise were believed to be the same 10 motor gunboats later noted passing through the Hainan Strait and probably represented the DRV's initial acquisition of modern naval craft. Augmentation of this force was continual after 1959, and as of late 1964 the DRV navy had a total complement of nearly 100 vessels. Armed with this background, and clear on the purpose of the mission, the USS MADDOX reached a point on the 17th parallel about 12 miles off the coast of the DRV on 31 July 1964 at 1300 hours' local time. From that point the MADDOX turned northward on a tack that was to take her up the coast for three days in what was believed to be another routine running of a DESOTO patrol.

Confrontation

Apparently the MADDOX was not the only was "going on a course of 52 degrees .9 nautical miles from Hon Me...Shortly after placement of the MADDOX near Hon Me Island by DRV tracking authorities, a message was passed to an identified DRV fighting vessel stating that it had been "decided to fight the enemy tonight." The MADDOX was apprised accordingly in a warning which preceded the actual attack by more than 12 hours.

DRV naval tracking stations were observed in continual surveillance from that time on. In addition, several messages were intercepted, apparently pre-positioning warships in preparation for the attack.

Between approximately 1130 and 1215 (Saigon local time) on 2 August, the MADDOX report—end sighting three PT's and two probable SWATOW class PGM's (motor gunboats) about 10 miles north of Hon Me Island. During the same time frame the MADDOX reached the northernmost point of its mission and observed a large junk fleet (approximately 75 craft), which it intended to avoid on its return route. There were no military ships intermingled with the junks, and there was still no apparent hostility.

It is not possible to ascertain exactly which element of the DRV naval command ordered the attack, but shortly after the MADDOX reached the apex of its mission, a message was passed stating that it was time to close with the "enemy" and use torpedoes. The MADDOX received this information some 50 minutes before the aggressive actions commenced.

At 1530, some 30 miles from shore, the MADDOX altered her course to the southeast, heading for the mouth of the Tonkin Gulf, and increased her speed to 25 knots, attempting to avoid the three DRV torpedo boats reflected on radar as closing at about 50 knots, within 20 miles of the DESOTO ship. At that time the pedo did not run. Air support from the T ICON—DEROGA arrived at that point and engaged the attacking vessels, and the MADDOX withdrew from the area. Total damage: one DRV PT boat dead and burning in the water; extensive but not' totally disabling damage to the other two PT ^{1}s; and slight damage to one gun on the MADDOX.

In order to assert the right of the U.S. to freedom on the seas, it was decided that the DESOTO patrol should be resumed as soon as possible. The strength of the patrol was doubled, with the USS TURNER JOY joining the MADDOX for a proposed four-day continuation of the mission; a formal warning was issued to the DRV authorities in Hanoi, stating that any further such unprovoked actions would result in severe retribution; and at 0900 on 3 August, the DESOTO mission was resumed. For this phase, continuous combat air support was provided.

During the day of the 3rd, the MADDOX reported that both she and the TURNER JOY had picked up radar signals and believed they both were being shadowed. This same suspect shadow activity occurred during the daylight hours on 4 August, but there were no provocations. Then the DRV naval communications facilities were observed alerting two SWATOW-class PGM' s to make ready for military operations on the night of the 4th. The DESOTO units were advised of the possible attack and headed for the mouth of the Gulf "at best speed."

The MADDOX reported several radar sightings of apparent hostile craft throughout the early evening hours of 4 August. Some of these sightings later broke away, but some of them continued to close. At about 2200, the MADDOX reported firing on an attacking PT boat which had presumably launched a torpedo. Three more probable PT' s were tracked closing rapidly on the DESOTO ships, and continual torpedo attack was reported through 0035 on 5 August. During the attack period the two DESOTO vessels engaged several radar contacts, and the TURNER JOY reported that one vessel was probably sunk. It was also reported that a DRV PT boat may have sunk one of its own companions in the conflict.

The weather throughout the attack was over-cast and cloudy, thus impairing the visibility of the support air fighters and making it impossible for them to sight the assailants. The DESOTO patrol initially reported that at least 21 torpedoes were launched during the battle. This figure was viewed as highly unlikely since the PT's carried only two torpedoes each, with no known on-sea reload capability, and the total DRV PT force was estimated at around 13, three of which had been damaged in the fighting of the 2nd. The figure was later amended when it was determined that the sonar operators may have seen their own propeller beats reflecting off the rudders during the zigzagging evasive action followed by the two DESOTO ships.

In retaliation for the second hostile action, JCS ordered sin pack to conduct a onetime maximum effort air strike against the selected DRV targets, to include several ports known to house SWATOW class PGM's and PT's, as well as priority one hit on the Vinh oil storage area,

this strike commenced on five August at 0700 hrs. and resulted in an estimated 90% destruction of the Vinh Oil storage area plus total or partial destruction of approximately 29 DRV naval vessels. The US lost two aircraft in the 64 sorties that were flown and suffered severe damage to a third in addition one US pilot was killed and another was captured. The Maddox and the Turner Joy resumed the Desoto mission of six August without further incident, and the rest is just painful history. (At the time of the Gulf of Tonkin incident the author, then in the Army, was on his way home from US am—nine, Clark Air Force Base, Philippines, to an SA, where he became a reporter for the Worth Vietnamese branch parentheses B261) it was in connection with one of the postmortems the incident that he gathered together the information presented in the story.

Feb-Mar crypto log page 10 responsive.

EXHIBIT 11

Excerpts from briefing book prepared for the November 1963 Honolulu Conference on Vietnam

"US COMPREHENSIVE PLAN—VIETNAM"

Background

1. The US Comprehensive Plan for the Republic of Vietnam resulted from discussions at the Secretary of Defense Conference in Hawaii in July 1962. Based on the assumption that the insurgent action would be reduced by the end of calendar year 1965, to a level which the Vietnamese themselves could control, the Plan develops the peak force structures for Vietnamese regular, paramilitary, and irregular forces during the active phases of the war, and provides for the phase-down of those forces—as well as the progressive reduction of all U.S. special military assistance as the tempo of the war diminishes.

SOURCE: JFK National Security Files 1961–1963 Country Files: Vietnam, Honolulu Meeting, Briefing Book, 11/20/63 (B), Box 204

EXHIBIT 12

Secretary of Defense Robert S. McNamara
General Maxwell D. Taylor

REPORTED TO THE PRESIDENT THIS morning and to the National Security Council this afternoon. Their report included a number of classified findings and recommendations which will be the subject of further review and action. Their basic presentation was endorsed by all members of the Security Council and the following statement of United States policy was approved by the President on the basis of recommendations received from them and from Ambassador [Henry Cabot] Lodge.

1. The security of South Viet-Nam is a major interest of the United States as other free nations. We will adhere to our policy of working with the people and Government of South Viet-Nam to deny this country to communism and to suppress the externally stimulated and supported insurgency of the Viet Cong as promptly as possible. Effective performance in this undertaking is the central objective of our policy in South Viet-Nam.
2. The military program in South Viet-Nam has made progress and is sound in principle, though improvements are being energetically sought.
3. Major U.S. assistance in support of this military effort is needed only until the insurgency has been suppressed or until the national security forces of the Government of South Viet-Nam are capable of suppressing it.

Secretary McNamara and General Taylor reported their judgment that the major part of the U.S. military task can be completed by the end of 1965, although there may be a continuing requirement for a limited number of U.S. training personnel. They reported that by the end of this year, the U.S. program for training Vietnamese should have progressed to the point where 1,000 U.S. military personnel assigned to South Viet-Nam can be withdrawn.

4. The political situation in South Viet-Nam remains deeply serious. The United States has made clear its continuing opposition to any repressive actions in South Viet-Nam. While such actions have not yet significantly affected the military effort, they could do so in the future.

5. It remains the policy of the United States, in South Viet-Nam as in other parts of the world, to support the efforts of the people of that country to defeat aggression and to build a peaceful and free society.

Source: U.S. Congress, Senate, Committee on Foreign Relations, 90th Congress, 1st Session, Background Information Relating to Southeast Asia and Vietnam (3d Revised Edition) (Washington, DC: U.S. Government Printing Office, July 1967), p. 115

EXHIBIT 13

NATIONAL SECURITY ACTION MEMORANDUM NO. 263

TO:
Secretary of State
Secretary of Defense
Chairman of the Joint Chiefs of Staff
SUBJECT: South Vietnam

AT A MEETING ON OCTOBER 5, 1963, the President considered the recommendations contained in the report of Secretary McNamara and General Taylor on their mission to South Vietnam.

The President approved the military recommendations contained in Section I B (1 -3) of the report but directed that no formal announcement be made of the implementation of plans to withdraw 1,000 U.S. military personnel by the end of 1963.

After discussion of the remaining recommendations of the report, the President approved the instruction to Ambassador Lodge which is set forth in State Department Telegram No. 534 to Saigon.

McGeorge Bundy

Copy furnished: Director of Central Intelligence Administrator, Agency for International Development 11/21/63

DRAFT

TOP SECRET

NATIONAL SECURITY ACTION MEMORANDUM

The President has reviewed the discussions of South Vietnam which occurred in Honolulu and has discussed the matter further with Ambassador Lodge. He directs that the following guidance be issued to all concerned:

1. It remains the central object of the United States in South Vietnam to assist the people and Government of that country to win their contest against the externally directed and supported Communist conspiracy. The test of all decisions and U.S. actions in this area should be the effectiveness of their contributions to this purpose.
2. The objectives of the United States with respect to the withdrawal of U.S. military personnel remain as stated in the White House statement of October 2, 1963.
3. It is a major interest of the United States Government that the present provisional government of South Vietnam should be assisted in consolidating itself in holding and developing increased public support. All U.S. officers should conduct themselves with this objective in view.
4. It is of the highest importance that the United States Government avoid either the appearance or the reality of public recrimination from one part of it against another, and the President expects that all senior officers of the Government will take energetic steps to insure that they and their subordinate go out of their way to maintain and to defend the unity of the United States Government both here and in the field. More specifically, the President approves the following lines of action developed in the discussions of the Honolulu meeting of November 20. The office or offices of the Government to which central responsibility is assigned is indicated in each case.
5. We should concentrate our own efforts, and insofar as possible we should persuade the government of South Vietnam to concentrate its efforts, on the critical situation in the Mekong Delta. This concentration should include not only military but political, economic, social, educational and informational efforts. We should seek to turn the tide not only of battle but of belief, and we should seek

to increase not only our control of land but the productivity of this area whenever the proceeds can be held for the advantage of anti-Communist forces.

(Action: The whole country team under the direct supervision of the Ambassador.)

6. Programs of military and economic assistance should be maintained at such levels that their magnitude and effectiveness in the eyes of the Vietnamese Government do not fall below the levels sustained by the United States in the time of the Diem Government. This does not exclude arrangements for economy on the MAP accounting for ammunition and any other readjustments which are possible as between MAP and other U.S. defense sources. Special attention should be given to the expansion of the import distribution and effective use of fertilizer for the Delta.

(Action: AID and DOD as appropriate.)

7. With respect to action against North Vietnam, there should be a detailed plan for the development of additional Government of Vietnam resources, especially for sea-going activity, and such planning should indicate the time and investment necessary to achieve a wholly new level of effectiveness in this field of action.

(Action: DOD and CIA)

8. With respect to Laos, a plan should be developed for military operations up to a line up to 50 kilometers inside Laos, together with political plans for minimizing the international hazards of such an enterprise. Since it is agreed that operational responsibility for such undertakings should pass from CAS to MACV, this plan should provide an alternative method of political liaison for such operations, since their timing and character can have an intimate relation to the fluctuating situation in Laos. (Action: State, DOD and CIA.)

9. It was agreed in Honolulu that the situation in Cambodia is of the first importance for South Vietnam, and it is therefore urgent that we should lose no opportunity to

exercise a favorable influence upon that country. In particular, measures should be undertaken to satisfy ourselves completely that recent charges from Cambodia are groundless, and we should put ourselves in a position to offer to the Cambodians a full opportunity to satisfy themselves on this same point.

(Action: State.)

10. In connection with paragraphs 7 and 8 above, it is desired that we should develop as strong and persuasive a case as possible to demonstrate to the world the degree to which the Viet Cong is controlled, sustained and supplied from Hanoi, through Laos and other channels. In short, we need a more contemporary version of the Jordan Report, as powerful and complete as possible.

(Action: Department of State with other agencies as necessary.)

McGeorge Bundy

EXHIBIT 14

Eyes-Only Telegram for 263

~~TOP SECRET~~ EYES ONLY   October 11, 1963

NATIONAL SECURITY ACTION MEMORANDUM NO. 263

TO: Secretary of State
           Secretary of Defense
           Chairman of the Joint Chiefs of Staff

SUBJECT: South Vietnam

At a meeting on October 5, 1963, the President considered the
recommendations contained in the report of Secretary McNamara
and General Taylor on their mission to South Vietnam.

The President approved the military recommendations contained
in Section I B (1-3) of the report, but directed that no formal
announcement be made of the implementation of plans to withdraw 1,000 U.S. military personnel by the end of 1963.

After discussion of the remaining recommendations of the report,
the President approved an instruction to Ambassador Lodge which
is set forth in State Department telegram No. 534 to Saigon.

McGeorge Bundy

EXHIBIT 15

NATIONAL SECURITY ACTION
MEMORANDUM NO. 273

THE WHITE HOUSE
WASHINGTON
November 26, 1963
TO:
The Secretary of State
The Secretary of Defense
The Director of Central Intelligence
The Administrator, AID
The Director, USIA

THE PRESIDENT HAS REVIEWED THE discussions of South Vietnam which occurred in Honolulu and has discussed the matter further with Ambassador Lodge. He directs that the following guidance be issued to all concerned:

1. It remains the central object of the United States in South Vietnam to assist the people and Government of that country to win their contest against the externally directed and supported Communist conspiracy. The test of all U. S. decisions and actions in this area should be the effectiveness of their contribution to this purpose.

2. The objectives of the United States with respect to the withdrawal of U.S. military personnel remain as stated in the White House statement of October 2, 1963.

3. It is a major interest of the United States Government that the present provisional government of South Vietnam

should be assisted in consolidating itself and in holding and developing increased public support. All U.S. officers should conduct themselves width this objective in view.

4. The President expects that all senior officers of the Government will move energetically to insure the full unity of support for established U.S. policy in South Vietnam. Both in Washington and in the field, it is essential that the Government be unified. It is of particular importance that express or implied criticism of officers of other branches be scrupulously avoided in all contacts with the Vietnamese Government and with the press. More specifically, the President approves the following lines of action developed in the discussions of the Honolulu meeting, of November 20. The offices of the Government to which central responsibility is assigned are indicated in each case.

5. We should concentrate our own efforts, and insofar as possible we should persuade the Government of South Vietnam to concentrate its efforts, on the critical situation in the Mekong Delta. This concentration should include not only military but political, economic, social, educational and informational effort. We should seek to turn the tide not only of battle but of belief, and we should seek to increase not only the control of hamlets but the productivity of this area, especially where the proceeds can be held for the advantage of anti-Communist forces.
(Action: The whole country team under the direct supervision of the Ambassador.)

6. 6. Programs of military and economic assistance should be maintained at such levels that their magnitude and effectiveness in the eyes of the Vietnamese Government do not fall below the levels sustained by the United States in the time of the Diem Government. This does not exclude arrangements for economy on the MAP account with respect to accounting for ammunition, or any other readjustments which are possible as between MAP and other U. S. defense resources. Special attention should be given

to the expansion of the import, distribution, and effective use of fertilizer for the Delta.

(Action: AID and DOD as appropriate.)

7. Planning should include different levels of possible increased activity, and in each instance there should be estimates of such factors as:

A. Resulting damage to North Vietnam.
B. The plausibility of denial.
C. Possible North Vietnamese retaliation.
D. Other international reaction.

Plans should be submitted promptly for approval by higher authority.

(Action: State, DOD, and CIA.)

8. With respect to Laos, a plan should be a developed and submitted for approval by higher authority for military operations up to a line up to 50 kilometers inside Laos, together with political plans for minimizing the international hazards of such an enterprise. Since it is agreed that operational responsibility for such undertakings should pass from CAS to MACV, this plan should include a redefined method of political guidance for such operations, since their timing and character can have an intimate relation to the fluctuating situation in Laos.

(Action: State, DOD, and CIA.)

9. It was agreed in Honolulu that the situation in Cambodia is of the first importance for South Vietnam, and it is therefore urgent that we should lose no opportunity to exercise a favorable influence upon that country. In particular, a plan should be developed using all available evidence and methods of persuasion for showing the Cambodians that the recent charges against us are groundless.

(Action: State.)

10. In connection with paragraphs 7 and 8 above, it is desired that we should develop as strong and persuasive a case as

possible to demonstrate to the world the degree to which the Viet Cong is controlled, sustained and supplied from Hanoi, through Laos and other channels. In short, we need a more contemporary version of the Jorden Report, as powerful and complete as possible.

(Action: Department of State with other agencies as necessary.)

s/ McGeorge Bundy
cc:
Mr. Bundy
Mr. Forrestal
Mr. Johnson
NSC Files

EXHIBIT 16

Third Oral History Interview with
ROBERT F. KENNEDY

April 30, 1964
New York, New York
By John Bartlow Martin
For the John F. Kennedy Library
[BEGIN TAPE V, REEL 1]
[snipping earlier portion of interview]

Martin:

All right. Now, Vietnam began in the first—on the 3rd of January started appearing rather prominently in the papers and, of course, still is, and was all through '63. Do you want to talk about it now? Do you want to wait till we come and pick up the coup later? In, on, in January, the Vietnamese killed three Americans and shot down five helicopters.

Kennedy:

Viet Cong, you mean.

Martin:

That's right. That's what I mean, I'm sorry, Viet Cong. A little later Mansfield said that we were, this thing was turning into an American war and wasn't justified by our national interest; we hadn't any business going in so deep, but we kept going in deeper. The president sent Maxwell Taylor and McNamara out there. And then, and Lodge, he appointed Lodge as the ambassador—and you remember the hassle between the CIA and Lodge. The president brought the CIA fellow back, and, in the end, there was the coup against the

Diem brothers. Do you want to discuss the whole thing now? You must have been in on a good deal of this.

Kennedy:

Yes. Well, yeah, what do you want to start with?

Martin:

All right. At the beginning we seemed to have our lines crossed. I mean, the majority leader in the Senate, Mansfield, was saying this was not an American war, and he didn't think it was—that our—it should be—not, not—should not be an American war. He didn't think our heavy commitment there was justified. How'd you feel about it; how'd the president feel about it; and at what point did we get our lines straightened out?

Kennedy:

Well, I don't think that...

Martin:

Did I make myself clear?

Kennedy:

No, I don't think that fact, Senator Mansfield or somebody in the Senate takes a position, necessarily means...

Martin:

Well, he was majority leader.

Kennedy:

Yeah, but, you know, he's frequently taken that, those, that line or that position on some of these matters. I don't think that the fact he has an independent view from the executive branch of the government, particularly in Southeast Asia, indicates that the lines aren't straight. I, no, I just, I think every... I, the president felt that the... He had a strong, overwhelming reason for being in Vietnam and that we should win the war in Vietnam.

Martin:

What was the overwhelming reason?

Kennedy:

Just the loss of all of Southeast Asia if you lost Vietnam. I think everybody was quite clear that the rest of Southeast Asia would fall.

Martin:

What if it did?

Kennedy:

Just have profound effects as far as our position throughout the world, and our position in a rather vital part of the world. Also, it would affect what happened in India, of course, which in turn has an effect on the Middle East. Just, it would have, everybody felt, a very adverse effect. It would have an effect on Indonesia, hundred million populations. All of these countries would be affected by the fall of Vietnam to the Communists, particularly as we had made such a fuss in the United States both under President Eisenhower and President Kennedy about the preservation of the integrity of Vietnam.

Martin:

There was never any consideration given to pulling out.

Kennedy:

No.

Martin:

But the same time, no disposition to go in all...

Kennedy:

No...

Martin:

...in an all-out way as we went into Korea. We were trying to avoid a Korea, is that correct?

Kennedy:

Yes, because I, everybody including General MacArthur felt that land conflict between our troops, white troops and Asian, would only lead to, end in disaster. So, it was... We went in as advisers, but to try to get the Vietnamese to fight themselves, because we couldn't win the war for them. They had to win the war for themselves.

Martin:

It's generally true all over the world, whether it's in a shooting war or a different kind of a war. But the president was convinced that we had to keep, had to stay in there...

Kennedy:

Yes.

Martin:

...and couldn't lose it.

Kennedy:

Yes.

Martin:

And if Vietnamese were about to lose it, would he propose to go in on land if he had to?

Kennedy:

Well, we'd face that when we came to it.

Martin:

Mm hm. Or go with air strikes, or—direct from carriers, I mean, something like that?

Kennedy:

But without...It didn't have to be faced at that time. In the first place, we were winning the war in 1962 and 1963, up until May or so of 1963. The situation was getting progressively better. And then I...

Martin:

But then it got progre—started going downhill, didn't it?

Kennedy:

Yes, and then we had all the problems with the Buddhists and the...

Martin:

Yeah.

Kennedy:

And, uh...

Martin:

Why did they go down, why did they get bad, Bob?

Kennedy:

Well, I just think he was just, Diem wouldn't make even the slightest concessions. He was difficult to reason with, well, with the... And then it was built up tremendously in an adverse fashion here in the United States and that was played back in Vietnam, and...And I think just the people themselves became concerned about it. And so, it began to, the situation began to deteriorate in the spring of 1962, uh, spring of 1963. I think David Halberstam's, from the *New York Times'* articles had a strong effect on molding public opinion: the fact that the situation was unsatisfactory. Our problem was that thinking of Halberstam's sort of as the Ma—what Matthews [uniden-tified] did in Cuba, that Batista [Fulgencio R. Batista] was not very satisfactory, but the important thing was to try to get somebody who could replace him and somebody who could keep, continue the war and keep the country united, and that was far more difficult. So that was what was of great concern to all of us during this period of time. Nobody liked Diem particularly, but how to get rid of him and get somebody that would continue the war, not split the country in two, and therefore lose not only the war but the country. That was the great problem.

EXHIBIT 17

President Johnson Chronology

PRESIDENTIAL CHRONOLOGY

THE GULF OF TONKIN ATTACKS OF AUGUST 1964

AUGUST 2

A. M.   The President is informed that North Vietnamese PT boats
        have attacked the destroyer USS Maddox in international
        waters of the Gulf of Tonkin.

P. M.   The President consults with his advisors, and decides not to
        retaliate against North Vietnam. He issues instructions:
        (1) to prepare a protest note to be sent to the North Vietnamese
        regime and (2) to strengthen the Tonkin patrol force and to
        counter attack and destroy any force attempting to repeat the
        attacks.

AUGUST 3

The President makes public his instructions issued the previous
day to U.S. Navy units in the Gulf of Tonkin.

The Department of State publicizes the U.S. protest note to
North Vietnam.

McNamara gives private briefing to Senate Foreign Relations
Committee members.

The President consults with Rusk, McNamara and Wheeler.

AUGUST 4

A. M.   The President is informed that North Vietnamese PT boats
9:12   have launched a second attack in the Gulf of Tonkin against the
        USS Maddox and the USS Turner Joy.

Noon   The President meets with the National Security Council

P. M.   The President has a luncheon meeting with Rusk, McNamara,
1:00   McCone, Bundy and Vance. The decision is made to retaliate.

6:15   The President reviews his decision with the National Security
        Council. All agree.

6:45   The President reviews his decision with the Congressional
        leadership at a White House meeting. All agree. The President
        indicated that he will ask the Congress for a Joint Resolution on
        Southeast Asia.

iv.

10:06   The President discusses his decision by telephone with
Republican Presidential candidate Goldwater. Goldwater
agrees.

11:36   The President addresses the Nation via Radio/TV. He
reviews the circumstances of the attack and his decision
to retaliate.

P. M.   The President approves personal messages sent by him
to several Heads of State and Heads of Government.

P. M.   The President reviews drafts of speech he will deliver on
Radio/TV that evening and at Syracuse the next morning.

AUGUST 5

A. M.   The President, in his speech at Syracuse University
reviews the Gulf of Tonkin events and his decision.

P. M.   The President sends a message to Congress reporting on
the Tonkin attacks and on his response and requests a
Joint Resolution.

In New York Ambassador Stevenson addresses a Security
Council Meeting to present U. S. charges against North
Vietnam.

In Bangkok the SEATO Council meets to review the Tonkin
events.

In Paris a special meeting of the North Atlantic Council
reviews the Tonkin events.

AUGUST 6

Congressional hearings and debate take place on the proposed
Gulf of Tonkin resolution. McNamara, Rusk and Wheeler
testify.

AUGUST 7

The President issues a statement hailing passage by the
Senate and House of the Joint Resolution on Southeast Asia.

AUGUST 8

A high level stock-taking conference is held on the White
House on developments in Southeast Asia.

v.

AUGUST 10

The President signs into law the Joint Congressional Resolution
on Southeast Asia.

At a White House meeting the President and his senior advisors
review the situation. The President expresses his conviction
that the present situation will not last long, and asks for recommendations to deal with future contingencies

EXHIBIT 17A

President Johnson's Message to Congress

August 5, 1964

LAST NIGHT I ANNOUNCED TO the American people that the North Vietnamese regime had conducted further deliberate attacks against U.S. naval vessels operating in international waters, and I had therefore directed air action against gunboats and supporting facilities used in these hostile operations. This air action has now been carried out with substantial damage to the boats and facilities. Two U.S. aircraft were lost in the action.

After consultation with the leaders of both parties in the Congress, I further announced a decision to ask the Congress for a resolution expressing the unity and determination of the United States in supporting freedom and in protecting peace in Southeast Asia.

These latest actions of the North Vietnamese regime has given a new and grave turn to the already serious situation in Southeast Asia. Our commitments in that area are well known to the Congress. They were first made in 1954 by President Eisenhower they were further defined in the Southeast Asia Collective Defense Treaty approved by the Senate in February 1955.

This treaty with its accompanying protocol obligates the United States and other members to act in accordance with their constitutional processes to meet Communist aggression against any of the parties or protocol states.

Our policy in Southeast Asia has been consistent and unchanged since 1954. I summarized it on June 2 in four simple propositions:

1. America keeps her word. Here as elsewhere, we must and shall honor our commitments.
2. The issue is the future of Southeast Asia as a whole. A threat to any nation in that region is a threat to all, and a threat to us.
3. Our purpose is peace. We have no military, political, or territorial ambitions in the area.
4. This is not just a jungle war, but a struggle for freedom on every front of human activity. Our military and economic assistance to South Vietnam and Laos in particular has the purpose of helping these countries to repel aggression and strengthen their independence.

The threat to the free nations of Southeast Asia has long been clear. The North Vietnamese regime has constantly sought to take over South Vietnam and Laos. This Communist regime has violated the Geneva accords for Vietnam. It has systematically conducted a campaign of subversion, which includes the direction, training, and supply of personnel and arms for the conduct of guerrilla warfare in South Vietnamese territory. In Laos, the North Vietnamese regime has maintained military forces, used Laotian territory for infiltration into South Vietnam, and most recently carried out combat operations—all in direct violation of the Geneva Agreements of 1962.

In recent months, the actions of the North Vietnamese regime have become steadily more threatening...

As President of the United States I have concluded that I should now ask the Congress, on its part, to join in affirming the national determination that all such attacks will be met, and that the United States will continue in its basic policy of assisting the free nations of the area to defend their freedom.

As I have repeatedly made clear, the United States intends no rashness, and seeks no wider war. We must make it clear to all that the United States is united in its determination to bring about the end of Communist subversion and aggression in the area. We seek the full and effective restoration of the international agreements signed in Geneva in 1954, with respect to South Vietnam, and again in Geneva in 1962, with respect to La.

Exhibit 17B

Geneva

Fighting in Laos resumed later in 1962 after the signing of the 1962 Declaration on the Neutrality of Laos in Geneva by fourteen nations including North Vietnam and the United States. An estimated 10,000 North Vietnamese were still present in Laos, despite the stipulation their government had signed at Geneva that withdrawal of all foreign troops be completed by October 7. Because the North Vietnamese did not respect the withdrawal requirement of the Geneva agreement, the United States stepped up military aid to the Kingdom of Laos, but it avoided deploying ground troops which would have violated the agreement.

As part of the American effort to support the Kingdom of Laos, United States Central Intelligence Agency (CIA) personnel operating from a base at Udon Thani, Thailand, took over the support of 30,000 to 36,000 irregulars, including Hmong guerrillas who bore the brunt of the fighting in northern Laos. The irregulars, who became known as the Secret Army, were instrumental in helping to rescue a large number of United States airmen who were shot down over Laos. By this time, the Hmong leader Vang Pao had risen to the rank of general in the Royal Lao Army and commanded the Second Military Region.

In October 1964, in response to an offensive by the Pathet Lao and North Vietnamese to expel the Laotian Neutralists from the Plain of Jars, the United States began providing air support against Pathet Lao positions and North Vietnamese supply lines. However, it was not until March 1966 at Phoukout, northwest of the Plain of Jars, that the Pathet Lao started to win major battles against the Royal Lao Army. In July 1966, the Pathet Lao won another major battle in the Nambak Valley in northern Louangphrabang Province by overrunning a Royal Lao Army base and inflicting heavy casualties. These victories gave the Pathet Lao new momentum in the war for control of Laos.

Meanwhile, in southern Laos, where the North Vietnamese had been working steadily every dry season to expand the Ho Chi Minh Trail network leading into the Republic of Vietnam (South Vietnam), the intensity of the air war also grew. The air war in Laos operated under a complicated command and control system that involved the United States embassy in Vientiane, the Military Assistance Command Vietnam in Saigon, Royal Thai air bases in Thailand, the commander in chief Pacific in Honolulu, and sometimes even the White House.

During the June 1969 rainy season, the Pathet Lao and two North Vietnamese battalions, using Soviet tanks, pushed the Royal Lao Army and the Neutralists out of their base at Muang Souy northwest of the Plain of Jars. Fighting continued during the monsoon season. In September 1969, Vang Pao's Hmong, supported by American bombing, launched a series of surprise attacks against key points on the Plain of Jars. A new North Vietnamese army division joined the battle shortly thereafter and by February 1970 had regained all of the devastated plain.

In 1970, despite eight years of ground offensives by the Royal Lao Army and massive United States air support, the Pathet Lao had grown into an army of 48,000 troops and was prepared to challenge Royal Lao Army forces on their own territory by mounting large offensives in the south engaging an even greater number of North Vietnamese forces. The introduction of Soviet-made long-range 130mm artillery pieces onto the battlefield in that year allowed the Pathet Lao and North Vietnamese to neutralize to some extent the Royal Lao Army's advantage of air superiority.

By December 1971, the Pathet Lao had taken Paksong on the Bolovens Plateau and had invested the main Hmong base at Longtiang. A major North Vietnamese-Pathet Lao offensive against Vang Pao and the Hmong began in mid-December 1971 and lasted until the end of April 1972. This battle involved more than twenty

North Vietnamese battalions and some 10,000 Hmong irregulars and Royal Lao Army defenders. Communist advances continued into 1972 and encircled Thakhek on the Mekong, and Vientiane.

The cease-fire of February 22, 1973 ended United States bombing and temporarily halted ground offensives. The Pathet Lao, however, used the cessation of military operations to resupply their forces over the long and exposed roads from North Vietnam.

References:
   Timelines of War, 475; Laos—A Country Study

EXHIBIT 17C

Joint Resolution of Congress

H.J. Res 1145
August 7, 1964

WHEREAS NAVAL UNITS OF THE Communist regime in Vietnam, in violation of the principles of the Charter of the United Nations and of international law, have deliberately and repeatedly attacked United States naval vessels lawfully present in international waters, and have thereby created a serious threat to international peace; and

Whereas these attacks are part of a deliberate and systematic campaign of aggression that the Communist regime in North Vietnam has been waging against its neighbors and the nations joined with them in the collective defense of their freedom; and

Whereas the United States is assisting the peoples of southeast Asia to protect their freedom and has not territorial, military or political ambitions in that area, but desires only that these peoples should be left in peace to work out their own destinies in their own way:

Now, therefore, be it resolved by the Senate and House of Representatives of the United States of America in Congress assembled,

That the Congress approves and supports the determination of the President, as Commander in Chief, to take all necessary measures to repel any armed attack against the forces of the United States and to prevent further aggression.

Section 2. The United States regards as vital to its national interest and to world peace the maintenance of international peace and security in southeast Asia. Consonant with the Constitution of the United States and the Charter of the United Nations and in accordance with its obligations under the Southeast Asia Collective Defense Treaty, the United States is, therefore, prepared, as the President determines, to take all necessary steps, including the use of armed force, to assist any member or protocol state of the Southeast Asia Collective Defense Treaty requesting assistance in defense of its freedom.

Section 3. This resolution shall expire when the President shall determine that the peace and security of the area is reasonably assured by international conditions created by action of the United Nations or otherwise, except that it may be terminated earlier by concurrent resolution of the Congress.

EXHIBIT 18

Pham Van Dong's Letter 1969

29968 Congressional Record—House October 14, 1969
(By unanimous consent Mr. Morten was allowed to speak out of order)

MR. MORTEN. MR. CHAIRMAN, a few moments ago there was handed to me by a messenger from the White House a letter from the premiere of North Vietnam, Pham Van Dong. The letter was sent from Hanoi in Vietnamese to Paris and transmitted from Paris to the United States, 1317 Greenwich Mean Time, October 14, 1969 it says:

> *Dear American friends: up until now the U. S. Progressive people have struggled against the war of aggression against Vietnam. This fall large sectors of the US people, encouraged and supported by many peace—and justice loving American personages, are also launching a broad and powerful offensive throughout the United States to demand that the Nixon administration put an end to the Vietnam aggressive war and immediately bring all American troops home.*
>
> *Your struggle eloquently reflects the U. S. People's legitimate an urgent demand, which is to save U. S. Honor and to prevent their sons from dying uselessly in Vietnam. This is also a very appropriate and timely answer to the attitude of the U. S. Authorities who are still obdurately intensifying and*

prolonging the Vietnam aggressive war in defiance of protests by U. Y. And world public opinion.

The Vietnamese and world people fully approve of and enthusiastically acclaim you're just struggle.

The Vietnamese people demand that the U. S. Government withdraw completely and uncon-ditionally U. S. Troops and those of other foreign countries in the American camp from Vietnam, thus allowing the Vietnamese people to decide their own destiny by themselves.

The Vietnamese people deeply cherish peace, but it must be peace in independence and free-dom. As long as the US government does not end its aggression against Vietnam, Vietnamese people will persevere in their struggle to defend their fundamen-tal national rights. Our people's patriotic struggle is precisely the struggle for peace and justice that you are carrying out.

We are firmly confident that, with the solidar-ity and bravery of the Peoples of our two countries and with the approval and support of peace-loving people in the world, the struggle of the Vietnamese people and U.S. Progressive people against U.S. Aggression will certainly be crowned with total victory.

May your fall offensive succeed splendidly,

Affectionately yours,

Pham Van Dong,
Premier of the DRV Government.

EXHIBIT 19

Dellums

Full text: December 1–3, 1970

National Veterans Inquiry on U.S. War Crimes in Vietnam (Washington D.C., December 1–3, 1970)
Witnesses:

NOTE: THIS IS THE FULL text of the transcript printed in the Congressional Record. That text, however, omits the testimony of

Michael J. Uhl, who later also testified at a Congressional hearing (August 2 1971), Joseph B. Neilands (Harvest of Death: Chemical Warfare in Vietnam and Cambodia, 1972), and perhaps other witnesses. It also omits commentary at the hearing by Noam Chomsky, Jeremy Rifkin, Robert Bowie Johnson, Jr. (the moderator), and perhaps others. -CJHj

> 117 Cong. Rec. 4238-4271 SuDoc: X.92/1:117/PT.4
> UNITED STATES OF AMERICA
> Congressional Record
> PROCEEDINGS AND DEBATES
> OF THE 92d CONGRESS
> FIRST SESSION
> VOLUME 117-PART 4
> FEBRUARY 26, 1971, TO MARCH 8, 1971
> (PAGES 4083 TO 5460)
> UNITED STATES GOVERNMENT PRINTING OFFICE, WASHINGTON, 1971
> Congressional Record
> PROCEEDINGS AND DEBATES
> OF THE 92d CONGRESS,
> FIRST SESSION
> * * * {4215} * * *
> HOUSE OF REPRESENTATIVES
> Monday, March 1, 1971
> The House met at 12 o'clock noon
> * * * {4238} * * *
> War Crimes: The Bitter Facts

(Mr. Dellums asked and was given permission to address the House for 1 minute, to revise and extend his remarks and include extraneous matter.)

Mr. Dellums. Mr. Speaker, as the war spreads, so does the possibility and danger of additional war atrocities committed by American soldiers.

Yet, the Military Establishment continues to ignore or down-play not only the factual existence of these ghastly horrors, but it also refuses to question the issue of ultimate responsibility for war crimes past and present.

Today, along with 21 of my colleagues, I am reintroducing a joint resolution proposing a full-scale congressional inquiry of American war crimes and war crime responsibility.

Joining with me in backing this resolution are Mr. Diggs, Mr. Rangel, Mrs. Abzug, Mr. Collins of Illinois, Mr. Roncallo, Mr. Mitchell, Mr. Rosenthal, Mr. Hawkins, Mr. Ryan, Mr. Scheuer, Mr. Edwards of California, Mr. Eckhardt, Mr. Conyers, Mr. Kastenmeier, Mr. Mikva, Mr. Seiberling, Mr. Burton, Mr. Koch, Mr. Helstoski, Mr. Dow, and Mr. Badillo. {4238c2}

Mr. Speaker, the Defense Department blatantly ignores its responsibility to deal with war crimes. Instead, the Military Establishment attempts to pin the blame on lower echelon person-nel—men such as Calley, Henderson, and soon, I presume, Medina—while refusing to acknowledge that the prime responsibility lies at the highest levels of civilian and military command.

Indeed, to all intent and purpose, the Military Establishment acts as if war crimes are minute aberrations, the deranged acts of men temporarily enraged by the horrors of combat. Of course, in some cases, that is true. But there have been far too many instances of pre-meditated atrocities for this excuse to be accepted anymore.

Mr. Speaker, the material I shall now insert into the Record is for the most part some of the most gruesome and beastly testimony that I have ever read.

The transcript which follows is that of the National Veterans Inquiry on U.S. War Crimes in Vietnam held last December here in Washington.

The inquiry was undertaken by the Citizens Commission of Inquiry in order that the American public and Government realize the terrible realities of war atrocities as an integral component of our illegal, insane, and immoral adventurism in Southeast Asia.

The testimony contained in the transcript is blunt.

But blunt also has been the Government's ridiculous efforts to bypass or soft-pedal the responsibility for these actions.

Congress represents the people of America, and I believe the people are sick of the war, sick of the war crimes, and sick of the Military Establishment's handling of these problems.

The transcript follows:

Transcript

Introduction

{Robert Bowie Johnson, Jr.}

Johnson. My name is Robert Bowie Johnson, Jr.

I'm a Vietnam veteran, ex-Army captain, and West Point graduate {1965}.

I'm currently a veteran coordinator of the National Citizens Commission of Inquiry on U.S. War Crimes in Vietnam.

On behalf of the Citizens Commission, I'd like to welcome you to the National Veterans Inquiry on U.S. War Crimes in Vietnam.

Most of you have received the schedules of when the veterans will testify. This afternoon, nine members of the Americal Division will testify. After that, Noam Chomsky will deliver a brief perspective; and after that the testimony on ground combat operations will continue until 4:30 pm.

Initially, six witnesses here will testify. They'll be interviewed by regional coordinators. After each witness testifies, we ask that the press hold their questions to about five minutes; then after all veterans have testified we will open the floor up again for questions. Should there be any question relating to procedure or scheduling, these questions will be directed to Mr. Tod Ensign or Mr. Jeremy Rifkin, national coordinators for the Citizens Commission.

Final Session

Moderator. Good morning.

I'd like to welcome you today to the final session of the National Veterans Inquiry into War Crimes in Indochina.

At this final session we will have the eyewitness testimonies of seven Vietnam veterans.

Source: Congressional Record (cited below).

By CJHjr: Photocopied, scanned, converted to text (OCR: FineReader 6.0), formatted (xhtml/css), links, text {in braces}, text beside a green bar ( ), text in yellow boxes, bold-face, bold-italics, highlighting, added paragraphing (for ease of reading) marked with this trailing paragraph symbol: The Congressional Record is formatted in three columns per page, and I've marked the beginning of each column {in green braces} (page number, column number).

SuWho?

SuDoc

CIS DL

This document: National Veterans Inquiry on U.S. War Crimes in Vietnam (Citizens' Commission of Inquiry on U.S. War Crimes, Washington D.C., December 1-3 1970), transcript, 117 Congressional Record 4238-4271 (U.S. Congress 92-1, March 1 1971, Permanent Edition (red bound)) {SuDoc: X.92/1:117/ PT.4, ISSN: 0883-1947, OCLC: 05058415, LCCN: 12036438, GPOCat, LL: paper, microfiche, DL, WorldCat}. Witnesses: Robert Bowie Johnson Jr., Michael Paul McCusker, Daniel K. Amigone, Greg Motoka, Kenneth Barton Osborn, Norman Kiger, Gail Graham, Steve Noetzel, Edward Murphy, Daniel Alfiero, Louis Paul Font, Robert Master, Peter Norman Martinsen, T. Griffiths Ellison, Ed Melton, Chuck Hamilton, Elliott Lee Meyrowitz, Gordon S. Livingston, Greg Turgeon, Richard Altenberger, Bob Connelly, Robert Lifton, Chaim Shatan, Donald Engel, Gary Thamer, Steven Hassett, Kenneth J. Campbell, Sam Rankin, Phillip Wingenbach, Tod Ensign, Larry Rottmann, Robert Osman. Citizen Soldier (New York City) is the present-day successor to the Citizens' Commission of Inquiry on U.S. War Crimes.

See also:

The first Phoenix hearings: Vietnam: Policy and Prospects, 1970: Hearings on Civil Operations and Rural Development Support Program (U.S. Congress 91-2, Senate Committee on Foreign Relations, Hearings, February 17, 18, 19, 20, and March 3, 4, 17, 19, 1970, and Appendix, 7+750 pages) {SuDoc Y 4.F 76/2:V 67/17, CIS: 71 S381-18, OCLC: 198272, LCCN: 76610214, DL, WorldCat}.

The second Phoenix hearings: U.S. Congress, House Hearings, U.S. Assistance Programs in Vietnam (U.S. Congress 92-1, House Committee on Government Operations, Subcommittee on Foreign Operations and Government Information, Hearings, July 15 {a.m., p.m.}, 16, 19, 21, and August 2 1971, 4+362 pages) {SuDoc: Y 4.G 74/7:V 67/4, CIS: 72 H401-3, OCLC: 235387, LCCN: 71616178, DL, WorldCat}. Ensuing report: U.S. Assistance Programs in Vietnam (U.S. Congress 92-2, House Report No. 92-1610, House Committee on Government Operations, October 17 1972, 5+107 pages) {SuDoc: [Y 1.1/8:]92-2:H.RP.1610, Serial Set: 12976-6, CIS: 72 H403-19, OCLC: 540690, LCCN: 72603272, WorldCat} {Full text: pages 1-46 (2394 kb pdf), pages 47-97 (2790 kb pdf), pages 99-107 (501 kb pdf)}.

The third Phoenix hearings: Nomination of William E. Colby to be Director of Central Intelligence (U.S. Congress 93-1, Senate Armed Services Committee, Hearings, July 2, 20 {a.m., p.m.}, 25, 1973, 3+186 pages) {SuDoc: Y 4.AR 5/3:C 67/3, CIS: 73 S201-27, OCLC: 800312, LCCN: 73603022, DL, WorldCat}.

Vietnam Policy Proposals: Hearings on nine posposed items of legislation to end the U.S. war in Vietnam (U.S. Congress 91-2, Senate Committee on Foreign Relations, Hearings, February 3, 4, 5, and March 16, 1970, 5+405 pages) {SuDoc: Y 4.F 76/2:V 67/16, CIS: 71 S381-7, OCLC: 78825, LCCN: 74606991, DL, WorldCat}.

Winter Soldier Investigation (Vietnam Veterans Against the War Inc., Detroit Michigan, January 31, February 1-2, 1971), transcript, 117 Congressional Record 9947-10055 (U.S. Congress 92-1, April 6 1971, Permanent Edition (red bound)) {SuDoc: X.92/1:117/ PT.8, ISSN: 0883-1947, OCLC: 05058415, LCCN: 12036438, GPOCat, LL: paper, microfiche, DL, WorldCat}; 117 Congressional Record E 2825-2936 (U.S. Congress 92-1, April 6-? 1971, Daily Edition (green bound)) {SuDoc: X/A.92/1:117/???-???, ISSN: 0363-7239, LCCN: 80646573, OCLC: 02437919, GPOCat, LL: paper, microfiche, DL, WorldCat}.

American Prisoners of War in Southeast Asia, 1971 (U.S. Congress 92-1, House Committee on Foreign Affairs, Subcommittee on National Security Policy and Scientific Developments, Hearings,

March 23, 24, 25, 30, 31, April 1, 6, 20 {vvaw}, 1971, 9+583 pages)
{SuDoc: Y 4.F 76/1:P 93/4/971/PT.1, CIS: 71 H381-9, OCLC:
15634210, LCCN: 77612471, WorldCat}. Witness: Larry Rottmann
(Vietnam Veterans Against the War), April 20 1971, pages 406-423.

Legislative Proposals Relating to the War in Southeast Asia
(U.S. Congress 92-1, Senate Committee on Foreign Relations,
Hearings, April 20, 21, 22, 28, May 3, 11, 12, 13, 25, 26, 27, 1971,
7+726+12 pages) {SuDoc: Y 4.F 76/2:AS 4/13, CIS: 71 S381-18,
OCLC: 198272, LCCN: 79614140, DL, WorldCat}. Witness: John
Kerry (Vietnam Veterans Against the War), April 22 1971, 11:05
a.m.-1:00 p.m., pages 180-210.

House Ad Hoc Hearing for Vietnam Veterans Against the
War (U.S. Congressmen Jonathon Bingham and Paul Findley,
presiding, Friday, April 23 1971, Venue: U.S. Congress, House of
Representatives), transcript, 117 Congressional Record 13104-
13118 (U.S. Congress 92-1, May 3 1971, Permanent Edition (red
bound)) {SuDoc: X.92/1:117/PT.10, ISSN: 0883-1947, OCLC:
05058415, LCCN: 12036438, GPOCat, LL: paper, microfiche,
DL, WorldCat}. Witnesses: Larry Rottmann, Forest Lindley, Les
Johnson, Arthur Egendorf, Kip A. Kypriandes, Phillip Lowley, Vinny
Giardina, Michael Paul McCusker, William W. Lemmer, Alex Prim,
Robert McLaughlin, Jack Smith, David B. Maize.

Senate Ad Hoc Hearing for Vietnam Veterans Against the War
(U.S. Senator George McGovern, presiding, Friday, April 23 1971,
Venue: U.S. Congress, Senate, Room G-103 New Senate Office
Building), transcript, 117 Congressional Record 15392-15405 (U.S.
Congress 92-1, May 17 1971, Permanent Edition (red bound))
{SuDoc: X.92/1:117/PT.12, ISSN: 0883-1947, OCLC: 05058415,
LCCN: 12036438, GPOCat, LL: paper, microfiche, DL, WorldCat}.
Witnesses: Scott Camil, Vinny Giardina, Melville L. Stephens, Basil
Paquet, Joe Nielsen, Dale Granata, Everett Carson, Forrest Lindley
Jr., Samuel Miller, David A. Lamenzo, Jon Bjornson, Ken Provan.

Ad Hoc Hearings on Command Responsibility for War
Atrocities in Vietnam {copy} (U.S. Congressman Ron Dellums, pre-
siding, April 26, 27, 28, 29, 1971, 9:30 a.m.-12:30 p.m., Venue: U.S.
Congress, House of Representatives, Caucus Room, Cannon House

Office Building), transcript, The Dellums Committee Hearings on War Crimes in Vietnam: An Inquiry into Command Responsibility in Southeast Asia (New York, Vintage Books, 1972, 13+355 pages) {LCCN: 79039897, ISBN: 0394717678, WorldCat}. Witnesses: Five West Point graduates (Fred Laughlin, Gordon Livingston {Iraq, copy}, Robert B. Johnson, Greg Hayward, Ron Bartek, Michael O'Mera), five former military intelligence special agents and PoW interrogators {to come: omitted from the linked source}, ten former Americal Division members (Gary Battles, Charles David Locke, Terry Mullen, Steve Padoris, Daniel S. Notley, John Beitzel, Guadalupe G. Villarreal, Daniel Barnes, Thomas Cole, William Toffling), overview of air war, pacification, and forced urbanization (John Sack, Kenneth J. Campbell, Randy Floyd, Elliot Lee Meyrowitz).

Bertrand Russell Tribunal (Stockholm Sweden, May 2-10 1967; Roskilde Denmark, November 20-December 1 1967).

Tiger Force: "Buried Secrets, Brutal Truths: Tiger Force, an elite fighting unit in Vietnam, left a trail of atrocities in that country that have been concealed from the public for three decades." (Toledo Blade, October 22, 2003, February 15, March 28, April 6, May 2, May 12, 2004).

This document is not copyrighted and may be freely copied.
Charles Judson Harwood Jr.
CJHjr

Posted August 28, 2004. Updated June 25, 2006.

EXHIBIT 19A

Daniel K. Amigone

Moderator: Danny Amigone will be speaking to the problem, the area of mistreatment of civilians in ground combat. Dan?

Amigone: Thank you, Chuck. Good afternoon. My name is Daniel K. Amigone. I'm from Buffalo, New York, the queen city of the Great Lakes.

I ENLISTED IN THE UNITED States Army after I received my master's degree from Arizona State. As you know Arizona State, or Arizona, is a big, conservative hotbed of American politics, and at the time I really thought that what all we were doing in Vietnam was the right thing to do. So, I enlisted in the United States Army and—for a three-year hitch by the way—and to this day I regret that.

At any rate, I went through basic and AIT because I had plans of going into OCS, but just before, just before my actual departure for OCS at Fort Benning, they had a review board in my behalf and they decided I was not officer material because of various views that I had had during basic and AIT. And this I believe starts the whole process.

But anyway, after they refused my application to OCS, they sent me to Germany and I was over in Germany for three months and I volunteered for Vietnam, not like a lot of these people who have testified here before. I actually volunteered.

At any rate, I went to Vietnam in March of 1968, March of 1968 I arrived at Bien Hoa and Bien Hoa just had been cleared of the Viet Cong. It was just right after Tet. I didn't have too much in-country training because we were really badly needed, and I was assigned to Company {4240} D, 3rd Battalion, 7th Infantry, 199th Infantry

Brigade and we were called the Red Catchers. And this began my career in Vietnam, I was assigned to an infantry unit as 11 Bravo, which is an infantryman because all the training I had was during basic and AIT.

And this training I think is very important to the whole philosophy that goes into the mind of a man that goes into the front lines over in Vietnam. Basic is just, as they say, basic, you know. They teach you how to fire usually a—in my case it was an M-14. They teach you the basic fundamentals of drill, and, etc. Once you get into advanced infantry training, the process gets stepped up and the process gets more involved.

And I heard a question before about racism. Well, racism starts in AIT, Advanced Infantry Training. It's not a racism designated against the Blacks and Puerto Ricans; its racism designed toward the Vietnamese people. On the ranges when you are firing for record score to qualify, you're taught by your platoon sergeant and the man who is the instructor to holler kill every time you squeeze that trigger, and you're killing a gook, as they call them.

And this is really where racism goes. They're not people anymore, they're gooks. They're not Vietnamese, they're gooks. So, on the bayonet range, your drill sergeant would holler, "What's the spirit of the bayonet?" And the people would as they lunged into their targets, would say, "kill, kill, kill." So that's—it's the spirit of killing that these infantrymen have when they go over to Vietnam. It's really imbedded into them.

And they get over to Vietnam and we practice what they have taught us.

There's one especially—topic I want to get into, and that's the question of McNamara's Brigade. In 1967, because of the drainage of manpower in the United States, Secretary of, I believe, Defense McNamara needed more manpower to fill the ranks over in Vietnam, in the infantry. So, what he did was: lowered the mentality, mentality standards for acceptance, accepting men into the armed forces especially the Army. What happens to these men—in particular I remember one man was in my company. He was a platoon sergeant in basic, acting platoon sergeant. I remember this one man who came up to me. He was only eighteen years old, a black boy from Newark, New Jersey, and he was married and had four kids, and he couldn't even read the letters that his wife wrote home to him. The Army had accepted him for combat duty. The Army was going to send him to paratrooper school and eventually to Vietnam. The man asked me to read his letter to him, and I read his letter to him and I said, "Well, what are you going—are you going to write to her?" And he said, "I don't know how to write."

What had happened was that the Army had drafted this man, and then put him through a three-week course so that he could learn how to write his name and sign his pay voucher. And what happens? These men go through this killing process. They learn to kill and they go to Vietnam and they do kill, and they do get killed, because given the fact that their reactions are a lot slower than a man with a normal intelligence, they haven't been told that when you hear a bullet fly you're supposed to duct. All they've been told how to do is to kill. So, they kill, and they get killed.

And if you look at Morning Reports—Morning Reports is a document, a document that registers your KIAs which are people killed in action, or your wounded people—you will find a disproportionately high number of people were these '67s. I say were because the Army had gotten a little grief about this, and they changed their system from using US or RA to social security numbers. That way they could hide anybody they wanted to. {4240c2}

At any rate, these people go to Vietnam and they die. And these people, I'd like to point out, they come from the ghettos. They come from the squalid areas of this country. They come from Appalachia, they're blacks, they're Puerto Ricans, they're poor whites. And I personally believe it's a sort of genocide, a genocide in both ways, a genocide in the effect that they're using the poor to fight the poor over in Vietnam.

So, what happens when we get over there? Well, as I say I arrived in the country just after Tet, and about the first week in the country I witnessed my first atrocity.

We were in the middle of a firefight, in the middle of a firefight, and this GI to the left of me, ahead, captured a peasant girl. And he raped her, raped her. In the middle of the firefight, raped her and then when she tried to get away, she killed—he killed her. And it was written off as a KIA, enemy casualty killed in combat.

And one more incident I'd like to bring up. I did not actually see it, but it happened when we were out on a patrol. We had captured three enemy prisoners and because of the lateness of the evening, we decided to hold them in our camp. And we held them and the next morning all three of them were dead, and they were shot in the back. And the—one of the platoon sergeants who were on duty at the time claimed the victory for killing them in the back saying that—he said that they tried to escape but what actually came out later, that he really just killed them. He loosened their binds and just killed them.

And we both times went to the CO, both times, and he said, "Well, that's war."

Moderator: Excuse me, Dan. How did it come out that he had killed them? Did anyone see him?

Amigone: Well, nobody really saw him kill them but he—one night he got drunk and it came out through his spirits.

Moderator: Are there any questions to be addressed to Mr. Amigone from the press?

Floor: You support that a disproportionate number of the poor were killed because I think you said their responses were slower. Would it be—would that be the case, or would it be the case that a disproportionate number of them are sent up to the front lines?

Amigone: Well—a very high rate of this 1967's that I'm talking about, that's where they go. The Army cannot use them anywhere else. And the real sad part of it is, after they have used them for two years and if they're still alive after their two-year period, they cannot re-enlist in the army because the Army's standards are too high for reenlistment. And yet they have fought their war for two years.

Floor: You said that you went to your CO after each of these incidents. Did you fear any kind of harassment or reprisal for doing that, or in fact did any such harassment or reprisal happen to you?

Amigone: Well, the first time I was like—as I said, I was brand new in the country. And he says, "Well, you'll see this happen all the time, just brush it off." The second time it happened late in my career and I soon after got wounded myself and was sent back.

Floor: So, you're—

Amigone: Nothing really happened, no.

Moderator: Are there any more questions?

Amigone: I'd like to add one more thing. We've heard about officers, and I'd like to just relate one incident. A fellow member of the 199, just back here; what happened was, I believe it was in May or April, in April of 1968—we were operating in a very dense, a very highly vegetated area called the Pineapple. It's outside Saigon.

And the night before, a sister company of mine went into this area and had suffered 60 per cent casualty. And it's very heavy booby-trapped.

So, what happened was that our company {4240c3} was given the orders to go into it the next night. And my CO said, "No, I will not go in." And the colonel said, "You go in or else I'll relieve you of the command." And my CO called back and said, "I stand relieved of my command." And we didn't go in that night. Well, another company went in and suffered almost 50 per cent casualties that night.

EXHIBIT 19B

Mr. Mike McCusker

McCusker. My name is Mike McCusker.

I am an ex-Marine. I was discharged as a sergeant. I enlisted in the reserves in 1959 in July; served six years in the reserves; and then in 1965 went active duty for two years, which means I had eight years of service. While in the reserves, I was trained in Recon, {4238c3} which meant that I became a jumper, a parachutist, scuba, and all the other John Wayne varieties.

In the two years that I was active I was what was called a combat correspondent for the First Marine Division in Vietnam, generally out of Chu Lai. In that position I saw damn near everything from command to the field.

Perhaps an indication of that is an interview—off the cuff, which I understand you know well enough—with the commanding general of the First Marine Division at that time, and said that Vietnamese society was ignorant and superstitious, the children were raised as thieves and liars; we could do nothing with the old; the children themselves should be taken from their families and indoctrinated all their lives in government camps.

A colonel, on an interview with him, said his job was to kill gooks—except I knew better what to write, and put it a different way, such as country, God, duty, and devotion, helping these people even though both of us knew it was a lie, and not worth considering as far as the military was concerned.

Lifers and NCOs continually referred to Vietnamese as gooks, inferior, of no worth.

As a reporter I could not write of these things, nor could I write of atrocities, nor could I write of the treatment of POW's; I could

397

not write of women fighting with the VC, nor of women or children taken prisoners, nor of harassment and interdiction fire, of even napalm, which was referred to as incender-gel about halfway through my tour.

My job essentially was to cover things up from the press, to be the PR, and come off with the Marine Corps looking like a shining knight on a white horse.

If anything was coming up that would embarrass the Marine Corps, we were to take reporters someplace else and make sure that they didn't know about it.

The general trend was to allude in our stories to all Vietnamese as Communists, not only dehumanizing them but indicting them as something that we are programmed to fear and abhor.

Every dead Vietnamese was counted as Viet Cong, because they would not be dead if they were not Viet Cong, whether they were ninety years old or six months old.

The body count was any pool of blood, and I used to think that perhaps multiplied by seven.

The villagers were destroyed or forcibly removed to New Life Hamlets—which is what they were called—which were nothing more than concentration camps with barbed wire and machine guns. The huts were too close, there was hardly any food—which forced beggars and whores of once-proud farmers.

And perhaps that was the most degrading atrocity: the garbage cans of the different battalions and companies, they would allow one or two Vietnamese to empty these garbage cans into their buckets—which also let the Marines think, after these farmers were reduced to nothing else, that these people must be inferior if they lived out of garbage cans.

Now there are two incidents, perhaps, that are of particular value as far as atrocity is concerned. They were SOP and they're examples of general procedure.

One happened on my mother's birthday, October 27, 1966, northwest of the Chu Lai perimeter, at a village called Duc Pho. It was a large village complex. A sniper killed a staff sergeant, so the skipper pulled us back and then ordered nape [Napalm] on the village itself. "Just napalm the hell out of it." When we went in later, after the fires burned down, there were many, many bodies of old women and men. But I think the worst was thirty dead children who had been laid out for us to see by the survivors, who got the hell out of there before we got in. They laid these children out for us to see in one courtyard, and from being completely—just their bodies mutilated, to some of these kids looking like they'd just been sunburned, all of them were dead, all of them were very young—boys and girls both. {4239}

Another time we destroyed two entire villages—which was a month earlier than that. One of our old men, a man who had been around for six months, got hit by a sniper. The battalion went into a frenzy and destroyed these two villages in the Pineapple Forest, which was southwest of Tam Ky about ten miles. Everything living died. It was just—it was mad, it was insane. Everything died and burned, and there was nothing left, nothing left of those two villages.

The general trend in Vietnam at that time that I was there, for the entire year, if you received incoming rounds, sniper rounds from a village, one or two or three, you called in artillery strikes on that village, you napalmed that village; whether it was artillery or air, whichever was the closest. And this was indiscriminate, and this was usual.

Moderator: Mike, in that village you last described, could you estimate the number of civilian casualties?

McCusker: The village—it's really very hard to estimate the casualties. I would say anywhere from fifty to one hundred fifty. I can't really say, because bodies even that day were burned, thrown into huts that were burning and tossed in there. So, it's very, very hard to get an estimate.

Of course, the situation report on it was essentially that we engaged a very large enemy force, and I forgot how many KIAs were listed; but then again, the body count you cannot take it for worth anything.

Moderator: Could you estimate the date of that incident, Mike?

McCusker: Yes, that was—if I remember the correct date, it would be 7 September 1966.

Moderator: Perhaps it would be good to have some questions at this point if there are any from any of the members of the press.

Floor: Was there ever any investigation of either of these incidents, 7 September or 27 October, by the 1st Marine Division or any other agency?

McCusker: No, there was no investigation.

Floor: Why not? Why do you think there was no investigation?

McCusker: Essentially because I would imagine nobody thought it out of—nobody thought to question it. It was, as I said by this time SOP, and you can consider the embarrassment of insanity on coming down from it.

Floor: Could there have been an investigation that you didn't know about?

McCusker: There could be a lot of things I didn't know about. As a matter of fact, generally we were kept in ignorance. One unit didn't know what the other unit was doing. So, the average troop really had no idea exactly what was going on except in his own platoon.

Now in that time when the thirty dead children were burned and napalmed, by the way, a captain came to me, because he knew I was the reporter, and he said,

"Look what the Viet Cong did to their own people."

And I got very angry and I said,

"The Viet Cong didn't do this. I saw the strikes and that's napalm."

And he said,

"Well I think, Sergeant McCusker, you had better write that the Viet Cong did this."

Floor: Did you write that?

McCusker: I didn't write anything on that story.

Floor: Who was the officer?

McCusker: He was a captain. I don't—I can't even remember his name. He was I think the battalion, perhaps the battalion S-1, if I remember correctly, but I'm not sure.

Another thing too, if we did write in or stories the things that we did see, there was absolutely no chance of them getting out anyway, because every story you turned in first went to your divisional office, through a staff sergeant, through a gunnery sergeant, through a lieutenant, and then a major, and then it was sent to the Combat Information {4239c2} Bureau at 3rd Marine Amphibious Headquarters in Danang, across the river from General Walt's headquarters. And each story which had already gone through this redlining procedure went through more lifers like gunnery sergeants, it went through a captain, for final analysis, and then up to a colonel for final analysis—before it was ever released to the press.

So, no matter what you tried to do, even through your stories, there were so many checks and counterbalances that by the time your story got out, if there was anything that you had put in, it was completely devoid of it; it was just—all the life was taken out and there was nothing but a shiny little shallow story about Vietnamese love us and the Marines succeeded again and every battle was a great victory.

Floor: Mr. McCusker, could you give us the names of the villages and the dates that this happened—pinpoint this just as close as you possibly can?

McCusker: The two villages that were destroyed.

Floor: Yes.

McCusker: It was, as I said, ten miles northwest—well, about ten miles due west of Tam Ky. It was down from Hill 488 where Howard got his medal of honor, and it was in the same area where the same battalion had gotten into a firefight the month before.

Floor: And the dates?

McCusker: The date, as I said, approximately, as closely as I can remember was 7 September that this happened, this incident.

Floor: Both of these incidents?

McCusker: The incident of the dead children was 27 October 1966, as I said it was my mother's birthday, which to me was an irony because it seemed like her children were dead.

Floor: Have you reported these incidents before?

McCusker: No, I'm afraid I never officially reported either of these two incidents.

Floor: Why haven't you, seeing as it happened four years ago and being—

McCusker: Oh, I have, I have, since I've been out of the Marine Corps, I've written of these incidents, I've spoken of these incidents, in the Marine Corps I've spoken of these incidents but I never did anything official.

Floor: What I'm driving at is why do you choose now to come here and instead of, if you feel this was an atrocity.

McCusker: All right, I wrote the Fulbright Commission about this. I received nothing but an innocuous answer.

Every time I've ever written anything to the government, and I have carbons of these, you just receive an answer that says, yes, we'll check into this, and we'll call you later about it, and you hear nothing.

I've done this many times, until you just throw up your hands in disgust, you know it's just going to be swept under the floor.

And I have, as I said, carbons of damn near every letter I've ever written, even to the prisoner of war issue—H. Ross Perrot, to which I never received an answer.

Also, the Saigon news correspondent who said the Army was lying—he was immediately made a chaplain's assistant.

I wrote to the Fulbright Commission which said it was going to begin to check into the management of news by the Pentagon, and military news, and I received nothing but a little answer saying, well, we don't have enough time to really call this commission right now. It's very interesting testimony you have, but we'll call you later.

Floor: Is it your impression that these incidents were the exception or were these the rule?

McCusker: No. These were not the exception. Oh, pardon me, these are not the rule. I'm sorry, I'm getting all fuddled up—these are not exceptions; these are generally the rule.

Now, what's an atrocity?

The killing down of one man running in the field.

Well, {4239c3} in other testimony, wherever you naped a village, the villagers were running from it, helicopters would shoot them down.

Under the general operating procedure that anybody running must be a Viet Cong or he wouldn't run from you. It was not taken into account that he might be just scared to death and he knows what the hell you're doing. And so, they were shot down in the field as they were running through the paddies.

No, these were the general rule, whether it was the shooting down of one man or whether two villages were hit.

Floor: What battalion was this?

McCusker: This was the First Battalion, Fifth Marine Regiment, First Marine Division.

Floor: In both these particular incidents.

McCusker: In both these particular incidents, yes.

Floor: Who was the commanding officer at that time?

McCusker: I'm sorry. We're not going to give names, it's on file who he is.

Floor: Well, if it's on file, can you tell us?

McCusker: Well—

Floor: What's the reasoning there?

McCusker: Okay. The reason for not giving any particular names is once again we're going to lay it back on individuals. And, the whole thing for this investigation is to take it away from individuals and not lay the blame back on them again and make it as if it were isolated.

That this is the highest policy possible; that field grade officers were present at this time and the field grade officers yet were under orders themselves.

Floor: You're absolving the CO of the battalion as just doing his duty under standing orders, are you?

McCusker: I'm absolving him as, in essence, the same way I'm absolving myself. That he was just as much a victim of the rigid structure in which he was involved, which especially his whole career was involved and so he was frozen within that position and could not do much more.

And he was under orders as I was under orders.

And I felt a great sense of powerlessness.

Michael Paul McCusker subsequently testified twice at the Winter Soldier Investigation (Detroit Michigan, January 31, February 1–2, 1971) and at the House Ad Hoc Hearing for Vietnam Veterans Against the War (April 23 1971).

—CJHjr

Moderator: We'd like to move to the next witness, Mr. McCusker, unless there is a really pressing other question. We've got five other guys.

Exhibit 19C

Kenneth Barton Osborn

Moderator: Gentlemen, our next witness will be Kenneth Barton Osborn, from Washington, D.C.

Osborn: Mike, here, just provided me with my own documentation, which I'd provided him with earlier. My name is Kenneth Barton Osborn. I live here in Washington and I'm a student here at American University, in the International Service Division. This is my DD 214, which proves that I was honorably discharged this past, let's see, October of 1969. I entered the Army—can you all hear me—I entered the Army in 1966 and was released from active duty in October of 1969, and this is the form that proves that.

I WAS IN VIETNAM FROM September of 1967 until December of 1968. My MOS in the Army was 97C40, which simply is described as an area intelligence specialist. I was trained at Fort Holabird from April of 1967 until right before leaving for Vietnam in September of 1967.

My job in the Army is described overtly—unclassifiedly—as that of an area intelligence specialist; that is, I'm supposedly familiar with the geographical area, culture in that area—and work to provide cross-cultural empathy facility for the Army, that is, so they can understand the culture into which they go on any operational basis.

In fact, when we started the program at Fort Holabird—we were there a couple of days for general orientation and when the class was organized, sat down and in walked a colonel who was a military intelligence—a full colonel in the Army—who gave us what they call the scare lecture.

He described to us that what we were going to be trained for was not, in fact, just area specialty, but the function of what they call a case officer, or an agent handler.

This is the job of spotting, analyzing, recruiting, training and running and terminating agents, who in fact are broken down as principal agents who run nets and sub-agents who are in fact the people in the field who are gathering information.

There are two basic functions in military intelligence: that of the counter-intelligence agent, who supposedly does just that—counter the enemy's intelligence—and the classified function, which is denied by our government, of the overt, active, aggressive collection of intelligence.

It was my job to perform that classified function.

Of course, the starting point with the orientation at Holabird was that, all this that we were going to be trained to do was against the Geneva Accords, and if we had moral compunctions about it, we could opt out of the program if we wanted to.

If we had none, you just go ahead and play along with the program—be trained this way, and then they would return to us as a result the privilege of autonomy from the military.

That is, at one point in our training we would be released from uniform, from military structure, {4242} we would be subservient to only a few people.

In other words, we would be more or less free agents.

This did happen when I got to Vietnam. I worked in the Danang area—that's the I Corps area—and ran agent nets there. I won't go into an awful lot of detail that's unnecessary; it's sufficient to say that I organized nets in the I Corps area and provided lead information to—I was with the 525th military intelligence group, with their 1st Battalion in the I Corps area. Traveled there under the cover of a GS-7 and later a GS-9 as I promoted myself during the year.

I lived under a cover name which is not my own name—which is not necessary to go into, I guess, and lived there in a house in Danang City and served using organizations being the 1st Marine Division, the 3rd Marine Division, the 3rd Marine Amphibious Force, Army units such as the American Division down in Lower

I Corps, the 7th Armored Cavalry, which was in An Kay, and later came up to Danang.

When I first got there, there was no liaison with the using units, and I had to establish that and also start from the beginning and establish nets and so forth. It took me a couple of months to get into business, and also to sell my services to the American military, who were reticent to use "foreign nationals," that is, indigenous Vietnamese personnel, for information.

When I proved on a retrospective plausibility basis, that is, look what I report and see what happens and if you believe it then accept my reports—when I sold them this information that way and they believed it, we were in business and I served in the 1st Marine Division, and the 3rd, and the 3rd Marine Amphibious Force primarily, because at that time the majority of the operations in the area were Marine operations.

My liaison was with the G-2 officers of those organizations, and with subordinate S-2 officers in regimental headquarters subservient to those divisions in the area.

So that was my function in Vietnam. I was there, in that function, for 16 months.

During that time, I worked with interrogations and I worked with the using units in their field operation at different times mostly to get a reading on what kind of information they needed—I needed requirements. I needed to know what to collect. I needed to know what to levy on my agents and as a result, since I couldn't get any specifics, other than things from the Pentagon like "Beware of troop movements around the western Czechoslovakian border," and so forth—couldn't be more specific than that, and we were in Southeast Asia, I had to go out and get my own requirements from the using units so that I could travel to the field with the Marine counter-intelligence investigating team.

During that time, I saw several incidents which I want to relate to you here.

There was a counter-intelligence team, an interrogation team, there on the compound of the 3rd Marine Amphibious Force, which is adjacent to the Danang air base in their G-2 shop, they have an investigation—they had at that time—I think it was 1967 or 1968—they had an intelligence team in there which were made exclusively of American Marines.

There were no Vietnamese there. These Marines were trained and spoke Vietnamese. They were interrogators.

In the course of collecting intelligence information, I would come up with what Ed Murphy referred to as VC infrastructure detail, personalities, descriptions of people working in the local committees in the villages which were VC organizations.

When I got this information—at first there was no function, that is, no use for it, because there was no program that could effectively deal with eliminating VC infrastructure on a combat-unit basis.

I later got into the Phoenix program on—as a result of searching around for a unit that could use this information.

At the time, early in the game, I used to give {4242c2} the information to the 3rd Marine Amphibious Force interrogating teams and they would pick up personally.

There was a lieutenant, first lieutenant Marine, who was later promoted to captain during his tour there that I knew him, who would go out to the village with other Marines, Marine EM—enlisted men—and scarf up these people who were described in my reports and bring them in for interrogation.

They had two hootches right there on that 3rd Marine Amphibious Force compound, which were devoted to interrogation and they used the following modus operandi:

At one point, I had described a certain individual of a local village—suburban village of Danang. They went out and scarfed her up and brought her in and simply put her in one of the wire mesh cages that were inside this hootch, which was divided into four cages. She was in one of them, and they simply put her in there. There were no facilities other than a wooden bench—regular, like a picnic bench, which stood on, like, a sawhorse—on which she could sit, sleep, do whatever she wanted to. There were no toilet facilities. There was no food and there was no water.

And the idea was that she should stay there until she talked. When they had weakened her, I was on the compound one day and the—a lieutenant said to me, I want to show you what we're doing with so-and-so whom you—who we got from your report there. Come on over next door and I'll show you the process and when we went over—and they had set this hootch up within the week.

And they were quite proud of the fact that they were just leaving the people there to starve. I said, well, we'll just leave her there until she talks. They did leave her there for about ten days until, finally, she was so weak that she couldn't respond to anything, and at that point, they just sent her back to her village and called it a loss—got no information from her.

At another point, I had identified one of the members of the village committees for VC logistical supply, as I remember. In any case, he was picked up and brought in as what was described earlier as a detainee, not a POW, but a detainee.

The fellow was put in the same hootch with the four cages, in another cage, and he was forced to lay on the floor with his hands tied behind his back and they would insert a bamboo peg—a wooden peg, I'm not sure if it was bamboo—a wooden peg, a dowel with a sharpened end, into the semicircular canal of the ear, which would be forced into the head little by little as he was interrogated. And eventually, did enter the brain and killed the subject, the detainee.

They never got any viable information out of him—they called that a loss but in any case, that was one thing that was a standard operating procedure.

And I asked the lieutenant, I said, how often do you do this kind of thing? He said, whenever we can't get information by easier methods.

These methods being, I won't re-describe the ringing up of the telephone sort of thing to the women's breast nipples and the men's genitals.

When these things failed, then they went further into—the, I think, worst of the torture methods that I saw was the one of the inserting the dowel into the ear.

With that same unit, the 3rd Marine Division, I went along twice when they would go up in helicopters which belonged to the Marine Division and take two detainees along.

409

They used one as a scare mechanism for the other. If they wanted to interrogate detainee A, they would take someone along who was either in bad health or whom they had already written off as a loss—take both these Vietnamese along in the helicopter and they would say, they would start investigating Detainee B, the one they had no interest in, and they wouldn't get any information out of him and so they would threaten to throw him out of the helicopter. {4242c3}

All the time, of course, the detainee they wanted information from was watching. And they would threaten and threaten and, finally, they would throw him out of the helicopter.

I was there when this happened twice and it was very effective, because, of course, at the time the step one was to throw the person out of the helicopter and step two was to say, "You're next."

And that quite often broke them down, demoralized them, and at that point they would give whatever information. Sometimes the information was accurate; sometimes this was considered an ineffective method of investigation. Sometimes the Vietnamese, when threatened with things like the dowel treatment or the telephone treatment or in one case, the helicopter incident, would start babbling anything at all—would say whatever you, he felt, wanted to hear, and this, again was ineffective.

But that was the modus operandi used, and those were the incidents that I actually was involved in.

Floor: Excuse me—you did actually see these two people thrown out of the helicopters?
Osborn: Yes, sir, on two different occasions, yes sir.
Floor: Could you tell me when and—
Osborn: Yes, sir, that was—
Floor: Be as specific as you can?
Osborn: Yes, sir, I will. That was in the month of April 1968, and it was northwest of Danang, perhaps fifteen miles just beyond the suburban villages there. The base of operations was the 3rd Marine Amphibious Force compound adjacent to the Danang air base in I Corps, and they would go from there up in a heli-

copter and go through this procedure and come back down again with what was considered a successful interrogation.

Floor: You went up there for that specific purpose?

Osborn: That's right.

Floor: Now, what was, what procedure did you follow, how did you do it?

Osborn: Simply go out to—from the Marine Wing, they called it, there, there were on the compound that were the interrogation headquarters, go out to the helicopter there in a jeep, take these people with us. They weren't badly restrained; they had their hands tied behind their backs. They walked, they were pushed and so forth onto the helicopter, and when they got up they would simply start on the subject that they didn't want to interrogate, to scare the one that they did want to interrogate, and they'd terminate—they would throw the second subject out to scare the first one into whatever they either wanted to hear or whatever was appropriate.

Floor: Who did the throwing?

Osborn: The throwing was done by Marine enlisted men.

Floor: On whose orders?

Osborn: On the lieutenant's orders.

Floor: Where were you when it happened?

Osborn: I was there in the helicopter on one of the side seats observing—

Floor: How far would you be from the door?

Osborn: Five feet.

Floor: What would you say? Did you ever make an attempt to stop it or—

Osborn: No, I did not. I was there to observe.

Moderator: Mr. Osborn has some additional testimony, sir. Could we—unless you have any objections—could we get that out before we have any additional questions.

Osborn: What else do you want to know?

Moderator: Bart, you said that you worked closely with the CIA in the Phoenix program; how closely did you work with the CIA, and what did the Phoenix program mean to you?

Osborn: As I had mentioned briefly earlier, sometimes the using combat units in the I Corps area, which is the area I basically {4243} served because that's where the nets were gathering information, had no use for potentially valuable information, accurate information and timely, that we would gather just in the course of getting reports in from the field, from the Vietnamese agents.

I was frustrated to let a lot of the information on a timely basis go down the drain. If I would have a VC who was the head of a committee or a fairly high-placed individual in the VC infrastructure and I found out where he was, where he would be, how he could be picked up and so forth, and I'd take this to the Marine Division and they'd say that's nice, but we really don't have the facilities to use it.

I lived in Danang and I happened to run into a fellow in the club where I—the Stone Elephants, the Navy officers' club—ate there, and I ran into a fellow who ran the I Corps area for CIA operations and I talked to him and found out through him that they had a program that could receive that kind of information.

On a discreet basis, I called him aside after dinner one night and asked him if he knew where I could disseminate this information on an effective basis. He put me in contact with an Army major who was at a house there rented by the CIA in Danang, and I established the liaison necessary in order to disseminate whatever VCI information I got with my reports, and did that for, I guess, for the last eight months or so that I was in Vietnam.

Moderator: Does the term exterminate, to terminate with extreme prejudice—are you familiar with that term?
Osborn: There are two ways—yes—there are two ways to terminate an agent. When you are through with the agent, that is, when he serves no more function to you, you can do one of two things.

You can terminate him by paying him an amount of money, thanking him for his service, swearing him to secrecy, and simply letting him go—that's without prejudice.

There is termination with prejudice where the agent constitutes a threat either to your operations, to you personally as a case officer, to whatever has determined the threat, and you terminate him with prejudice by either killing the individual or perhaps relocating him in the—

I remember one incident of an agent up in Phu Bi who was relocated as a prisoner of war into a Chieu Hoy camp and reoriented—

I'm not really familiar with the details of that, but the main idea was to, of course, neutralize the individual.

I got orders a couple of times to terminate agents with prejudice because of things they had done which were considered illegal or in bad taste or threatening—bad security—while I was there.

Floor: Did you follow those orders out, sir?

Osborn: I had an agent, for instance, in Danang who was an effective principal agent—ran a net in the I Corps area around Danang. And who had worked—had told me when I hired him that he had never worked for American intelligence before. That was a starting point when I hired him. He spoke English so we communicated well—he was fluent in French and English, and he told me, no, he had never worked for the American intelligence community before.

It turned out, though, that while he had been working for us for some time, in March of 1968, a list came out from the CIA, from CSD, they're in Danang. And it was called the catalog of undesirable personalities, and we called that a blacklist. People who had done no-nos and were to be left untouched by the American military intelligence community.

His name was on that list and I was shocked to find that out.

I went—I went to a captain, an Army military intelligence captain, and I asked him what he thought I ought to do in that method of termination. He said, well, you do whatever you want to do, he's your {4243c2} man, and generally that was the case, that the case officers were able to use their own discretion.

But he said, "I want the man dead," and so I said, "All right."

And I went out and he was a resident of Danang, had a family, a wife who also spoke English and a fine woman, also two children, two or three children. And so this would be eliminating the father of two children, obviously, and for no real reason, because what he had done was to have worked previously for the CIA as an interpreter and they didn't like his interpreting because he had been feeding information to agents on the side in order to corroborate their information and get them better pay. He'd sit down with two agents and say, what do you have and what do you have, and he'd cross the information.

They found this out and they fired him, on the blacklist as a result.

He was an active agent with me, he was blacklisted, so he had to go.

I took him aside; at the time he had quite a number of pieces of equipment. He had a Yamaha motorcycle that I had lent him for running around, he had a two-way radio, a little Motorola set that we communicated with on an emergency basis, he had a number of things and he owed me a lot of piasters which he's drawn on his salary—which I had done in order to get a handle on him, in order to make him work effectively.

And so, he was strung out, and he was obligated in this way, and I sat him down and said I need these things back—it was a period of about ten days.

And when I had gotten all these things back, which, of course, were compromising logistics, I then told him what I had been told to do and told him that if he did not disappear from the city, with his family or without his family but in any case disappear for at least three months, I would have to come back and kill him. That was a hollow threat, but it worked. And he left and whether it was followed up or not, I don't know, but that's an example of going beyond what the orders were in neutralizing agents.

Floor: What about the other orders?
Osborn: I had an agent in Phu Bai, which was the 3rd Marine
    Division base, and he had been involved in some black market

activities, and that came up in the course of an interview one time that I had with him one time.

And I reported it to—in a report which was standard after every interrogation, after every what they call personal meeting with your agent.

Because he would be compromised by having his finger in the black market and was not working exclusively for me or for the American intelligence community, he was considered a threat.

I was told to terminate him.

I went up to Phu Bai and I brought him down to Danang to live with some relatives, and that's what happened.

Moderator: Are you familiar, Bart, with any incident where a person was actually terminated, liquidated, with extreme prejudice?

Osborn: Yes, I'm afraid I had at one point in my employ a woman who was Chinese and who lived in Vietnam. She was a Chinese Vietnamese citizen. She was educated to the point where she spoke several languages, she spoke fluent English. And I used her as an interpreter and also as a guide to the culture that I was working in because as a Westerner, there were a lot of things there that I couldn't have been sensitive to. She was my guide in that respect.

She also was my direct contact with agents, that is, I had people I didn't want to meet because I didn't want them to know me because in case they got compromised, they couldn't compromise me.

So, she was my go-between. She acted as an interpreter, guide, and support agent, that is, a courier.

And at one point she had been—because we were short of people who were that well trained in Vietnamese, she was cross-exposed to operations. She was into a lot of my operations. {4243c3}

She worked with—and incidentally, I ran only unilateral operations, American operations only, not in cooperation with the Vietnamese, which is against the Geneva Convention.

And so, this was a sensitive area.

When it was determined by a military intelligence captain that she was too cross-exposed, he reported that to Saigon and he got the reading back that she ought to be terminated from the scene. She ought to be let go. It was not determined—it wasn't said whether she ought to be terminated with prejudice or not.

He took it upon himself to terminate her by murdering her.

He murdered her with a .45 in a street in Danang, shot her in the neck and let her lay in the street there.

It was said that there were Viet Cong agents, or terrorists, or sappers, or something in the area who shot her, and it was plausible because we knew that she was heavily involved in intelligence and would have been targeted by the unfriendlies—that's the Viet Cong.

Moderator: I have one further question before I turn this over to the press. Bart, since your return to the United States have you ever worked, have you ever been in contact with the CIA since that time?

Osborn: Yes, I have, Mike. I had been pretty deeply involved in a number of operations in Vietnam, as I said, and as a result when you recruit agents you usually do it by recruiting their loyalty to you, and then get them to relate to the mission.

When I left Vietnam I turned over my operation to my successor, but because a number of these things were CIA-supported, like the Phoenix program, VCI operations, and so forth, I was recontacted when I got back to the states, back a couple of months.

They recontacted me and asked if I would serve on an advisory basis, and I did for a while. I don't think that that's all that relevant to this whole thing, but it is true that these things continue.

I terminated that whole thing this June, and I have no association with the CIA anymore.

Moderator: Gentlemen, any questions, please.

Floor: When you were recruiting these agents, you were working for the CIA?

Osborn: Yes, sir, these were military intelligence modus operandi—
you know, method of operation—nets. They were serving military combat units for combat intelligence and the Phoenix
program for VC infrastructure, and they were laterally disseminated on a discretionary basis.

If I had only combat information, I'd only send it to combat
units. If I had only VCI I'd send it only to the Phoenix program, the
Phoenix coordinator there in Danang.

Floor: Mr. Osborn, in that first incident you mentioned, about the
termination, you said that was a hollow threat. Why did you
say that?
Osborn: Because at the time that I said that, I didn't have any intention of killing him, but just of exercising a second threat if the
first one didn't work. I may have killed him eventually if he
became a viable threat. That is, he may have gotten bitter and
compromised a number of things I was involved in and as a
result have threatened my life. I may have. But I didn't. But as I
say, at the time that was a hollow threat because I didn't intend
to kill him, when I told him I did.
Floor: You would have killed him if necessary?
Osborn: Yes, I would have.
Floor: Why are you spilling all the beans now? Because we haven't
won the war?
Osborn: No, ma'am, it's not.
Floor: Well, will you tell us why?
Osborn: Yes. I feel as if this standard operating procedure, which is
authorized by the American military community, and by the
CIA, is against the American value system.

I don't feel that I can come back with a clear conscience from
Vietnam and con- {4244} sider myself a good Christian, or I don't
feel I can have a clear conscience, knowing that my government is
working despicable methods of operation in other parts of the world,
and denying it; working against the Geneva Conference and blam-

ing other nations for doing the same; taking action against foreign interests which are doing the same thing that we're doing, it's just that we classify it as they do—we catch them, they catch us, and it constitutes one heck of a hypocrisy.

The reason I've said these things today is simply to document or add evidence to the fact that we are doing these things, and my suggestions would be that we don't have to.

We should not criticize others for doing the same things that we're doing, or we ought to cut it out. One of the two.

I simply want to add to what the others have said, and that's why I'm here today.

Floor: Do you consider yourself a war criminal, under Nuremberg?

Osborn: Yes, for some of the things that I did in Vietnam I feel that they definitely were criminal. Then why wasn't he arrested and charged during this confession?

Floor: Mr. Noetzel, did you ever terminate an agent yourself?

Osborn: Mr. Noetzel?

Floor: No, I'm sorry.

Osborn: Mr. Osborn. I beg your pardon.

Floor: Did you ever terminate an agent by death yourself? Did you ever kill an agent?

Osborn: No, I didn't. I never killed an agent.

Floor: In that first case, the case of the agent with the Yamaha. Is it possible that when he was working for the CIA, he was not aware of that?

Osborn: No, it is not possible that he was not aware that he was working for the American military intelligence community, and that was my question to him that he had denied. So, in essence he had lied to me. And the interest in lying was simply this: the American intelligence community was hiring him, and they were the only force hiring him in the area, and if he wanted a job—and he was qualified because of his multi-language capability—he had to get on with somebody. And he had been fired by the CIA, and as a matter of fact he had not re-approached us, we had approached him.

Floor: With the Chinese agent who was killed, did you have any advance news that he was going to be killed?

Osborn: No, I had not advance news.

Floor: In that case, what was your reaction, if you felt it was unnecessary? Did you protest?

Osborn: Yes, I protested to the fellow who had murdered her and asked him why, and he simply explained that she was too cross-exposed and was too involved in operations. And I didn't feel that since she had been asked to help us, and had never done anything actively or passively that was against our interest, but had only followed through and had gotten involved in as many operations as we had asked her to get involved in, then to determine her fair bait for murder seemed wrong.

Floor: Sir, did you ever kill anyone other than an agent?

Osborn: In Vietnam?

Floor: In Vietnam.

Osborn: Not that I can tell you about. In fact, during the fifteen months that I was in Vietnam I was responsible for deaths, yes.

Floor: In what respect?

Osborn: Several respects. One of our functions in supplying combat information to the 1st Marine Division, especially their G-2 office, was to get targeting areas for B-52 strikes, and we would follow these up to see how effective we had been.

For instance, if we had gotten an NVA unit reported in an area, and they would come in with the B-52s and they would target them as they came in and they would plough an area—that is, they'd drop bombs and plough an {4244c2} area there—and we'd follow up occasionally, and I'd find that we had killed civilians in the process.

And whether or not they were Viet Cong agents or not I don't know. There were civilian's dead as a result who were not, in fact, part of the NVA units that were targeted.

Floor: Did you ever kill any civilians or POWs yourself?

Osborn: Not myself, no.

Floor: Did you ever make any attempts to tell anybody, any government authorities, about these things?

Osborn: In other words, bring charges or make an official complaint? No, never did.

Floor: Will you tell us why?

Osborn: Yes. Because it was so much the SOP, and my entire peer group had been doing the same thing, and to bring this up as a subject was old news.

And as a matter of fact the people to whom I talked privately, private citizens, when I came back to the United States, doubted this—frankly didn't believe me, or if they believed me generally, and knew that I was not known to be a liar, knew that I wouldn't have any reason to lie about this, thought it was sad that I had been exposed to a war, but that's war.

Floor: Have you ever told this in public before?

Floor: What about your peer group, what is their attitude about these cages, and throwing people out of helicopters and that sort of thing, as you say?

Osborn: They vary. They do vary in their attitudes. I know people who are conscience-stricken about the methods of operations that we described, I know other people who just looked on it as a dirty necessity, of being in Vietnam for a year. And you get your year over and you go home and forget about it. There were all levels of conscience about it. Generally, though, it was an accepted thing.

Floor: Tell us what your rank was.

Osborn: Yes, sir, I was in Vietnam, when I first got there, a Pfc, an E-3 in the Army, and when I left Fort Holabird an E-3. It was a long time before I was promoted to an E-4. I was an E-4 when I left Vietnam and was promoted to E-5 by administrative process just before I left the Army.

Floor: Did you ever get extra pay? Did you have a living allowance, or that sort of thing?

Osborn: Yes. We had allowance for separate rations, because we had to eat, we had to live in the status and keep up—GS-9s make a good bit of money in Vietnam. They have a 25 per cent pay increment and so forth. On Pfc salary I couldn't necessarily do that, and so there were separate rations, separate living allowance, and then a lot of our expenses were paid through a separate intelligence fund, so we didn't have to put it out of our own pockets.

Floor: Would you explain what you understand to be your violations of the Geneva Accords?

Osborn: Yes. Primarily it was this.

I mentioned the scare lecture that we had at Holabird, and it mentioned that we would be working in an area, that is, agent operations, that is plausibly denied by the American government. If we didn't want to associate with it that was up to us, but we had to make that value judgment and do it voluntarily.

In fact, out of a class of thirty-seven people only one opted out, and we were told that it would not be a mark against us if we decided not to continue with this at that point, but that we would have the rest of the day to think about it, and we were let go that day from class. And the next day we came back and a fellow had opted out, and the rest stayed because about half the class knew that that was the case, that area intelligence specialists were in fact agent handlers, and the others, who were surprised, accepted it. {4244c3}

Floor: Sir, what were the violations, though?

Osborn: Oh, all right. Yes.

And we were told, we were told at the time that our function would be to run illegal operations, that is, active collection of intelligence by utilization of spies, nets, agent nets—and this was illegal. It alludes to the thing about if you are caught or compromised, we'll deny the whole thing. And that's basically why we lived in cover status in Vietnam.

Because if John Smith, and that's a fictional name, was caught doing so and so, he would be pulled back to Saigon and perhaps sent out of country, perhaps changed back to uniform, and he would simply evaporate—and so if charges were officially ever brought against the government that said, "We know of a John Smith in the I Corps area, who was in fact recruiting agents," they'd say, well, you document that, and that's fine.

That was plausible denial, and it worked very effectively. This was illegality number one.

Another example of what we were doing illegally, I mentioned before, we were running unilateral operations only. Just unilateral. They were an American effort, no cooperation whatsoever with the Vietnamese, based on the assumption that whatever the Vietnamese did was compromising because they might be infiltrated by the Viet Cong.

In any case, it is, in fact, it is in conflict with our agreement with the government of South Vietnam to have exclusively unilateral collection of intelligence operations, which is what we had.

Floor: Sir, do you feel in any personal danger as a result of your appearance here today?

Osborn: I don't feel as if, if somebody came out and reported to the press involvement with classified operations which are still classified, to which I have agreed not to speak, and I have signed agreements with the Department of Defense saying that I would not go into specific detail, which I, in fact, have not named names today—this is not a crucifying session of any kind—I have agreed not to go into this in detail.

It was implicit in my agreement with the Department of Defense, that if anyone asked me what I did in Vietnam, I was an area intelligence specialist; "What was that?" Well, you were kind of familiar with the area and you studied geography and knew map reading and things, but I don't know map reading and things very well, so that was not very plausible.

And so I don't think that this would do me any good, if I went to apply for top-secret clearance, like I had before, I probably wouldn't make out too well, but what I plan to do is go into private industry on the basis of my education when I complete it, and so forth.

And I hope to be able to stand on my own two feet—not a precarious process like investigation.

Is the "pinko" questionable?

I feel as though the classification system is closed to me as a result of today, and whatever else I get into.

Floor: You say you are at George Washington?

Osborn: I'm at American.

Floor: And what is your major?

Osborn: My major is languages and linguistics. I'm in a master's degree for International Services program, in the school there, and I'm Western Europe oriented—German and so forth.

Floor: What was your analysis of the Green Beret case in 1969, in Nha Trang? The way in which the Administration and the Department of the Army handled that?

Osborn: I mentioned plausible denial to you before. And I think that if you were familiar with the method of operation that went on, and it was a part of your life, you lived with it—and if that were your goal, your mission, your assignment, and so forth, if you heard of having a double agent through the 5th Special Forces, who was to {4245} be terminated, and it flapped, that is, it became known, and it was necessary for our government to deny it, to see them deny it, and go through the legal process to divert attention from it or whatever they were trying to do, was not surprising at all.

That's the way I saw it.

Floor: Sir, you say you saw Marines push Vietnamese out of helicopters. Could you tell me what the reaction of the Marines aboard the helicopters was when this occurred? Was there any reaction, or this sort of thing, and what was the reaction of the victims?

Osborn: The victims fell.

Floor: Before.

Osborn: Before they left the helicopter? That's two questions, sir.

Floor: I'd like to know a little about what was going on in the helicopter.

Osborn: Right. We'd go up, and the interrogation team chief—the lieutenant—and one, two, three EM, I'm not—there were two or three EM, I guess. And they would have these people with them, and they would have their hands tied behind their back, and they would load them on the helicopters, and the helicopter would take off and the

The Marines, you have to understand that wherever they were in a function like interrogation, any support function at all, they considered it less dangerous than a combat mission.

They would go out in the boonies and kill via their M-16 rifles. And so, I didn't ever see any moral compunctions about that being done; as a matter of fact, when they were told to go ahead and push the fellow they would go ahead and push him

And on both occasions that happened.

Moderator: I'm sorry to interrupt this right now. We're already five minutes over the time of this session, and we have two more witnesses. Mr. Osborn will be available for additional interviews, he'll be here during the day, so I'd like to move on right now.

Kenneth Barton Osborn subsequently testified before two Congressional committees: A House Government Operations subcommittee (August 2 1971) and the Senate Armed Services Committee (July 20 1973). -CJHjr

EXHIBIT 20

Appendix: Text of Proposed or Enacted Provisions Funding Restrictions on Military Operations

1. Cooper-Church Amendment, P.L. 91-652, H.R. 19911

Sec. 7. (a) In line with the expressed intention of the President of the United States, none of the funds authorized or appropriated pursuant to this or any other act may be used to finance the introduction of United States ground troops into Cambodia, or to provide United States advisers to or for Cambodian military forces in Cambodia; (b) military and economic assistance provided by the United States to Cambodia and authorized or appropriated pursuant to this or any other act shall not be construed as a commitment by the United States to Cambodia for its defense.

2. Continuing Appropriations, P.L. 93-52, H.J. Res. 636

Sec. 108. Notwithstanding any other provision of law, on or after August 15, 1973, no funds herein or heretofore appropriated may be obligated or expended to finance directly or indirectly combat activities by United States military forces in or over or from off the shores of North Vietnam, South Vietnam, Laos or Cambodia.

3. Continuing Appropriations, 1974, P.L. 93-124, H.J. Res. 727

Resolved by the Senate and House of Representatives of the United States of America in Congress assembled, That clause (c) of section 102 of the joint resolution of July 1, 1973 (Public Law 93-52), is hereby amended by striking out "September 30, 1973" and inserting in lieu thereof "the sine die adjournment of the first session of the Ninety-third Congress".

4. Second Supplemental Appropriations Act, P.L. 93-50, H.R. 9055

Sec. 304. No funds appropriated in this Act shall be expended to aid or assist in the reconstruction of the Democratic Republic of Vietnam (North Vietnam). Sec. 307. None of the funds herein appropriated under this Act may be expended to support directly or indirectly combat activities in or over Cambodia, Laos, North Vietnam and South Vietnam or off the shores of Cambodia, Laos, North Vietnam and South Vietnam by United States forces, and after August 15, 1973, no other funds heretofore appropriated under any other Act may be expended for such purpose.

5. Department of State Authorization, P.L. 93-126, H.R. 7645

Sec. 13. Notwithstanding any other provision of law, on or after August 15, 1973, no funds heretofore or hereafter appropriated may be obligated or expended to finance the involvement of United States military forces in hostilities in or over or from off the shores of North Vietnam, South Vietnam, Laos, or Cambodia, unless specifically authorized hereafter by the Congress. Notwithstanding any other provision of law, upon enactment of this Act, no funds heretofore or hereafter appropriated may be obligated or expended for the purpose of providing assistance of any kind, directly or indirectly, to or on behalf of North Vietnam, unless specifically authorized hereafter by the Congress.

CRS-29

6. Cooper-Church Amendment, H.R. 15628, Senate Foreign Relations Committee Amdt. No. 3, H.R. 15628

In concert with the declared objectives of the President of the United States to avoid the involvement of the United States in Cambodia after July 1, 1970, and to expedite the withdrawal of American forces from Cambodia, it is hereby provided that unless specifically authorized by law hereafter enacted, no funds authorized or appropriated pursuant to this act or any other law may be expended after July 1, 1970 for the purpose of:

(1) retaining United States forces in Cambodia.

(2) paying the compensation or allowances of, or otherwise supporting, directly or indirectly, any United States personnel in Cambodia who furnish military instruction to Cambodian forces or engage in any combat activity in support of Cambodian forces; (3) entering into or carrying out any contract or agreement to provide military instruction in Cambodia or to provide persons to engage in any combat activity in support of Cambodian forces; or (4) conducting any combat activity in direct support of Cambodian forces; nothing contained in this section shall be deemed to impugn the constitutional power of the President as Commander in Chief, including the exercise of that constitutional power which may be necessary to protect the lives of U.S. armed forces wherever deployed; nothing contained in this section shall be deemed to impugn the constitutional powers of the Congress including the power to declare war and to make rules for the government and regulation of the armed forces of the United States.

14. Cooper-Church Amendment, H.R. 9910

Withdrawal of United States Forces from Indochina Sec. 406. (a) The Congress hereby finds that the repeal of the joint resolution entitled "Joint Resolution to promote the maintenance of international peace and security in Southeast Asia", approved August 10, 1964 (Public Law 88-408), known as the Gulf of Tonkin Resolution, has left the Government of the United States without congressional authority for continued participation in the war in Indochina. Therefore, in order to bring an end to the involvement of the armed forces of the United States in the hostilities in Indochina, to secure the safe return of the United States' prisoners of war held by North Vietnam and its allies, and to help bring about a political settlement of the war in Indochina, it is the sense of the Congress that it should be the policy of the United States to provide for the expeditious withdrawal from Indochina of all United States armed forces.

CRS-33

(b) On and after the date of enactment of this Act, in order to carry out the policy of withdrawal of all United States armed forces from Indochina, funds authorized for use by such forces by this or any other Act may be used only for the purpose of withdrawal of all such forces from Indochina and may not be used for the purpose of engaging such forces in hostilities in North or South Vietnam, Cambodia, or Laos, except for actions necessary to protect those forces against imminent danger as they are withdrawn.

EXHIBIT 21

War Powers Resolution of 1973

Public Law 93-148
93rd Congress, H. J. Res. 542
November 7, 1973
Joint Resolution
Concerning the war powers of Congress and the President.
Resolved by the Senate and the House of Representatives of the
    United States of America in
Congress assembled,
SHORT TITLE
SECTION 1. This joint resolution may be cited as the "War Powers
    Resolution".

PURPOSE AND POLICY

SEC. 2. (A) IT IS the purpose of this joint resolution to fulfill the intent of the framers of the Constitution of the United States and insure that the collective judgments of both the Congress and the President will apply to the introduction of United States Armed Forces into hostilities, or into situations where imminent involvement in hostilities is clearly indicate by the circumstances, and to the continued use of such forces in hostilities or in such situations.

(b) Under article I, section 8, of the Constitution, it is specifically provided that the Congress shall have the power to make all laws necessary and proper for carrying into execution, not only its own powers but also all other powers vested by the Constitution in the Government of the United States, or in any department or officer thereof.

(c) The constitutional powers of the President as Commander-in-Chief to introduce United States Armed Forces into hostilities, or into situations where imminent involvement in hostilities is clearly indicated by the circumstances, are exercised only pursuant to (1) a declaration of war, (2) specific statutory authorization, or (3) a national emergency created by attack upon the United States, its territories or possessions, or its armed forces.

CONSULTATION

SEC. 3. The President in every possible instance shall consult with Congress before introducing United States Armed Forces into hostilities or into situation where imminent involvement in hostilities is clearly indicated by the circumstances, and after every such introduction shall consult regularly with the Congress until United States Armed Forces are no longer engaged in hostilities or have been removed from such situations.

REPORTING

SEC. 4. (a) In the absence of a declaration of war, in any case in which United States Armed Forces are introduced—

(1) into hostilities or into situations where imminent involvement in hostilities is clearly indicated by the circumstances;

(2) into the territory, airspace or waters of a foreign nation, while equipped for combat, except for deployments which relate solely to supply, replacement, repair, or training of such forces; or

(3) in numbers which substantially enlarge United States Armed Forces equipped for combat already located in a foreign nation; the president shall submit within 48 hours to the Speaker of the House of Representatives and to the President pro tempore of the Senate a report, in writing, setting forth—

(A) the circumstances necessitating the introduction of United States Armed Forces;

(B) the constitutional and legislative authority under which such introduction took place; and

(C) the estimated scope and duration of the hostilities or involvement.

(b) The President shall provide such other information as the Congress may request in the fulfillment of its constitutional responsibilities with respect to committing the Nation to war and to the use of United States Armed Forces abroad

(c) Whenever United States Armed Forces are introduced into hostilities or into any situation described in subsection (a) of this section, the President shall, so long as such armed forces continue to be engaged in such hostilities or situation, report to the Congress periodically on the status of such hostilities or situation as well as on the scope and duration of such hostilities or situation, but in no event shall he report to the Congress less often than once every six months.

CONGRESSIONAL ACTION

SEC. 5. (a) Each report submitted pursuant to section 4(a)(1) shall be transmitted to the Speaker of the House of Representatives and to the President pro tempore of the Senate on the same calendar day. Each report so transmitted shall be referred to the Committee on Foreign Affairs of the House of Representatives and to the Committee on Foreign Relations of the Senate for appropriate action. If, when the report is transmitted, the Congress has adjourned sine die or has adjourned for any period in excess of three calendar days, the Speaker of the House of Representatives and the President pro tempore of the Senate, if they deem it advisable (or if petitioned by at least 30 percent of the membership of their respective Houses) shall jointly request the President to convene Congress in order that it may consider the report and take appropriate action pursuant to this section.

(b) Within sixty calendar days after a report is submitted or is required to be submitted pursuant to section 4(a)(1), whichever is earlier, the President shall terminate any use of United States Armed Forces with respect to which such report was submitted (or required to be submitted), unless the Congress (1) has declared war or has enacted a specific authorization for such use of United States Armed Forces, (2) has extended by law such sixty-day period, or (3) is physically unable to meet as a result of an armed attack upon the United States. Such sixty-day period shall be extended for not more than an additional thirty days if the President determines and certifies to the Congress in writing that unavoidable military necessity respecting the safety of United States Armed Forces requires the continued use of such armed forces in the course of bringing about a prompt removal of such forces.

(c) Notwithstanding subsection (b), at any time that United States Armed Forces are engaged in hostilities outside the territory of the United States, its possessions and territories without a declaration of war or specific statutory authorization, such forces shall be removed by the President if the Congress so directs by concurrent resolution.

CONGRESSIONAL PRIORITY PROCEDURES FOR JOINT RESOLUTION OR BILL

SEC. 6. (a) Any joint resolution or bill introduced pursuant to section 5(b) at least thirty calendar days before the expiration of the sixty-day period specified in such section shall be referred to the Committee on Foreign Affairs of the House of Representatives or the Committee on Foreign Relations of the Senate, as the case may be, and such committee shall report one such joint resolution or bill, together with its recommendations, not later than twenty-four calendar days before the expiration of the sixty-day period specified in such section, unless such House shall otherwise determine by the yeas and nays.

(b) Any joint resolution or bill so reported shall become the pending business of the House in question (in the case of the Senate the time for debate shall be equally divided between the proponents and the opponents), and shall be voted on within three calendar days thereafter, unless such House shall otherwise determine by yeas and nays.

(c) Such a joint resolution or bill passed by one House shall be referred to the committee of the other House named in subsection (a) and shall be reported out not later than fourteen calendar days before the expiration of the sixty-day period specified in section 5(b). The joint resolution or bill so reported shall become the pending business of the House in question and shall be voted on within three calendar days after it has been reported, unless such House shall otherwise determine by yeas and nays.

(d) In the case of any disagreement between the two Houses of Congress with respect to a joint resolution or bill passed by both Houses, conferees shall be promptly appointed and the committee of conference shall make and file a report with respect to such resolution or bill not later than four calendar days before the expiration of the sixty-day period specified in section 5(b). In the event the conferees are unable to agree within 48 hours, they shall report back to their respective Houses in disagreement. Notwithstanding any rule in either House concerning the printing of conference reports in the Record or concerning any delay in the consideration of such reports, such report shall be acted on by both Houses not later than the expiration of such sixty-day period.

CONGRESSIONAL PRIORITY PROCEDURES FOR CONCURRENT RESOLUTION

SEC. 7. (a) Any concurrent resolution introduced pursuant to section 5(b) at least thirty calendar days before the expiration of the sixty-day period specified in such section shall be referred to the Committee on Foreign Affairs of the House of Representatives or the Committee on Foreign Relations of the Senate, as the case may be, and one such concurrent resolution shall be reported out by such committee together with its recommendations within fifteen calendar days, unless such House shall otherwise determine by the yeas and nays.

(b) Any concurrent resolution so reported shall become the pending business of the House in question (in the case of the Senate the time for debate shall be equally divided between the proponents and the opponents), and shall be voted on within three calendar days thereafter, unless such House shall otherwise determine by yeas and nays.

(c) Such a concurrent resolution passed by one House shall be referred to the committee of the other House named in subsection (a) and shall be reported out by such committee together with its recommendations within fifteen calendar days and shall thereupon become the pending business of such House and shall be voted on within three calendar days after it has been reported, unless such House shall otherwise determine by yeas and nays.

(d) In the case of any disagreement between the two Houses of Congress with respect to a concurrent resolution passed by both Houses, conferees shall be promptly appointed and the committee of conference shall make and file a report with respect to such concurrent resolution within six calendar days after the legislation is referred to the committee of conference. Notwithstanding any rule in either House concerning the printing of conference reports in the Record or concerning any delay in the consideration of such reports, such report shall be acted on by both Houses not later than six calendar days after the conference report is filed. In the event the conferees are unable to agree within 48 hours, they shall report back to their respective Houses in disagreement.

INTERPRETATION OF JOINT RESOLUTION

SEC. 8. (a) Authority to introduce United States Armed Forces into hostilities or into situations wherein involvement in hostilities is clearly indicated by the circumstances shall not be inferred—

(1) from any provision of law (whether or not in effect before the date of the enactment of this joint resolution), including any provision contained in any appropriation Act, unless such provision specifically authorizes the introduction of United States Armed Forces into hostilities or into such situations and stating that it is intended to constitute specific statutory authorization within the meaning of this joint resolution; or

(2) from any treaty heretofore or hereafter ratified unless such treaty is implemented by legislation specifically authorizing the introduction of United States Armed Forces into hostilities or into

such situations and stating that it is intended to constitute specific statutory authorization within the meaning of this joint resolution.

(b) Nothing in this joint resolution shall be construed to require any further specific statutory authorization to permit members of United States Armed Forces to participate jointly with members of the armed forces of one or more foreign countries in the headquarters operations of high-level military commands which were established prior to the date of enactment of this joint resolution and pursuant to the United Nations Charter or any treaty ratified by the United States prior to such date.

(c) For purposes of this joint resolution, the term "introduction of United States Armed Forces" includes the assignment of member of such armed forces to command, coordinate, participate in the movement of, or accompany the regular or irregular military forces of any foreign country or government when such military forces are engaged, or there exists an imminent threat that such forces will become engaged, in hostilities.

(d) Nothing in this joint resolution—

(1) is intended to alter the constitutional authority of the Congress or of the President, or the provision of existing treaties; or (2) shall be construed as granting any authority to the President with respect to the introduction of United States Armed Forces into hostilities or into situations wherein involvement in hostilities is clearly indicated by the circumstances which authority he would not have had in the absence of this joint resolution.

SEPARABILITY CLAUS

SEC. 9. If any provision of this joint resolution or the application thereof to any person or circumstance is held invalid, the remainder of the joint resolution and the application of such provision to any other person or circumstance shall not be affected thereby.

EFFECTIVE DATE

SEC. 10. This joint resolution shall take effect on the date of its enactment.

CARL ALBERT
Speaker of the House of Representatives.
JAMES O. EASTLAND
President of the Senate pro tempore.
IN THE HOUSE OF REPRESENTATIVES, U.S.,
November 7, 1973.

The House of Representatives having proceeded to reconsider the resolution (H. J. Res 542) entitled "Joint resolution concerning the war powers of Congress and the President", returned by the President of the United States with his objections, to the House of Representatives, in which it originated, it was Resolved, That the said resolution pass, two-thirds of the House of Representatives agreeing to pass the same.

Attest:
W. PAT JENNINGS
Clerk.

I certify that this Joint Resolution originated in the House of Representatives.

W. PAT JENNINGS
Clerk.
IN THE SENATE OF THE UNITED STATES
November 7, 1973

The Senate having proceeded to reconsider the joint resolution (H. J. Res. 542) entitled "Joint resolution concerning the war powers of Congress and the President", returned by the President of the United States with his objections to the House of Representatives, in which it originate, it was Resolved, That the said joint resolution pass, two-thirds of the Senators present having voted in the affirmative.

Attest:
FRANCIS R. VALEO
Secretary.

Exhibit 22

Col. Homes Notarized Statement

As Entered in Congressional Record (Page: H5551) 7/30/93

September 7, 1992. Memorandum for Record:
Subject: Bill Clinton and the University of Arkansas ROTC Program:

There have been many unanswered questions as to the circumstances surrounding Bill Clinton's involvement with the ROTC department at the University of Arkansas. Prior to this time, I have not felt the necessity for discussing the details. The reason I have not done so before is that my poor physical health (a consequence of participation in the Bataan Death March and the subsequent three and a half years interment in Japanese POW camps) has precluded me from getting into what I felt was unnecessary involvement. However, present polls show that there is the imminent danger to our country of a draft dodger becoming Commander-in-Chief of the Armed Forces of the United States. While it is true, as Mr. Clinton has stated, that there were many others who avoided serving their country in the Vietnam war, they are not aspiring to be the President of the United States.

The tremendous implications of the possibility of his becoming Commander-in-Chief of the United States Armed Forces compels me now to comment on the facts concerning Mr. Clinton's evasion of the draft. This account would not have been imperative had Bill Clinton been completely honest with the American public concerning this matter. But as Mr. Clinton replied on a news conference this evening (September 5, 1992) after being asked another particular about his dodging the draft, "Almost everyone concerned with these

438

incidents are dead. I have no more comments to make". Since I may be the only person living who can give a firsthand account of what actually transpired, I am obligated by my love for my country and my sense of duty to divulge what actually happened and make it a matter of record.

Bill Clinton came to see me at my home in 1969 to discuss his desire to enroll in the ROTC program at the University of Arkansas. We engaged in an extensive, approximately two (2) hour interview. At no time during this long conversation about his desire to join the program did he inform me of his involvement, participation and actually organizing protests against the United States involvement in South East Asia. He was shrewd enough to realize that had I been aware of his activities, he would not have been accepted into the ROTC program as a potential officer in the United States Army.

The next day I began to receive phone calls regarding Bill Clinton's draft status. I was informed by the draft board that it was of interest to Senator Fullbright's office that Bill Clinton, a Rhodes Scholar, should be admitted to the ROTC program. I received several such calls. The general message conveyed by the draft board to me was that Senator Fullbright's office was putting pressure on them and that they needed my help. I then made the necessary arrangements to enroll Mr. Clinton into the ROTC program at the University of Arkansas.

I was not "saving" him from serving his country, as he erroneously thanked me for in his letter from England (dated December 3,1969). I was making it possible for a Rhodes Scholar to serve in the military as an officer. In retrospect I see that Mr. Clinton had no intention of following through with his agreement to join the Army ROTC program at the University of Arkansas or to attend the University of Arkansas Law School. I had explained to him the necessity of enrolling at the University of Arkansas as a student in order to be eligible to take the ROTC program at the University. He never enrolled at the University of Arkansas, but instead enrolled at Yale after attending Oxford. I believe that he purposely deceived me, using the possibility of joining the ROTC as a ploy to work with the draft board to delay his induction and get a new draft classification.

The December 3rd letter written to me by Mr. Clinton, and subsequently taken from the files by Lt. Col. Clint Jones, my executive officer, was placed into the ROTC files so that a record would be available in case the applicant should again petition to enter the ROTC program. The information in that letter alone would have restricted Bill Clinton from ever qualifying to be an officer in the United States Military. Even more significant was his lack of veracity in purposefully defrauding the military by deceiving me, both in concealing his anti-military activities overseas and his counterfeit intentions for later military service. These actions cause me to question both his patriotism and his integrity. When I consider the caliber, the bravery, and the patriotism of the fine young soldiers whose deaths I have witnessed, and others whose funerals I have attended…When I reflect on not only the willingness but eagerness that so many of them displayed in their earnest desire to defend and serve their country, it is untenable and incomprehensible to me that a man who was not merely unwilling to serve his country, but actually protested against its military, should ever be in the position of Commander-in-Chief of our armed Forces.

I write this declaration not only for the living and future generations, but for those who fought and died for our country. If space and time permitted I would include the names of the ones I knew and fought with, and along with them I would mention my brother Bob, who was killed during World War II and is buried in Cambridge, England (at the age of 23, about the age Bill Clinton was when he was over in England protesting the war). I have agonized over whether or not to submit this statement to the American people. But, I realize that even though I served my country by being in the military for over 32 years, and having gone through the ordeal of months of combat under the worst of conditions followed by years of imprisonment by the Japanese, it is not enough. I'm writing these comments to let everyone know that I love my country more than I do my own personal security and well-being. I will go to my grave loving these United States of America and the liberty for which so many men have fought and died. Because of my poor physical condition this will be my final statement. I will make no further comments to any of the media regarding this issue.

Eugene Holmes Colonel, U.S.A., Ret.
September 1992

EXHIBIT 23

Clinton's ROTC Letter

As Entered in Congressional Record (Page: H5550) 7/30/93

Dear Col. Holmes,

I AM SORRY TO BE so long in writing. I know I promised to let you hear from me at least once a month, and from now on you will, but I have to have some time to think about this first letter. Almost daily since my return to England I have thought about writing, about what I want to and ought to say.

First, I want to thank you, not only for saving me from the draft, but for being so kind to me last summer, when I was as low as I have ever been. One thing that made the bond we struck in good faith somewhat palatable to me was my high regard for you personally. In retrospect, it seems that the admiration might not have been mutual had you known a little more about me, about my political beliefs and activities. At least you might have thought me more fit for the draft than for ROTC.

Let me try to explain. As you know, I worked in a very minor position on the Senate Foreign Relations Committee. I did it for the experience and the salary but also for the opportunity, however small, of working every day against a war I opposed and despised with a depth of feeling I had reserved solely for racism in America before Vietnam. I did not take the matter lightly but studied it carefully, and there was a time when not many people had more information about Vietnam at hand than I did.

I have written and spoken and marched against the war. One of the national organizers of the *Vietnam Moratorium* is a close friend

442

of mine. After I left Arkansas last summer, I went to Washington to work in the national headquarters of the Moratorium, then to England to organize the Americans here for demonstrations October 15 and November 16.

Interlocked with the war is the draft issue, which I did not begin to consider separately until early 1968. For a law seminar at Georgetown I wrote a paper on the legal arguments for and against allowing, within the Selective Service System, the classification of selective conscientious objection, for those opposed to participation in a particular war, not simply to "participation in war in any form."

From my work, I came to believe that the draft system itself is illegitimate. No government really rooted in limited, parliamentary democracy should have the power to make its citizens fight and kill and die in a war they may oppose, a war which even possibly may be wrong, a war, which in any case, does not involve immediately the peace and freedom of the nation. The draft was justified in World War II because the life of the people collectively was at stake. Individuals had to fight, if the nation was to survive, for the lives of their country and their way of life. Vietnam is no such case. Nor was Korea an example where, in my opinion, certain military action was justified but the draft was not, for the reasons stated above.

Because of my opposition to the draft and the war, I am in great sympathy with those who are not willing to fight, kill, and maybe die for their country (i.e. the particular policy of a particular government) right or wrong. Two of my friends at Oxford are conscientious objectors. I wrote a letter of recommendation for one of them to his Mississippi draft board, a letter I am prouder of than anything else I wrote at Oxford last year. One of my roommates is a draft resister who is possibly under indictment and may never be able to go home again. He is one of the bravest, best men I know. His country needs men like him more than they know. That he is considered a criminal is an obscenity.

The decision not to be a resister and the related subsequent decisions were the most difficult of my life. I decided to accept the draft in spite of my beliefs for one reason only, to maintain my political viability within the system. For years I have worked to prepare myself for a political life characterized by both practical political ability and concern for rapid social progress. It is a life I still feel compelled to try to lead. I do not think our system of government is by definition corrupt, however dangerous, and inadequate it has been in recent years. (The society may be corrupt, but that is not the same thing, and if that is true, we are all finished anyway.)

When the draft came, despite political convictions, I was having a hard time facing the prospect of fighting a war I had been fighting against, and that is why I contacted you. ROTC was the one way in which I could possibly, but not positively, avoid both Vietnam and the resistance. Going on with my education, even coming back to England, played no part in my decision to join ROTC. I am back here and would have been at Arkansas Law School because there is nothing else, I can do. I would like to have been able to take a year out perhaps to teach in a small college or work on some community action project and in the process to decide whether to attend law school or graduate school and how to begin putting what I have learned to use.

But the particulars of my personal life are not near as important to me as the principals involved. After I signed the ROTC letter of intent I began to wonder whether the compromise I had made with myself was not more objectionable than the draft would have been, because I had no interest in the ROTC program itself and all I seem to have done was to protect myself from physical harm. Also, I had begun to think that I had deceived you, not by lies—there were none—but by failing to tell you all of the things I'm telling you now. I doubt I had the mental coherence to articulate them then.

Page 2.

At that time, after we had made our agreement and you had sent my 1D deferment to my draft board, the anguish and loss of myself regard and self-confidence really set in. I hardly slept for weeks and kept going by eating compulsively and reading until exhaustion brought sleep. Finally, on September 12 I stayed up all night writing a letter to the chairman of my draft board, saying basically what is in the preceding paragraph, thanking him for trying to help in a case

444

where he really couldn't, and stating that I couldn't do the ROTC after all and would he please draft me as soon as possible.

I never mailed the letter, but I did carry it with me every day until I got on the plane to return to England. I didn't mail the letter because I didn't see, in the end, how my going in the army and maybe going to Vietnam would achieve anything except a feeling that I had punished myself and gotten what I deserved. So, I came back to England to try to make something of the second year of my Rhodes scholarship.

And that is where I am now, writing to you because you have been good to me and have a right to know what I think and feel. I am writing too in the hope that my telling this one story will help you understand more clearly how so many fine people have come to find themselves loving their country but loathing the military, to which you and other good men have devoted years, lifetimes and the best service you could give. To many of us, it is no longer clear what is service and what is dis-service, or if it is clear, the conclusion is likely to be illegal.

Forgive the length of this letter. There was much to say. There is still a lot to be said, but it can wait. Please say hello to Colonel Jones for me.

Merry Christmas.

Sincerely,

Bill Clinton

EXHIBIT 24

VVAW Minutes

Executive Committee Meeting Minutes/ Thurs. 11 Sept. 1970(?)

Members Attending:

Jan Crumb - Pres. Scott Moore - Vice-Pres. Al Hubbard - Exec. Sect. Jason Gettinger Treas. Joe Urgo-Chairman Pub. Rel. Bill Craddell Mid-West Rep. John Kerry-NE Rep.

The meeting was chaired by & Al Hubbard ,

Al Hubbard gave a report of finances; Cash on hand $4337.07
Credits   900.00
Debts   219.00

Approximate cost of Operation RAW $8812.41
No debts outstanding from Operation RAW

Motion was made and seconded to appt. Jason Gettinger interim Treasurer, motion carried without objection.

The following issues were discussed and VVAW responses decided.

1) National Gaurd Association - It was decided that VVAW would send a letter to Mayor Lindsay demanding he not welcome the NGA, it was further decided that VVAW will maintain a picket line in front of the Americana Hotel throughout the convention 13-17 sep.

2) It was decided that VVAW would sponsor a Vietnam War display (anti) in the capital.

3) It was decided that VVAW will support the MAN U.N. effort.

4) VVAW will determine response to Oct 3 D.C. rally (Ky) upon receipt of more info.

5) VVAW will generate 1000 signatures for Winter Soldier by Sep. 23, will call press conference no later then Sep 23.

6) VVAW will sponsor turn in of war crimes testimony to UN following winter soldier.

7) VVAW will consider appropiate induction center action for purpose of making clear transition from citizen to war criminal.

8) VVAW for purpose of protecting credtbility will engage in only unilateral actions until after winter soldier.

9) VVAW will call a weekend cordon of White House (date to be announced) also will demand opportunity to address joint session of congress.

10) Al Hubbard will make speaking tour with Fonda.

11) General membership meeting will be called during week of Sep 20th.

12) It was decided that membership will continue to be restricted to Vietnam (SE Asia) vets, all other vets will be encouraged to support our programs.

The meeting was adjourned at XXXXX 2200hrs.

EXHIBIT 25

Distribution

CRYPTOLOGIC QUARTERLY IS PUBLISHED FOUR times a year by the Center for Cryptologic History, NSA. The publication is designed as a working aid and is not subject to receipt, control, or accountability. Distribution is made to branch level; further dissemination is the responsibility of each branch. Extra copies or those for which there is no further need should be returned to the Editor for disposition.

Contributions

Contributions to Cryptologic Quarterly should be sent to

Managing Editor, Cryptologic Quarterly E05, SAB 2, Door 22 Suite 6886

(b) (3) -P. L. 86-36

Electronic submissions can be made via email. Such submissions should include a pdf (portable document format) version, as well as a txt (text) version of the article. Each article should include an abstract. Authors are responsible for determining the classification of submitted articles. If computer disks are submitted. authors must ensure that they are virus-free. All material used in the publication of an article is destroyed when no longer needed unless the author requests that it be returned. Cryptologic Quarterly will not accept articles written anonymously or with a pseudonym.

Cryptologic quarterly

(U) Skunks, Bogies, Silent Hounds, and the Flying Fish: The Gulf of Tonkin Mystery, 2-4 August 1964

ROBERT J. HANYOKHSÐ The Gulf of Tonkin incidents of 2 to 4 August 1964 have come to loom over the subsequent American engagement in Indochina. The incidents, principally the second one of 4 August, led to the approval of the Gulf of Tonkin Resolution by the U.S. Congress, which handed President Johnson the carte blanche charter he had wanted for future intervention in Southeast Asia. From this point on, the American policy and programs would dominate the course of the Indochina War. At the height of the American involvement, over a half million U.S. soldiers, sailors, airmen, and marines would be stationed there. The war would spread across the border into Cambodia and escalate in Laos. Thailand assumed a Beater importance as a base for supporting the military effort, especially for the air war, but also for SIGINT purposes of intercept and direction finding.

(U) At the time, the Gulf of Tonkin incidents of August were not quite so controversial. According to the Johnson administration, the issue of the attacks was pretty much cut and dried. As the administration explained, our ships had been in international waters—anywhere from fifty to eighty miles from the DRV coastline by some calculations, during the alleged second attack—and were attacked even though they were innocent of any bellicose gestures directed at North Vietnam. Secretary of Defense Robert McNamara had assured the Senate that there had been no connection between what the U.S. Navy was doing and any aggressive operations by the South Vietnamese. [1] Washington claimed that the United States had to defend itself and guarantee freedom of navigation on the high seas.

Derived from: NSACSSM 123-2

24 February 1998

Declassify On: Xl

(U) However, within the government, the events of 4 August were never that clear. Even as the last flare fizzled in the dark waters of the South China Sea on that August night, there were conflicting narratives and interpretations of what had happened. James Stockdale, then a navy pilot at the scene, who had "the best seat in the house from which to detect boats," saw nothing. "No boats," he would later write, "no boat wakes, no ricochets off boats, no boat impacts, no torpedo wakes—nothing but black sea and American firepower."[2] The commander of the Maddox task force, Captain John J. Herrick, was not entirely certain what had transpired. (Captain Herrick actually was the commander of the destroyer division to which the Maddox belonged. For this mission, he was aboard as the on-site commander.) Hours after the Incident, he would radio the Commander-in-Chief, Pacific (CINCPAC) telling them that he was doubtful of many aspects of the "attack."

(U) It would be years before any evidence that an attack had not happened finally emerged in the public domain, and even then, most reluctantly. Yet, remarkably, some of the major participants in the events still maintained that the Gulf of Tonkin incident had occurred just as it had been originally reported. Secretary of Defense Robert McNamara, in his memoirs in Retrospect, considered the overall evidence for an attack still convincing.[3] The U.S. Navy's history of the Vietnam conflict, by Edward J. Marolda and Oscar P. Fitzgerald (hereafter referred to as the "Marolda-Fitzgerald history"), reported that the evidence for the second attack, especially from intelligence, including a small amount of SIGINT, was considered conclusive.[4]

(U) The public literature on the Gulf of Tonkin for years has been overwhelmingly skeptical about the 4 August battle. Articles that appeared in magazines within a few years illustrated the general inconsistency in the descriptions of the incident of 4 August by simply using the conflicting testimony from the officers and crews of both ships. The first major critical volume was Joseph Goulden's Truth Is the First Casualty, published in 1969. The most complete work to date is Edwin Moise's Tonkin Gulf and the Escalation of the Vietnam War. Moise's work has the dual advantage of using some Vietnamese sources, as well as small portions of a few SIGNT reports released to the author under a Freedom of Information Act request. Yet, even what few scraps he received from NSA were enough to raise serious questions about the validity of the SIGINT reports cited by the administration which related to the 4 August incident.[5]

-fSffSÐ the issue of whether the available SIGÜNT "proved" that there had been a second attack has been argued for years. In 1968, Robert McNamara testified before Senator William Fulbright's Foreign Relations Committee's hearings on the Gulf of that the supporting signals intelligence was "unimpeachable." On the other hand, in 1972 the deputy director of NSA, Inuis Tordella, was quoted as saying that the 4 August intercepts pertained to the 2 August attacks.

In a 1975 article in the NSA magazine Crypto log, the Gulf of Tonkin incident was retold, but the SIGINT for the night of August 4 was not mentioned, except for the "military operations" intercept, and even then without comment.[6] The Navy's history of the Vietnam War would misconstrue the SIGINT (disguised as unsourced "intelligence") associating portions of two critical intercepts and implying a connection in the evidence where none could be established.'

-€ffStj Except for the sizable collection of SIGINT material within NSA, and a much smaller amount from the archives of the Naval Security Group (which essentially duplicates portions of the NSA holdings), almost all relevant material relating to the Gulf of Tonkin incidents has been released. Although the questions about what happened in the Gulf of Tonkin on the night of 4 August have been fairly well answered by the evidence from all of the other sources—radar, sonar, eyewitness, and archival—the SIGINT version needs to be told. This is because of the critical role that SIGINT played in defining the second attack in the minds of Johnson administration officials. Without the signal's intelligence information, the administration had only the confused and conflicting testimony and evidence of the men and equipment involved in the incident. It is difficult to imagine the 5 August retaliatory air strikes against North Vietnamese naval bases and installation-ions being ordered without the SIGINT "evidence."[8] Therefore, it is necessary to recount in some detail what signals intelligence reported.

-fSffS9 for the first time ever, what will be presented in the following narrative is the complete SIGINT version of what happened in the Gulf of Tonkin between 2 and 4 August 1964. Until now, the NSA has officially maintained that the second incident of 4 August occurred. This position was established in the initial SIGINT reports of 4 August and sustained through a series of summary reports issued shortly after the crisis. In October 1964, a classified Chrono low of events for 2 to 4 August in the Gulf of Tonkin was published by NSA which furthered the contention that the second attack had occurred.

-£HS9-In maintaining the official version of the attack, the NSA made use of surprisingly few published SIGINT reports—fifteen in all. The research behind the new version which follows is based on the discovery of an enormous amount of never-before-used SIGNT material. This included 122 relevant SIGINT products, along with watch center notes, oral history interviews, and messages among the various SIGINT and military command centers involved in the Gulf of Tonkin incidents. Naturally, this flood of new information changed dramatically the story of that night of 4/5 August. The most important element is that it is now unknown what the North Vietnamese Navy was doing that night. And with this information a nearly complete story finally can be told.

—f&ffSÐ Two startling findings emerged from the new research. First, it is not simply that there is a different story as to what happened; it is that no attack happened that night. Through a compound of analytic errors and an unwillingness to consider contrary evidence, American SIGINT elements in the region and at NSA HQs reported Hanoi's plans to attack the two ships of the Desoto patrol. Further analytic errors and an obscuring of other information led to publication of more "evidence." In truth, Hanoi's navy was engaged in nothing that night but the salvage of two of the boats damaged on 2 August.

-fSffS±) The second finding pertains to the handling of the SIGINT material related to the Gulf of Tonkin by individuals at NSA Beginning with the period of the crisis in early August, into the days of the immediate aftermath, and continuing into October 1964, SIGINT information was presented in such a manner as to preclude responsible decision makers in the Johnson administration from having the complete and objective narrative of events of 4 August 1964. Instead, only SIGINT that supported the claim that the communists had attacked the two destroyers was given to administration officials.

4S7ffSf) This mishandling of the SIGINT was not done in a manner that can be construed as conspiratorial, that is, with manufactured evidence and collusion at all levels. Rather, the objective of these individuals was to support the Navy's claim that the Desoto patrol had been deliberately attacked by the North Vietnamese. Yet, in order to substantiate that claim, all of the relevant SIGINT could not be provided to the White House and the Defense and intelligence officials. The conclusion that would be drawn from a review of all evidence would have been that the North Vietnamese not only did not attack but were uncertain as to the location of the ships.

fSffStl Instead, three things occurred with the SIGINT. First of all, the overwhelming portion of the SIGINT relevant to 4 August was kept out of the post-attack summary reports and the final report written in October 1964. The withheld information constituted nearly 90 percent of all available SIGINT. This information revealed the actual activities of the North Vietnamese on the night of 4 August that included salvage operations of the two torpedo boats damaged on 2 August, and coastal patrols by a small number of DRV craft. As will be demonstrated later in this chapter, the handful of SIGINT reports which suggested that an attack had occurred contained severe analytical errors, unexplained translation changes, and the conjunction of two unrelated messages into one translation. This latter product would become the Johnson administration's main proof of the 4 August attack.

CHSÐ Second, there were instances in which specious supporting SIGINT evidence was inserted into NSA summary reports issued shortly after the Gulf of Tonkin incidents. This SIGINT was not manufactured. Instead, it consisted of fragments of legitimate intercept lifted out of its context and inserted into the summary reports to support the contention of a premeditated North Vietnamese attack on 4 August. The sources of these fragments were not even referenced in the summaries. It took extensive research before the original reports containing these items could be identified,

-6ffSfrFinally, there is the unexplained disappearance of vital decrypted Vietnamese text of the translation that was the basis of the administration's most important evidence—the so-called Vietnamese after-action report of late 4 August. The loss of the text is important because the SIGINT record shows that there were critical differences in the English translations of it issued both by the navy intercept site in the Philippines and NSA. Without the individual texts (there were two of them), it is difficult to determine why there are critical differences in the translations and more importantly, to understand why two separate North Vietnamese messages were combined into one translation by NSA.

(U) Before a discussion can begin, it is necessary to understand how the Gulf of Tonkin incidents came to happen, the way they did, and what their significance was for the Johnson administration. To do that, we need to consider the Desoto mission that the Maddox was conducting at the time, as well as the Defense Department's OPLAN-34A missions against the Democratic Republic of Vietnam (DRV). It was the convergence of the two that embroiled that ship in the crisis in the Tonkin Gulf.

(U) The Desoto Missions-4S+SB Desoto was the cover name for a U.S. Navy signals intelligence collection program begun in 1962 in which naval SIGINT direct support units (DSU) were placed on board American destroyer patrols along the Asiatic coastline in the western Pacific

-679'*' Physically, Desoto mission destroyers were unique in their configuration—a small van lashed to the ship which housed intercept positions for voice and manual Morse communications. There also was a position which intercepted no communications emissions such as radars, referred to as electronic intelligence or ELINT. Finally, a communications position, which allowed the detachment to send and receive messages from the other monitoring stations in the area, as well as other SIGINT organizations and commands, via the Criticomm communications system, was located in the hut. The hut was manned in shifts from a complement of twelve to eighteen officers and men from the Navy's cryptologic element, known as the Naval Security Group (NSG). However, contrary to some assertions, the Desoto missions were not the functional or operational equivalent of the ubiquitous Soviet electronic collection trawlers.[9] The Desoto missions primarily settled the mission needs of local commanders, although they received technical support in the way of technical working aids and intercept data from NSA.

-f+The Desoto patrols had a two-part mission: to collect intelligence in support of the embarked commander and higher-level authorities and to assert freedom of navigation in international waters. The earl Desoto missions in the waters of coastal tracking radars in viligeance networks belonging to the naval forces =While an

Occasional communist patrol ship would come out and shadow the U.S. patrol, little else happened.

(U) However, when the Desoto patrol first was proposed for the waters in Southeast Asia, its Desoto mission van mission was expanded. First of all, the commander, Seventh Fleet, wanted the patrol to move in closer than the original twenty-mile limit—as close as twelve miles. Additionally, the Desoto mission was expanded to include a broader collection of "all-source intelligence," namely, photographic, hydrographic, and meteorological information.[10]

(U) In mid-January 1964, COMUSMACV requested that the Desoto patrol scheduled for February (USS Radford, DD-446) be designed to provide the forthcoming OPLAN-34A program with critical intelligence regarding North Vietnam's ability to resist its projected commando operations. However, in this case, the Radford's mission was canceled so as to not interfere with OPLAN-34A missions planned for the first two weeks of February.[11]

(U) This is an important point, although a subtle one, for understanding the events of 2 to 4 August. Inasmuch as there was an interworking between the two programs, and this remained a point of contention in later congressional hearings, as well as a source for speculation by the press, the Desoto mission remained merely one of collection of intelligence which could be of use to the OPLAN-34A planners and commanders back in Danang and the Pentagon. There was no direct operational connection between the two programs. They were managed under separate offices and were not known to coordinate mission planning, except for warnings to the Desoto patrol to stay clear of 34A operational areas. At least that was the understanding back in Washington.12

(U) In early July, General Westmoreland requested more intelligence on Hanoi's forces which were capable of defending against an expanded OPLAN-34A program. Specifically, Westmoreland required intelligence on the DRVs defenses in those areas targeted for July operation—Hon Me, Hon Nieu, and Hon Matt Islands, as well as the area around the port of Vinh Son, south of the islands. In response, Admiral Sharp, CINCPAC, issued a new directive for a

Desoto patrols whose purpose was "determining DRV coastal patrol activity."[13]

That the two missions might run up physically against one another was a consideration at both

MACV in Saigon and CINCPAC (and CINCPACFLT) in Honolulu.

But Westmoreland assured the navy commanders that as long as the Desoto patrol stayed within

its schedule and area of operations, there would be no problem.

Westmoreland added that all the Studies and Observations Group (SOG), which ran the

OPLAN-34A missions, needed in the way of anGulf of Tonkin region of interest to OPLAN-34A and Desoto missions' alphabetic points denote Desoto mission start and stop positions (Courtesy of Naval Historical Center)

alert was thirty-six hours' notice of any change. They could then adjust any planned 34A operation. The navy accepted these reassurances from MACV.[14]

-fSffSt) The first Desoto mission in the Tonkin Gulf region ran from February to March 1964. The USS Craig (DD-885) sailed near Hainan Island towards the Vietnamese coast and then turned back north towards Macao and Taiwan. The North Vietnamese tracked the Craig as it swung south of Hainan Island, but had made no reaction even though they knew that it was a U.S. warship. It was uncertain to the Americans what the Vietnamese precisely knew of the Craig or its mission,

-fSffS+ During this mission, there was a Naval Security Group DSU aboard whose task was to provide tactical intelligence to the Craig's commander, as well as intercept unique communications and electronic intelligence in reaction to the vessel's presence. The Craig also received support from the SIGINT facilities in the region: the navy and air force COMINT sites in the Philippines

No Vietnam-based sites were involved since the area of Craig's mission barely touched on the DRVs territorial waters, and then only briefly, although it was suspected that the North Vietnamese navy at least once did report the Craig's position. [17]

(U) However, there were two critical differences between the Craig's Desoto mission and that of the Maddox which followed it in late July and August: The Maddox would sail along the entire DRV coastline, while, at the same time, OPLAN-34A maritime missions against North Vietnamese coastal installations were being carried out. By July, the North Vietnamese were reacting aggressively to these raids, pursuing, and attacking the seaborne commando units.

CSHSÐ in mid-July 1964, the JCS approved another Desoto mission, which would concentrate on collecting intelligence on North Vietnam's coastal defense posture. The USS Maddox, under the command of Captain John Herrick, loaded up its intercept van in the e sixteen members of the DSU boarded, and the ship departed for the Gulf of Tonkin. The Maddox had received no additional instructions to its standard collection mission and apparently was not aware of specific OPLAN 34A missions in the area. [18] However, the Maddox was not on a purely passive mission. U.S. intercept sites in the area were alerted to the real reason for the Desoto missions, which was to stimulate and record (my italics) North Vietnamese reactions in support of the U.S. SIGINT effort.

CINCPAC's orders to Herrick were equally explicit and ambitious: locate and identify all' coastal radar transmitters, note all navigational aids along the DRV's coastline, and monitor the Vietnamese junk fleet for a possible connection to DRV/Viet Cong maritime supply and infiltration routes. [20] Whether these missions could be completed was questionable: the DSU was limited by its few positions and equipment in collecting such a large amount of communications. The Maddox had been ordered by CNCPAC to stay eight nautical miles from the North Vietnamese coastline, but only four miles from needs of internal security plan is admitted that the operations of this level would involve per CIA needs of internal security. The planners admitted that the operations at this level would involve large enough forces that they would be necessary

—ffSffS±)- At the beginning of 1964, the Department of Defense, which had started its own program, assumed control of all of these covert missions. It me ed i own project and organized o e new missions under PLAN 4A-

34 ongn y wasp n to last twelve months and was to be a program of selective intrusions and attacks of graduated intensity. The purpose of these actions was to "convince the Democraüc Republic of Vietnam leadership that their continued direction and support of insurgent activities in the RVN and Laos should cease."[24]

OPLAN reflected the current American strategy of escalation of the war through graduated response. The U.S. established four levels of actions; each proceeding one was a qualitative and quantitative increase in the sensitivity of target selector and the intensity of the application of force. It began with harassment attacks and operations, whose cumulative effect, though labeled "unspectacular," was to make Hanoi aware of them to the extent it would allocate forces to counter them.[25] If this approach failed, then the next level—tagged as attritional—was to attack important military and chill installations whose loss could cause "temporary immobilization of important resources" which, in turn, might create or increase opposition amongst the North Vietnamese population to the government in Hanoi. The third level, termed punitive by the 34A planners, was meant to cause damage, displacement, or destruction of those facilities or installations considered critical to the DRV economy, industry, or security. To protect itself from further attacks would mean that the DRV would have to redeploy resources originally meant to support the war in the south to the ly overt. But the planners felt that these attacks could be attributable to the South Vietnamese. [26]

—eSHSĐ-The final step of the plan was the initiation of an aerial bombing campaign designed to damage the DRV's capacity to support the southern insurrection or cripple its economy to such an extent that it would realize the extent of its losses was not worth the support of the war in the South. At this point, the planners in Washington believed that Hanoi's reaction to the attacks would be based on two factors: its willingness to accept critical damage to its own economy by continuing supporting the war in the South, and the possible support of the People's Republic of China. The plan did suggest that the communists would choose to continue to support the southern front, and it left open the possibility of further operations to offset the anticipated Chinese aid.[27]

—ffSffSÐ-The major operational components of OPLAN 34A were airborne operations that inserted intelligence and commando teams into North Vietnam, and maritime operations (MAROPS) which consisted of hit-and-run raids on coastal installations and facilities. These latter missions were known under the operational title Timberwork. The teams were made up of mostly South Vietnamese Special Forces, known as Luc Luong Dac Biet or Biet Kich, with some foreign mercenaries (mostly Chinese and Koreans) to crew the attack craft. The American involvement, though extensive in the planning, training, and logistics portions, was minimized to achieve the usual "no attribution" status in case the raids were publicized by the North. No Americans were allowed to participate in the actual raids.

(U) Despite all of the planning, there was little confidence in the effectiveness of the OPIAN 34A operations. CIA chief John McCone suggested that they "will not seriously affect the DRV or Nontvegianbuilt '*Nastv[g] fast patrol boat, the primary platform for maritime operations

OPIAN cause them to change their policies.' Defense Secretary McNamara, when he returned from an inspection trip to South Vietnam in March 1964, described OPLAN 34A as "a program so limited that it is unlikely to have any significant effect." The operations were described by other officials as "pinpricks" and "pretty small potatoes."[9]

(U) The Johnson administration was dissatisfied with the initial results of OPLAN 34A and sought a stronger approach. By June 1964, a new OPLAN, designated 37-64, had been developed jointly by the National Security Council, the JCS, and MACV. This new OPLAN called for a three-pronged approach to "eliminate to negligible proportions DRV support of VC insurgency in the Republic of Vietnam." Three military options were put forward: ground action in Cambodia and Laos to eliminate VC sanctuaries and supply points, increased levels of 34A attacks on Hanoi's coastal installations, and South Vietnamese and United States bombing of ninety-eight "preselected" targets in North Vietnam.[30]

(U) If the commando raids had been such failures, why did they continue to be staged? The truth is, Washington was anxious to support the shaky regime of General Khanh, who had succeeded to the presidency of South Vietnam after Diem's assassination. Until a better plan, such as 37-64, could be implemented, then doing "something," even as ineffective as the raids, was the course Washington chose to follow. In spite of Hanoi's gains for the first six months of 1964, if America's determination to succeed could be communicated to Khanh, then the South Vietnamese might be reassured of the prospects for victory.[31] This was Washington's policy: to prop up Saigon. Yet, this was a structure built on unsupported assertions.

-ffSffS±) The reality for Washington was that the increased tempo of maritime commando raids had only raised Hanoi's determination to meet them head on. Through June and July 1964, NSA and the navy monitoring site in the Philippines reported that the conflict along the coast of North Vietnam was heating up. Communications about small boat actions, commando landings, and high-speed chases out at sea were intercepted and reported back to Washington. What the reports showed was a North Vietnamese navy emboldened to more aggressive reactions to incursions by the commandos from the south. For example, on 28 July, after an attack on the island of Hon Gio, DRV Swatow-class patrol boats pursued the enemy for forty-five nautical miles before giving up the chase.[32] Earlier, on 30 June, another patrol boat had taken potshots at two jet aircraft flying along the coast and claimed a hit.[33]

4.Sk/.SB By early June, Hanoi's stepped-up defensive posture had registered in its radio traffic. On 8 June, NSA reported that the level of North Vietnamese tactical radio communications had increased almost fourfold during the early part of June from the previous period in May, probably in reaction to attacks along its coast. It also reported that DRV naval patrols now seemed to cover its entire coastline" Clearly, Hanoi was determined to defend itself resolutely. Whether or not the Vietnamese believed that the Americans were preparing for a larger war was not important. What was critical was that the situation along North Vietnam's territorial waters had reached a near boil.[35]

-ffS17'Sf) The SIGINT support to OPLAN 34A started at almost the same time as the operations began. Codenamed Kit Kat, the effort required that the then current ceiling of 660 cryptologic personnel in South Vietnam had to be raised. In February 1964, an increase of 130 personnel for Kit Kat was approved by CINCPAC.[36] The ASA moved personnel from the Philippines to Phu Bai, and the Naval Security Group added coverage of North Vietnamese naval communications to its mission at San Miguel in the Philippines. The Air Force Security Sew ice units at Monkey Mountain near Danang increased their coverage of the communications of DRV navy and coastal surveillance posts. A small special SIGINT unit at Tan Son Nhut Airbase, known as the Special Support Group (SSG), was formed in late February to coordinate Kit Kat support between the intercept sites and the Studies and Observations Group.

-t&ffSf) A few last notes before we review the attacks. It will be necessary to limit the discussion to the role SIGINT played during the incident. Other evidential sources, such as that from the American ships' own radar, sonar, and sightings, will be mentioned in passing simply because they are part of the story and cannot be altogether ignored. However, the brunt of the following discussion center on the SIGNT evidence because of its critical role in convincing the
Johnson administration that the attack actually occurred.

fSñSÿBesides the NSG detachment aboard the Maddox (USN-467N), other SIGINT elements that were involved in the events of the next three days included a Marine SIGINT detachment (USN-414T), collocated with the Army Security Agency intercept site at Phu Bai (USM626J), and the NSG site at San Miguel, Philippines (USN-27), which also had a Marine SIGNT contingent, but the latter was not designated separately as was the Marine group at Phu Bai. It would be the intercept and reporting by the Marine unit at Phu Bai and the navy site in the Philippines which would prove critical to the events in the Gulf of Tonkin.

—suffix large number of the reports by the various field sites and NSA were issued contemporaneously with the events themselves. A few of these would be cited in the various after-action analyses and postmortems that attended the Gulf of Tonkin. However, many more field translations and reports based on the intercept during the period of the incidents would be issued as late as two to four days after the crisis. The reason for the apparent delay was that the request from NSA for ALL intercept came only on 7 August.[38]

-€ffSò-Because of the nature and enormous amount of the SIGINT evidence used here for the very first in discussing the Gulf of Tonkin crisis, we will need to present it in a format which will highlight that information. Rather than try to retell the story all at once and incorporate the new evidence into the narrative, which could be overwhelming, especially to those readers not intimately familiar with the events of 4 August, a different tack will be used. We will break down the events into their separate days. First, we will review the details of the known engagement of the afternoon of 2 August. While there is no controversy surrounding this fight—at least there is no question that it occurred—there is an important point to draw from it: that is, the North Vietnamese communications profile during a naval combat engagement was revealed. For ease of reference, we shall refer to this communications profile as the "command and control communications and intelligence" system or C31. This is a functional description used widely in the intelligence and defense communities to describe the process whereby the individual elements of intelligence (information/ intelligence), command and control (interaction by command authorities), and communications (communications links among all operating elements and units) are combined in military operations.

(U) After looking at the "uneventful" day of 3 August, we will consider the "official" version of the engagement of 4 August. Although, as we progress through the narrative, we will consider the problems with the various other pieces of evidence which support the contention that an attack occurred, the emphasis will be on the SIGINT "clinchers," that is, those reports that convinced the Johnson administration that an attack had occurred. These items will be presented when and how they appeared to the participants,

(U) Finally, we will go back over the clinching SIGINT "evidence" of 4 August and illustrate what problems exist with the individual pieces. In this section, the entire scenario of what was reported and, more importantly, what was not reported, will be considered. We will review closely the technical problems with the two critical

SIGINT reports which prop up all of the other evidence of an attack by the North Vietnamese. In this approach we will consider how the product was developed and the serious problems in translation, composition, and reporting of the information.

-. &+SB One last item. For purposes of clarity, all time references will be marked either Zulu time ("Z," or Greenwich Mean Time) or Golf ("G," or Zulu +7), which is the time zone for the Gulf of Tonkin. While the actual time of the incidents was in local, or Golf time, SIGINT reports were issued in Zulu time. This is done because of the worldwide nature of SIGINT reporting. The use of Zulu time allows for a consistent and universal benchmark for analysts and recipients of the intelligence. To further confuse the issue, the U.S. Navy used Hotel time (Zulu +8) in all of its messages, which is carried over into its history of the Vietnam War. Then there are the events in Washington, D.C., and NSA HQ, Fort Meade,

MD, which are in the Eastern time zone, or Romeo ("R," or Zulu-5 hours). The latter times will be notated "EST" for Eastern Standard Time. All times will be in given in the military twenty-four-hour clock. So, all "P.M." times after 1200 hours can be determined by subtracting 1200 from the time: e.g., 1700 hours equals 5:00 P.M. Also, it must be remembered that events in the Gulf of Tonkin occurred west of the international date line, so that certain events in the region were occurring the next day in terms of Washington's time. For example, if something happened at 1500 hours Zulu, it is reflected as 2200 hours Golf, 2300 hours Hotel and 1000 hours Romeo of the same day. However, a two-hour advance in Zulu time, that is, 1700 hours on 4 August, means 0000 hours Golf and 0100 hours Hotel time on 5 August, while Washington will be 1200 hours on 4 August. For ease of reference, the reader can observe that there is a twelve-hour difference between Washington and the Gulf of Tonkin.

(U) Round One: The 2 August Battle

It all began with the fireworks of the night of 30/31 July 1964, when South Vietnamese commandos struck at Hon Me Island (19°21 'N, 105 56'E), located off the central coast of North Vietnam. At first the commandos tried to land and attack a radar station but were driven off. The raiders then stood offshore in their boats and peppered the installation with machine gun and small cannon fire. At the same time, two other commando boats bombarded Hon Ngu Island (18 °48'N, 105°47'E) near the port of Vinh. During the attack, the Maddox had drawn off from the scene as required by its orders to stay well out at sea during the night. On the morning of 31 July, as the Maddox made for its patrol station near the coast, Captain Herrick observed the retreating commando boats (called "Nasties" after the manufacturer of their boat, "Nast")

heading south. Communist communications were intercepted by the navy monitoring site in the Philippines, which reported the vain attempts by their patrol craft to catch the "enemy. „ 39

4S+SB-On the morning of 1 August, the ASA site at Phu Bai, Republic of Vietnam, monitored a DRV patrol boat, T-146, a Swatow-class patrol craft communicating tracking data on the Maddox to another Swatow. At the time, between 0700G to 0730G (0030Z), the Maddox was located nine miles southeast of Hon Me Island moving northeasterly. The Swatow-class patrol craft was one of a group supplied by the People's Republic of China. It was a fairly large patrol craft displacing sixty-seven tons. It had a top speed of forty-four knots and a cruising speed of twenty knots. It was armed with two 37-millimeter (mm) antiaircraft (AA) gun mounts, two 20-mm AA mounts, and carried up to eight depth charges. This armament limited the Swatow's role to countering other small vessels. The Swat0W carried the Skin Head surface search radar. The Swatow's often worked in tandem with P-4 torpedo boats, acting as communications relays between North Vietnamese naval command centers and the P-4s, whose long-distance communications capability was limited. This was a role that the Swatow's filled all during the next few days' action.40

(V) Swatow-class patrol boat

-£HSĐ the T-146 patrol craft also ordered the other craft to turn on its "equipment," which probably referred to its Skin Head radar. However, the Maddox did not intercept any emissions from the Swatow's radar. The North Vietnamese boats referred to the frack as the "enemy"; the equation of the term to the Maddox was made by Phu Bal.[41]

Shortly after 2300G (1600Z) on I August, the naval intercept site in the Philippines reported that the DRV naval base at Ben Thuy (18°39'N, 105°42'E) had informed an unidentified entity, possibly the T-146 patrol boat, that it had been "DECIDED TO FIGHT THE ENEMY TONIGHT [1 Group unreadable] WHEN YOU RECEIVE DIRECTING ORDERS." The base also queried the boat if it had received the "enemy*s" position change from another naval entity, possibly an authority on Hon Matt Island (18°48'N, 105° 56'E).[42] The Maddox was informed of this intercept. A half hour after receiving the most recent report, Captain Herrick informed Seventh Fleet and CNCPAC that he had terminated the Desoto mission because of indications of an imminent attack and was now heading east out of the patrol area at ten knots. These indications of an attack were from Vietnamese communications intercepted by the two field sites, as well as the NSG detachment aboard the Maddox. Throughout the rest of the day, these stations would monitor the North Vietnamese ship-to ship and ship-to-shore manual Morse and voice communications nets. They intercepted the all-important vectoring information, the orders from shore commands, and all the tactical communications. However, the DRV boats made no hostile moves against the Maddox that day.

—4S•HS+} Throughout the night of 1/2 August, according to the intercepted communist messages, the North Vietnamese continued to track the destroyer as it remained east of Hon Me Island, some twenty-five miles offshore. Still, nothing had happened that night, and so the

Maddox returned to its patrol line off the DRV coast on 2 August.

-fSffSB—During the early morning, the Maddox, which was heading along the northern track of its patrol area, was notified of further North Vietnamese tracking of its movements. The North Vietnamese naval motor torpedo boat squadron stationed at Port Wallut command was receiving the tracking. A coastal surveillance radar station on Hon Me may have been ordered to begin tracking the destroyer "continuously." (It is possible that this station had been inactive during the previous day so as to deny any information on its operation parameters from the American monitoring effort.)

R-S#SÐ More ominously for the Maddox, the communists also had ordered P-4 patrol torpedo boats (MTB) and Swatow-class patrol boats to begin concentrating near Hon Me Island later in the morning" These patrol torpedo boats had been supplied by the Soviet Union. The P-4 boat displaced twenty-five tons. Its top speed was fifty knots; its cruising speed was thirty knots. It had two twin 12.7-mm machine-gun mounts and two eighteen-inch torpedo tubes. The P-4 boat also carried a Skin Head surface search radar. The reporting from the American intercept sites construed the Vietnamese boat concentration near Hon Me as a prelude to an attack on the Maddox."

<SHSÐ NSA feared that an attack on the Maddox was in the offing. At 1002G (0302Z) on 2 August, NSA sent an urgent message to a number of commands and sites in the region warning of a possible attack. Included in this message was CINCPACFLT, MACV, and the Commander, 7th Fleet. Ironically, the Maddox was not on distribution for this message; the DSU would have received the message, but it was not addressed either. The gist of the message was simple: repeated attacks by "enemy vessels" on Hon Me Island had led Hanoi to make preparations to repel any further assaults. NSA added that C^r

"...THE INDICATED SENSITIVITY ON PART OF DRV AS AS THEIR INDICATED PREPARATION TO COUNTER, POSSIBLE THE DRV

REACTION TO DESOTO PATROL MIGHT BE MORE SEVERE THAN WOULD BE OTHER-

WISE BE ANTICIPATED." The problem with the Maddox not receiving these critical warnings would not be resolved until after the first attack. [46]

-a-S-HS±•) Shortly before noon, at 1144G (0444Z), the Marine SIGINT group attached to the ASA site at Phu Bai, RVN, intercepted a message from the T-142 Swatow-class patrol boat to the DRV naval base at Port Wallut which stated that "[WE] HAVE RECEIVED

THE ORDERS. [T]146 AND [T]142 DID USE [1 Group unreadable] HIGH SPEED TO GET TOGETHER [PARALLEL] WITH ENEMY FOLLOWING LAUNCHED TORPEDOES. 47 The Phu Bai station issued a Critic, short for a critical message, that alerted all relevant commands, and the Maddox, of the planned attack. In the same report, the Phu Bai site added that four boats, T142, T-146, T-166, and T-135, had been engaged in tracking and following an "enemy" which "is probably the current Desoto mission." The final paragraph of the message added that the DRV naval facility in Port Wallut was acting as the shore-based "coordinator/director" for the surveillance of the probable Desoto vessel.[48]

-f•S79'St)- About a half hour later, at 1218G (0518Z), another Marine SIGINT detachment stationed with the navy monitoring station at San Miguel, Philippines, intercepted the same message. This later intercept is not unusual; it meant that the Vietnamese were retransmitting the message to ensure its reception. However, this intercept was reported in a different manner than Phu Bai's version. The second version was reported as a translation instead of a report. In essence, this meant that the actual intercept was reported, and not a restatement of its contents. Therefore, some interesting items of intelligence, which were missing from the first report, were included.

4S++S+) First of all, the second version contained what is known as the "file time" of the DRV message, that is, the time when the message was entered into a log prior to its transmission by the Vietnamese radio operator on the T-142. In this case, a file time of 1113G was noted. This time reference tells us that there was a half-hour delay between the receipt of the message from the originator and the initial transmittal of the "attack" message (1144G/0444Z), as well as an hour's difference in the second intercept (1218G/ ()518Z). The differences are interesting for two reasons. First of all, if the intercept times from both American sites reflect the beginning of the actual intercept of the Vietnamese transmission, then the half-hour difference suggests that the "attack" message was sent more than once. Why more than once? It is possible that Port Wallut had not received the first transmission from T-142, although the reports from both Marine sites imply that the message was received each time.

Secondly, the lag between the file then and the actual transmission by the Vietnamese, if figured from the American thane of intercept, suggests that the Vietnamese were having difficulties in transmitting messages in a timely manner. This delay, as we shall see, becomes an important element in determining the DRV intentions.

(U) At about this time, the three torpedo boats had arrived at Hon Me Island. The Maddox, which was steaming on a northeast heading away from the island, had observed visually the arrival of the three boats. Shortly afterwards, the two Swatow's were seen by the Maddox in the area of Hon Me. The five North Vietnamese boats now were concentrated at the island.

4SHS9-The "attack" message was followed up by another message, this time from Port Wallut to T-146, which was intercepted at 1306G (0612Z) by the Marines in the Philippines. The message instructed T-146 (and probably T-142) to "LEAVE 135 AND TURN BACK TO [THE PATH] OF THE ENEMY." The "135" that T-146 was told to leave turns out not to have been an individual boat, as earlier reported by the Marines, but the squadron designator for the three P-4 torpedo boats which would take part in the upcoming attack These three boats made up the Section 3 of Squadron 135.

-fSHSĐ The five boats, which included the P-4 boats, T-333, T-336, and T-339, departed Hon Me Island at about 1300G, quite possibly on their way to seek out the Maddox.[49] Within the next hour a set of apparently conflicting orders was sent to the Vietnamese boats. At 1409G (07090, Port Wallut notified both Swatow craft that the "enemy" was a large ship bearing 125 degrees (from My Duc?) at a distance of nineteen miles at a speed of eleven knots on a heading of twenty-seven degrees. This put the target on a north-by northeast heading, which matched that of the Maddox. The same message also included a garbled phrase to "THEN DETERMINE," but it is unclear what this phrase meant.[50] However, according to Edwin Moise, the North Vietnamese said that Section 3 received its order to attack the destroyer at 1350G.[51] Since the file time of the message from Port Wallut was 1400G, this may have been the "attack" message.

-£HSB-However, there is a complicating factor. At 1403G (0703Z), just six minutes earlier, the site at San Miguel had copied a message from Haiphong to the two Swatow patrol boats which told them to "ORDER 135 NOT TO MAKE WAR BY DAY." Furthermore, the message added that all of the boats were ordered to head towards shore (though an intercept of the same transmission by the Marines at Phu Bai ordered the boats first to pretend to head towards shore), and then return to Hon Me Island.[52] Although this message was sent shortly after 1400G (07000, it contains a file time of 1203G (05030. This means that this message, which constitutes an order to recall the boats, was originated some two hours before the order to attack was transmitted! A second intercept of the same message added that T146 was supposed to order the recall of Squadron 135's torpedo boats.[53] According to Moise, the North Vietnamese claimed that a recall order was sent after the attack message, but T-146 never relayed it in time.

-fSHS9-This conflict in orders by command elements from Port Wallut and Haiphong indicates that there was a loss of control of the situation. It further suggests that the DRV naval authority in Haiphong had never wanted the attack to occur, at least not during the day, when conditions were not favorable for surprising the Maddox. Since the boats continued their attack on the destroyer, it appears that the recall order was ignored. The deciding factor for the Vietnamese boat commander may have been the much earlier file fame of the recall order; the attack message with the more current file time probably superseded everything else in his decision.

-fSffSB at around 1400G, the Maddox's radar detected the approach from the southwest of the three P-4 torpedo boats. Forewarned by the SIGINT of the Vietnamese intentions to attack, the Maddox then started turning eastward, then to the southeast and increased its speed from eleven to twenty-five knots. The North Vietnamese boats initially may have missed the turn to the southeast by the Maddox. They probably had been visually tracking the American vessel.[55] There is no SIGINT evidence that their Skin Head radars were active, though the Vietnamese claimed the boats used it. Pictures from the action appear to show the radar masts still upright and not lowered in a combat position. By the time, the Vietnamese did react to the Maddox's change in course, they found themselves in an unfavorable attack position. They were chasing the Maddox from its rear starboard, that is, from the northwest, which meant it would take some time, even with a near twenty-knot advantage in speed, to achieve an optimal firing position for their torpedo run—perhaps as long as thirty minutes before they could execute a turn on an attack heading.

(U) VS

Ticonderoga

By 1430G, Commander Ogier ordered the Maddox to go to general quarters.

(U) At about 1440G (0740Z) the Maddox sent a flash precedence message to various commands in the Pacific that she was being approached by high-speed craft with the intention of attacking with torpedoes. Herrick announced that he would fire if necessary, in self-defense.[56] He also requested air cover from the carrier Ticonderoga, which was then 280 miles to the southeast. Four F-8E Crusaders from the carrier, already aloft, were vectored to the Maddox. The destroyer Turner Joy (DD-951) was ordered to make best speed to the Maddox.

(U) For the next twenty minutes, the chase continued. The Vietnamese boats inexorably closed the gap between themselves and the destroyer. At 1500G, Captain Herrick ordered Ogier's gun crews to open fire if the boats approached within ten thousand yards. At about 1505G, the Maddox fired three rounds to warn off the communist boats. This initial action was never reported by the Johnson administration, which insisted that the Vietnamese boats fired first.

(U) A few minutes later the Maddox resumed fire. Through the shellfire, the DRV boats bore in on the Maddox. But their attacks were ineffective. Within fifteen minutes of Maddox's first salvo, jets from the carrier Ticonderoga had arrived and attacked the Vietnamese boats, leaving one dead in the water and the other two damaged. As for the Maddox, she was unscathed except for a single bullet hole from a Vietnamese machine gun round.

(U) There would continue to be confusion over losses for some time. The DRV claimed that two aircraft had been shot down. In reality, one of the navy's jets had sustained wing damage during its maneuvering for the attack and was escorted out of the area by another jet. Both aircraft departed the area under full power, the black exhausts trailing from their engines probably appeared as battle damage to the Vietnamese sailors.[57] The damaged navy jet would be forced to land at Danang.

As for the attacking communist vessels, eventually all three struggled back to their bases. The one craft, T339, thought to be dead in the water and claimed to have been sunk by the 2 August naval action. Note the use of Hotel time (Z+8/G+1). (Courtesy of Naval Historical Center)

sunk by the Vietnamese as well, actually restarted its engines and managed to limp back to shore. On board were four dead and six wounded Vietnamese sailors out of a crew complement of 12. However, the other Vietnamese boats were unaware of what had happened and reported T-339 as sunk and would continue to do so for days afterwards.[58]

-tsnsr•) At 1630G (23300, the Vietnamese patrol boat, T-142, received orders to Concentrate back at a location north of Hon Me Island, and to make contact with another posse) le Swatow class patrol boat, T-165. T-146 also received orders from Haiphong to send two boats out and help the P-4s of Squadron 135 to return.[59] Two days later, on the afternoon of 4 August, T-146 would report to Haiphong the damage to the boats during the attack. T-333 had been hit three times and suffered scattered damage to its water pipes and lifeboat. Its auxiliary engine had been hit and oil pressure was low, suggesting a leak. Still, the boat was assessed as being "lightly damaged." On the other hand, T-336 was deserted as being "heavily damaged with many holes." Its fuel oil was contaminated, possibly by sea water, and the barrel of one of its deck guns was ruined.[60] The boat's crew had suffered at least two wounded as well. The status of both boats and T-333's crew is important to remember when we look at the events of the later evening of 4 August.

(U) In Washington, the reaction to the attack was relatively sub-dued. Since no Americans had been hurt, President Johnson wanted the event downplayed while a stern note of protest was sent to the North Vietnamese. (Ironically, this message was the first diplomatic note ever sent to North Vietnam by the United States.) The president had said that we would not "runaway"; yet we were not going to 'be provocative." However, Hanoi was to be informed in no unambig-uous terms that any more unprovoked actions would entail "grave consequent 61

-€ffSf)-The lack of any reprisal was surprising, especially since freedom of navigation was one of the official reasons for the Desoto missions. However, it is likely that there were mitigating factors which caused Washington to pause. Secretary of Defense McNamara was incorrect to claim that the Vietnamese had fired first.[62] At the same time, the Johnson administration had seriously miscalculated the reaction by Hanoi to the OPLAN 34A missions. It had never considered that the communists might correlate the attacks with the presence of the American destroyer.[63] NSA, monitoring the increas-ing aggressiveness in DRV naval communications, had seen the pos-sibility, and had warned everyone, except the Maddox.

-£SHSB Furthermore, Washington, through the intercept of the DRVs naval communications, had seen the confused set of orders sent to the boats, which suggested that Hanoi had lost control of the situation. McNamara would state, "We believed it possible that it had resulted from a miscalculation or an impulsive act of a local com-mander."[64] It seemed that everyone was trying to defuse the crisis.

(U) The Pentagon was not going to wait around for another incident to happen, either. Plans were put into motion to augment U.S. forces in the region, including deployment of United States Air Force combat aircraft to the Philippines and the dispatch of the carrier Constellation to join the Ticonderoga. A second destroyer, the Turner Joy, already had been dispatched to rendezvous with the Maddox. CINCPAC ordered both ships back to the patrol area, see-ing it "in our interest that we assert right of freedom of the seas." CNCPACFLT issued new rules of engagement for the next three days which allowed both ships to approach the North Vietnamese coast as close as eight nautical miles and four miles from its islands. The two destroyers were ordered to arrive at their daylight patrol point about one hour before dawn. One hour before sunset they were ordered to retire east out to sea during the night.[67]-O If the Pentagon brass was anxious to insert its ships into harm's way, Captain Herrick was more cautious. In an after-action report transmitted that evening, which reviewed the attack and the successful American defense, he added a warning: the concerned about aggressive reactions ordered all e sites in e region to maintain extreme collection, processing, and reporting vigilance on part of all with reporting accomplished LAW [in accordance with] established procedures and at precedence a radiate to activity, especially in regards teaction."[65] A SIGINT Readiness Level Bravo Lantern was declared. Under this readiness level, eight field sites were tasked b NSA to monitor for any North Vietnamese reaction to the patrols. The brunt of e Intercept and reporting was handed to the navy at San Miguel and the Army and Marine missions at Phu Bal.[66]

"DRV HAS DOWN THE GAUNTLET AND NO[W] CONSIDERS ITSELF AT WAR WITH US." He added a concern that the DRV's torpedo boats, especially at night, could hide and then approach the destroyers with little warning.[68] He stated that the Maddox and the Turner Joy, with their five-inch guns and top speed of thirty-three knots, were inadequately armed for defense against such boats. He suggested that the Desoto patrol would be safe only with a cruiser and continuous air cover. One last item was reported by Captain Herrick: the Maddox's long-range, air search radar (AN/SPS40) was inoperative, and the fire control radar

(AN/SPG-53) belonging to the USS Turner Joy, with ammunition and supplies while under way. They had been ordered to return to the coast at daybreak.

-fS7'7'St)-The SIGINT community could be proud of its efforts during the day. The field sites and NSA had intercepted, processed, and reported North Vietnamese naval communications in such a rapid and clear way that everyone in the Pacific command was aware of the approaching attack. It also had provided the information to Washington that suggested that Hanoi's grip on events was less certain than was expected. At the same time, by monitoring the DRVs naval communications, the cryptologists had developed a picture of the command and control elements prior to an attack: extensive tracking by coastal observation posts; the identification of a target and the communication of an attack command; and the use, if limited, of radars in locating the target. The Maddox had never been explicitly named as the target of the attack; in fact, there was just the notation of an "enemy"; however, the analysts at Phu Bai, San Miguel, and inside the Desoto hut had correlated the North Vietnamese tracking with the American ship. The Maddox had been fixed in the minds of the American cryptologists as an "enemy vessel" to the North Vietnamese; they would be on the lookout for possible new attacks. The question was, though, was Hanoi spoiling for another round with the

U.S. Navy? (U) Interlude: Maneuvers and Watchfulness, 3 August

(U) On 3 August, President Johnson made public the instructions he had issued to the Navy earlier. He said that the patrols would continue in the Gulf of Tonkin, that they would be reinforced by another destroyer with combat aircraft overhead. He added that if attacked in international waters, U.S. forces would attack any force with the intention of not just driving it off, but of "destroying it."

(U) At the same Time, the State Department publicized the note it had sent Hanoi Protesting the attacks. It concluded with the words 'The United States Government expects that the authorities of the regime in North Vietnam will be under no misapprehension as to the grave consequences which would inevitably result from any further unprovoked military action against the United States forces."[70]

(U) Despite the increased North Vietnamese vigilance and the observed sensitivity to American and South Vietnamese naval activity in Hanoi's territorial waters, COMUSMACV went ahead with an OPLAN 34A mission scheduled for the night of 3-4 August. In accordance with an earlier agreement, the Maddox and Turner Joy were advised to avoid sailing in the area bounded by the 17th and 18th parallels. A 34A mission against the radar site at Vinh Son (17°57'N, 106°30'E), which involved a four-boat task group, set sail at 1510G (0810Z) on 3 August. At midnight it shelled the radar station. One of the boats broke off and attacked a nearby security post and was pursued for a short distance by a North Vietnamese patrol craft.

(U) By midmorning of 3 August, the two destroyers were heading to their patrol Station, which was about 100 miles northwest of the new 34A mission area. They expected to be on station by early afternoon. However, this location kept them in the area of the island of Hon Me, which was the focus of DRV naval activity during the ensuing day and night.

-fSffS9 Meanwhile, the North Vietnamese were concerned with the salvage of their damaged boats. Just past midnight on 3 August, T-142 and T-146 were in the area of Hon Me Island trying to contact another Swatow, T-165, as well as find the missing boats from Squadron 135. At 0300G (2000Z), T-142 sent an after-action report to the T-146 (for relay to Port Wallut), which highlighted the previous afternoon's combat. It included a Chronology of the various actions the squadron's boats carried out from 0935G to 1625G when they attacked the Maddox

-69S)-Even by midafternoon of 3 August, naval headquarters in Haiphong still did not know where the torpedo boats were and demanded that the Swatow's inform it when they knew their situation.[72] However, the SIGINT site at Phu Bai misconstrued this search and salvage activity as a prelude to a potentially dangerous concentration of enemy boats. It issued a Critic at 1656G (0956Z), which placed six DRV patrol and torpedo boats near Hon Me Island.[73] However, the report was wrong in that it identified the squadron reference "135" as a boat, as well as locating the two torpedo boats, which, at the time, were still missing. The ominous concentration of boats simply was not occurring. However, this incident revealed how tense the situation had become. It also illustrated a precedent by the field site at Phu Bai for misinterpreting Hanoi's intentions.

-ff+SĐ Almost as soon as the two destroyers arrived on station south of Hon Me Island in early afternoon, they were shadowed by a DRV patrol boat which tracked them using its Skin Head radar.[74] The tracking continued through the afternoon into early evening.

The Haiphong naval authority and the Swatow boats near Hon Me exchanged position information on the two destroyers as they moved from the north to south and back north on their patrol.[75] At one point, another Swatow, T-379, erroneously identified as an SO-I class subchaser, was ordered to go out and observe "different targets," which probably referred to the American ships.[76] The North Vietnamese also detected aircraft in the area of the Desoto patrol, though it is unclear from their report whose aircraft these were. However, the commander, 7th Fleet, had ordered a continuous combat air patrol accompanying the two destroyers. The navy jets flew their cover to the east of the Desoto position so as to avoid infringing on DRV air space.

-67ffSt) By early evening, Haiphong ordered T-142 to track the Desoto patrol. T-379, which earlier had been Instructed to observe the Desoto patrol, had sailed to Hon Ngu Island (18°48'N, 105°47'E). It had arrived at 2250G (15500 and reported that the situation at sea was "peaceful."78

fS} T-142 took up a position to the north of the two destroyers and stayed with them, reporting the location of the American ships to Haiphong either directly to naval HQs or relaying reports through T-146. Both U.S. ships reported being followed from the north at a distance of thirty-eight miles by a DRV patrol craft using its Skin Head radar. By this time, 2252G (1552Z), the Desoto patrol was heading southeast out of the patrol area as had been instructed earlier. Tracking of the destroyers ended soon after when they were out of range.

4SHSĐ Meanwhile, the main concern of the DRV navy was the recovery operation for the boats damaged during the 2 August attack. late in the night of 3 August, Haiphong informed T142 that the salvage tug Bach Dang would soon leave Haiphong (it was not clear from the intercept if the time of departure was 0100G, 4 August/1800Z, 3 August) and head towards Hon

Me Island to tow T-333 and T-336 back to

Haiphong or Port Wallut, which was their unit's base.[80] It was expected that the tug would arrive at about noon on 4 August.

Meanwhile, T-146 was ordered to stay with the two damaged boats from Squadron 135 and report their position and status.

(U) So ended 3 August. That evening's 34A raid on Vinh Son was protested by Hanoi. In its complaint, it accused the two destroyers of participating in the raid. Although the DRVs own tracking of the two ships had ceased some hours before, and they could not be certain of where the American ships were, the Vietnamese had inferred anyway that the Desoto ships were involved. It may not have been the right conclusion, but the Vietnamese believed it. Washington still did not think that Hanoi would act.

(U) Round 2: "Everything in Doubt"—

The 4 August Action

-£ffSÿ at 0600G (2300Z) on the morning of August 4, the two destroyers turned westward towards the DRV coastline to begin their day's patrol. By 1300G (0600Z) they returned to their duty station off the coast of North Vietnam near Thanh Hoa (20°08'N, 105°30'E), known as point "Delta," where they began to steam to the southwest along the Vietnamese coast. The air cover from the Ticonderoga again was overhead and to the east. An hour later, the Maddox reported that it had another shadow, this time fifteen miles to the east. The identity of this shadow cannot be determined.

(S#S9- The North Vietnamese had been tracking the Americans. Haiphong informed T142 at 1610G (09100 that they had located the destroyers near 19°36'N and 106°19'E traveling on a southwest heading. However, this last position of the two ships had been acquired by the North Vietnamese some two and one-half hours earlier at 1345G (06450.[81] At approximately 1600G (0900Z), following his operational directive from

CINCPAC to be clear of the patrol area by dark, Herrick ordered the patrol to head due east.

-fS79'SÐ at 1115z (18159, the naval SIGINT detachment aboard the Maddox received a Critic from the Marine SIGINT unit collocated with the ASA at Phu Bai, which stated, "POSS DRV NAVAL OPERATIONS PLANNED AGAINST THE DESOTO PATROL TONITE 04 AUG. AMPLIFYING DATA FOL."[82] Twenty-five minutes later, Phu Bai issued a follow-up report at

1140Z (1840G) which reported, "IMMNENT PLANS OF DRV NAVAL ACTION POSSIBLY AGAINST DESOTO MISSION."83 The report went on to add that three DRV boats, T-142, T146, and T-333 had been ordered at 0927Z (16279, the time the message was intercepted by Phu Bai, to "make ready for military operations the night of 4 August." Although the report did not specify the nature of the military operations, the Marines appear to have concluded that it was an attack against the Desoto. The NSG detachment informed Herrick. Within an hour, at 12404 he informed CNCPAC and other commands that he had received "NFC) NDICATING AITACK BY PGN P-4 IMMINENT. MY POSITION 19-10N 107-OOE. PROCEEDNG SOUTHEAST."84 At this point, the two ships were about eighty to eighty-five nautical miles from the nearest DRV coastline and began to head southeast at twenty knots.

—S) A short time later, just after 1300Z (2000G), the Desoto vessels acquired their first radar contacts. The Maddox reported that it had detected "two skunks" (surface contacts) and three "bogies" (air contacts) on its radars. The surface contacts were about forty to forty-five miles to the northeast of the two destroyers, putting them about 100-110 miles away from the Vietnamese coast at sea, but very close to Hainan Island. 85 (The appearance of aircraft returns (bogies) on the destroyer's radar has generally gone unremarked upon by various commentators. Herrick speculated that these were terrain returns. Whatever the case, these false "boos" suggest Maddo£s air surveillance radar was still malfunctioning.) The Ticonderoga ordered the four jets on CAP to cover the two ships. It scrambled four more A-IH Sky raiders. Within an hour, the aircraft were overhead.

fS)-At about 2045G (1345Z), Herrick reported he had lost the original surface contacts: they had never closed to less than twen-ty-seven miles from his own ships. At 2108G (1408Z), Maddox detected another return—first identified as one boat, later thought to be several boats in a tight formation—this time only fifteen miles away to the southwest, moving towards the destroyers at thirty knots. Nine minutes later, naval A-4 Skyhawk's flying air cover were vectored towards the supposed boats. Although the pilots could see the wakes of the destroyers clearly, they could see no boats at the point the radar indicated. At 2131G (143 IZ), this radar return disappeared.[86]

(U) Then at 2134G (1434Z) came the most important radar contact of the entire incident. What appeared to be a single boat suddenly appeared on the Maddox's radar screen east of the two destroyers at 9,800 yards and closing at nearly 40 knots. The Turner Joy detected another object approaching, but on a different heading, distance, and speed. According to Marolda and Fitzgerald, the navy claimed that this was the same return as the Maddox's.[87] At 2137G (1437Z) at a distance of 6,200 yards from the Desoto vessels, the return tracked by the Maddox appeared to make a sharp turn to the south. This maneuver was interpreted by the Maddox combat information center as a turn after a torpedo run. If this was a torpedo launch, then it was an extraordinarily desperate one. Hanoi's tactical Specifications for its P-4s called for torpedo launches at ranges under 1,000 yards. At over 6,000 yards, it was unlikely a torpedo launched at a moving target could hit anything.[88] The sonar operator aboard the Maddox detected a noise spike on his equipment but did not report it as a torpedo. This conclusion was reached on the CIC. However, the Turner Joy never detected any torpedoes on its sonar. Nor did it detect any torpedoes at all on its sonar that night.[89]

(U) At 2140G (1440Z), Herrick informed CNCPACFLT that he had commenced firing on the attacking PT boat. The Turner Joy had begun firing at its return shortly before this. Both destroyers had a difficult time holding a radar Lock on their targets. Within five minutes, the return on Maddox's radar, which was moving away from the destroyers, disappeared from its screen at a distance of about 9,000 yards. The one that the Turner Joy was kept approaching, and at a distance of about 4,000 yards, it disappeared as well.[90]

(U) For the next fifteen minutes all surface contacts were gone from the radars of the two destroyers. Then, at 2201G (15010, more contacts were detected coming from the west. Now the thickest part of the naval action commenced. The two destroyers Weighted wildly in the dark waters of the Gulf of Tonkin, the Turner Joy firing over 300 rounds madly at swarms of attacking North Vietnamese boats— maybe as many as thirteen—and dodging over two dozen torpedoes.

Another twenty-four-star shells had been fired to illuminate the area and four or five depth charges had been dropped to ward off the pursuing boats and the torpedoes. The Maddox vectored overhead aircraft to the surface contacts, but time and again the aircraft reached the designated point, dropped flares, and reported they could not find any boats. By the time the attack was considered over at 2335G (1635Z), Herrick reported two enemy patrol boats sunk and another damaged. (The count of the damaged boats varied; Herrick believed that the DRV boats sank one of their own accidentally. It is not understood how he arrived at this conclusion, except as a misinterpretation of the radar data which itself was of dubious quality.)

(U) It should be mentioned again that the radar returns from both ships were not continuous Tracking's. Rather, they were mostly flashing returns, that is, they appeared on the scope, held for a few sweeps of the radar, then disappeared. Other targets would suddenly appear a few miles from the destroyers, hold for a while and then disappear. They came from all directions. As each return was logged, it was assigned a target desi maintained that the ship was never able to acquire any of the targets during the battle; he figured he was shooting at the high swells brought on by the storms.[92] Ironically, during all of this latter action, the Maddox never fired a round; its radar never acquired another target after the initial one detected two hours earlier.[93]

(U) The sonar returns of the supposed torpedo attacks were later determined to be a result of the high-speed maneuvering by both U.S. ships. As we saw above, the first "evidence" of a torpedo launch by the enemy boats came from radar. When one of the radar tracks turned away to the south from a westerly heading, this was interpreted by the Americans as a torpedo launch. The sonar rooms in both destroyers were then alerted to a possible torpedo attack. Four crewmen aboard the Turner Joy thought they saw a "white streak" in the water as the ship turned.[94] Both vessels had then gone into wild evasive maneuvers to avoid the torpedoes that were thought to have been launched against them. It was this high-speed writing by the American warships through the waters that created all of the additional sonar reports of more torpedoes. Every time one of the destroyers changed course, the sonar reported the distinctive high-speed sounds of torpedoes. Eventually, Herrick and the other officers realized what was happening: the rudders of the two ships had caused the high-speed returns when they reflected the turbulence of the ships' own propellers.[95]

—S Within an hour of the end of the attack, Herrick relayed his doubts about the attack in an after-action report. After reviewing the number of contacts and possible sinking's, he stated, "ENTIRE ACTION LEAVES MANY DOUBTS EXCEPT FOR APPARENT ATTEMPTED AMBUSH AT BEGINNING." [96] Herrick then suggested in the morning that there be a thorough air reconnaissance of the area for wreckage. In a follow-up message, Herrick added that the Maddox had "NEVER POSITIVELY IDENTIFIED A BOAT AS SUCH. „ 97

(U) Herrick's doubts did not sit well with Washington. Since the first Critic warning of the attack, which had arrived at 0740 EST, Washington had been following the action in the Gulf of Tonkin. At 0925 EST, Secretary McNamara had called the president with the news of the imminent attack. At 1000 EST the flash message from the destroyers that they were under attack reached the Pentagon. Within three hours after the attack ended, 1400 EST, President Johnson had already approved a retaliatory strike against North Vietnamese naval bases to be carried out at 1900 EST, 4 August (0700G, 5 August).

(U) Precisely why President Johnson ordered a retaliatory strike so quickly is not totally clear, especially when there was conflicting evidence as to whether it had actually occurred. Johnson was in the midst of a presidential campaign and his opponent, Republican senator Barry Goldwater from Arizona, a noted hawk, would have gained in the race if Johnson had hesitated or refused to retaliate. Johnson, even in his pose as a moderate relative to Goldwater, could hardly appear weak before a public audience demanding a counterstrike.[98] It also has been suggested that when Johnson first learned of the possible attack, that is, the first Critic issued by Phu Bai, he decided to use the warning as an excuse to get Congress to pass what was soon to be known as the Gulf of Tonkin Resolution.

-fS)-Whatever the president's own rationale for ordering the air strike, he required immediate verification of the North Vietnamese attack because of the doubts that started to be openly expressed within the administration. At around 1400 EST, Admiral Ulysses S. Sharp, CINCPACFLT, called the Pentagon with the news that "a review of the action makes many reported contacts and torpedoes fired 'appear doubtful' because of freak weather, over-eager sonar Operators, and the absence of visual sightings.[100] McNamara called Sharp, who added that there was "a little doubt on just what exactly went on. „101 Messages buzzed back and forth between Washington and the Pacific, demanding information, and then getting contradictory evidence of the attack. The Desoto mission reported that except for possibly the first torpedo report at 2159G (14597), all others were caused by reflections off the two destroyers' screws.[102] At the same time, Herrick reported that the air cover from the two carriers was unable to locate the targets because of poor weather. Yet the carrier Ticonderoga transmitted its own evaluation in which the pilots had "REPORT[ED] NO VISUAL SIGHTINGS OF VESSELS OR WAKES OTHER THAN TURNER JOY AND M[ADDOX]. WAKES FROM TURNER JOY AND M[ADDOX] VISIBLE FROM 2-3000 YARDS. „ 103 Crews from the two destroyers reported seeing nothing for certain. One sailor thought he had seen flashes of gunfire but wasn't sure.

Then, like a classic deus ex machine, along came a second SIGINT report that seemed to clinch the case for an attack. This report was a translation issued by NSA on the 4th of August at 1933Z (1433 EST in Washington) and was leaped upon by administration officials, especially the secretary of defense, Robert McNamara, as direct evidence of the attack. What this translation appeared to be was a sort of North Vietnamese after-action report. An unidentified North Vietnamese naval authority had been intercepted reporting that the DRV had "SHOT DOWN TWO PLANES IN THE BATTLE AREA," and that "WE HAD SACRIFICED SHIPS AND ALL THE REST ARE OKAY." It also added that "THE ENEMY SHIP COULD ALSO HAVE BEEN DAMAGED. „ 104

(U) At 1640 EST, Admiral Sharp again called McNamara with more information on the attack. Just before 1700 EST, McNamara and the JCS met to evaluate the evidence on the attack. They concluded that it had occurred and that five factors were critical: "(1) The Turner Joy was illuminated [by a searchlight] when fired on by automatic weapons; (2) One of the destroyers observed cockpit [bridge] lights [of one of the DRV patrol boats]; (3) A PGM 142 had shot at two U.S. aircraft (from COMINT); (4) A North Vietnamese announcement that two of its boats were 'sacrificed' (from COMINT); (5) Admiral Sharp's determination that there was indeed an attack.„ 105

(U) Of the five pieces of "evidence," two were from the same NSA product issued that afternoon (EST). If the two pieces of visual evidence—the searchlight and cockpit light reports—were contentious, the SIGINT was, in the minds of the secretary of defense, the JCS, and the president, the "smoking gun" evidence needed to justify the air strikes on North Vietnam.[106] so, at 0700G

(V) Burning North Vietnamese patrol! boat after 5 August strike

(00000 on 5 August, CINCPAC received the order to execute the retaliatory raid, codenamed Pierce Arrow. At 1030G (0330Z), naval strike aircraft from Ticonderoga were launched. By early afternoon they hit several targets in the DRV, including almost all of its naval installations.

(U) The Silent Dogs: What the SIGINT Really Did (and Did Not) Report

-6++SD Events surrounding the apparent second attack had been driven almost exclusively by SIGINT. Herrick's personal doubts, the false sonar readings, the confused radar returns, and the pilots' reports, all subverted the validity of the attack reports. But not the SIGINT. For the Johnson administration, both reports—the initial Critic reporting the North Vietnamese preparations for operations, and the after-action report—acted as factual bookends, propping up the other pieces of contentious evidence. The details of the attack, as contradictory as they were, could be massaged or explained to fit the scenario set by the SIGINT. For example, since there were no reported shoot downs of American aircraft that night, then the

North Vietnamese report of downed U.S. planes must have resulted when they had confused illuminating flares for falling aircraft. [107]

-'Shⁱ* However, there were many problems specific to the SIGINT information which emerged almost as soon as it was being reported. In this section we will reconsider what happened that night using all of the relevant SIGINT. We will begin with the initial order to the Vietnamese boats ordering them to make ready for military operations.

Exhibit A: The First Attack Message

•fS+•fSf} The first product, the "attack" message, issued at 1115Z (1815G), reported only the fact that there was a possible DRV naval operation planned against the Desoto patrol. At 1140Z (1840G), this was followed up by a second report from Phu Bai which contained a number of details, such as that T-146 and T-333 were to carry out military operations with T-142. Unlike the messages of 2 August, there was no reference to an "enemy," no tracking to equate to the Desoto patrol, or any indication of the nature of the operations to be carried out by the boats. In the fact, the original intercepted message was only the first part of a larger message, the rest of which was not intercepted. So, what might have been in the latter part is unknown, except that it might have amplified the meaning of the type of operation the boats were involved in.

-CHSfrWhat made this intercept a Critic was the interpretation put to it by the Marine SIGINT site at Phu Bai, which stated that this was an "OPERATION PLANNED AGAINST THE DESO-TO PATROL. „ [108] The follow-up report from Phu Bai amplified the original Critic and maintained, as well, that the attack was against the Desoto mission.[109] When one considers the events of 2 August, this interpretation was not totally unfounded; one could see a reference to a military operation being directed against the American warships. However, the text of the intercept never mentioned a target or any objective of the military operation, or even the nature of the operation. As we shall see soon, not everyone who saw this intercept jumped to the same conclusion that an attack against the American ships was being planned.

-fSffSB Another problem is that the decrypted Vietnamese phrase for military operations, Hanh Quan, has an alternate meaning of "forced or long march or movement," which, in a nautical context, could refer to a voyage by both T-146 and T333. As it turns out, this is the activity that the intercept was actually alluding to.

...6HSB. -For at 1440Z, almost at the precise moment that Herrick ordered his two destroyers to open fire on the approaching radar returns, the Phu Bai intercept site issued a spot report which DRV torpedo craft, T-336 and T333, the latter of which earlier had been reported to attack the Desoto patrol, were, in fact, being readied to be towed to either Haiphong or Port Wallut. This second report carried two points: First, at 1946G (12460, Swatow Haiphong that the tug Bach unable to return to port. T-142 also statement that if the ship [Bach THEM."[110] Besides being a warning further on in this narrative Phu Baj Critic alerting Desoto patrol to possible attack

6.HSĐ the second point of the Phu Bai report was that at 2031G (1331Z) T-142 had informed an authority in Port Wallut that the tug was towing the two craft from Squadron 135. The analysts at Phu Bai added this comment to the end of their report which read, "WITH THE MTB 336 ADDED TO ITS STRING, ITAP[PE

THAT T333 WILL NOT PARTICIPATE IN ANY MILITARY OPERATIONS." so, the boats originally reported being ready to attack the Desoto patrol, were incapable of even moving on their own!

-fSffSiù in fact, this attempted salvage of the two damaged torpedo boats would occupy the efforts of Hanoi's sailors for much of the night of 4/5 August. The Vietnamese would try various methods of getting the two damaged P-4s to a port for repairs. During the 2300G hour, T-146 was ordered by Haiphong to escort the Bach Dang as it returned to base. When that was completed, T-146 was ordered to Bay Chay, a point near Haiphong harbor Shortly afterwards, T142 informed Haiphong that the very busy T-146 was now to tow T-336 back, but since the latter boat was short of fuel, the T-333, which was short of oil but under tow from the Bach Dang, could transfer one to five tons of its fuel to its sister vessel.[112] At 1830Z on 4 August (0130G on 5 August), the navy monitoring site at San Miguel intercepted T-142's report to Haiphong that T-146 had completed its preparations for the two torpedo boats by 0100G 5 August (1800Z 4 August).[113] So, in reality, none of the boats named in the original attack Critic in fact participated in anything but salvage efforts.

fS)-Remember, Captain Herrick did not know that the original Critic was really an interpretation, and that there was no explicit reference to an attack on his ships. He accepted the Critic's contents as intercept of actual Vietnamese plans to attack his ships when he informed the Ticonderoga task group commander of his decision to leave the area. He added his own twist to the report to include specifically the unsupported amplification mentioning the involvement of North Vietnamese P-4 torpedo boats when only one was mentioned as a potential participant in the unidentified operations, and then only if it could be refueled.[114]

-GSHSĐ The possibility that, even if the interpretation was incorrect, the Marine Critic was justified in light of the events from two days earlier, does not stand up when we consider that another site, the navy intercept station at San Miguel, Philippines, had translated the same "operations order," but reported it in a much different fashion. The navy translated the same intercept and then reported it at a Priority precedence, two levels below a Critic (or one level above Routine). The navy analysts titled the report "REPLENISHMENT OF DRV NAVAL VESSEL." The San Miguel report translated the critical sentence as: "T146 SUPPLY FUEL FOR THE 333 ORDER TO GIVE ORDERS TO PUT NTO OPERATION ((2 GR G)) WITH T146. 115

-£S++SB- The difference (and correctness/ incorrectness) between the translations is not important as much as the fact that San Miguel viewed the information as nothing more than the refueling of the damaged torpedo boats. This was in line with an earlier intercept of a query from Haiphong to T-142 asking if T-333 had been refueled yet. [116] Unfortunately, because the San Miguel version was a lower precedence, it was released much later. In fact, it came out at 1838Z (0038G), some two hours after the destroyers had stopped shooting.

€+fSB The quandary created by the reports about the salvage operations is this: If the original suspect vessels, the two Swatow-class patrol and damaged P-4 torpedo boats, were not participating in the anticipated "attack" against the Desoto patrol, then who exactly was going to attack? No other messages had been intercepted which suggested that any other DRV boats were handed the mission of attacking the American destroyers. In fact, there was no intercept at all which hinted at an attack; nothing at all like what had been intercepted on 2 August. So, if the original culprits were involved in salvage operations, then just what was going on in the Gulf of Tonkin?

+/SI.) For NSA and the rest of the SIGINT participants, the second Phu Bai report should have acted as a brake to any further reporting about an attack. It directly contradicted the interpretation—remember, it was an interpretation only—contained in the initial Critic which claimed an attack was being prepared. At this point, all the SIGINT community could accurately state was that there was no signals intelligence reflecting a planned or ongoing attack against the Desoto mission.

-ffSffSf) Except this is not what happened. The second Phu Bai report was not used to report what was going on in the Gulf of Tonkin. Instead, the problem posed by the second Phu Bai report was handled in a curious manner. late on 4 August, Washington (050130Z August 1964), NSA issued a Gulf of Tonkin situation report which covered the events of 4 to 5 August. At the end of the report, NSA added these interesting sentences: "ALTHOUGH NITIAL MESSAGES INDICATED 'H•wr THE T142, T146, AND 1333 WOULD BE INVOLVED THE ATTACK. SUBSEQUENT MESSAGES [not further identified in the report—a curious lapse by NSA which we will address in detail later] SUGGEST THAT NONE OF THESE [BOATS] WAS NVOLVED. REPORTS FROM THE MADDOX THAT IT WAS UNDER ATTACK SOME SEVENTY NAUTICAL MILES NORTHEAST OF THE NAVAL BASE AT QUANG KHE SUGGEST THAT NAVAL UNITS SUBORDNATE TO THE SOUTHERN FLEET COMMAND...WERE INVOLVED...„ 117

-affSfrHowever, the effort to find "culprits" only compounded the errors: the only boats known to be stationed permanently at Quang Khe were Swatow-class Patrol boats which did not carry torpedoes.[118] All P-4 torpedo boats staged from Port Wallut far northwest of the action. Accusing the Swatow craft of participating in the attack was no "solution"; in fact, it only added to the confusion. In reality, though, this statement by NSA was a vain attempt to cover the problem of the contradictory report from Phu Bai. It was nothing but speculation—ignorant speculation at that. Furthermore, this summary report did not address the issue of the total lack of intercept of any North Vietnamese attack command and control communications.

(U) Fingering the Swatow's as the culprits only made the "attack" scenario more improbable for another reason. The distance from Quang the naval base (17°46'N, 106°29'E) to the reported first radar plot by the Maddox, forty to forty-five nautical miles northeast of its position, is about 120 nautical miles. However, this distance should not be construed as a "straight line" dash from Quang Khe. Because the DRV boats were "detected" coming from the east, they would have had to travel in a long arc northward and then southeast around the American destroyers which were speeding to the southeast. Also, remember that the Maddox and Turner Joy did not "detect" these boats until they approached from the east, so the route to the north of the American destroyers had to be at a distance sufficient to avoid discovery by radar. This lengthens to a distance of around 180 nautical miles. Since the "attack order" was issued at 1115Z and the initial radar plot was at 1336Z (and we are presuming that the postulated boats left at the exact time of the first intercept, or were soon under way at the time), then the boats would have had to have been traveling at a speed of nearly seventy miles per hour (about 110 mph) to have been where the Maddox first detected them—at a rate some 58 percent higher than the Swatow's known top speed!

(U) The only other base from which the "attack" could have been staged was Port Wallut, which was the base for the P-4 Squadron 135. The distance from Port Wallut (21°13'N, 107°34'E) to the initial point of detection by the Desoto radars is about 140 nautical miles. However, the same problem exists here as for Quang Khe, though not quite as extreme, for the P-4s. The scenario presumes that they would have been moving at a little less than seventy miles per hour, or a good 40 percent higher than the boat's listed maximum speed.

4SHSĐ-Another possibility to consider when looking at the "attack message" is that there was some other activity to which the "military operations" (if that is the interpretation one could have) might have referred. In fact, there was something else going on that night of 4/5 August which is seldom mentioned in the public record: a maritime OPLAN-34A mission was, in fact, moving northward along the DRV coastline at the time when the American destroyers were shooting away at those radar returns. The Marolda and Fitzgerald history of the U.S. Navy in Vietnam fails to mention the ongoing 34A mission. Official Washington as well never mentioned this 34A mission. In classified hearings in February 1968, Secretary of Defense McNamara never mentioned this mission, claiming that the last one prior to the 4 August attack occurred on the night of 3-4 August. Obviously, if the 34A mission of the night of 4-5 August were at the time, it would have undercut Washington's claim that nothing else was happening that night which might have provoked Hanoi.

(U) This 34A mission had been scheduled back at the end of July by COMUSMACV, which then had informed Washington of the missions planned for all of August. This particular foray main objective was the shelling of the island of Hon Matt. It is not certain when this mission left Danang, though it was normal for the boats to depart in the late afternoon to take advantage of darkness by the time they reached the DRV coastline. So, a departure time between 1500G and 1600G (0900Z) would not be too far off.

-fSffS±) At 2316G (1616Z) the Marine mission at Phu Bai intercepted a message from the DRV naval HQ in Haiphong to T-142 that six enemy raiding vessels had been located somewhere south of Thanh Hoa (20°00'N, 105°30'E). (The actual position is confusing due to a garble in the text transmitted from Phu Bai. Neither the time of the enemy boats' position nor their course is clear.)[119] This intercept occurred only a few minutes before the JCS approved an urgent recall order from CINCPACFLT for the 34A mission to be discontinued and return to Danang immediately.[120] It is possible that the Kit support element may have passed this intelligence to the MACV/SOG, which in turn began the recall.

(-SHSÐIn light of what finally transpired with T-142 and the two P-4 torpedo boats, it seems that they were not part of a defensive plan against the raiders. That this Swatow received the message about the raiders does not seem odd in light of the fact that T-142 seems to have served as some sort of radio relay for other boats or as a communications guard vessel for all DRV naval operations: a majority of intercepted messages during the period seem to have been sent to or through T-142. From other intercepts, we know that at least another Swatow, T-379, was near Hon Matt; two others, T-130 and T-132, were near Hon Me Island; and T-165 had deployed, as well. If the DRV was planning to attack the 34A raiders on 4 August, these craft would have been the local ones to use because of their substantial deck gun armament. However, no other communications activity related to any other Swatow patrol craft was intercepted that night. So, it remains uncertain what, if anything, Hanoi was planning to do to fend off the 34A mission of 4 August.

Exhibit B: The Lack of Vietnamese Command, Control, Communications, and Intelligence

-fSffS1) To our initial question as to who was involved in the apparent attack of the two American destroyers, we must add a corollary question: How did the North Vietnamese carry out the "attack"; that is, how were the boats controlled and vectored to the American ships? If we recall the three elements of the command, control, communications and intelligence (C31) observed during the previous two days' activities—communications from Haiphong and Port Wallut, relayed through the Swatow-class boats; the relay of tracking information on the American ships; and the use of the Skin Head surface search radar—then we have another serious problem with the engagement of the night of 4 August because none of these elements was present during the so-called attack.

-tans- During the entire day of 4 August, most of the communications intercepted from either DRV naval command entities in Port Wallut or Haiphong either were directed to the craft involved in the salvage and recovery of the two Squadron 135 torpedo boats, or else were relays of tracking reports of the Desoto patrol, and those latter messages were exchanged with T-142, which was involved in the ongoing recovery operations. The only other messages which were intercepted contained orders for other Swatow-class patrol boats to move to positions along the coast: T-130 and T-132 were ordered to Hon Me Island, while T-165 was ordered to leave Haiphong at 1448G (0748Z) and move to the entrance of an unspecified bay.[121]

-fSHSĐ-During the 2 August attack, there were elements of high-level control from the naval commands at Port Wallut and Haiphong, both of whom sent orders and tracking reports to the attacking boats. The Swatow's, principally T142, acted as a communications relay between the torpedo boats and the onshore commands. The messages were transmitted using high frequency manual Morse communications which were intercepted throughout the day, even during the fighting. Finally, there were sporadic boat-to-boat VHF, tactical voice communications which the intercept positions aboard the Maddox's hut could intercept, at least until the destroyer activated its fire control radars, which interfered with the navy's monitoring.

-fSf++ However, not one of these elements was detected during the night of 4 August. Trying to find more evidence of the purported attack, NSA had queried the NSG detachment aboard the Maddox on 6 August to supply urgently all intercept that "PROVIDES PROOF OF DRV ATTACK

ON FOUR AUGUST UPON U.S. NAVAL VESSELS. „ 122Within five hours came the disheartening reply from the DSU. There was no manual Morse intercept to prove the DRV attack of 4 August. Furthermore, voice intercept was nil, except for signal checks between two unidentified stations.123

-4SffSÙThe tracking messages Locating the Desoto patrol ships had been intercepted by the Americans early in the day of 4 August. However, the last credible position of the American ships was passed at 1610G (0910Z) from Haiphong to T-142. The position, 19°36'N, 106°19'E, was fairly close to the Desoto patrol's position at the time. This was just about two hours before Herrick ordered his ships to head east in reaction to the Phu Bai Critic.[124] However, it should be pointed out that this position report was sent to the T-142, which was involved in the salvage of the two torpedo boats. There is no evidence that the T-142 relayed it to any other boat or command.

-CSffSB- One more position report on the Desoto patrol was sent from Port Wallut to a probable vessel at 2246G (1546Z), which was about an hour after the supposed engagement had begun. This position report might seem as related to the action, except for two problems. First of all, the report located the American ships thirty-five nautical miles east of Hon Matt Island, which places the destroyers some eighty nautical miles northwest of where they actually were at the then! In addition, the report does not carry the time associated with the Americans' position. (The reported location suggests, however, at least from the track the Desoto patrol took that night, that this position report was about four to five hours old.) So, this information could hardly be used by any North Vietnamese boats intending to attack the Americans. Secondly, the message includes an order (or advisory) to the recipient to maintain a continuous communication watch with an unidentified entity, as well as to "go close to shore. „ 125 This latter command seems to be hardly intended for boats looking to attack the American ships; rather it appears suited for the boats involved in the salvage operations or the other patrol boats spread out along the DRV coast.

...6+9...The issue of DRV tracking of the Desoto patrol is important. For in September 1964 NSA would release a report on Vietnamese coastal radar operations during the period. In this report, NSA would contend that active tracking by the coastal observation posts equipped with coastal surveillance radars would indicate hostile intentions by Hanoi. The report pointed out that there was no tracking of the Craig earlier in March.[126] This was not quite Done: the DRV was aware of the location of the destroyer, but its time off the Vietnamese coast was quite short so the tracking was spotty.

++9 The same report also pointed out that the Maddox was under "constant" radar surveillance before it came under attack on 2 August. However, the report then ducks the issue of the observed sporadic tracking by the North Vietnamese on 4 August with the claim that "The evidence is feel inconclusive in light of the virtual absence of tracking's on 3-4 August before the second attack. „127 The evidence would never be found. The final report from the DSU aboard the Maddox showed only occasional coastal tracking from shore stations and North Vietnamese boats on 4 August. And it had ended by midafternoon.128

-B-Finally, the Americans detected no Skin Head emissions during the "attack" on 4 August. Keep in mind that during 3 August the DRV boats that shadowed the Desoto patrol used their Skin Head surface search radars, and that these emissions were detected by the ELINT position in the intercept hut aboard the Maddox. These signals were also intercepted during the morning and early afternoon of 4 August.[129]

-fS+SĐ While it is true that no North Vietnamese radar emissions were detected during the 2 August attack on the Maddox, it must be remembered that this attack occurred in the daytime under nearly ideal conditions.[130] Yet, the DRV boats had difficulty visually locating and then following the Maddox. What we are confronted with in the second "attack" is the proposition that the North Vietnamese boats themselves, which the Turner Joy and Maddox detected using only their radars, could find the Americans so far out at sea (over 100 nautical miles), in heavy swells (three to six feet), at night, with a low cloud cover, without using their radars. Even if the North Vietnamese had the equipment to receive the American radar pulses, this information would have given them only a crude bearing on which to track. They could not determine distance, speed, or anything else which to plot any sort of torpedo attack.[131] Besides that, how could they even begin to track the American ships when the latest valid position was almost five hours old!

(U) In the Sherlock Holmes story "Silver Blaze," the great Victorian detective and his assistant, Dr. Watson, are confronted with the paradox of a crime which cannot be proven to have happened. In the story there is this exchange:

Is the-' any point to which you wish to draw my attention?

To the curious incident of the dog in the nighttime.

The dog did nothing in the night-time.

That was the curious incident, remarked Sherlock Holmes.132

-fSHSÐ And so it is with the 4 August incident: there were no DRV naval communications or radar emissions which were normally associated with a naval engagement. Just two days prior, the Americans had an opportunity to observe Vietnamese naval communications during the attack on the Maddox. Among other things, they had seen that the Vietnamese had difficulties in setting up and maintaining control of an attack, as the incident with the conflicting orders illustrated. And so there should have been a generous amount of intercept of any communications which would have supported the claims of the two American destroyers.

4+9 Yet, nothing as much as a single bark was intercepted. As Holmes would come to conclude that no crime was committed, so we must conclude that, since U.S. SIGINT never intercepted anything associated with an attack, none ever occurred. And the contention that all possible communications and emissions reflecting an attack might have gone unheard can be dismissed. As Gerrel Moore, the officer-in-charge of the DSU on board the Maddox, observed: "I can't believe that somebody wouldn't have picked up something." Finally, a review of the DSU intercept log for 4 August showed no variation in Vietnamese communications procedures which could suggest that any change or changes, such as new operating frequencies, call signs, or procedures, were implemented just for the "attack" that could elude American intercept.

C: The "After-Action" Report

-fSffS9-With there being no SIGINT evidence of an attack, and the rest of the evidence from visual, radar, and sonar sources so unsupportive, we are left with attempting to explain the intercept of late 4 August, which was interpreted as an after-action report. Remember, it was this intercept which was so critical to McNamara's contention that an attack had occurred—two of the five pieces of his list of "convincing" evidence. Yet, when we look closely at the intercept, there are four major problems with the assertion that it was a report on the supposed engagement from just a few hours earlier on 4 August. The translation, "TIO-64," issued by NSA at 1933Z on 4 August (0233G, 5 August) is shown on this page.

...4SHS9 the first difficulty with the intercept is that it does not resemble an after-action report of the type which had been intercepted early on 3 August by the Marine element at Phu Bai. That intercept, sent by T-142 to T-146 and the Port Wallut HQ of Squadron 135, contained a chronology of events beginning at 0925G on 2 August when T-146 met the three boats from Squadron 135 and guided them to Hon Me Island. The report noted that the attack against the Americans began at 1525G, and that by 1625G, all the boats had received the orders to break off the attack.135

-4S++SĐ in the 4 August translation, there is no Chronology associated with the supposed down-

-SHY The supposed Vietnamese communist naval after-action report

in of the aircraft. There is no mention of any participating boats or units, except to mention that two were "SACRIFICED...AND ALL THE REST ARE OKAY." The only sense of when anything happened comes with the beginning phrase, "AFTER THE 135 HAD ALREADY STARTED TO REPORT TO YOU." In fact, the entire report seems incoherent, not the type one expected to see sent by an officer on the scene, as had been intercepted on 3 August. It rambles, mixing morale boosting statements with seemingly repetitious references to planes being shot down and then seeing them "sink."

-.4. *SĐ Secondly, there is a problem the translation of a critical passage: "WE SACRIFICED MO SHIPS AND ALL THE REST ARE OKAY." Unfortunately, the original, decrypted Vietnamese language version of the message cannot be located in the NSA Archives. Also, a possible original Translation of the entire message (or part of it), numbered "T162-64" and issued by the navy site at San Miguel, cannot be found in the NSA Archives file of that site's 1964 translations. Without either document, we are left with the conjecture of what Vietnamese words were seen by the new analysts and linguists at San Miguel and their counterparts at NSA.

-fSffSĐ However, from the existing records, what we do know is that the translation finally issued by NSA was not what was initially reported by San Miguel. At 1550Z (2250G) on 4 August, when the American destroyers were shooting away at those radar returns, San Miguel intercepted a message which it identified as being sent from T-142 to an unidentified entity at My Duc (19°52'N, 105°5'E). In total, the report, numbered "08," read:

WE SHOT AT TWO ENEMY AIRPLANES AND AT LEAST ONE WAS DAMAGED. WE SACRID TWO COMRADES BUT ALL ARE BRAVE AND RECOGNIZE OUR OBLIGA'HON.136

(U) How the translation changed from "comrades" in the San Miguel version to "boats" in the NSA version is unknown. Edwin Moise, in his study of the Tonkin Gulf, suggests that a Vietnamese sentence to the effect of losing two comrades could hardly be construed to mean two ships: "HAI DONG CHI HY SNH" or "HAI DONG CHI BI HY SINH" are possible

Vietnamese phrases which could be translated to "sacrificing two comrades."137 The Vietnamese word for boat, "TAU," had been seen in earlier intercepted messages. This would be consistent, since Hanoi's messages usually shortened the word to just the letter "T" from where the same letter designators for Hanoi's boats comes from, such as "T-142," "T-146," etc.

-.6ᵗ+Sò A possible argument that there was a garble in the inception of the message which could have led to confusion does not hold.

(U) There is an additional point of interest: President Johnson in his memoirs noted that "The North Vietnamese skipper reported that his unit had 'sacrificed two comrades'. "Our experts said that this meant either two enemy boats or two men in the attack group." 139(My italics in all cases.) This is an interesting admission, for it suggests, and rather strongly, that even the day that the NSA translation was issued, the intercept was considered, at best, ambiguous in its meaning. Why NSA opted for 't) oats" instead of "comrades" in its final Translation is not clear, especially if the difference was enough to tell the president.

-fSffSf) The third problem is with the time of the intercept and the file time listed on the NSA translation. The file time, 2242G (1542Z), is barely one hour after the Turner Joy and Maddox opened fire on the first radar returns. As we saw with the messages from 2 August, this entry is the time that the Vietnamese communications center (or a radio operator) assigned to the message when it arrived ready for transmission, which, as it turns out, in this case took another eight minutes to complete. If we allow any time for the message's drafting, coordination, and encryption (remember, this is a manual system three charts), then the actual time of the composition of the message must be pushed back close to the beginning of the so-called engagement. Even if we are generous with our appreciation of the skill of the Vietnamese communications personnel in encrypting the message, we fall have to concede some fine to get the message from composition to transmission. The more fame we allow for this process, then the closer its origin comes up to the time that the destroyers first opened fire. In that case, then, the intercept cannot be considered an action report of the events currently occurring at sea in the Gulf of Tonkin.

-fSffSÐ the question of the time of origin for the information in the Vietnamese message gets even more suspect when we consider the identities of the Vietnamese who may have sent and received it. The NSA translation carries the two call words "TM" and "LAP" as unidentified. Actually, this is not true. San Miguel, in its reports, identified the transmitting station, known by the cover name "TRA," as the T-142 patrol boat. The receiving station, "LAP," was identified as a shore station at My Duc, possibly the coastal observation post which earlier had tracked the American ships.

-fS79'Sfî in reality, these equations probably were incorrect. The probable identities for the cover names had been known for some time; it is just that San Miguel confused them. "TRA" had been associated with a DRV naval HQs in Haiphong as recently as 2 August. "LAP" had been identified with T-142 on 30 July.[141] However, the exact identities are not important. What is critical is that Haiphong could not have originated the information in the intercept; it had to come from some other source. Another station had to compose a report, encrypt, and transmit the information to Haiphong before it could, in turn, send its message. This means that the very first version of this "after-action" report probably was composed at or before the time the two destroyers opened fire!

fSHSĐ the message file time, 2242G (1542Z) and the intercept time, 1550Z (2250G), should have been highlighted in the translation. These times would have indicated that the intercept could not have been construed as an after-action report. Neither critical time element was noted in the translation. Instead, it seems that the time NSA released the translation, 1933Z (or 1955Z if it had been relayed), was the critical element. That the translation was issued some two and one-half hours after the incident was over probably was the reason it was interpreted by its Washington recipients as a North Vietnamese after-action report.

81ST) The translation as issued is hardly helpful in providing a useful background to explain its significance. The title, "DRV NAVAL ENTITY REPORTS LOSSES AND CLAIMS TWO ENEMY AIRCRAFT SHOT DOWN," does not indicate any context for the translation. That being so, it would not be difficult to infer that the translation referred to the recently ended combat action. So, it just hung there waiting for someone to claim it, and the Johnson administration jumped on it. Remember, this translation arrived in Washington midway in the afternoon of 4 August just at the time that the administration was trying to resolve the doubts about the attack that Captain Herrick had reported. And, as we have seen, it was to be the answer to all of the lingering doubts as to the validity of the attack. NSA itself would use the translation to support the contention that there had been a second attack as well, quoting excerpts from it in several Gulf of Tonkin Summary reports issued from 4 to 6 August. The problem 'With the file and intercept times is a critical one, and it reflects a failure by the analysts who issued the translation to draw attention to them.

Yet it is the fourth problem with the translation which is the most troublesome: that is, specifically, how it was put together. It was mentioned above that the original intercept of the translation was missing from NSA files on the Gulf of Tonkin. We also mentioned that the possible English translation of the entire or part of the intercept, "T162-64," issued by San Miguel, was missing. This situation is odd since crucial earlier and original intercepts, such as the "attack message" and several tracking reports, were available and placed in the allegedly "complete" NSA Chrono low of the attacks, the latter document of which we will discuss shortly. But neither the original intercept nor the translations from San Miguel are in the Chrono low. It would seem that they should be there to buttress the validity of the all-important "after-action" report.[142] However, they are not; therein lies the problem.

For only four minutes (1554Z) after San Miguel reported the transmission about "sacrificing two comrades," it published the following intercept from T-142 to My Duc:

((3GR G)) THE NEWS BECAUSE THEY DID CONTINUOUSLY SEE WITH THEIR EYES ENEMY AIRCRAFT FALL -INTO THE SEA. ENEMY VESSEL PERHAPS IS DAMAGED. REPORT THIS NEWS TO THE MOBILIZED UNIT.[143]

-fSffSB If we take the two intercepts from San Miguel in the sequence in which they were monitored and put them together, we have constructed, with the addition of some transitional words, the so-called "after-action" translation, "T-10," issued by NSA at 1933Z on 4 August. Since the messages were transmitted by the Vietnamese in this sequence, both spoke of aircraft, and were transmitted shortly after one another with little or no interval, it probably was not difficult to conflate the Ova as parts of the same message.

-.4SHSi) However, are these two intercepts really parts of the same message? The answer turns out to be no. This is because the English translation of the second intercept exists. San Miguel transmitted it to NSA on 8 August as part of the post-crisis review. It carried an important item—the Vietnamese-assigned message file number, "NR24," which indicates that the second intercept was a separate message after all, and not part of the first intercept![144]

fSffSf)-So, if we look at the NSA translation, "TIO," specifically beginning at the phrase "BECAUSE THEY THEMSELVES SAW..." to the end, what we actually are looking at is a separate

North Vietnamese message. The reason for two messages is easy to explain. The second one is reporting what the Vietnamese observed of the 4 August action from either one of their boats near the coast, or coastal installations.[145] What the Vietnamese actually saw was either the flares dropped by the carrier Ticonderoga's aircraft to illuminate the DRV boats they were told were there by the two destroyers, or any of the fifty or so star shells fired by the two American ships to illuminate targets. Note that the second intercept reports only that "ENEMY AIRCRAFT FALLING INTO THE SEA." There is no mention by the Vietnamese of shooting at them, as we would expect if it were a report after an engagement with the Americans as there is in the first intercept. In the same fashion, the flashes from the destroyers' guns and shells exploding observed from over the horizon must have suggested to the Vietnamese that one of the American ships had been hit. San Miguel's analysts recognized that the second intercept dealt with that evening's actions. San Miguel, then, reported it first at 1632Z, while the first intercept about "sacrificing comrades" was reported later at 1646Z.

-6+9 If we again look at the first intercept from San Miguel, we note that the Vietnamese claim they shot at two planes and damaged one. This happens to be in line with their later claims from the action on 2 August. Additionally, the loss of two comrades probably refers to the casualties suffered by T-336 from the same day's fighting.[146] (Keep in mind that the whereabouts and condition of T-339 were unknown to the DRV command as late as 4 August. It was still considered sunk.)

(U) The congruence of the NSA and the San Miguel reports has been noted elsewhere. In Edwin Moise's book on the Tonkin Gulf, he discusses the resemblance between a "longer" message and a "shorter" one he had received from NSA in response to a FOIA request. Since he had received heavily redacted versions of "TIO" and "R38" and "R39" from San Miguel, it was difficult for him to determine the critical fact that the two reports from the Philippines were issued before the NSA translation. However, he did catch the similarity among them, especially the phrases about the downed planes.[147]

-679'Sf)- This finding that San Miguel had issued two separate reports, which probably had been conflated into a single translation by NSA, may explain the description by President Johnson of the discussions with the so-called technical experts at the White House the afternoon of the attack The major point that Johnson related was the explanation that the expression "sacrificing two comrades" could have meant two enemy boats or two men. The fact that this issue was brought up strongly suggests that the reports from San Miguel probably were circulating among intelligence and defense officials, and that questions were being raised as to which version was correct, the boats or the comrades. But it is still not clear from this incident what the source was of the NSA version which claimed that two boats were lost instead of two men. As we stated earlier, without the original Vietnamese text, we are left with conjecture. However, with the great divergence between the reports issued by San Miguel and NSA, attention must fall primarily on the actions of the NSA analysts. Why did they change San Miguel's original translation?

-fSffSÐ-This analysis of the NSA translation of the so-called after-action report may appear excessive. Yet it is warranted because of the crucial role played by it in convincing the Johnson administration of the validity of the claim that the two destroyers indeed had been attacked by the North Vietnamese. The critical analysis of the translation has revealed several problems with the text itself, the context and timing of the intercept, that is, whether it was really related to the attack, and finally, the circumstances of the original analysis of the intercept.

—fSffSÐ-If the results of this analysis of the translation were not enough to make one suspect its validity, the difficulties with the documentary source record undermine it all the more. For the sources we do not have, that is, the missing technical supplements and the translation, "T162," leave us with a serious gap: we have only the two field reports and single NSA English translation. The differences between the field version and the one published by NSA are too large to ignore; depending on which translation one accepts, the possible interpretations of the incident of 4 August are either that nothing happened or that there was an attack

(U) Exhibit D: A Matter of Certainty

(U) A question remains, what were the circumstances surrounding the issuance of this last translation? The answer is that we do not exactly know the details of how it was put together. However, we do have some clues as to the environment in which the analysis reporting by NSA was done.

-fSffSB-After the 2 August attack, the analytic division concerned with the North Vietnamese problem, B26, had established an informal twenty-four-hour watch center to handle the SIGINT reporting from the Gulf of Tonkin, A relatively small team, perhaps fewer than ten, of analysts, linguists, and supervisory personnel, staffed the center. Unfortunately, there were what can be called "environmental pressures" on the staff. Notably, a crisis atmosphere surrounding everyone and everything, which, combined with twelve- to sixteen-hour days, probably led to serious problems of pressure and fatigue. There was also the problem that the linguists available were relatively inexperienced, some being barely a year or two removed from language school. Besides just reviewing the field intercept, people from this crisis cell also briefed the Pentagon and National Security Council.[148]

-fSffSf) It appears that there was little in the way of control or interaction between this cell and senior NSA leadership. The director, NSA, General Blake, was out of town at the time. The various briefings at the Pentagon, and possibly the White House, were handled by midlevel managers and staffers operating out of the crisis cell and NSA liaison positions in the Pentagon and the White House. In fact, for the most part, it seems that senior NSA leadership stayed out of the proceedings, exercising little control or over 149

(U) That there might have been a lot of pressure on the NSA people to produce "proof" is quite likely. Regarding that charged period, Ray Cline, the former CIA deputy director, recalled that "Everybody was demanding the signet (signals intelligence; intercepts); they wanted it quick, they didn't want anybody to take any time to analyze it." [150] It was certainly a crisis moment. We know from the chronology mentioned earlier, that the translation of the "after-action" report arrived about two hours after the time that the first news of Captain Herrick's doubts about the action had arrived in Washington. Also, as we have seen, McNamara's evidence contained at least two points from the NSA translation. Of this, there is little to doubt. However, it remains a question as to whether the analysts and managers in NSA were certain of the second attack.

…4SHSÐIt has been reported in other histories that the NSA analyst (or analysts) who actually decrypted and translated the intercepts were doubtful of the second incident from the very beginning, believing that the message referred to the 2 August attack.[151] Furthermore, a review of oral histories suggests that in the watch center there was a sort of division between those who were certain the second attack occurred, which was composed of midlevel management, and the analysts who were not so sure.152

fSffSÐ Actually, the doubters were not as skeptical about the reality of the attack as much as they as were uncertain as how to label the intercept about the Vietnamese shooting at/down the aircraft. Was it related to what was happening in the Gulf of Tonkin? As one linguist recalled, the problem came down to "Was this, or was this not?" The deciding element for the analysts was the fact that the intercept time (1550Z or 1559Z) of the "after action" intercept coincided with the •time frame of the attack on the two destroyers: an "coin toss" was made, and the translation went out which was interpreted as supporting the validity of the second attack.[153] There was no explicit connection between the intercept and events: it was inferred from the coincidence of the time of the intercept and the time of the ongoing "attack." Also implicit in this decision was a lack of confidence concerning the validity of the information; it could not stand by itself as the evidence, at least in the minds of the analysts.

(U) On such small things as a mental "coin toss," then, does history often turn.

-fSffSfrAs to the nature of the translation, according to the same linguist, reportedly there were no enforced "word changes" in this report (or any others which were issued), though arguments over translation "styles" did occur. These arguments were over the rendering of the translations from the Vietnamese original "into suitable English."[154]

-affS±} This analysis by coin flip left the door open for follow-up reports which more openly supported the notion of an attack. Barely six hours after it issued the "after-action" translation, NSA released its first summary report of the action. This summary contained quotes from the earlier after-action translation. These quotes were placed in summary in such a way as to substantiate collateral radar, sonar, and visual information from the Desoto patrol. On 6 August two more summaries were released by NSA which carried more SIGINT which the Agency asserted supported the second attack scenario. Publicly, at least, and probably from the very beginning, NSA supported the Johnson Administration claim for a second attack[155] These reports are important in understanding the post-attack position taken by NSA

-4SHSfl as for the doubts about the second attack among the analysts at NSA, it appears that none of them were ever publicized during the briefings with officials at the Defense Department. Or, if they were mentioned, they were downplayed. In fact, it seems that the NSA position was a fairly straightforward one: that the second attack occurred.[156] So firm was NSA's position, that one previous NSA historian has suggested that this allowed President Johnson to shift the blame for the final decision from himself to the "experts" who had assured him of the strength of the evidence from the SIGINT.[157]

(U) Officially, everyone else in Washington supported the notion that there had been an attack. Later statements by various intelligence and Defense Department officials suggest that there was a large group who simply did not believe that the attack had happened or that the evidence even pointed to an attack. Many high-ranking officials from CIA, the Department of State, and the Pentagon could not see the evidence assembled by McNamara as supporting a Vietnamese attack. Some of them were skeptical (or claim to have been so) from almost the beginning of the incident. This group of doubters included the then U.S. Army's deputy chief of staff for military operations, General Bruce Palmer Jr., Ray Cline, the CIA's deputy director for intelligence, the heads of the Department of State's Intelligence and Far Eastern Divisions, as well as a host of staffers on the National Security Council and in the Defense Department, who, in years to come, would become notable: Daniel Ellsberg, Alvid Friedman, and Alexander Haig.

(U) Yet, despite doubts, people in the intelligence and defense communities kept their silence. As much as anything else, it was an awareness that President Johnson would brook no uncertainty that could undermine his position. Faced with this attitude, Ray Cline was quoted as saying: we knew it was bum dope that we were getting from the Seventh Fleet, but we were told only to give the facts with no elaboration on the nature of the evidence. Everyone knew how volatile LBJ was. He did not like to deal with uncertainties."[158]

-fSffSÐ and there were plenty of people in NSA and the cryptologic community who doubted that the SIGINT was convincing evidence of an attack. Notable among these were the chief of B Group, who seems to have been skeptical from the morning of 5 August, and the NSA Pacific Representative (NSAPAC), who sent a message to DIR-NSA listing his doubts after reviewing a CINCPAC study of the affair.[159]

-eS++SÐWith all of the doubters about the attack, whether they were uncertain from the beginning, or saw the problems with the "evidence" later on, it is surprising that what emerged from various intelligence and Defense Department studies of the 4 August event were even more confirmations that the attack had occurred. Within weeks of the event, teams from the navy commands in the Pacific region, CINCPAC and Seventh Fleet, conducted reviews which verified the attack. A Defense Department team arrived in mid-August and conducted interviews of the pilots and the crews of the destroyers. They found strong evidence for the attack as well.[160] The Joint Reconnaissance Center issued a Chrono low of events, while ASA Pacific Headquarters conducted a critique of the reporting by Phu Bai during SIGINT Readiness Bravo Lantern, the enhanced SIGINT coverage ordered during the Gulf of Tonkin crisis.[161] Both documents supported the idea of a second attack

Exhibit E: And Some More Silent Dogs

-fSffSÐ Various elements of the Naval Security Group, which oversaw and provided the manning for the Desoto missions, issued reports on the incidents in the Gulf of TonHn which were strangely reticent about the evidence of the attack on the night of the 4th. For example, in the report issued by the commanding officer of NSG detachment aboard the Maddox, two and one-half pages are devoted to SIGINT reflections of the 2 August attack. The follow-up air Strikes of 5 August warrant another half page. Yet the statement summarizing the SIGINT activity of 4 August is rendered in just in one sentence:

H. On 4 August information received from USN 414T and USM 626J [Phu Bail indicated a possible attack on the Desoto ships by the DRV 162 naval vessels.

—tS77SÎi A report from the director, Naval Security Group Pacific, of 24 August was similar. Twelve paragraphs of the message are devoted in recounting the SIGINT detail of the 2 August attacks. The recounting of the "attack" of 4 August was done in a short entry of two paragraphs, the first of which contained the information that T-142 was "again shadowing" the U.S. ships. It also refers to "moderately heavy tracking" by two DRV tracking sites at Thanh Hoa

(20²00'N, 105⁰30'E) and Hon En (18⁰18'N,

-fSffSf)-Further evidence, and perhaps one of the strongest pieces available indicating that no attack had happened, came from the North Vietnamese themselves. On 6 August, an unidentified DRV naval entity, possibly the naval HQ at Port Wallut, transmitted to an unidentified station a recap of the previous combat with the Americans. It summarized the events of 2 August and mentioned their boats fighting the "American warship." It also recounted that their naval and air defense forces had shot down some American warplanes on 5 August and had captured one American pilot alive. Yet, there is no mention of anything occurring on the night of 4 August in this recap.[164] The absence of any reference to 4 August cannot be attributed to North Vietnamese embarrassment over the results of the "action"; they lost heavily on both 2 and 5 August. The only

---

[2] 10609'E)."The site at Than Hoa would have tracked the two ships early on 4 August, but the attack was several hours later. When Hon En tracked the ships is unknown. The second paragraph mentions only the two reports from Phu Bai, stating that they indicated "a possible attack."163

conclusion that this intercept points to is that there was no attack on the night of 4 August.

-6ffSf)-Oddly, this last intercept has never been used in any evaluation of the Gulf of Tonkin incidents. Understandably, those evaluations have tended to rely on the evidence from the time period of the incidents themselves. Surely, a North Vietnamese accounting of the operations for the previous three days would have been considered as part of the body of evidence concerning the attack. Yet it was not used, although NSA summaries issued on the same day were. Was that because the intercept says nothing about an attack on 4 August?

—f'S7'7'Stÿ Maintaining the Line: The NSA Summary Reports and the "Del Lang Chronology"

-6ffSi)-As the field sites submitted their reports on what intercept they did or did not have, as in the case of the NSG element aboard the Maddox, and the analysts had the luxury of time to review all of the SIGINT, the various evaluations they produced continued to reflect the official position that the second attack had occurred. The most important early response from Fort Meade was a series of summary reports issued between 5 and 7 August. It is these reports which make up first official NSA judgment on what happened. Because of this, they deserve a close look, since they establish the tone and form for the later Chrono low, which became, in a way, the final NSA statement on what had happened.

-g-SHSÐNSA issued five summary and situation reports after the incident, beginning early on 5 August. Of the five, numbers "ROI" through "R05," the pertinent ones are the first three, especially the first and third. These three reports explicitly state that the 4 August attack occurred. Report "ROI" notes that the reports from the destroyer that it had sunk two torpedo boats were later "confirmed by a DRV message which stated 'that we had sacrificed two ships and the rest are okay. „ 165 Where this idea that two boats were sunk came from is hard to say. NSA received all messages from the Desoto patrol via the JCS. All through the afternoon of 4 August, the destroyers reported at first that three boats had been sunk, then later changed it to one sunk and one, possibly two, damaged.[166] The second post-incident report, known as "Gulf of Tonkin SIGINT Situation Report No. 1," included the statement "f0110%ãng the 4 August attack"

It was the third report that was the most open in supporting the idea of the second attack. It was stated in the lead sentence of the report that 'This report is a summary of those DRV naval communications during the period 15 August which demonstrate irrefutably that DRV naval boats did, in fact, engage in preplanned combat against U.S. destroyers patrolling in international waters.„ 167

-•æffSB- However, the confident tone of the third report is belied by its thin layer of evidence. And this problem was noticed by some of its recipients. late on the afternoon of 6 August, a DIA representative queried NSA if additional SIGINT was available from the 4 August incident. He reported that Secretary McNamara was not satisfied with the contents of this third summary report, "that it was insufficient for his purposes." In reviewing the SIGINT from the incident, it was discovered that there was a large gap with no intercept—specifically, leading up to the actual attack. Based on this discovery, urgent messages were sent to the field sites requesting all intercept.[168] And, as we have seen, the field sites had nothing else to add.

-affSÐ There are problems with the way this series of reports portrays the information in them. For example, the first report mentions the salvage operations of the two damaged DRV torpedo boats which had been discussed earlier. However, unlike what we discovered; the summary does not go on to report that these operations continued into the time of the attack as reported by the marines at Phu Bai. The authors of the third report tried to address this with the speculation that the attacking boats might have come from Quang Khe or some other base in the DRV Southern Command.[169] But this has already been shown to be wrong since the distance traveled for the boats to have attacked from the east could not have been accomplished because of the limitations of the boats' speed.

-8+SÐ-Perhaps the most serious problem, though, is the lack of any citation of source reports which made up the summaries. This is a critical point, since the information referred to in the summaries is coming from already published, serialized NSA and field site reports and translations. The very lack of notes is odd since this type of summary reporting required that source notes be included. It seems that if the Agency was attempting to build a case demonstrating that an attack had occurred, then the source reports and translations which substantiated the position would have been included. However, this was not the case. In fact, there were cases in which information used in the summaries as evidence, was, in fact, not related at all, or impossible to verify. -ffSffSf)- For example, the first summary, "ROI," issued early on 5 August, contained this section which strongly suggests that the Desoto patrol was surveyed by DRV aircraft. The entry read:

During 3 August, DRV Naval Communications reflected the tracking and shadowing of the two destroyers throughout the day; this activity was reported by both destroyers. They were also apparently shadowed by two presumably DRV aircraft. A DRV merchant ship advised its shipping office in Haiphong that 'two bombers' would 'fly' in the direction of the ship and investigate. No further identification of the aircraft was provided.170

-ffSffSf) This entry was lifted from a San Miguel report on DRV merchant shipping. In it, a single North Vietnamese merchant ship, the Thong Mat, reported that two single-propeller aircraft (Chong chongs), and not bombers, were flying to investigate the ship, presumably a reference to itself.[171] Hanoi's aircraft inventory contained two single-prop planes—the AN-2 (Colt), a small transport biplane and the YAK-18 (Max) trainer—both of which were unsuitable to maritime patrols. Since the report never specified the nationality of the aircraft, it is likely that they were American A-IH single propeller fighter bombers from the Ticonderoga.

-696B at the time of the intercept, 1018Z on 3 August, the Desoto patrol was some sixty muse to the south of the Thong Mat', it seems reasonable that the Desoto combat air patrol would have gone to investigate the North Vietnamese freighter.[172] A few hours after the Thong Mat reported the aircraft, the Haiphong shipping office transmitted an urgent message to three DRV merchant ships to "take precautions against enemy airplanes and ships." [In]

-••••&Skis in addition, the third report, "R03," refers to intercept at 1054Z on 4 August that the DRV was Trying to keep "activities under cover" when it was claimed that it had intercepted a message with the sentence "YOU CANNOT PUBLICIZE THE SITUATION OF THE BOATS OF FLOTILLA 135 TO THE BACH DANG. 174 Who is sending this message, and to whom, is not mentioned in the summary. To date, the source of this sentence has not been found; its context, the correctness of the Translation, or even its correlation to the attack, cannot be determined.

-ffS79'SÙ Report "R03" also carried another curious entry supporting the idea of an attack. This read "KHOAI HAD MET THE ENEMY." Over the ensuing years this entry bothered people researching the incident. No one could find the original intercept, and no one could seem to explain it. [175] No wonder. The sentence was a rewrite of a San Miguel intercept. The original intercept was of a message from Haiphong to T146, which originally read: "WHEN (YOU)) MEET THE ENEMY T333 MUST MOBILIZE."

Since the local time of the intercept is 0211G (2011Z) on 5 August, the reference to meeting the enemy has nothing to do with the prior evening's incident. In fact, the tense of the original translation suggests that this was a message anticipating a possible future clash »ñth the Americans, and it was expected that torpedo boat T-333 had to be ready to defend itself.[176] The name "KHOAI" was seen in other intercepts over the prior two days, including the infamous "military operations" one of early 4 August. In reality, "KHOAI" probably was Le Duy Khoai, the commander of Squadron 135. That he, the commanding officer, accompanied Section 3 in its attack against the Maddox on 2 August, and stayed on to supervise the recovery operations of his two damaged boats, was standard procedure for DRV naval officers.[177]

•ffSffS•9 The main NSA effort at producing a record of the events of 2-5 August 1964 centered on a joint postmortem with the Defense Intelligence Agency, begun in late August 1964 and released on 14 October 1964. What was produced was a chronology of events which supported the contention that there had been a second attack. The NSA version of the Chrono low stayed within the cryptologic community with a very narrow distribution totaling ten recipients. later, after the second Gulf of Tonkin "incident" of 19 September 1964, a second volume was added to cover that event.[178]

—ffS77STThis chronology, specifically the volume titled "Chrono low of Events of 2-5 August in the Gulf of Tonkin," was bound in a black binder and came to be popularly referred to as the "Del Lang Chrono low," named after the B Group staff officer, Lieutenant Colonel Delmar Lang, USAF, who compiled it. Colonel Lang was a veteran cryptologic staff officer with a great deal of liaison experience with various SIGINT missions in Asia, starting with work during the Korean War. He would be instrumental later in implementing various SIGINT support efforts for Rolling Thunder and Linebacker air campaigns. The Chrono low he produced solidified the official position that the attack had occurred. In the introduction, Lang claimed it to be as complete as far as the SIGINT involvement necessitated. The SIGNT material included product reports, translations, and selected messages between NSA and various field sites and liaison offices. The Chrono low also made heavy use of non-SIGINT sources, in this case messages from the Desoto patrol, CINCPAC, and the JCS. The Chrono low was arranged with an introductory timeline which highlighted events between 2 to 5 August, followed by the documents which were notated with "tabs" numbered sequentially and cross-referenced in the introduction&

-fSHSĐ-Like the summaries discussed above, there are serious problems in the Chrono low with both the amount and subject matter of the SIGNT evidence and the way it is presented. For example, in reference to the 4 August incident, the chronology makes use of only six SIGINT products (not counting the summaries which were a review of published product) as evidence. Now, we have been referring to a large number of these products about the 4 August "attack" throughout this article. All told, 3 and 6 August, fifty-nine SIGINT products can be identified as being relevant to that purported attack, that is, containing information related in some way to it. These include serialized reports, translations, critics, follow-ups to the Critics, and technical supplements. The fifty-nine products include status reports on the North Vietnamese boats, DRV tracking of the Desoto patrol from coastal observation posts and boats, salvage operations of the damaged boats originally thought to be involved, DRV boat movement and location reports, and intelligence reports. So, the six products used in the Chrono low constitute a bit more than 10 percent of the total available.

-saffron, the introduction to the chronology refers to using "representative samples of DIRNSA's COMINT reporting of the activities directly and indirectly related to the situation of the activities in the Gulf of Tonkin. „ 180 How merely six out of fifty-nine is "representative" is difficult to understand. Furthermore, these six reports are the only ones which can be construed to demonstrate an aggressive intent on the part of Hanoi's navy. They include a 3 August report of a concentration of DRV vessels near Hon Me Island, the three Critics and follow-ups concerning the "attack" being planned for the night of 4 August, the translation of the so-called "after-action" report, and an early 5 August message reporting DRV plans for combat operations on the night of 5 August, which turned out to be related to the ongoing salvage operations.[181]

-4S+fSB-None of the other fifty-three products were included in the Chrono low. These include all of the ones that have been cited earlier in this article, and which demonstrated that no attack was planned, or proved that the North Vietnamese did not know the location of the American destroyers, or indicated that the salvage operations were the primary activity of

Hanoi's navy, or the outright statements in some intercept for the DRV boats to stay away from the Americans. These products were available at the time of the composition of the Chrono low. Yet why they were not included is unknown. Obviously, their absence leaves the reader with the impression of Hanoi's overt aggression against the American ships.

-fSffSÐ the way the material is presented is also curious. Almost all of the SIGNT product included for both 2 and 4 August has attached the reproduction of the original intercept of the DRV navy's messages: that is, the cipher and its decrypted Vietnamese text. This allows the reader to see the unfolding of the SIGNT process, from intercept to report.

-fSHS9 However, there is one glaring exception to this: the 4 August translation of the so called "after-action" report used by Secretary McNamara and President Johnson as primary evidence of the attack in fact, only the translation is included, and it is there only as "a sample." Considering the importance attached to it by the administration, as we saw earlier, this is a very odd way of presenting this piece of critical evidence. It would seem that the NSA originators of the Chrono low would have added the complete Vietnamese cipher and text to bolster the case for an attack. Yet the translation stands alone. Since we know that the intercept used to produce the translation currently is missing, might we ask if they were already "missing" shortly after the incident itself?

-fSffSò-Finally, the chronology does not address the problem of the total lack of North Vietnamese C31 related to the supposed 4 August attack. Not surprisingly, there are samples of the C31 from the 2 August attack. Yet, aside from the so-called "attack" message and the purported "after-action" report, there is nothing. We have commented on this before. The argument that the material may not have been available in early August might have had some slight relevance.

The chronology might have been the vehicle for addressing this shortcoming. However, filly two months later, there is still nothing included of the enemy's C31—the huge gap is not addressed, much less explained, by NSA

-•fSffSfî Over the years, the chronology came to be the source book for responses to congressional inquiries into the Gulf of Tonkin incidents. That is, the other 90 percent of related SIGINT product was not offered to any congressional investigating committees. Instead, the chronology became, by virtue of its position as an "official" report, the only source for background on the Gulf of Tonkin incidents.

—ffSff6Ð-The first investigation came in early 1968 when the Senate Foreign Relations Committee, under the chairmanship of Senator William Fulbright, who had steered the Gulf of Tonkin Resolution through the Senate, opened hearings on the incident. Secretary of Defense Robert McNamara was called in to testify. Prior to his testimony, he requested that the pertinent COMINT on the incidents be given to him. The NSA and the Defense Intelligence Agency were reluctant to have the SIGINT used; both agencies were fearful that the exposure would compromise the then current capabilities against the North Vietnamese.[182] Ultimately, Secretary McNamara was given the contents of the chronology, as was the Senate committee as well. The resulting hearings did nothing to clear up the confusion. McNamara argued for the attack, citing the various SIGINT reports, though he seemed to mix up what was in them, and left observers sometimes confused.[183] Many senators, looking at the same Chrono low, remained skeptical.

-fSffSf)- In August 1975, the Senate Select Committee on Intelligence, under the chairmanship of Senator Frank Church of Idaho, approached NSA about the Gulf of Tonkin incident. The committee's interest, though, may not have been in establishing the validity of the incident; their attention was focused on information concerning the covert OPLAN 34A and Desoto missions, and what exactly was being done by both operations. NSA's response to the Church Committee's request was similar to that of Fulbright's: limited release of materials from the chronology. In fact, NSA was concerned that the Church Committee get exactly what Fulbright had received.[184] Again, the chronology of the events of 2 to 4 August was the source used for material to be released. Interestingly, a major figure in these latter deliberations on what to release to the Senate was the then-retired, former deputy director of NSA, Dr. Inuis Tordella. He had advised the NSA staff as to what to release and hold back. Curiously, one of the few things held back was a similar Chrono low of the events of mid-September 1964, in which another Desoto patrol claimed it had been attacked.

-fSffSB-Gulf of Tonkin Redux:

The 18 September "Attack"

—tS17SI) In an interesting and ironic repeat of the Gulf of Tonkin incidents, on 18 September 1964 another Desoto patrol would undergo the same experience as the Maddox and Turner Joy. In this incident, two destroyers, the USS Morton (DD 948) and the USS Richard S. Edwards (DD 950), were assigned a Desoto mission for MI September. The ships began their operations on 16 September. The North Vietnamese knew almost from the start that the two vessels would be in the area and were trading it. The DRV naval authorities also ordered their ships and posts to be on alert and to be aware for "provocations" by the Americans. [185]

-fSffS±) North Vietnamese tracking of the two destroyers held through the 17th and into the 18th of September. At 1738G (1038Z) on 18 September, a message was passed from an unidentified DRV naval authority that ordered all ships to take precautions against possible South Vietnamese maritime commandos who might take advantage of the presence of the American ships in the area to launch an attack. The North Vietnamese ships were also ordered to "avoid provocation" and to disperse and camouflage. [186]

(U) At about 1729G (1029Z), the two destroyers acquired radar contacts following them. Both ships began to maneuver and increase speed to clear the apparent vessels trailing them. About forty-five minutes later, the Morton fired a warning shot at one of the contacts. By this time, the Americans counted on their radar scopes five ships trailing them. However, the warning shot did not deter the threatening vessels. About ten minutes later, both ships opened fire. For about the next hour, both American ships engaged the contacts as they appeared on their radar screens. Oddly, at no fame did the contacts return any fire, nor did they launch any torpedoes. Even more curious, only one of the enemy ships ever closed faster than twenty-three knots. In fact, the contacts pretty much matched the speeds of the destroyers. Meanwhile, the Morton and Edwards fired almost 300 rounds at the contacts and claimed to sink as many as five of the vessels (there were now more than the original five contacts) which had been menacing them.

-€The JCS ordered a search, to begin the next morning, of the area for debris to confirm the attacks. At the same time, plans were put under way for another retaliatory strike against the DRV. More air force and navy aircraft were dispatched to the region to reinforce the proposed strikes. [187] Yet, nothing happened. The area was searched, but no debris nor even an oil slick was found. The JCS continued to request data on the attacks from all the intelligence and combat commands. Yet even by the 19th there still was no concrete evidence of an attack. [188]

++SB-Available SIGINT information indicated that the North Vietnamese were well aware of the presence of the two destroyers but remained in a defensive posture. The DRV was looking to react to a possible maritime raid by the South Vietnamese, but there were no reflections of any hostile intent against the two destroyers.[189] In fact, on 20 September NSA corrected a Critic by San Miguel which claimed that the DRV was planning to attack the Desoto patrol that evening. Fort Meade pointed out that the intercepted information could apply equally to an attack on South Vietnamese "raiders. „ 190

(U) By the end of 20 September, the issue remained unresolved. The Edwards and Morton were ordered to return to the nearby carrier task group, and the Desoto missions were indefinitely suspended, and, in fact, except for an occasional training cruise, they were never carried out again. [191]

(U) In certain histories of the Indochina War, it has been fashionable to maintain that, in the final accounting, whether or not there was an attack on U.S. Navy destroyers on 4 August in the Gulf of Tonkin may not have mattered at all. The Johnson administration had been looking for a way to expand America's role in South Vietnam. In June 1964, two months before the August attacks, a resolution had been prepared by William Bundy, assistant secretary of state for Far Eastern Affairs, which would give the president the right to commit U.S. forces to the defense of any nation in Southeast Asia threatened by communist aggression or subversion. Furthermore, the draft resolution gave Johnson both the discretion to determine the extent of the threat and, by virtue of this evaluation, the leeway to define what forces and actions were necessary to counter it. At first, the resolution was planned to be put before the Senate as soon as possible. But President Johnson demurred, fearing that it would ruin the image of moderation he had been cultivating for the presidential election in November. The draft resolution was quietly shelved until another opportunity could come along.[192]

(U) The Johnson administration used the 4 August incident to ride the resurrected resolution, now popularly referred to as the

Tonkin Gulf Resolution, through the Senate, with only two dissenting votes. It was portrayed as a moderating measure "calculated to prevent the spread of war. „ 193 However, President Johnson now had the legal cover to use whatever military force he wanted. When he heard of its passage by both houses, he laughed and told an aide that the resolution "was like Grandma's nightshirt. It covers everything." [194]

(U) Yet, even with the resolution in his pocket, President Johnson ignored the similar September Gulf of Tonkin "incident," and did not order a retaliation against North Vietnam. It would take another communist attack on American forces, the strike at the American base at Pleiku in February 1965, to make Washington escalate the war a further step, this time initiating the Rolling Thunder air campaign.[195]

(U) The problem, of course, was the nature of the provocation which made possible the passage of the resolution. If the resolution had been tied to the naval action of the afternoon of 2 August, or to the communist bombing of the officers' quarters in Saigon on Christmas Eve 1964, or even to the VC sapper attack on the air base at Bien Hoa on 1 November 1964, then the administration at least would have had an actual incident upon which to base support for it. Then any reconsideration of the resolution would have centered solely on it and not the incident on which it was based.

(U) Unfortunately, the administration chose to hang the rationale for expanding its war-making franchise in Southeast Asia on an incident which could not stand up to any kind of objective examination of the full documentation. So, as eventually happened in 1968, when the Gulf of Tonkin Resolution came to be reviewed, the incident that it was based on also came under scrutiny. When the events of 4 August were revealed to have been based on very thin evidence, it concurrently was demonstrated that the Johnson administration had indulged in a very selective use of information. If the administration had not lied exactly, it had not been exactly honest with the public, or, for that matter, even honest within its own deliberations. The question no longer was about the appropriateness of the resolution, but the basic honesty of the administration. It would cast a pall on an already distrusted Johnson presidency. As Senator Barry Goldwater, who had run against Johnson in the 1964 presidential election, bitterly noted years later in 1972, "I had no reason to believe that Mr. Johnson's account of the gravity existing in the Gulf of Tonkin was not legitimate.„ 196

(U) As for the Tonkin Gulf incident itself,

August 1964. President Johnson summed it up best just a few

days later: "Hell, those damn, stupid sailors were just shooting at flying fish."

(U) In this article we have done something quite apart from most Agency histories: Using virtually hitherto untouched material from a variety of sources, we have told a radically different version of an important event in cryptologic history which, in turn, had a critical effect on the course of American history. In doing so, a great deal of unfamiliar ground, in terms of source material, had to be covered, and the new information could not be presented in a typical, historical narrative format. Instead, we had to painstakingly analyze a series of documents which were quite important if we were to grasp what happened on 4 August 1964. Admittedly, this was a difficult task, but it was necessary if we were to be as comprehensive as possible in our analysis of what happened.

(U) After recounting all of the events and analyzing the sources, the remaining task for the historian is to attempt to characterize them, to offer a summation or a judgment that will place the narrative into a coherent framework. But before that can be done, it is necessary to review what has been presented. In this way we can consider again what we have learned about the events in early August.

...4S.H. S.9We have seen that the Gulf of Tonkin incidents occurred as a result of the congruence of the Desoto patrols and the maritime commando raids along the North Vietnamese coast carried out under OPIAN 34A. In the period leading up to the Maddox mission, the DRV had been reacting with increasing force to the OPLAN 34A attacks. Monitoring Hanoi's more aggressive response to the raids, NSA had warned the major commands in the region of the potential danger for the Desoto patrols, but the warning did not register. The decision makers in Washington believed that Hanoi would not see the two missions as related.

-fSffSf) On 2 August, the SIGINT system performed admirably when it provided sufficient warning to the Maddox to allow it to defend itself against the attack by the three DRV torpedo boats. At the same time, the American cryptologists were able to observe the DRV naval C31 system in action. From this they should have developed a profile from which further timely warnings could be deduced. During 3 August, both sides maintained a distant watchfulness, though tensions remained high—high enough, perhaps, for the field site at Phu Bai to confuse salvage operations around the island of Hon Me for a pre attack concentration of forces.

—fS79'Sfi the 4 August incident began in the early afternoon due to an analytic error by the Marine contingent at Phu Bai. This mistake set in the minds of the crew of the two destroyers the idea that they shortly would be attacked. This was an error of interpretation by the Marine unit at Phu Bai, a mistake, as we have seen, which was not committed by the navy site at San Miguel. Nor was the Critic transmitted by Phu Bai questioned or corrected at NSA. This may have been in line with an unspoken policy of not second-guessing field sites since they were "closer" to the action. However, under Critic procedures, Phu Bai had to supply the technical information upon which it based its alert. When the discrepancy between what the intercept actually said and what the Marine detachment reported became known, NSA should have cautioned the recipients of the Critic. However, this did not happen.

4SHSfrThree hours later, at almost the same moment that the American destroyers opened fire on the approaching radar return, Phu Bai issued another report which stated that the specific boats, which had been identified as being readied for an attack, in reality, were to be towed to Haiphong for repairs. This salvage operation would be the subject of several more reports during the rest of the evening of 4 August. Since no other boats were referenced in the original "attack" message, the cryptologists at NSA found themselves without any SIGINT evidence supporting the reports of an ambush. The Phu Bai reports had effectively cancelled out the original Critic.

However, the response by NSA was to counter the SIGINT evidence with an unfounded speculation that the boats the Desoto patrol thought were attacking it came from Quang Khe. And it has been demonstrated how impossible this scenario was.

-fSffSĐIt also has been established that none of the C31 associated with DRV naval attack of 2 August was present on 4 August. Aside from sporadic North Vietnamese coastal tracking, which ended hours before the two destroyers turned east, there was no intercept to suggest the North Vietnamese had anything more than the usual interest in the two ships. Nor, for that matter, was there any intercept of any DRV naval communications which suggested in any manner that an attack was planned, much less that one actually was occurring. In fact, Hanoi seemed more interested in warning its boats of the patrol's presence, viewing the Americans as a threat to its new. For the cryptologic community, this lack of any attack C31 is one of the most critical points of the Gulf of Tonkin crisis. Yet, NSA never addressed the issue in any reports or activity summaries it published concerning the 4 August incident.

-f+SB-Instead, NSA would issue summaries with scattered tidbits of contentious and unreferenced intercept ("Khoai had met the enemy" and the purported aerial tracking) to support the notion that an attack had been planned and that it had been carried out. The extensive amount of SIGINT evidence that contradicted both the Initial attack order and the notion that any North Vietnamese boats were involved in any "military operations," other than salvage of the two damaged torpedo boats, was either misrepresented or excluded from all NSA produced post-incident summaries, reports, or chronologies. NSA's failure to deal with both issues, the lack of any attack C31 and the Contradictory SIGINT, especially during the critical hours leading up to the retaliatory air strikes of 5 August, remains its most glaring shortcoming in this incident.

-fSf+SĐ4•Ve have seen the many technical problems as well with the supposed "after-action" translation. This product, upon which the administration based so much of its case, appears to have been the result of an analytic error of combining two separate messages, each dealing with separate incidents, into a single translation.

There were more problems, such as the actual translation of the term "comrades" and how it was rendered into "boats" by NSA Here, the analytic problems mix with those discovered about the available records: the original decrypted Vietnamese text, and an important translation from San Miguel cannot be located. Considering the importance of this translation to the administration's case, the fact that the original text cannot be found (and was not used as early as October 1964) is unusual. That these original texts and translation are the only missing papers in the San Miguel reports allows for suspicion to shade any further discourses.

-fSffSf)-What we are confronted with is the same conundrum that confronted the NSA analysts at the time. We have discussed earlier that, for the most part, the NSA personnel in the crisis center who reported the second Gulf of Tonkin incident believed that it had occurred. The problem for them was the SIGINT evidence. The evidence that supported the contention that an attack had occurred was scarce and nowhere as strong as would have been wanted. The overwhelming body of reports, if used, would have told the story that no attack had happened. So, a conscious effort ensued to demonstrate that the attack occurred.

-fSffSff the exact "how" and "why" for this effort to provide only the SIGINT that supported the claim of an attack remain unknown. There are no "smoking gun" memoranda or notes buried in the files that outline any plan or state a justification. Instead, the paper record speaks for itself on what happened: what few product (six) were actually used, and how 90 percent of them were kept out of the Chrono low; how contradictory SIGINT evidence was answered both with speculation and fragments lifted from context; how the complete lack of Vietnamese C31 was not addressed; and, finally, how critical original Vietnamese text and subsequent product were no longer available. From this evidence, one can easily deduce the deliberate nature of these actions. And this observation makes sense, for there was a purpose to them: This was an active effort to make SIGINT fit the claim of what happened during the evening of 4 August in the Gulf of Tonkin.

-fifty-three question why the NSA personnel handled the product the way they did will probably never be answered. The notion

that they were under "pressure" to deliver the story that the administration wanted simply cannot be supported. If the participants are to be believed, and they were adamant in asserting this, they did not bend to the desires of administration officials. Also, such "environmental" factors as overworked crisis center personnel and lack of experienced linguists are, for the most part, not relevant when considering the entire period of the crisis and follow-up. As we have seen, the efforts to ensure that the only SIGINT publicized would be that which supported the contention that an attack had occurred continued long after the crisis had passed. While the product initially issued on the 4 August incident may be contentious, thin, and mistaken, what was issued in the Gulf of Tonkin summaries beginning late on 4 August was deliberately skewed to support the notion that there had been an attack. What was placed in the official Chrono low was even more selective. That the NSA personnel believed that the attack happened and rationalized the contradictory evidence away is probably all that is necessary to know in order to understand what was done. They walked alone in their counsels.

DRV Navy on Desoto Patrol," B205/981-64, 020302Z August 1964; NSA Command Center Record of Events 2 August 1964. The new intercept sits the Responsibility for relaying Critical communication messages to the DSU aboard the Maddox. However, the initial Critic for 2 August was NOT passed until much later. NCA ACC#

85.4SH-SĐ an interesting speculation emerged after Captain Herrick's initial radar contact placed the suspect boats so far to the northeast of his position that these craft could have been Chinese Communist naval vessels on patrol from nearby Hainan Island. As Marolda, 408; bomb damage assessments from 5 August indicate that some P-4s may have been at Quang Khe. However, there is no SIGINT reflection to support any activity during this period by P-4s in the Southern Naval Command.

August1964. This serialized report was sent at a precedence ("Z") reserved for Critics. This was a technical error and did not affect warning or then lines. However, it makes tracking down the reports more difficult.

(U) Moise, 200.

B26 COMINT Technical Report #009-65, 9 March 1965, CCH Series. NN.

(U) Moise, 200; Lyndon B. Johnson, 114. -•æ•ffSÐ in the matter of who the "experts" were that President Johnson is referring to, it appears that they were members of the White House Intelligence Advisory Staff. According to one source, they examined "all available intelligence having even the most remote relevance [to the Gulf of Tonkin]." According to this source, SIGINT alone provided "positive evidence of DRV premeditation." Whether this evidence refers to the 2 or 4 August incidents is unclear. It is also not certain if all "relevant intelligence" was pursued. Furthermore, it is not clear if any of the "experts" were Vietnamese linguists, or if they were being prompted by the analysts at NSA. Source: NSA Memorandum for the Record: "Intense with Mr. Arthur McCafferty, White House Staff, on the use of SIGINT in Shaping White House Decisions on Southeast Asia," CCH Series XII.NN., undated.

Call words/codenames were used to designate units, entities, and individuals. It was not uncommon to see(b) (3) -50 USC 403 (b) (3) -18 USC 798 (b) (3) -P. L. 86-36a particular entity, such as T-142, addressed with as many as three call words over this period. However, these call words equated to any number of differing entities that would have been aboard. The missing intercept would have arrived in the form of so-called technical supplements to the San Miguel reports "38" and "39." Generally, these supplements were sent anywhere from fifteen to forty-five minutes after the report was issued. They included the original Vietnamese text. These supplements were sent to a small audience of SIGNT-producing elements. The supplements probably were what the B26 crisis center used in generating the after-action report, "T-10."-CHS9-As a general practice, once the technical supplements were received, they were attached to the original reports. A review of the NSA archival file containing the San Miguel reports issued in 1964 revealed that reports in the preceding and following series have their supplements attached, while the two reports in questions stand alone, sans supplements.

EXHIBIT 25A

The Gulf of Tonkin Mystery: The SIGINT Hounds Were Howling

5 December 2005

IN HIS ARTICLE, SKUNKS, BOGIES, Silent Hounds, and the Flying Fish: The Gulf of Tonkin Mystery, 2-4 August 1964, NSA historian Robert Hanyok reaches two conclusions—that the reported second attack by North Vietnamese PT boats on 4 August never happened and that "SIGINT information was presented in such a manner as to preclude responsible decision makers in the Johnson administration from having the complete and objective narrative of events of 4 August 1964."

As noted by Mr. Hanyok, many historians now believe the supposed attack by North Vietnam naval forces on the Desoto patrol on 4 August did not occur. Mr. Hanyok provides an even more convincing argument for this position based upon previously unreleased SIGINT. Evidence supporting the attack on 4 August is based principally upon eyewitness accounts, as well as radar and sonar data from the U.S. destroyers Maddox and Turner Joy. Additionally, analysis of communications intelligence (COMINT) intercepted immediately after the purported attack appeared to confirm that such an attack did indeed occur and this COMINT was used by Secretary of Defense McNamara and President Johnson as supporting evidence to order a U.S. retaliation strike.

While later reports questioned the intensity of the attack, Captain Herrick as well as other officers and seamen were adamant then and remain adamant to this day that the ships were attacked. From an NSA perspective, however, it is important to note that the COMINT evidence was supporting evidence to justify the U.S retaliation attacks. In testimony before the Committee on Foreign Relations in 1968, Secretary McNamara responded to a question asking if he would have proceeded with the attacks without the COMINT by stating, "Yes, it was not the deciding factor, but it justified the decision." Thus, it is clear that the U.S. retaliation was based principally on eyewitness accounts from the destroyers on the scene, not from intelligence.

This article does not dispute Mr. Hanyok's ultimate conclusion—an attack did not occur. Nevertheless, while Mr. Hanyok's analysis of the available COMINT evidence is convincing, on its own, the COMINT does not prove that an attack did or did not occur. Unlike the 2 August COMINT where an actual attack message was intercepted, circumstantial evidence and the absence of a 4 August COMINT attack message cannot conclusively prove there was not an attack.

However, this article does dispute Mr. Hanyok's assertion that SIGINT was mishandled, deliberately skewed, or not provided to the Johnson administration. In fact, the record shows that NSA performed magnificently during this period of crisis, providing all SIGINT available in a timely manner to a broad spectrum of customers. With only a few trained Vietnamese linguists at NSA Headquarters and field stations analyzing encrypted North Vietnamese communications, NSA still provided U.S. forces advance warning of possible intended attacks that quite likely prevented the sinking of a U.S. destroyer on 2 August.

NSA notified U.S. forces approximately twelve hours before the attack on 2 August and notified Maddox approximately 1800 local time on 4 August that the DRV navy had been ordered to make ready for military operations that night, possibly against the Desoto patrol. Mr. Hanyok correctly notes that the intercepted communications did not specifically state that the military operations were to be against the Desoto patrol and that the Marine SIGINT unit made this assumption. However, given the events of the preceding days, this was a prudent assumption by the Marine unit. Most commanders would prefer to obtain prior warning of a possible attack that later proves to be incorrect than to obtain no warning.

Mr. Hanyok principally uses the Delmar Lang chronology published on 14 October 1964 to support his argument that NSA purposely misled the Johnson administration. However, as noted by Mr. Hanyok in his article, the report received a very limited distribution and then only within the NSA community. As stated in the memorandum accompanying the report, the chronology was written per the direction of Chief B2 for internal historical use only. It was not intended to be a Department of Defense chronology nor an Intelligence Community chronology; such official chronologies had already been written by that time. This was confirmed by a recent conversation between this author and Milton Zaslow, Chief B2 at the time. Given this intent, Mr. Lang states, "In-so-far as the SIGINT aspects of the action are concerned the report is as complete as the need for documentation of SIGINT involvement appeared to necessitate."

Nevertheless, it is indeed curious that Lang would draft an internal NSA report in October 1964 that did not specifically address the general consensus of analysts at the time that the COMINT was, at best, inconclusive regarding the 4 August attack. In his oral history, Lang himself admits, "me and the guys had some reservations at the time about whether that attack had really occurred. And then there was no question that the second attack a couple of days later was not an attack."

While this is curious, it is not necessarily surprising. NSA was not in a position to contradict the eyewitnesses. Thus, while Lang in his chronology discusses the "attack" on 4 August, consistent with the official DOD position at the time, he appears careful to never state that COMINT supported such a conclusion. As Mr. Hanyok notes, there was no higher-level direction from his superiors at NSA to take a position, nor, according to NSA Director General Blake, no such pressure coming from outside NSA. Certainly, from a COMINT perspective, the NSA analysis that began to appear on August 5 and was consistently maintained afterwards—was that the COMINT was inconclusive.

From the SIGINT reporting and discussions this author has had with several analysts present during that time, it appears that most analysts at NSA believed on 4 August that the COMINT indeed supported an attack on that day. The real time reports from the Navy destroyers coupled with field COMINT reporting shortly after the time of the encounter led analysts to believe they were seeing an after-action report regarding an attack on 4 August.

Shortly thereafter, however, it appears that doubts began to arise at NSA concerning whether the messages in question were in actuality after action reports from the 2 August encounter rather than from 4 August. Subsequent NSA reporting used language such as "the actual attack on the 2 nth and noted that the ships initially thought to be involved in the attack, the T 142, T 146 and T333, could not have been. NSA suggested, based on "reports from the Maddox that it was under attack, "possibly naval units subordinate to the Southern fleet command at Ben Thuy were involved. It is clear that NSA analysts were trying to reconcile the SIGINT with eyewitness reports from the Maddox of an attack and were having difficulty doing so. It cannot be emphasized enough that all of this reporting, unlike the Lang chronology, was distributed widely to NSA customers, including CIA, JCS and DIA

Mr. Hanyok carefully analyzes the action report issued by NSA, 2/0/VHN/TIO-64, used by Secretary McNamara as evidence of an attack on 4 August, and provides a convincing argument that NSA combined two field reports into one and that the report was in actuality an after action report on the attack on 2 August. Mr. Hanyok provides an excellent discussion of this reporting especially on the phrase "sacrificed two comrades" as reported by the field versus "sacrificed two boats" as reported by NSA, noting that it is not clear why NSA opted for "boats" instead of "comrades". What is clear, however, as noted by Mr. Hanyok, was that the uncertainty was communicated ultimately to President Johnson. DOD chronologies written in late August 1964 also note the uncertainty of "boats" or "comrades".

This episode alone makes it clear that NSA was not presenting information in such a manner as to preclude responsible decision makers in the Johnson administration from having the complete and objective narrative of events of 4 August 1964. Instead, NSA was informing its customers of uncertainties in NSA analysis of even single words in the COMINT,

In this regard, Mr. Hanyok notes the "unexplained disappearance" of the original decrypted text of this translation from the NSA archives. While indeed, the original translation of this message does not exist, it is only one of many original translations of messages from this period that is missing. One explanation, as noted by General Blake in his interview with William Gerhard, is the information was destroyed because NSA did not have the capacity to store the volume of information being produced. In fact, NSA records disposition schedules, then, as now, allow raw COMINT material to be destroyed once the final report is issued. Another explanation, discussed in the Blake interview, suggests the raw material was not destroyed but was provided to DIA for a Defense chronology.

Further evidence refuting the claim that COMINT information was presented in such a manner as to preclude responsible decision makers in the Johnson administration from having the complete and objective narrative of events of 4 August 1964 can be found in the NSA review of Secretary McNamara's testimony before Congress. NSA noted that McNamara systematically used overkill language with COMINT and that the COMINT surrounding Tonkin was "flexible for interpretation". Again in 1972, as noted by Mr. Hanyok, NSA Deputy Director Dr. Tordella provided Senator Fulbright's staff director Carl Marcy access to all NSA material relating to the Gulf of Tonkin and told Mr. Marcy that the intercept of 4 August could indeed refer to events that occurred on 2 August.

These facts make it clear that NSA consistently provided the Administration, as well as Congress, all COMINT information related to the events of 2-4 August. In fact, one NSA manager present during the August 1964 events has stated, "the folks' downtown was provided all of the COMINT as they wanted to do their own analysis. They weren't overly interested in what we thought." Some Would argue that NSA should have explicitly informed decision makers in formal SIGINT reporting that COMINT showed there was no attack on 4 August. However, the available COMINT could not support such a position. While some analysts did indeed come to such a conclusion, the COMINT itself, as noted by Dr. Tordella, was "flexible for interpretation".

In the final analysis, it is clear that not only was SIGINT information not presented in such a manner as to preclude responsible decision makers in the Johnson administration from having the complete and objective narrative of events of 4 August 1964, but that all of the COMINT produced was distributed to CIA, JCS, DIA and other customers and that NSA uncertainties, even of single words, were made known to decision makers.

Louis F. Giles
Director of Policy and Records

EXHIBIT 26

THE CONSTITUTION OF THE UNITED STATES OF AMERICA

We the people of the United States, in order to form a more perfect union, establish justice, insure domestic tranquility, provide for the common defense, promote the general welfare, and secure the blessings of liberty to ourselves and our posterity, do ordain and establish this Constitution for the United States of America.

Article I

SECTION 1. ALL LEGISLATIVE POWERS herein granted shall be vested in a Congress of the United States, which shall consist of a Senate and House of Representatives.

Section 2. The House of Representatives shall be composed of members chosen every second year by the people of the several states, and the electors in each state shall have the qualifications requisite for electors of the most numerous branch of the state legislature.

No person shall be a Representative who shall not have attained to the age of twenty five years, and been seven years a citizen of the United States, and who shall not, when elected, be an inhabitant of that state in which he shall be chosen.

Representatives and direct taxes shall be apportioned among the several states which may be included within this union, according to their respective numbers, which shall be determined by adding to the whole number of free persons, including those bound to service for a term of years, and excluding Indians not taxed, three fifths of all other Persons. The actual Enumeration shall be made within three years after the first meeting of the Congress of the United States, and within every subsequent term of ten years, in such manner as they shall by law direct. The number of Representatives shall not exceed one for every thirty thousand, but each state shall have at least one Representative; and until such enumeration shall be made, the state of New Hampshire shall be entitled to choose three, Massachusetts eight, Rhode Island and Providence Plantations one, Connecticut five, New York six, New Jersey four, Pennsylvania eight, Delaware one, Maryland six, Virginia ten, North Carolina five, South Carolina five, and Georgia three.

When vacancies happen in the Representation from any state, the executive authority thereof shall issue writs of election to fill such vacancies.

The House of Representatives shall choose their speaker and other officers; and shall have the sole power of impeachment.

Section 3. The Senate of the United States shall be composed of two Senators from each state, chosen by the legislature thereof, for six years; and each Senator shall have one vote.

Immediately after they shall be assembled in consequence of the first election, they shall be divided as equally as may be into three classes. The seats of the Senators of the first class shall be vacated at the expiration of the second year, of the second class at the expiration of the fourth year, and the third class at the expiration of the sixth year, so that one third may be chosen every second year; and if vacancies happen by resignation, or otherwise, during the recess of the legislature of any state, the executive thereof may make temporary appointments until the next meeting of the legislature, which shall then fill such vacancies.

No person shall be a Senator who shall not have attained to the age of thirty years, and been nine years a citizen of the United States and who shall not, when elected, be an inhabitant of that state for which he shall be chosen.

The Vice President of the United States shall be President of the Senate, but shall have no vote, unless they be equally divided.

The Senate shall choose their other officers, and also a President pro tempore, in the absence of the Vice President, or when he shall exercise the office of President of the United States.

The Senate shall have the sole power to try all impeachments. When sitting for that purpose, they shall be on oath or affirmation. When the President of the United States is tried, the Chief Justice shall preside: And no person shall be convicted without the concurrence of two thirds of the members present.

Judgment in cases of impeachment shall not extend further than to removal from office, and disqualification to hold and enjoy any office of honor, trust or profit under the United States: but the party convicted shall nevertheless be liable and subject to indictment, trial, judgment and punishment, according to law.

Section 4. The times, places and manner of holding elections for Senators and Representatives, shall be prescribed in each state by the legislature thereof; but the Congress may at any time by law make or alter such regulations, except as to the places of choosing Senators.

The Congress shall assemble at least once in every year, and such meeting shall be on the first Monday in December, unless they shall by law appoint a different day.

Section 5. Each House shall be the judge of the elections, returns and qualifications of its own members, and a majority of each shall constitute a quorum to do business; but a smaller number may adjourn from day to day, and may be authorized to compel the attendance of absent members, in such manner, and under such penalties as each House may provide.

Each House may determine the rules of its proceedings, punish its members for disorderly behavior, and, with the concurrence of two thirds, expel a member.

Each House shall keep a journal of its proceedings, and from time to time publish the same, excepting such parts as may in their judgment require secrecy; and the yeas and nays of the members of either House on any question shall, at the desire of one fifth of those present, be entered on the journal.

Neither House, during the session of Congress, shall, without the consent of the other, adjourn for more than three days, nor to any other place than that in which the two Houses shall be sitting.

Section 6. The Senators and Representatives shall receive a compensation for their services, to be ascertained by law, and paid out of the treasury of the United States. They shall in all cases, except treason, felony and breach of the peace, be privileged from arrest during their attendance at the session of their respective Houses, and in going to and returning from the same; and for any speech or debate in either House, they shall not be questioned in any other place.

No Senator or Representative shall, during the time for which he was elected, be appointed to any civil office under the authority of the United States, which shall have been created, or the emoluments whereof shall have been increased during such time: and no person holding any office under the United States, shall be a member of either House during his continuance in office.

Section 7. All bills for raising revenue shall originate in the House of Representatives; but the Senate may propose or concur with amendments as on other Bills.

Every bill which shall have passed the House of Representatives and the Senate, shall, before it become a law, be presented to the President of the United States; if he approve he shall sign it, but if not he shall return it, with his objections to that House in which it shall have originated, who shall enter the objections at large on their journal, and proceed to reconsider it. If after such reconsideration two thirds of that House shall agree to pass the bill, it shall be sent, together with the objections, to the other House, by which it shall likewise be reconsidered, and if approved by two thirds of that House, it shall become a law. But in all such cases the votes of both Houses shall be determined by yeas and nays, and the names of the persons voting for and against the bill shall be entered on the journal of each House, respectively. If any bill shall not be returned by the President within ten days (Sundays excepted) after it shall have been presented to him, the same shall be a law, in like manner as if he had signed it, unless the Congress by their adjournment prevent its return, in which case it shall not be a law.

Every order, resolution, or vote to which the concurrence of the Senate and House of Representatives may be necessary (except on a question of adjournment) shall be presented to the President of the United States; and before the same shall take effect, shall be approved by him, or being disapproved by him, shall be repassed by two thirds of the Senate and House of Representatives, according to the rules and limitations prescribed in the case of a bill.

Section 8. The Congress shall have power to lay and collect taxes, duties, imposts and excises, to pay the debts and provide for the common defense and general welfare of the United States; but all duties, imposts and excises shall be uniform throughout the United States;

To borrow money on the credit of the United States.

To regulate commerce with foreign nations, and among the several states, and with the Indian tribes.

To establish a uniform rule of naturalization, and uniform laws on the subject of bankruptcies throughout the United States.

To coin money, regulate the value thereof, and of foreign coin, and fix the standard of weights and measures.

To provide for the punishment of counterfeiting the securities and current coin of the United States.

To establish post offices and post roads.

To promote the progress of science and useful arts, by securing for limited times to authors and inventors the exclusive right to their respective writings and discoveries.

To constitute tribunals inferior to the Supreme Court.

To define and punish piracies and felonies committed on the high seas, and offenses against the law of nations.

To declare war, grant letters of marque and reprisal, and make rules concerning captures on land and water.

To raise and support armies, but no appropriation of money to that use shall be for a longer term than two years.

To provide and maintain a navy.

To make rules for the government and regulation of the land and naval forces.

To provide for calling forth the militia to execute the laws of the union, suppress insurrections and repel invasions.

To provide for organizing, arming, and disciplining, the militia, and for governing such part of them as may be employed in the service of the United States, reserving to the states respectively, the appointment of the officers, and the authority of training the militia according to the discipline prescribed by Congress;

To exercise exclusive legislation in all cases whatsoever, over such District (not exceeding ten miles square) as may, by cession of particular states, and the acceptance of Congress, become the seat of the government of the United States, and to exercise like authority over all places purchased by the consent of the legislature of the state in which the same shall be, for the erection of forts, magazines, arsenals, dockyards, and other needful buildings;—And

To make all laws which shall be necessary and proper for carrying into execution the foregoing powers, and all other powers vested by this Constitution in the government of the United States, or in any department or officer thereof.

Section 9. The migration or importation of such persons as any of the states now existing shall think proper to admit, shall not be prohibited by the Congress prior to the year one thousand eight hundred and eight, but a tax or duty may be imposed on such importation, not exceeding ten dollars for each person.

The privilege of the writ of habeas corpus shall not be suspended, unless when in cases of rebellion or invasion the public safety may require it.

No bill of attainder or ex post facto Law shall be passed.

No capitation, or other direct, tax shall be laid, unless in proportion to the census or enumeration herein before directed to be taken.

No tax or duty shall be laid on articles exported from any state.

No preference shall be given by any regulation of commerce or revenue to the ports of one state over those of another: nor shall vessels bound to, or from, one state, be obliged to enter, clear or pay duties in another.

No money shall be drawn from the treasury, but in consequence of appropriations made by law; and a regular statement and account of receipts and expenditures of all public money shall be published from time to time.

No title of nobility shall be granted by the United States: and no person holding any office of profit or trust under them, shall, without the consent of the Congress, accept of any present, emolument, office, or title, of any kind whatever, from any king, prince, or foreign state.

Section 10. No state shall enter into any treaty, alliance, or confederation; grant letters of marque and reprisal; coin money; emit bills of credit; make anything but gold and silver coin a tender in payment of debts; pass any bill of attainder, ex post facto law, or law impairing the obligation of contracts, or grant any title of nobility.

No state shall, without the consent of the Congress, lay any imposts or duties on imports or exports, except what may be absolutely necessary for executing it's inspection laws: and the net produce of all duties and imposts, laid by any state on imports or exports, shall be for the use of the treasury of the United States; and all such laws shall be subject to the revision and control of the Congress.

No state shall, without the consent of Congress, lay any duty of tonnage, keep troops, or ships of war in time of peace, enter into any agreement or compact with another state, or with a foreign power, or engage in war, unless actually invaded, or in such imminent danger as will not admit of delay.

Article II

Section 1. The executive power shall be vested in a President of the United States of America. He shall hold his office during the term of four years, and, together with the Vice President, chosen for the same term, be elected, as follows:

Each state shall appoint, in such manner as the Legislature thereof may direct, a number of electors, equal to the whole number of Senators and Representatives to which the State may be entitled in the Congress: but no Senator or Representative, or person holding an office of trust or profit under the United States, shall be appointed an elector.

The electors shall meet in their respective states, and vote by ballot for two persons, of whom one at least shall not be an inhabitant of the same state with themselves. And they shall make a list of all the persons voted for, and of the number of votes for each; which list they shall sign and certify, and transmit sealed to the seat of the government of the United States, directed to the President of the Senate. The President of the Senate shall, in the presence of the Senate and House of Representatives, open all the certificates, and the votes shall then be counted. The person having the greatest number of votes shall be the President, if such number be a majority of the whole number of electors appointed, and if there be more than one who have such majority, and have an equal number of votes, then the House of Representatives shall immediately choose by ballot one of them for President; and if no person have a majority, then from the five highest on the list the said House shall in like manner choose the President. But in choosing the President, the votes shall be taken by States, the representation from each state having one vote; A quorum for this purpose shall consist of a member or members from two thirds of the states, and a majority of all the states shall be necessary to a choice. In every case, after the choice of the President, the person having the greatest number of votes of the electors shall be the Vice President. But if there should remain two or more who have equal votes, the Senate shall choose from them by ballot the Vice President.

The Congress may determine the time of choosing the electors, and the day on which they shall give their votes, which day shall be the same throughout the United States.

No person except a natural born citizen, or a citizen of the United States, at the time of the adoption of this Constitution, shall be eligible to the office of President; neither shall any person be eligible to that office who shall not have attained to the age of thirty five years, and been fourteen Years a resident within the United States.

In case of the removal of the President from office, or of his death, resignation, or inability to discharge the powers and duties of the said office, the same shall devolve on the Vice President, and the

Congress may by law provide for the case of removal, death, resignation or inability, both of the President and Vice President, declaring what officer shall then act as President, and such officer shall act accordingly, until the disability be removed, or a President shall be elected.

The President shall, at stated times, receive for his services, a compensation, which shall neither be increased nor diminished during the period for which he shall have been elected, and he shall not receive within that period any other emolument from the United States, or any of them.

Before he enter on the execution of his office, he shall take the following oath or affirmation:—"I do solemnly swear (or affirm) that I will faithfully execute the office of President of the United States, and will to the best of my ability, preserve, protect and defend the Constitution of the United States."

Section 2. The President shall be commander in chief of the Army and Navy of the United States, and of the militia of the several states, when called into the actual service of the United States; he may require the opinion, in writing, of the principal officer in each of the executive departments, upon any subject relating to the duties of their respective offices, and he shall have power to grant reprieves and pardons for offenses against the United States, except in cases of impeachment.

He shall have power, by and with the advice and consent of the Senate, to make treaties, provided two thirds of the Senators present concur; and he shall nominate, and by and with the advice and consent of the Senate, shall appoint ambassadors, other public ministers and consuls, judges of the Supreme Court, and all other officers of the United States, whose appointments are not herein otherwise provided for, and which shall be established by law: but the Congress may by law vest the appointment of such inferior officers, as they think proper, in the President alone, in the courts of law, or in the heads of departments.

The President shall have power to fill up all vacancies that may happen during the recess of the Senate, by granting commissions which shall expire at the end of their next session.

Section 3. He shall from time to time give to the Congress information of the state of the union, and recommend to their consideration such measures as he shall judge necessary and expedient; he may, on extraordinary occasions, convene both Houses, or either of them, and in case of disagreement between them, with respect to the time of adjournment, he may adjourn them to such time as he shall think proper; he shall receive ambassadors and other public ministers; he shall take care that the laws be faithfully executed, and shall commission all the officers of the United States.

Section 4. The President, Vice President, and all civil officers of the United States, shall be removed from office on impeachment for, and conviction of, treason, bribery, or other high crimes and misdemeanors.

Article III

Section 1. The judicial power of the United States shall be vested in one Supreme Court, and in such inferior courts as the Congress may from time to time ordain and establish. The judges, both of the supreme and inferior courts, shall hold their offices during good behavior, and shall, at stated times, receive for their services, a compensation, which shall not be diminished during their continuance in office.

Section 2. The judicial power shall extend to all cases, in law and equity, arising under this Constitution, the laws of the United States, and treaties made, or which shall be made, under their authority;—to all cases affecting ambassadors, other public ministers and consuls;—to all cases of admiralty and maritime jurisdiction;—to controversies to which the United States shall be a party;—to controversies between two or more states;—between a state and citizens of another state;— between citizens of different states;—between citizens of the same state claiming lands under grants of different states, and between a state, or the citizens thereof, and foreign states, citizens or subjects.

In all cases affecting ambassadors, other public ministers, and consuls, and those in which a state shall be party, the Supreme Court shall have original jurisdiction. In all the other cases before mentioned, the Supreme Court shall have appellate jurisdiction, both as to law and fact, with such exceptions, and under such regulations as the Congress shall make.

The trial of all crimes, except in cases of impeachment, shall be by jury; and such trial shall be held in the state where the said crimes shall have been committed; but when not committed within any state, the trial shall be at such place or places as the Congress may by law have directed.

Section 3. Treason against the United States shall consist only in levying war against them, or in adhering to their enemies, giving them aid and comfort. No person shall be convicted of treason unless on the testimony of two witnesses to the same overt act, or on confession in open court.

The Congress shall have power to declare the punishment of treason, but no attainder of treason shall work corruption of blood, or forfeiture except during the life of the person attainted.

Article IV

Section 1. Full faith and credit shall be given in each state to the public acts, records, and judicial proceedings of every other state. And the Congress may by general laws prescribe the manner in which such acts, records, and proceedings shall be proved, and the effect thereof.

Section 2. The citizens of each state shall be entitled to all privileges and immunities of citizens in the several states.

A person charged in any state with treason, felony, or other crime, who shall flee from justice, and be found in another state, shall on demand of the executive authority of the state from which he fled, be delivered up, to be removed to the state having jurisdiction of the crime.

No person held to service or labor in one state, under the laws thereof, escaping into another, shall, in consequence of any law or regulation therein, be discharged from such service or labor, but shall be delivered up on claim of the party to whom such service or labor may be due.

Section 3. New states may be admitted by the Congress into this union; but no new states shall be formed or erected within the jurisdiction of any other state; nor any state be formed by the junction of two or more states, or parts of states, without the consent of the legislatures of the states concerned as well as of the Congress.

The Congress shall have power to dispose of and make all needful rules and regulations respecting the territory or other property belonging to the United States; and nothing in this Constitution shall be so construed as to prejudice any claims of the United States, or of any particular state.

Section 4. The United States shall guarantee to every state in this union a republican form of government, and shall protect each of them against invasion; and on application of the legislature, or of the executive (when the legislature cannot be convened) against domestic violence.

Article V

The Congress, whenever two thirds of both houses shall deem it necessary, shall propose amendments to this Constitution, or, on the application of the legislatures of two thirds of the several states, shall call a convention for proposing amendments, which, in either case, shall be valid to all intents and purposes, as part of this Constitution, when ratified by the legislatures of three fourths of the several states, or by conventions in three fourths thereof, as the one or the other mode of ratification may be proposed by the Congress; provided that no amendment which may be made prior to the year one thousand eight hundred and eight shall in any manner affect the first and fourth clauses in the ninth section of the first article; and that no state, without its consent, shall be deprived of its equal suffrage in the Senate.

Article VI

All debts contracted and engagements entered into, before the adoption of this Constitution, shall be as valid against the United States under this Constitution, as under the Confederation.

This Constitution, and the laws of the United States which shall be made in pursuance thereof; and all treaties made, or which shall be made, under the authority of the United States, shall be the supreme law of the land; and the judges in every state shall be bound thereby, anything in the Constitution or laws of any State to the contrary notwithstanding.

The Senators and Representatives before mentioned, and the members of the several state legislatures, and all executive and judicial officers, both of the United States and of the several states, shall be bound by oath or affirmation, to support this Constitution; but no religious test shall ever be required as a qualification to any office or public trust under the United States.

Article VII

The ratification of the conventions of nine states, shall be sufficient for the establishment of this Constitution between the states so ratifying the same.

Done in convention by the unanimous consent of the state's present the seventeenth day of September in the year of our Lord one thousand seven hundred and eighty-seven and of the independence of the United States of America the twelfth. In witness whereof We have hereunto subscribed our Names,

G. *Washington* -Presidt. and deputy from Virginia

New Hampshire: *John Langdon, Nicholas Gilman*

Massachusetts: *Nathaniel Gorham, Rufus King*

Connecticut: *Wm: Saml. Johnson, Roger Sherman*

New York: *Alexander Hamilton*

New Jersey: *Wil: Livingston, David Brearly, Wm. Paterson, Jona: Dayton*

Pennsylvania: *B. Franklin, Thomas Mifflin, Robt. Morris, Geo. Clymer, Thos. FitzSimons, Jared Ingersoll, James Wilson, Gouv Morris*

Delaware: *Geo: Read, Gunning Bedford jun, John Dickinson, Richard Bassett, Jaco: Broom*

Maryland: *James McHenry, Dan of St Thos. Jenifer, Danl Carroll*

Virginia: *John Blair——, James Madison Jr.*

North Carolina: *Wm. Blount, Richd. Dobbs Spaight, Hu Williamson*

South Carolina: *J. Rutledge, Charles Cotesworth Pinckney, Charles Pinckney, Pierce Butler*

Georgia: *William Few, Abr Baldwin*

Exhibit 26A

AMENDMENTS TO THE CONSTITUTION OF THE UNITED STATES

Amendment I (1791)

Congress shall make no law respecting an establishment of religion, or prohibiting the free exercise thereof; or abridging the freedom of speech, or of the press; or the right of the people peaceably to assemble, and to petition the government for a redress of grievances.

Amendment II (1791)

A well-regulated militia, being necessary to the security of a free state, the right of the people to keep and bear arms, shall not be infringed.

Amendment III (1791)

No soldier shall, in time of peace be quartered in any house, without the consent of the owner, nor in time of war, but in a manner to be prescribed by law.

Amendment IV (1791)

The right of the people to be secure in their persons, houses, papers, and effects, against unreasonable searches and seizures, shall not be violated, and no warrants shall issue, but upon probable cause, supported by oath or affirmation, and particularly describing the place to be searched, and the persons or things to be seized.

Amendment V (1791)

No person shall be held to answer for a capital, or otherwise infamous crime, unless on a presentment or indictment of a grand jury, except in cases arising in the land or naval forces, or in the militia, when in actual service in time of war or public danger; nor shall any person be subject for the same offense to be twice put in jeopardy of life or limb; nor shall be compelled in any criminal case to be a witness against himself, nor be deprived of life, liberty, or property, without due process of law; nor shall private property be taken for public use, without just compensation.

Amendment VI (1791)

In all criminal prosecutions, the accused shall enjoy the right to a speedy and public trial, by an impartial jury of the state and district wherein the crime shall have been committed, which district shall have been previously ascertained by law, and to be informed of the nature and cause of the accusation; to be confronted with the witnesses against him; to have compulsory process for obtaining witnesses in his favor, and to have the assistance of counsel for his defense.

Amendment VII (1791)

In suits at common law, where the value in controversy shall exceed twenty dollars, the right of trial by jury shall be preserved, and no fact tried by a jury, shall be otherwise reexamined in any court of the United States, than according to the rules of the common law.

Amendment VIII (1791)

Excessive bail shall not be required, nor excessive fines imposed, nor cruel and unusual punishments inflicted.

Amendment IX (1791)

The enumeration in the Constitution, of certain rights, shall not be construed to deny or disparage others retained by the people.

Amendment X (1791)

The powers not delegated to the United States by the Constitution, nor prohibited by it to the states, are reserved to the states respectively, or to the people.

Exhibit 26B

ADDITIONAL AMENDMENTS TO THE CONSTITUTION OF THE UNITED STATES

Amendment XI (1798)

THE JUDICIAL POWER OF THE United States shall not be construed to extend to any suit in law or equity, commenced or prosecuted against one of the United States by citizens of another state, or by citizens or subjects of any foreign state.

Amendment XII (1804)

The electors shall meet in their respective states and vote by ballot for President and Vice-President, one of whom, at least, shall not be an inhabitant of the same state with themselves; they shall name in their ballots the person voted for as President, and in distinct ballots the person voted for as Vice-President, and they shall make distinct lists of all persons voted for as President, and of all persons voted for as Vice-President, and of the number of votes for each, which lists they shall sign and certify, and transmit sealed to the seat of the government of the United States, directed to the President of the Senate;—The President of the Senate shall, in the presence of the Senate and House of Representatives, open all the certificates and the votes shall then be counted;—the person having the greatest number of votes for President, shall be the President, if such number be a majority of the whole number of electors appointed; and if no person have such majority, then from the persons having the highest numbers not exceeding three on the list of those voted for as

President, the House of Representatives shall choose immediately, by ballot, the President. But in choosing the President, the votes shall be taken by states, the representation from each state having one vote; a quorum for this purpose shall consist of a member or members from two-thirds of the states, and a majority of all the states shall be necessary to a choice. And if the House of Representatives shall not choose a President whenever the right of choice shall devolve upon them, before the fourth day of March next following, then the Vice-President shall act as President, as in the case of the death or other constitutional disability of the President. The person having the greatest number of votes as Vice-President, shall be the Vice-President, if such number be a majority of the whole number of electors appointed, and if no person have a majority, then from the two highest numbers on the list, the Senate shall choose the Vice-President; a quorum for the purpose shall consist of two-thirds of the whole number of Senators, and a majority of the whole number shall be necessary to a choice. But no person constitutionally ineligible to the office of President shall be eligible to that of Vice-President of the United States.

Amendment XIII (1865)

Section 1. Neither slavery nor involuntary servitude, except as a punishment for crime whereof the party shall have been duly convicted, shall exist within the United States, or any place subject to their jurisdiction.

Section 2. Congress shall have power to enforce this article by appropriate legislation.

Amendment XIV (1868)

Section 1. All persons born or naturalized in the United States, and subject to the jurisdiction thereof, are citizens of the United States and of the state wherein they reside. No state shall make or enforce any law which shall abridge the privileges or immunities of citizens of the United States; nor shall any state deprive any person of life, liberty, or property, without due process of law; nor deny to any person within its jurisdiction the equal protection of the laws.

Section 2. Representatives shall be apportioned among the several states according to their respective numbers, counting the whole number of persons in each state, excluding Indians not taxed. But when the right to vote at any election for the choice of electors for President and Vice President of the United States, Representatives in Congress, the executive and judicial officers of a state, or the members of the legislature thereof, is denied to any of the male inhabitants of such state, being twenty-one years of age, and citizens of the United States, or in any way abridged, except for participation in rebellion, or other crime, the basis of representation therein shall be reduced in the proportion which the number of such male citizens shall bear to the whole number of male citizens twenty-one years of age in such state.

Section 3. No person shall be a Senator or Representative in Congress, or elector of President and Vice President, or hold any office, civil or military, under the United States, or under any state, who, having previously taken an oath, as a member of Congress, or as an officer of the United States, or as a member of any state legislature, or as an executive or judicial officer of any state, to support the Constitution of the United States, shall have engaged in insurrection or rebellion against the same, or given aid or comfort to the enemies thereof. But Congress may by a vote of two-thirds of each House, remove such disability.

Section 4. The validity of the public debt of the United States, authorized by law, including debts incurred for payment of pensions and bounties for services in suppressing insurrection or rebellion, shall not be questioned. But neither the United States nor any state shall assume or pay any debt or obligation incurred in aid of insurrection or rebellion against the United States, or any claim for the loss or emancipation of any slave; but all such debts, obligations and claims shall be held illegal and void.

Section 5. The Congress shall have power to enforce, by appropriate legislation, the provisions of this article.

Amendment XV (1870)

Section 1. The right of citizens of the United States to vote shall not be denied or abridged by the United States or by any state on account of race, color, or previous condition of servitude.

Section 2. The Congress shall have power to enforce this article by appropriate legislation.

Amendment XVI (1913)

The Congress shall have power to lay and collect taxes on incomes, from whatever source derived, without apportionment among the several states, and without regard to any census of enumeration.

Amendment XVII (1913)

The Senate of the United States shall be composed of two Senators from each state, elected by the people thereof, for six years; and each Senator shall have one vote. The electors in each state shall have the qualifications requisite for electors of the most numerous branches of the state legislatures.

When vacancies happen in the representation of any state in the Senate, the executive authority of such state shall issue writs of election to fill such vacancies: Provided, that the legislature of any state may empower the executive thereof to make temporary appointments until the people fill the vacancies by election as the legislature may direct.

This amendment shall not be so construed as to affect the election or term of any Senator chosen before it becomes valid as part of the Constitution.

Amendment XVIII (1919)

Section 1. After one year from the ratification of this article the manufacture, sale, or transportation of intoxicating liquors within, the importation thereof into, or the exportation thereof from the United States and all territory subject to the jurisdiction thereof for beverage purposes is hereby prohibited.

Section 2. The Congress and the several states shall have concurrent power to enforce this article by appropriate legislation.

Section 3. This article shall be inoperative unless it shall have been ratified as an amendment to the Constitution by the legislatures of the several states, as provided in the Constitution, within seven years from the date of the submission hereof to the states by the Congress.

Amendment XIX (1920)

The right of citizens of the United States to vote shall not be denied or abridged by the United States or by any state on account of sex.

Congress shall have power to enforce this article by appropriate legislation.

Amendment XX (1933)

Section 1. The terms of the President and Vice President shall end at noon on the 20th day of January, and the terms of Senators and Representatives at noon on the 3d day of January, of the years in which such terms would have ended if this article had not been ratified; and the terms of their successors shall then begin.

Section 2. The Congress shall assemble at least once in every year, and such meeting shall begin at noon on the 3d day of January, unless they shall by law appoint a different day.

Section 3. If, at the time fixed for the beginning of the term of the President, the President elect shall have died, the Vice President elect shall become President. If a President shall not have been chosen before the time fixed for the beginning of his term, or if the President elect shall have failed to qualify, then the Vice President elect shall act as President until a President shall have qualified; and the Congress may by law provide for the case wherein neither a President elect nor a Vice President elect shall have qualified, declaring who shall then act as President, or the manner in which one who is to act shall be selected, and such person shall act accordingly until a President or Vice President shall have qualified.

Section 4. The Congress may by law provide for the case of the death of any of the persons from whom the House of Representatives may choose a President whenever the right of choice shall have devolved upon them, and for the case of the death of any of the persons from whom the Senate may choose a Vice President whenever the right of choice shall have devolved upon them.

Section 5. Sections 1 and 2 shall take effect on the 15th day of October following the ratification of this article.

Section 6. This article shall be inoperative unless it shall have been ratified as an amendment to the Constitution by the legislatures of three-fourths of the several states within seven years from the date of its submission.

Amendment XXI (1933)

Section 1. The eighteenth article of amendment to the Constitution of the United States is hereby repealed.

Section 2. The transportation or importation into any state, territory, or possession of the United States for delivery or use therein of intoxicating liquors, in violation of the laws thereof, is hereby prohibited.

Section 3. This article shall be inoperative unless it shall have been ratified as an amendment to the Constitution by conventions in the several states, as provided in the Constitution, within seven years from the date of the submission hereof to the states by the Congress.

Amendment XXII (1951)

Section 1. No person shall be elected to the office of the President more than twice, and no person who has held the office of President, or acted as President, for more than two years of a term to which some other person was elected President shall be elected to the office of the President more than once. But this article shall not apply to any person holding the office of President when this article was proposed by the Congress, and shall not prevent any person who may be holding the office of President, or acting as President, during the term within which this article becomes operative from holding the office of President or acting as President during the remainder of such term.

Section 2. This article shall be inoperative unless it shall have been ratified as an amendment to the Constitution by the legislatures of three-fourths of the several states within seven years from the date of its submission to the states by the Congress.

Amendment XXIII (1961)

Section 1. The District constituting the seat of government of the United States shall appoint in such manner as the Congress may direct:

A number of electors of President and Vice President equal to the whole number of Senators and Representatives in Congress to which the District would be entitled if it were a state, but in no event more than the least populous state; they shall be in addition to those appointed by the states, but they shall be considered, for the purposes of the election of President and Vice President, to be electors appointed by a state; and they

shall meet in the District and perform such duties as provided by the twelfth article of amendment.

Section 2. The Congress shall have power to enforce this article by appropriate legislation.

Amendment XXIV (1964)

Section 1. The right of citizens of the United States to vote in any primary or other election for President or Vice President, for electors for President or Vice President, or for Senator or Representative in Congress, shall not be denied or abridged by the United States or any state by reason of failure to pay any poll tax or other tax.

Section 2. The Congress shall have power to enforce this article by appropriate legislation.

Amendment XXV (1967)

Section 1. In case of the removal of the President from office or of his death or resignation, the Vice President shall become President.

Section 2. Whenever there is a vacancy in the office of the Vice President, the President shall nominate a Vice President who shall take office upon confirmation by a majority vote of both Houses of Congress.

Section 3. Whenever the President transmits to the President pro tempore of the Senate and the Speaker of the House of Representatives his written declaration that he is unable to discharge the powers and duties of his office, and until he transmits to them a written declaration to the contrary, such powers and duties shall be discharged by the Vice President as Acting President.

Section 4. Whenever the Vice President and a majority of either the principal officers of the executive departments or of such other body as Congress may by law provide, transmit to the President pro tempore of the Senate and the Speaker of the House of Representatives their written declaration that the President is unable to discharge the powers and duties of his office, the Vice President shall immediately assume the powers and duties of the office as Acting President.

Thereafter, when the President transmits to the President pro tempore of the Senate and the Speaker of the House of Representatives his written declaration that no inability exists, he shall resume the powers and duties of his office unless the Vice President and a majority of either the principal officers of the executive department or of such other body as Congress may by law provide, transmit within four days to the President pro tempore of the Senate and the Speaker of the House of Representatives their written declaration

that the President is unable to discharge the powers and duties of his office. Thereupon Congress shall decide the issue, assembling within forty-eight hours for that purpose if not in session. If the Congress, within twenty-one days after receipt of the latter written declaration, or, if Congress is not in session, within twenty-one days after Congress is required to assemble, determines by two-thirds vote of both Houses that the President is unable to discharge the powers and duties of his office, the Vice President shall continue to discharge the same as Acting President; otherwise, the President shall resume the powers and duties of his office.

Amendment XXVI (1971)

Section 1. The right of citizens of the United States, who are 18 years of age or older, to vote, shall not be denied or abridged by the United States or any state on account of age.

Section 2. The Congress shall have the power to enforce this article by appropriate legislation.

Amendment XXVII (1992)

No law varying the compensation for the services of the Senators and Representatives shall take effect until an election of Representatives shall have intervened.

Prepared by Gerald Murphy (*Cleveland Free-Net—aa300*)
Converted to HTML by Jawaid Bazyar (*bazyar@hypermall.com*)

Distributed by the Cybercasting Services Division of the National Public Telecommuting Network (NPTN).

Permission is hereby granted to download, reprint, and/or otherwise redistribute this file, provided appropriate point of origin credit is given to the preparer(s) and the National Public Telecommuting Network.

EXHIBIT 27

Communist Goals (1963)

Congressional Record—Appendix, pp. A34–A35
January 10, 1963
Current Communist Goals

EXTENSION OF REMARKS OF HON. A. S. HERLONG, JR. OF FLORIDA IN THE HOUSE OF REPRESENTATIVES

Thursday, January 10, 1963

MR. HERLONG. MR. SPEAKER, MRS. Patricia Nordman of De Land, Fla., is an ardent and articulate opponent of communism, and until recently published the De Land Courier, which she dedicated to the purpose of alerting the public to the dangers of communism in America.

At Mrs. Nordman's request, I include in the RECORD, under unanimous consent, the following "Current Communist Goals," which she identifies as an excerpt from "The Naked Communist," by Cleon Skousen:

[From "The Naked Communist," by Cleon Skousen]
CURRENT COMMUNIST GOALS

1. U.S. acceptance of coexistence as the only alternative to atomic war.
2. U.S. willingness to capitulate in preference to engaging in atomic war.

3. Develop the illusion that total disarmament of the United States would be a demonstration of moral strength.

4. Permit free trade between all nations regardless of Communist affiliation and regardless of whether or not items could be used for war.

5. Extension of long-term loans to Russia and Soviet satellites.

6. Provide American aid to all nations regardless of Communist domination.

7. Grant recognition of Red China. Admission of Red China to the U.N.

8. Set up East and West Germany as separate states in spite of Khrushchev's promise in 1955 to settle the German question by free elections under supervision of the U.N.

9. Prolong the conferences to ban atomic tests because the United States has agreed to suspend tests as long as negotiations are in progress.

10. Allow all Soviet satellites individual representation in the U.N.

11. Promote the U.N. as the only hope for mankind. If its charter is rewritten, demand that it be set up as a one-world government with its own independent armed forces. (Some Communist leaders believe the world can be taken over as easily by the U.N. as by Moscow. Sometimes these two centers compete with each other as they are now doing in the Congo.)

12. Resist any attempt to outlaw the Communist Party.

13. Do away with all loyalty oaths.

14. Continue giving Russia access to the U.S. Patent Office.

15. Capture one or both of the political parties in the United States.

16. Use technical decisions of the courts to weaken basic American institutions by claiming their activities violate civil rights.

17. Get control of the schools. Use them as transmission belts for socialism and current Communist propaganda. Soften

the curriculum. Get control of teachers' associations. Put the party line in textbooks.

18. Gain control of all student newspapers.

19. Use student riots to foment public protests against programs or organizations which are under Communist attack.

20. Infiltrate the press. Get control of book-review assignments, editorial writing, policymaking positions.

21. Gain control of key positions in radio, TV, and motion pictures.

22. Continue discrediting American culture by degrading all forms of artistic expression. An American Communist cell was told to "eliminate all good sculpture from parks and buildings, substitute shapeless, awkward and meaningless forms."

23. Control art critics and directors of art museums. "Our plan is to promote ugliness, repulsive, meaningless art."

24. Eliminate all laws governing obscenity by calling them "censorship" and a violation of free speech and free press.

25. Break down cultural standards of morality by promoting pornography and obscenity in books, magazines, motion pictures, radio, and TV.

26. Present homosexuality, degeneracy, and promiscuity as "normal, natural, healthy."

27. Infiltrate the churches and replace revealed religion with "social" religion. Discredit the Bible and emphasize the need for intellectual maturity which does not need a "religious crutch."

28. Eliminate prayer or any phase of religious expression in the schools on the ground that it violates the principle of "separation of church and state."

29. Discredit the American Constitution by calling it inadequate, old-fashioned, out of step with modern needs, a hindrance to cooperation between nations on a worldwide basis.

30. Discredit the American Founding Fathers. Present them as selfish aristocrats who had no concern for the "common man."

31. Belittle all forms of American culture and discourage the teaching of American history on the ground that it was only a minor part of the "big picture." Give more emphasis to Russian history since the Communists took over.

32. Support any socialist movement to give centralized control over any part of the culture—education, social agencies, welfare programs, mental health clinics, etc.

33. Eliminate all laws or procedures which interfere with the operation of the Communist apparatus.

34. Eliminate the House Committee on Un-American Activities.

35. Discredit and eventually dismantle the FBI.

36. Infiltrate and gain control of more unions.

37. Infiltrate and gain control of big business.

38. Transfer some of the powers of arrest from the police to social agencies. Treat all behavioral problems as psychiatric disorders which no one but psychiatrists can understand.

39. Dominate the psychiatric profession and use mental health laws as a means of gaining coercive control over those who oppose Communist goals.

40. Discredit the family as an institution. Encourage promiscuity and easy divorce.

41. Emphasize the need to raise children away from the negative influence of parents. Attribute prejudices, mental blocks and retarding of children to suppressive influence of parents.

42. Create the impression that violence and insurrection are legitimate aspects of the American tradition; that students and special-interest groups should rise up and use united force to solve economic, political or social problems.

43. Overthrow all colonial governments before native populations are ready for self-government.

44. Internationalize the Panama Canal.

45. Repeal the Connally reservation so the United States can-
    not prevent the World Court from seizing jurisdiction over
    nations and individuals alike.

EXHIBIT 28

How North Vietnam Won the War Taken from the *Wall Street Journal*, Thursday August 3, 1995

WHAT DID THE NORTH VIETNAMESE leadership think of the American antiwar movement? What was the purpose of the Tet Offensive? How could the U.S. have been more successful in fighting the Vietnam War? Bui Tin, a former colonel in the North Vietnamese army, answers these questions in the following excerpts from an interview conducted by Stephen Young, a Minnesota attorney and human-rights activist. Bui Tin, who served on the general staff of North Vietnam's army, received the unconditional surrender of South Vietnam on April 30, 1975. He later became editor of the People's Daily, the official newspaper of Vietnam. He now lives in Paris, where he immigrated after becoming disillusioned with the fruits of Vietnamese communism.

Question: How did Hanoi intend to defeat the Americans?
Answer: By fighting a long war which would break their will to help South Vietnam. Ho Chi Minh said, "We don't need to win military victories, we only need to hit them until they give up and get out."
Q: Was the American antiwar movement important to Hanoi's victory?
A: It was essential to our strategy. Support of the war from our rear was completely secure while the American rear was vulnerable. Every day our leadership would listen to world news over the radio at 9 a.m. to follow the growth of the American antiwar movement. Visits to Hanoi by people like Jane Fonda, and former Attorney General Ramsey Clark and ministers gave us confidence that we

should hold on in the face of battlefield reverses. We were elated when Jane Fonda, wearing a red Vietnamese dress, said at a press conference that she was ashamed of American actions in the war and that she would struggle along with us.

Q: Did the Politburo pay attention to these visits?

A: Keenly.

Q: Why?

A: Those people represented the conscience of America. The conscience of America was part of its war-making capability, and we were turning that power in our favor. America lost because of its democracy; through dissent and protest it lost the ability to mobilize a will to win.

Q: How could the Americans have won the war?

A: Cut the Ho Chi Minh trail inside Laos. If Johnson had granted [Gen. William] Westmoreland's requests to enter Laos and block the Ho Chi Minh trail, Hanoi could not have won the war.

Q: Anything else?

A: Train South Vietnam's generals. The junior South Vietnamese officers were good, competent, and courageous, but the commanding general officers were inept.

Q: Did Hanoi expect that the National Liberation Front would win power in South Vietnam?

A: No. Gen. [Vo Nguyen] Giap [commander of the North Vietnamese army] believed that guerrilla warfare was important but not sufficient for victory. Regular military divisions with artillery and armor would be needed. The Chinese believed in fighting only with guerrillas, but we had a different approach. The Chinese were reluctant to help us. Soviet aid made the war possible. Le Duan [secretary general of the Vietnamese Communist Party] once told Mao Tse-tung that if you help us, we are sure to win; if you don't, we will still win, but we will have to sacrifice one or two million more soldiers to do so.

Q: Was the National Liberation Front an independent political movement of South Vietnamese?

A: No. It was set up by our Communist Party to implement a decision of the Third-Party Congress of September 1960. We always said there was only one party, only one army in the war to liberate the South and unify the nation. At all times there was only one-party commissar in command of the South.

Q: Why was the Ho Chi Minh trail so important?

A: It was the only way to bring sufficient military power to bear on the fighting in the South. Building and maintaining the trail was a huge effort, involving tens of thousands of soldiers, drivers, repair teams, medical stations, communication units.

Q: What of American bombing of the Ho Chi Minh trail?

A: Not very effective. Our operations were never compromised by attacks on the trail. At times, accurate B-52 strikes would cause real damage, but we put so much in at the top of the trail that enough men and weapons to prolong the war always came out the bottom. Bombing by smaller planes rarely hit significant targets.

Q: What of American bombing of North Vietnam?

A: If all the bombing had been concentrated at one time, it would have hurt our efforts. But the bombing was expanded in slow stages under Johnson and it didn't worry us. We had plenty of times to prepare alternative routes and facilities. We always had stockpiles of rice ready to feed the people for months if a harvest were damaged. The Soviets bought rice from Thailand for us.

Q: What was the purpose of the 1968 Tet Offensive?

A: To relieve the pressure Gen. Westmoreland was putting on us in late 1966 and 1967 and to weaken American resolve during a presidential election year.

Q: What about Gen. Westmoreland's strategy and tactics caused you concern?

A: Our senior commander in the South, Gen. Nguyen Chi Thanh, knew that we were losing base areas, control of the rural population and that his main forces were being pushed out to the borders of South Vietnam. He also worried that Westmoreland might receive permission to enter Laos and cut the Ho Chi Minh Trail. In January 1967, after discussions with Le Duan, Thanh proposed the Tet Offensive. Thanh was the senior member of the Politburo in South Vietnam. He supervised the entire war effort. Thanh's struggle philosophy was that "America is wealthy but not resolute," and "squeeze tight to the American chest and attack." He was invited up to Hanoi for further discussions. He went on commercial flights with a false passport from Cambodia to Hong Kong and then to Hanoi. Only in July was his plan adopted by the leadership. Then Johnson had rejected Westmoreland's request for 200,000 more troops. We realized that America had made its maximum military commitment to the war. Vietnam was not sufficiently important for the United States to call up its reserves. We had stretched American power to a breaking point. When more frustration set in, all the Americans could do would be to withdraw; they had no more troops to send over. Tet was designed to influence American public opinion. We would attack poorly defended parts of South Vietnam cities during a holiday and a truce when few South Vietnamese troops would be on duty. Before the main attack, we would entice American units to advance close to the borders, away from the cities. By attacking all South Vietnam's major cities, we would spread out our forces and neutralize the impact of American firepower. Attacking on a broad front, we would lose some battles but win others. We used local forces nearby each target to frustrate discovery of our plans. Small teams, like the one which attacked the U.S. Embassy in Saigon, would be sufficient. It was a guerrilla strategy of hit-and-run raids.

Q: What about the results?

A: Our losses were staggering and a complete surprise; Giap later told me that Tet had been a military defeat, though we had gained the planned political advantages when Johnson agreed to negotiate and did not run for re-election. The second and third waves in May and September were, in retrospect, mistakes. Our forces in the South were nearly wiped out by all the fighting in 1968. It took us until 1971 to re-establish our presence, but we had to use North Vietnamese troops as local guerrillas. If the American forces had not begun to withdraw under Nixon in 1969, they could have punished us severely. We suffered badly in 1969 and 1970 as it was.

Q: What of Nixon?

A: Well when Nixon stepped down because of Watergate we knew we would win. Pham Van Dong [prime minister of North Vietnam] said of Gerald Ford, the new president, "he's the weakest president in U.S. history; the people didn't elect him; even if you gave him candy, he doesn't dare to intervene in Vietnam again." We tested Ford's resolve by attacking Phuoc Long in January 1975. When Ford kept American B-52's in their hangers, our leadership decided on a big offensive against South Vietnam.

Q: What else?

A: We had the impression that American commanders had their hands tied by political factors. Your generals could never deploy a maximum force for greatest military effect.

BIBLIOGRAPHY

A.) Article: *Treason by Henry Mark Holzer September 19,* 2005

B.) Article: *Treason by Henry Mark Holzer September 19, 2005*

C.) Article: *Treason by Henry Mark Holzer September 19, 2005*

D.) Wikipedia internet: References

Arnold, Benedict. Encyclopedia Britannica. Retrieved on 2007-09-18.

Roget's New Millennium™ *Thesaurus, First Edition (v 1.3.1).* Lexico Publishing Group, LLC. 03 Aug. 2007.

Martin, James Kirby. *Benedict Arnold, Revolutionary Hero: An American Warrior Reconsidered.* New York University Press.

Randall, William Stearn: *Benedict Arnold: Patriot and Traitor.* William Morrow and Company, 1990.

U-S-History.com (2005). The French and Indian War, Fort William Henry "Massacre" August 1757. Retrieved on 2006-06-01.

Dictionary of Canadian Biography Online. Library and Archives, Canada. Retrieved on 2007-09-18.

Siege of Quebec and Death of General Montgovery. Retrieved on 2007-09-18. [unreliable source?]

The Battle of Quebec. theamericanrevolution.org. Retrieved on 2007-09-18.

Quigley, Louis. *Treachery and Fidelity, the Love Letters of Benedict Arnold Reveal a True Heart.* (2002). Retrieved on 2006-06-01.

Gold Selleck Silliman. famousamericans.ne. Retrieved on 2007-09-18.

David Wooster. famousamericans.ne. Retrieved on 2007-09-18.

Edward Shippen (1729–1806). University of Pennsylvania. Retrieved on 2007-09-18.

D.) Wikipedia internet: References

Bell, E. T. (1937). *Men of Mathematics. New York: Simon and Schuster.* ISBN 0-671-46400-0. (Excerpt)

Christianson, Gale (1984). *In the Presence of the Creator: Isaac Newton and His Times.* New York: Free Press. ISBN 0-02-905190-8. This well-documented work provides, in particular, valuable information regarding Newton's knowledge of Patristics.

Interview with James Gleick: "Isaac Newton" (Pantheon). *WAMU's The Diane Rehm Show Friday, June 13 2003* (RealAudio stream). Retrieved on 8 March 2005.

Sir Isaac Newton. *School of Mathematics and Statistics,* University of St. Andrews, Scotland. Retrieved on 8 March 2005.

The Newton Project. *Imperial College London.* Retrieved on 8 March 2005.

Westfall, Richard S. *(1980, 1998). Never at Rest. Cambridge University Press.* ISBN 0-521-27435-4.

Craig, John (1963). *Isaac Newton and the Counterfeiters, Notes and Records of the Royal Society (18). London: The Royal Society.*

"The Invisible Science." *Magical Egypt.* Chance Gardner and John Anthony West. 2005.

D.) Wikipedia internet

Hồ applied for the French Colonial Administrative School

Adam Weiss. *Boston behind the Scenes* http://www.bostonbe-hindthescenes.com/ *Podcast accessed on* 2007-14 March.

[abc]Sophie Quinn-Judge, *Hồ Chí Minh: The Missing Years* pp. 20–21, 25 http://www.londontourist.org/attractions.html

Joseph Buttinnger, *Vietnam: A Dragon Embattled,* vol. 1. (New York: Praeger, 1967)

See: *The Black Book of Communism* ^ Cecil B. Currey, *Victory At Any Cost* (Washington: Brassey's, 1997), p. 126

D)Wikipedia internet

Currey, Cecil B., *Senior General Vo Nguyen Giap Remembers,* in *Journal of Third World Studies,* Fall 2003 (see link below).Currey, Cecil B., *Victory at Any Cost: The Genius of Viet Nam's Gen. Vo Nguyen Giap.* Dupuy, Trevor N., Curt Johnson, and David L. Bongard, *The Harper Encyclopedia of Military Biography.* New

York: Castle Books, 1995.Giap, Vo Nguyen., *The Military Art of People's War*. New York: Monthly Review Press, 1970. Karnow, Stanley., *Vietnam: A History*. New York: Penguin, 1991.Pribbenow, Merle, Trans.' *Victory in Vietnam: A History of the People's Army of Vietnam, 1954–1975*. Military History Institute of Vietnam. Lawrence, KS: University of Kansas Press, 2002.

D.) Wikipedia internet

Although there is an inconsistency among published sources about Stalin's year and date of birth, Iosif Dzhugashvili is found in the records of the Uspensky Church in Gori, Georgia as born on December 18 (old style: December 6), 1878. This birth date is maintained in his School Leaving Certificate, his extensive tsarist Russia police file, a police arrest record from April 18, 1902 which gave his age as twenty-three years, and all other surviving pre-revolution documents. Stalin himself listed December 18, 1878, in a curriculum vitae as late as 1921 in his own handwriting. However, after his coming to power in 1922, the date was changed to December 21, 1879 (December 9, old style), and that was the day his birthday was celebrated in the Soviet Union. Russian playwright Edvard Radzinsky argues in his book *Stalin* that he changed the year to 1879 to have a nationwide birthday celebration of his 50th birthday. He could not do it in 1928 because his rule was not absolute enough. [1]

Bullock, p. 548, "both dictators."

Ulam, p. xiv, "the dictator not only deprived."

Davies, Harris, p.108, "Stalin as dictator."

Mawdsley, p. 1, "effectively a dictator."

Overy, p. 17, "and, later, as dictator."

[ab]Simon Sebag Montefiore. *Stalin: The Court of the Red Tsar*, Knopf, 2004 (ISBN 1-4000-4230-5).

Russia's War: A History of the Soviet Effort: 1941-1945, ISBN 0-14-027169-4.

Richard Overy, *The Dictators: Hitler's Germany, Stalin's Russia*, ISBN 0-393-02030-4.

[2]

Hoober 15

See Service's biography below

Biography of Dolganev (Russian)

[3]

Volume 1, page 43

The last days of Lieutenant Jakov Stalin Colin Simpson and John Shirley, *Sunday Times*, January 24, 1980

[4]

Koba the Dread, p. 133, ISBN 0-7868-6876-7; *Stalin: The Man and His Era*, p. 354, ISBN 0-8070-7001-7, in a footnote he quotes the press announcement as speaking of her "sudden death"; he also cites pp. 103-105 of his daughter's book, *Twenty Letters to a Friend*, the Russian edition, New York, 1967.

Knight, Ami W. (1991), Beria and the Cult of Stalin: Rewriting Transcaucasian Party History. *Soviet Studies*, Vol. 43, No. 4, pp. 749–763.

Shanin, Teodor (July 1989), Ethnicity in the Soviet Union: Analytical Perceptions and Political Strategies. *Comparative Studies in Society and History*, Vol. 31, No. 3, pp. 409–424.

Stalin's relationship with Lenin.

Joseph Stalin (January 30, 1924). On the Death of Lenin. *Pravda* magazine. Retrieved on May 9, 2007.

Robert Lewis. *The Economic Transformation of the Soviet Union*, ed. Mark Harrison, R. W. Davies, S.G Wheatcroft, p. 188

The rise of Stalin: AD1921-1924. *History of Russia*. HistoryWorld. Retrieved on 2006-04-03.

Alan Bullock, p. 269

[5]

[6]

[7]

Oliver Freire Jr. "Marxism and the Quantum Controversy: Responding to Max Jammer's Question"

Péter Szegedi "Cold War and Interpretations in Quantum Mechanics"

Ethan Pollock, *Stalin and the Soviet Science Wars*, Princeton University Press, 2006; introduction available online at [8] Montefiore. p.638, Phoenix, Reprinted paperback.

Joseph V. Stalin (1950-06-20). "Concerning Marxism in Linguistics," *Pravda*. Available online as *Marxism and Problems of Linguistics*, including other articles and letters published (also in *Pravda*) soon after February 8 and July 4, 1950.

Russia. (2007). In Encyclopædia Britannica. Retrieved July 14, 2007, from Encyclopædia Britannica Online: [9].

Alexander N. Yakovlev: *A Century of Violence in Soviet Russia* (Yale University Press, 2002), pg 165

Richard Pipes: *Communism: A History* (Modern Library Chronicles, 2001), p. 66

abLegacy of famine divides Ukraine BBC, November 24, 2006

SBU documents show that Moscow singled out Ukraine in famine5 Kanal: First News Channel of Ukraine, 22.11.2006

Revelations from the Russian Archives: UKRAINIAN FAMINE Library of Congress

Donald Rayfield. *Stalin and His Hangmen: The Tyrant and Those Who Killed for Him.* Random House, 2004. p. 193.

US Commission on the Ukraine Famine, "Findings of the Commission on the Ukraine Famine" [10], Report to Congress, Washington, DC, April 19, 1988.

US House of Representatives Authorizes Construction of Ukrainian Genocide Monument.

Statement by Pope John Paul II on the 70th Anniversary of the Famine.

HR356 "Expressing the sense of the House of Representatives regarding the man-made famine that occurred in Ukraine in 1932-1933," US House of Representatives, Washington, DC, October 21, 2003.

Yaroslav Bilinsky (1999). "Was the Ukrainian Famine of 1932-1933 Genocide?" *Journal of Genocide Research 1 (2):* 147-156.

Lisova, Natasha. "Ukraine Recognize Famine as Genocide," Associated Press, 28.11.2006.

[11]

Alan Bullock, pp. 904–905

Philip Boobbyer. The Stalin Era

[12]

Aleksandr Solzhenitsyn: *The Gulag Archipelago 1918-1956*, 1973-76
    ISBN 0-8133-3289-3

[13]

Anne Applebaum. *Gulag: A History* 2004 ISBN 1-4000-3409-4

Robert Gellately. *Lenin, Stalin, and Hitler: The Age of Social
    Catastrophe.* Knopf, 2007 ISBN 1400040051 p. 584: "Anne
    Applebaum is right to insist that the statistics 'can never fully
    describe what happened.' They do suggest, however, the mas-
    sive scope of the repression and killing."

Robert Gellately. *Lenin, Stalin, and Hitler: The Age of Social
    Catastrophe.* Knopf, 2007. ISBN 1400040051 p. 256

Simon Sebag Montefiore. *Stalin: The Court of the Red Tsar.* Knopf,
    2004. ISBN 1400042305 p. 246

[14]

[15]

[16]

Vadim Erlikman. *Poteri narodonaseleniia v XX veke: spravochnik.*
    Moscow 2004. ISBN 5-93165-107-1

[17]

R. W. Davies, Stephen G. Wheatcroft: *The Years of Hunger: Soviet
    Agriculture, 1931-1933 (The Industrialization of Soviet Russia),*
    2004 ISBN 0-333-31107-8

Andreev, EM, et al, *Naselenie Sovetskogo Soiuza, 1922–1991.* Moscow,
    Nauka, 1993. ISBN 5-02-013479-1

Simon Sebag Montefiore. Stalin: The Court of the Red Tsar. p. 649:
    "Perhaps 20 million had been killed; 28 million deported, of
    whom 18 million had slaved in the Gulags."

Dmitri Volkogonov. Autopsy for an Empire: The Seven Leaders Who
    Built the Soviet Regime. p. 139: "Between 1929 and 1953 the
    state created by Lenin and set in motion by Stalin deprived
    21.5 million Soviet citizens of their lives."

Alexander N. Yakovlev. A Century of Violence in Soviet Russia., Yale University Press, 2002, p. 234: "My own many years and experience in the rehabilitation of victims of political terror allow me to assert that the number of people in the USSR who were killed for political motives or who died in prisons and camps during the entire period of Soviet power totaled 20 to 25 million. And unquestionably one must add those who died of famine—more than 5.5 million during the civil war and more than 5 million during the 1930s."

Robert Gellately. *Lenin, Stalin, and Hitler: The Age of Social Catastrophe.* Knopf, 2007 ISBN 1400040051 p. 584: "More recent estimations of the Soviet-on-Soviet killing have been more 'modest' and range between ten and twenty million."

Stéphane Courtois. The Black Book of Communism: Crimes, Terror Repression. Harvard University Press, 1999. p. 4: "U.S.S.R.: 20 million deaths."

Robert Conquest. The Great Terror: A Reassessment, Oxford University Press, 1991 (ISBN 0-19-507132-8).

[18]

[19]

[20]

Robert Gellately. *Lenin, Stalin, and Hitler: The Age of Social Catastrophe.* Knopf, 2007 ISBN 1400040051 p. 391

Anne Applebaum. *Gulag: A History,* Doubleday, 2003 (ISBN 0-7679-0056-1)

Richard Rhodes (2002). *Masters of Death: The SS-Einsatzgruppen and the Invention of the Holocaust.* New York: Alfred A. Knopf. ISBN 0-375-40900-9. pp. 46-47

Allen Paul. *Katyn: Stalin's Massacre and the Seeds of Polish Resurrection,* Naval Institute Press, 1996, (ISBN 1-55750-670-1), p. 155

Anthony Eden (1965). *Memoirs: The Reckoning.*

Richard Overy The Dictators Hitler's Germany, Stalin's Russia p.568–569

Alan Bullock, *Hitler and Stalin: Parallel Lives,* Vintage; Reprint edition, 1993 (ISBN 0-679-72994-1), p. 905

See, *e.g.*, Brown, Philip Marshall. "The Recognition of Israel," *American Journal of International Law*, Vol. 42, No. 3 (Jul. 1948), p. 620.

Joseph V. Stalin. "Voprosy leninizma," 2nd ed., Moscow, p. 589; (1951) "Istoricheskij materializm", ed. by F. B. Konstantinov, Moscow, p. 402; P. Calvert (1982). "The Concept of Class," New York, pp. 144-145.

Jonathan Brent, Vladimir Naumov. *Stalin's Last Crime: The Plot Against the Jewish Doctors, 1948–1953*. HarperCollins, 2003. ISBN 0-06-019524-X.

Arvo Tuominen. *The Bells of the Kremlin*, p. 162.

Modern Poll—Votes for Stalin

http://www.findarticles.com/p/articles/mi_qn4158/is_20060420/ai_n16146985

http://thescotsman.scotsman.com/international.cfm?id=69292005

Rayfield, p.18.

"The human monster," page 4. O'Hehir, A. *Salon.com*. May 5, 2005.

D.) Wikipedia internet

McCullough, p. 38

Ferrell, Robert Hugh *(1996)*. *Harry S. Truman: A Life. Columbia: University of Missouri Press*, 87. ISBN 0826210503.

Drugstore Clerk at 14 His First Job. Truman Library. Retrieved on 2007-07-26.

Harry Truman joins Battery B of the Missouri National Guard. Truman Library. Retrieved on 2007-07-26.

[abcd]Hanlon, Michael E. (2000). Capt. Harry Truman, Artilleryman and Future President. *Doughboy Center: The Story of the American Expeditionary Forces*. Worldwar1.com Magazine. Retrieved on 2007-07-19.

Ferrell, p. 87 McNulty, Bryan. The great atomic bomb debate. *Perspectives*. Ohio University. Retrieved on 2007-04-02.

D) Wikipedia internet

"Supreme commander," Encyclopædia Britannica, Dwight D. Eisenhower article, p. 3 of 6. URL retrieved on January 21, 2007.

D.) Wikipedia internet

Goldzwig, Steven R. and Dionisopoulos, George N., eds. *In a Perilous Hour: The Public Address of John F. Kennedy*, text and analysis of key speeches (1995)

D.) Wikipedia internet

Lyndon Baines Johnson Library and Museum—Religion and President Johnson.

Caro, Robert A. Volume I

735—Remarks at a Rally in San Bernardino. October 28, 1964.

The Ultimate San Bernardino Trivia Quiz.

Remarks at Southwest Texas State College Upon Signing the Higher Education Act of 1965. Lyndon Baines Johnson Library and Museum. Retrieved on 2006-04-11.

Woods, Randall (2006), p. 131

Caro, Robert A. (1982) is full of details.

Hove, Duane T. (2003). American Warriors: Five Presidents in the Pacific Theater of World War II. Burd Street Press. ISBN 1-57249-070. [1]

Dallek, Robert. *Lone Star Rising*, p. 237

Woods, Randall (2006), p. 217; Caro, Robert A. (1989)

Woods, Randall (2006), p. 262

http://www.afterimagegallery.com/nytjohnson.htm

Rowland Evans and Robert Novak. *Lyndon B. Johnson: The Exercise of Power* (1966), p. 104

John A. Farrell (2001). Tip O'Neill and the Democratic Century: A Biography. Little, Brown. ISBN 0-316-26049-5.

The Assassination Records Review Board noted in 1998 that Johnson became skeptical of some of the Warren Commission findings. See: Final Report, chapter 1, footnote 17 at http://www.fas.org/sgp/advisory/arrb98/index.html

Dallek, Robert (1998). Chapter 2

Dallek, Robert (1998). Chapter 3

Evans and Novak (1966), pp. 451-456; Taylor Branch. *Pillar of Fire: America in the King Years 1963-65*, pp. 444-470

Risen, Clay. "How the South Was Won," The Boston Globe, 2006-03-05. Retrieved on 2007-02-11.

Woods, Randall (2006), pp. 759-787

Public Papers of the Presidents of the United States: Lyndon B. Johnson, 1965. Volume II, entry 301, pp. 635-640 (1966)

Woods, Randall (2006), pp. 563-68; Dallek, Robert (1988), pp. 196-202

Patricia P. Martin and David A. Weaver. "Social Security: A Program and Policy History," *Social Security Bulletin*, volume 66, no. 1 (2005), see also online version

Woods, Randall (2006), pp. 790-795; Michael W. Flamm. *Law And Order: Street Crime, Civil Unrest, and the Crisis of Liberalism in the 1960s* (2005).

Dallek, Robert. *Flawed Giant*, pp. 391-396; quotes on pp. 391 and 396

http://siwmfilm.net/Vietnam_War/Military_Casualty_Information.html

Lawrence R. Jacobs and Robert Y. Shapiro. "Lyndon Johnson, Vietnam, and Public Opinion: Rethinking Realist Theory of Leadership." *Presidential Studies Quarterly* 29 #3 (1999), p. 592

John E. Mueller. *War, Presidents and Public Opinion* (1973), p. 108

http://news.yahoo.com/s/ap/20061117/ap_on_re_us/lbj_tapes

http://www.lbjlib.utexas.edu/johnson/Press.hom/tape_release_11_2006.shtm

Dallek, Robert (1998). Flawed Giant: Lyndon B. Johnson and His Times, 1961-1973. Oxford: Oxford University Press, 754. *ISBN 0-19-505465-2.*

Lewis L. Gould (1993), p. 98

Lewis L. Gould (1993). *1968: The Election That Changed America.*

Harris, Marvin (December 1999). "Taming the Wild Pecan at Lyndon B. Johnson National Historical Park." *Park Science 19 (2).*

Elsen, William A. "Ceremonial Group Had Busy 5 Weeks." *The Washington Post*, January 25, 1973.

LBJ Library Staff. Religion and President Johnson. Lyndon Baines Johnson Library and Museum. Retrieved on 2006-04-11.

Caro, Robert A. (2002).

Gulley, Bill; Mary Ellen Reece (1980). *Breaking Cover.* New York: Simon & Schuster, 78-79. ISBN 0-671-24548-1.

http://www.nndb.com/lists/050/000140627/

Caro, Robert A. (2002). *Master of the Senate: The Years of Lyndon Johnson.* New York: Knopf, 122. *ISBN 0-394-52836-0.*

Dallek, Robert (2004), p. 139

D.) Wikipedia internet

Primary sources

Foreign Relations of the United States: Nixon-Ford Administrations

By Richard Nixon

The Challenges We Face: Edited and Compiled from the Speeches and Papers of Richard M. Nixon (1960) ISBN 0-7581-8739-4

Six Crises. Doubleday (1962) ISBN 0-385-00125-8

RN: The Memoirs of Richard Nixon, Simon & Schuster (Reprint, 1978) ISBN 0-671-70741-8

The Real War. Sidgwich Jackson (1980) ISBN 0-283-98650-6. Written as a *cri de coeur* against what RN saw as serious threats to US security from Soviet expansionism in the late 1970s

- *Leaders.* Random House (1982) ISBN 0-446-51249-4. A character study of various leaders that RN came to know during his career.
- *Real Peace.* Sidgwick & Jackson Ltd (1984) ISBN 0-283-99076-7
- *No More Vietnams.* Arbor House Publishing (1987) ISBN 0-87795-668-5
- *1999: Victory Without War.* Simon & Schuster (1988) ISBN 0-671-62712-0
- *In the Arena: A Memoir of Victory, Defeat, and Renewal.* Simon & Schuster (1990) ISBN 0-671-72318-9. A more personal memoir than *RN: The Memoirs of Richard Nixon,* shows RN's reflections on life, politics, and personal philosophy
- *Seize the Moment: America's Challenge in a One-Superpower World.* Simon & Schuster (1992) ISBN 0-671-74343-0
- *Beyond Peace.* Random House (1994) ISBN 0-679-43323-6

By other authors
- Ehrlichman, John D. *Witness to Power. The Nixon Years* (1982).

- Gergen, David. *Eyewitness to Power: The Essence of Leadership* (2000).
- Haldeman, H. R. (Bob). *The Haldeman Diaries: Inside the Nixon White House* (1994), abridged version; complete diaries were published on CD-ROM by SONY.
- Kissinger, Henry *White House Years*. Little Brown & Co. (1979).
- *Years of Upheaval* (1982).
- Price, Raymond. *With Nixon* (1977).
- Safire, William. *Before the Fall: An Inside View of the Pre-Watergate White House* (1975)
- Stans, Maurice H. *One of the President's Men: Twenty Years with Eisenhower and Nixon* (1995
- Secondary sources

Biographies
- Aitken, Jonathan. *Nixon: A Life* (1993). Favorable.
- Ambrose, Stephen E. *Nixon: Ruin and Recovery 1973-1990* (1991). The most detailed scholarly biographies (hostile).
- Ambrose, Stephen E. *Nixon: The Triumph of a Politician, 1962-1972* (1989).
- Ambrose, Stephen E. *Nixon: The Education of a Politician 1913-1962* (1987).
- Greenberg, David. *Nixon's Shadow: The History of an Image* (2003). Important study of how Nixon was perceived by media and scholars.
- Hoff, Joan. *Nixon Reconsidered* (1994). Quite favorable.
- Morgan, Iwan. *On Nixon* (2002). Favourable British view.
- Morris, Roger. *Richard Milhous Nixon: The Rise of an American Politician* (1990).
- Parmet, Herbert S. *Richard Nixon and His America* (1990).
- Reeves, Richard. *President Nixon: Alone in the White House* (2002).
- Wicker, Tom. *One of Us: Richard Nixon and the American Dream* (1991).

Political studies

- Bochin, Hal W. *Richard Nixon: Rhetorical Strategist* Greenwood Press 1990.
- *Dallek, Robert (2007). Nixon and Kissinger: Partners in Power. HarperCollins.* ISBN 0060722304.
- Friedman, Leon and William F. Levantrosser, eds. *Richard M. Nixon: Politician, President, Administrator* (1991), essays by scholars.
- Genovese, Michael A. *The Nixon Presidency: Power and Politics in Turbulent Times* (1990).
- Greene, John Robert. *the Limits of Power: The Nixon and Ford Administrations* (1992).
- Gellman, Irwin. *The Contender: Richard Nixon: The Congress Years, 1946 to 1952* (1999).
- Mason, Robert. *Richard Nixon and the Quest for a New Majority* (2004). 289 pp.
- Matusow, Allen J. *Nixon's Economy: Booms, Busts, Dollars and Votes.* U. Press of Kansas, 1998. 323 pp.
- Marvillas, Anthony Rama. "Nixon in Nixonland," *Southern California Quarterly* 2002 84(2): 169-181. ISSN 0038-3929 examines the Nixonlanders, loyal supporters of Nixon throughout his political career, and how well Nixon fit their perception of his political views. Mostly Protestants and prosperous small business owners, the Nixonlanders opposed the New Deal's domestic programs and the Democrats' foreign policy. They believed in individualism, self-reliance, and thrift and stood fast against the Soviet Union and Communism. These old guard Republicans believed Nixon shared these views, but in reality, Nixon was far more pragmatic, distrusting wealthy Republicans and open to change. He considered himself a moderate Republican as defined by his mentor, Dwight Eisenhower, and thus was an "extremely imprecise fit" to the Nixonlander definition.
- Reichley, A. James. *Conservatives in an Age of Change: The Nixon and Ford Administrations* (1981).

- Small, Melvin. *The Presidency of Richard Nixon* (2003).
- Summers, Anthony. *The Arrogance of Power the Secret World of Richard Nixon* (2000).
- White, Theodore. *The Making of the President 1968: A narrative History of American politics in Action* (1969).
- White, Theodore. *The Making of the President, 1972* (1973).

Foreign policy

- Bundy, William. *A Tangled Web: The Making of Foreign Policy in the Nixon Presidency.* 1998. 647 pp. online review.
- Daum, Andreas W.; Gardner, Lloyd C.; Mausbach, Wilfred, eds. *America, the Vietnam War, and the World: Comparative and International Perspectives.* (Publications of the German Historical Institute) (2003).
- Gaddis, John Lewis *Strategies of Containment: A Critical Appraisal of Postwar American National Security Policy* 1982.
- Goh, Evelyn. "Nixon, Kissinger, and the 'Soviet Card' in the US Opening to China, 1971-1974." *Diplomatic History* 2005 29(3): 475-502. ISSN 0145-2096. Full text in Ingenta and Ebsco; Kissinger's use of the "Soviet card" in relations with China between 1971 and 1974 offers diplomatic historians an interesting, if not yet conclusive, perspective on the rise and fall of détente and the problems of "triangular diplomacy." Kissinger sought to play up the Soviet threat to the Chinese as a way of promoting closer relations with the PRC. While at times he suggested a US-PRC alliance, declassified sources indicate that his suggestions were more hyperbole than actual US policy. He was really using the Soviet threat as a means to a closer relationship with China, but one that was still subordinated to improved US-Soviet relations. Unfortunately for Kissinger and the Nixon administration, the triangular diplomacy failed because of Chinese suspicions and the Watergate crisis.
- Kimball, Jeffrey P. *Nixon's Vietnam War* (2002).

- Levantrosser, William F. ed. *Cold War Patriot and Statesman, Richard M. Nixon* (1993), essays by scholars and senior officials.
- Shawcross, William. *Sideshow: Kissinger, Nixon, and the Destruction of Cambodia* (1979), Simon and Schuster. Strong critique of Cambodia policy. Kissinger responds directly to Shawcross's claims in appendix to *Years of Upheaval.*
- Thornton, Richard C. *The Nixon-Kissinger Years: Reshaping America's Foreign Policy* (1989).
- Tucker, Nancy Bernkopf. "Taiwan Expendable? Nixon and Kissinger Go to China" *Journal of American History* 2005 92(1): 109-135. ISSN 0021-8723 Full text in History Cooperative and Ebsco. Analyzes U.S. policy toward China and finds that Nixon and Kissinger pursued a deeply flawed and ultimately harmful path toward establishing relations with Communist China. Nixon and Kissinger operated in secrecy in order to hide the "collateral damage" of their China policy, particularly the damage it did to the former U.S. client state of Taiwan.
- Warner, Geoffrey, "Nixon, Kissinger, and the Breakup of Pakistan, 1971," *International Affairs* (London), 81 (Oct. 2005), 1097-1118.

Domestic policy

- Burke, Vincent J. *Nixon's Good Deed: Welfare Reform* (1974).
- Hood, J. Larry. "The Nixon Administration and the Revised Philadelphia Plan for Affirmative Action: A Study in Expanding Presidential Power and Divided Government," *Presidential Studies Quarterly* 23 (Winter 1993): 145-67.
- Flippen, J. Brooks. *Nixon and the Environment* (2000).
- Kotlowski, Dean J. *Nixon's Civil Rights: Politics, Principle, and Policy* (2001).

- Kotlowski, Dean J.; "Richard Nixon and the Origins of Affirmative Action," *The Historian*. Volume: 60. Issue: 3. 1998. pp. 523 ff.
- Kotlowski, Dean J. "Deeds Versus Words: Richard Nixon and Civil Rights Policy." *New England Journal of History* 1999-2000 56(2-3): 122-144. Abstract: Political considerations and his own personal views gave President Nixon a mixed record in the area of civil rights, which included such advances as the implementation of affirmative action, school desegregation, and other types of economic support promoting racial equality, but opposed busing, ignored women, and made compromises to placate Southern conservatives.
- McAndrews, Lawrence J.; "The Politics of Principle: Richard Nixon and School Desegregation," *The Journal of Negro History*, Vol. 83 #3, 1998 pp 187+.
- O'Reilly, Kenneth. *Nixon's Piano: Presidents and Racial Politics from Washington to Clinton* (1995).
- Matusow, Allen J. *Nixon's Economy: Booms, Busts, Dollars, and Votes* (1998).
- Schell, Jonathan "The Time of Illusion" Vintage (1976).
- Sussman, Glen and Daynes, Byron W. "Spanning the Century: Theodore Roosevelt, Franklin Roosevelt, Richard Nixon, Bill Clinton, and the Environment." *White House Studies* 2004 4(3): 337-354. ISSN 1535-4768 Watergate
- Bernstein, Carl; Woodward, Bob. *All the President's Men* (1974).
- Friedman, Leon and Levantrosser, William F. eds. *Watergate and Afterward: The Legacy of Richard M. Nixon* (1992), essays by scholars
- Kutler, Stanley I. *The Wars of Watergate: The Last Crisis of Richard Nixon*. (1990).
- Olson, Keith W. *Watergate: The Presidential Scandal That Shook America*. (2003). 220 pp.
- Schudson, Michael *Watergate in American Memory: How We Remember, Forget, and Reconstruct the Past* (1993)

D) Wikipedia internet

Summers, JR., Harry G. *Historical Atlas of the Vietnam War.* New York: Houghton Mifflin, 1995. ISBN 0-395-72223-3.

- Wiest, Andrew (editor). *Rolling Thunder in a Gentle Land.* Oxford: Osprey Publishing, 2006. ISBN 978-1-84693-020-6.
- Windrow, Martin. *The French Indochina War 1946-1954 (Men-At-Arms, 322).* London: Osprey Publishing, 1998. ISBN 1-85532-789-9.
- Sino-French War (Franco-Chinese War, 1884-1885)
- Indochina Wars
- Vietnam War (Second Indochina War, 1957-75)
- Cambodian-Vietnamese and Sino-Vietnamese Wars (Third Indochina War, 1978-1989; 1979)
- Algerian War (Algerian War of Independence, 1954–1962) 1 to 51

Windrow, Martin (1998). *The French Indochina War 1946–1954 (Men-At-Arms, 322).* London: Osprey Publishing, p. 11. ISBN 1855327899.

Windrow p. 23

Those named Martin, Their history Is Ours: The Great History, (1946–1954). The Indochina War (French), documentary. Channel 5 (France). Retrieved on 2007-05-20.

[abc]Ruscio, Alain. "Guerre d'Indochine: Libérez Henri Martin," l'Humanité, 2003-08-02. Retrieved on 2007-05-20. (French)

Allies Reinforce Java and Saigon, British Paramount News rushes, 1945

Philipe Leclerc de Hauteloque (1902–1947), La légende d'un héro, Christine Levisse-Touzé, Tallandier/Paris Musées, 2002.

Philipe Leclerc de Hauteloque (1902–1947), La légende d'un héro, Christine Levisse-Touzé, Tallandier/Paris Musées, 2002.

Barnet, Richard J. (1968). Intervention and Revolution: The United States in the Third World. World Publishing, 185. ISBN 0529020149.

Prados, John (August 2007, Volume 20, Number 1). The Smaller Dragon Strikes. MHQ: The Quarterly Journal of Military History, 50. ISSN 1040-5992.

[ab]La Guerre En Indochine (video). Newsreel (1950-10-26). Retrieved on 2007-05-20.

[ab]Bigeard et Dien Bien Phu (video). TV news. Channel 2 (France) (2004-05-03). Retrieved on 2007-05-20.

DienBienPhu.org the official website of the battle.

June 17, 1954 discourse of Mendès-France on the website of the French National Assembly.

Five columns on the cover's dossiers: Communism in the United States (May 4th 1965) French public channel ORTF.

William M. Leary, CAT at Dien Bien Phu, Aerospace Historian 31 (fall/September 1984).

[abcde]Hercombe, Peter (2004). Dien Bien Phu, Chronicles of a Forgotten Battle. Documentary. Transparences Productions/ Channel 2 (France).

[ab]France's war against Communists rages on (video). Newsreel. News magazine of the Screen/Warner Bros. (May 1952). Retrieved on 2007-05-20.

A Bernard Fall Retrospective, presentation of Bernard Fall, Vietnam Witness 1953–56, New York, Praeger, 1966, by the Ludwig von Mises Institute.

Nhu Tang, Truong. "A Vietcong Memoir: An Inside Account of the Vietnam War and Its Aftermath," Vintage, 1986-03-12. Retrieved on 2007-06-27. (English).

[abc]France History, IV Republic (1946–1958) (French). Quid Encyclopedia. Retrieved on 2007-05-20.

Patrick Pesnot, Rendez-vous Avec X—Dien Bien Phu, France Inter, December 4, 2004 (Rendez-vous With X broadcasted on public station France Inter).

"We wanted a newspaper to tell what we wanted" interview by Denis Jeambar and Roland Mihail.

The war in Indo-China goes on (video). Newsreel. News magazine of the Screen/Warner Bros. (December 1953). Retrieved on 2007-05-20.

Boudarel affair in the ANAPI official website.

[ab]USS Skagit and Operation Passage To Freedom. self-published. Retrieved on 2007-05-20.

Alf Andrew Heggoy and *Insurgency and Counterinsurgency in Algeria*, Bloomington, Indiana, Indiana University Press, 1972, p.175.

*The 317th Platoon*s script.

French Defense Ministry archives, ECPAD.

Service Spéciaux—GCMA Indochine 1950/54, Commandant Raymond Muelle and Eric Deroo, Crépin-Leblond editions, 1992, ISBN 2703001002.

Guerre secrète en Indochine—Les maquis autochtones face au Viêt-Minh (1950-1955), Lieutenant Colonel Michel David, Lavauzelle editions, 2002, ISBN 2702506364.

Dien Bien Phu—Le Rapport Secret, Patrick Jeudy, TF1 Video, 2005.

French Defense Ministry archives

French Defense Ministry archives

French Defense Ministry archives

Replacing France: The Origins of American Intervention in Vietnam (PDF). Book. University Press of Kentucky (2007-07). Retrieved on 2007-06-28.

[abcde]French-American relations. Embassy of France in the US (2005-02-24). Retrieved on 2007-05-20.

French Defense Ministry archives

http://www.ina.fr/archivespourtous/index.php?vue=corpus&code=C0524208764# Indochina War: The "good offices" of the Americans (National Audiovisual Institute)

US Defense service

French Defense Ministry archives

French Defense Ministry archives

Chinese General Hoang Minh Thao and Colonel Hoang Minh Phuong quoted by Pierre Journoud researcher at the Defense History Studies (CHED), Paris University Pantheon-Sorbonne, in *Paris Hanoi Beijing* published in *Communisme* magazine and the Pierre Renouvin Institute of Paris, July 20, 2004.

French Defense Ministry archives.

French Defense Ministry archives.

Pierre Schoendoerffer interview with Jean Guisnel in *Some edited pictures.*

Roman Karmen, un cinéaste au service de la révolution, Dominique Chapuis and Patrick Barbéris, Kuiv Productions/Arte France, 2001.

The Cinematheque of Toulouse

(D) Wikipedia internet

Brigham, *Guerrulla Diplomacy,* p. 6; Marcus Raskin & Bernard Fall, *The Viet-Nam Reader,* p. 89; William Duiker, *U.S. Containment Policy and the Conflict in Indochina,* p. 212.

(D) Wikipedia internet

[abcd]*Feklisov, Aleksandr; Kostin, Sergei (2001). The Man Behind the Rosenbergs.* Enigma Books. ISBN 1-929631-08-1.

Feklisov, Aleksandr; Kostin, Sergei (2001). *The Man Behind the Rosenbergs.* Enigma Books. 140–147. ISBN 1-929631-08-1.

See Joseph Albright and Marcia Kunstell. *Bombshell,* Times Books, 1997 (ISBN 0-8129-2861-X) with reference to Theodore Alvin Hall and Saville Sax and their motives.

Roberts, Sam (2001). *The Brother: The Untold Story of the Rosenberge Case.* Random House, 425–426,432. ISBN 0-375-76124-1.

Judge Kaufman's Statement Upon Sentencing the Rosenbergs on the site of the University of Kansas City-Missouri School of Law. Accessed September 28, 2006.

"KGB agent says Rosenbergs were executed unjustly," 1997-03-06. Retrieved on 2006-09-25.

The content and value of Fuchs's data for the Soviet program is discussed thoroughly in David Holloway's *Stalin and the Bomb: The Soviet Union and Atomic Energy, 1939–1956* (New Haven, CT: Yale University Press, 1994). Holloway based his assessment of the value of Fuchs's data in particular from the intelligence transcripts and the reactions of key Soviet personnel— especially Igor Kurchatov—to Fuchs's data. The exact use of espionage information by the Soviets was somewhat complicated, due to mutual distrust of the espionage data and the Soviet scientists themselves by Stalin and Beria (see Soviet atomic bomb project for more information).

(D) Wikipedia internet
Domino Theory
D.) Wikipedia internet
SDS in chapter 12
(P) From Enemy To Friend: *By Bui Tin*
(Q) Wikipedia internet: Chronology of Opposition

References

1. Nonrandom Risk: The 1970 Draft Lottery, Norton Starr, Journal of Statistics Education v.5, n.2, 1997
2. Anti-war campaigners to donate documents to Vietnamese museum, Keiji Hirano, Kyodo News, *The Japan Times*, February 16, 2002. (Web edition hosted by lbo-talk under the title "What Japanese Anti-Vietnam War Activists Are Up To").
3. 1961-1973: GI Resistance in the Vietnam War, libcom. org.
4. *War Tax Resistance.* War Resisters League (2003) p. 75.
5. http://www.levity.com/aciddreams/samples/pentagon. html.

(R) http://userpages.aug.com/captbarb/femvetsnam.html.
(D) Wikipedia internet: References

1. *1969: Millions march in US-Vietnam Moratorium.* BBC On This Day, 15 October. Accessed May 05, 2007.
2. Oral History Transcript: David E. Kennell.
3. The University of Delaware: A History, chapter 12.
4. The Australian, 9 May 1970, estimated the crowd as 100,000. Also, Strangio, Paul. "Farewell to a Conscience of the Nation," The Age, 2003-10-13. Retrieved on 2006-07-01.
5. Silence kills; events leading up to the Vietnam Moratorium on 8 May by J. F. Cairns, M.P., Vietnam Moratorium Committee, 1970. Retrieved from "http://en.wikipedia. org/wiki/Moratorium_to_End_the_War_in_Vietnam."

D) Wikipedia internet, Bill Ayers

References

1. [abcdef]Terry, Don (Chicago Tribune staff reporter, "The calm after the storm", *Chicago Tribune Magazine*, p 10, September 16, 2001 June 8, 2008
2. Obituary: Thomas Ayers Served as Board Chair from 1975 to 1986*Northwestern University*, June 19, 2007
3. Thomas G Ayers, 1915-2007 *Cinnamon Swirl*, June 18, 2007
4. [abcd]Barber, David, *Fugitive Days: A Memoir*. Book review, Journal of Social History, Winter 2002, retrieved June 10, 2008.
5. *Fugitive Days: A Memoir.*
6. Cathy Wilkerson (2001-12-01). *Fugitive Days*. Book review, *Zmag* magazine.
7. Jacobs, Ron. *The Way the Wind Blew: A History of the Weather Underground*, London & New York: Verso, 1997. ISBN 1-85984-167-8
8. [abc]Avrich. *The Haymarket Tragedy*, p. 431.
9. Adelman. Haymarket Revisited, p. 40.
10. [abcdef]Dinitia Smith, "No Regrets for a Love Of Explosives: In a Memoir of Sorts, a War Protester Talks of Life With the Weathermen," *The New York Times*, September 11, 2001.
11. Marcia Froelke Coburn, "No Regrets," *Chicago Magazine*, August 2001.
12. Staples, Brent, "The Oldest Rad," book review of *Fugitive Days* by Bill Ayers in *New York Times Book Review*, September 30, 2001, accessed June 5, 2008
13. Jesse Lemisch, Weather Underground Rises from the Ashes: They're Baack!, *New Politics*, Summer 2006
14. Farber, David, "Radical on the run—Bill Ayers recounts his life outside the law as a member of the Weather Underground," book review of *Fugitive Days: A Memoir* by Bill Ayers, *Chicago Tribune*, Books section, p 1, August 26, 2001, retrieved June 8, 2008

15. NB that although the interview was published on 9/11, it was completed prior to that and cannot be properly construed as a reaction to the events of that day.
16. Bill Ayers, "Clarifying the Fact—a Letter to the *New York Times*," 9-15-2001, Bill Ayers (blog), April 21, 2008.
17. [ab]Bill Ayers, Episodic Notoriety—Fact and Fantasy, Bill Ayers (blog), April 6, 2008
18. Bill Ayers. "I'M SORRY! I think," Bill Ayers (blog).
19. Ayers, Bill, letter to the editor, *Chicago Tribune*, September 23, 2001, retrieved June 8, 2008.
20. Cite error: Invalid <ref> tag; no text was provided for refs named rcabc830.
21. Web page titled "Weather Underground/Exclusive interview: Bernardine Dohrn and Bill Ayers," Independent Lens website, accessed June 5, 2008.
22. Chepesiuk, Ron. "Sixties Radicals, Then and Now: Candid Conversations with Those Who Shaped the Era." McFarland & Company, Inc., Publishers: Jefferson, North Carolina, 1995, "Chapter 5: Bill Ayers: Radical Educator," p. 102.
23. Flint, Jerry, M. "2d Blast Victim's Life Is Traced: Miss Oughton Joined a Radical Faction After College," news article, *The New York Times*, March 19, 1970.
24. Kifner, John. "That's what the Weathermen are supposed to be." "Vandals in the Mother Country" article, *The New York Times* magazine, January 4, 1970, page 15.
25. Berger, Dan (2006). *Outlaws of America: The Weather Underground and the Politics of Solidarity.* AK Press, 95.
26. See document 5, Revolutionary Youth Movement (1969). "You Don't Need a Weatherman to Know Which Way the Wind Blows." Retrieved on 2008-04-11.
27. Franks, Lucinda. "US Inquiry Finds 37 in Weather Underground," news article, *The New York Times*, March 3, 1975.
28. [ab]William Ayers. University of Illinois at Chicago, College of Education.

29. Before "going underground" he published an account of this experience, *Education: An American Problem.*

30. Mike Dorning and Rick Pearson, Daley. "Don't Tar Obama for Ayers," *The Chicago Tribune*, April 17, 2008.

31. Burger, Timothy, J., [http://www.bloomberg.com/apps/news?pid=newsarchive&sid=adgAs9YOxRSc "Obama's Ties Might Fuel 'Republican Attack Machine' (Update2)", Bloomberg News, February 15, 2008, retrieved August 30, 2008

32. http://blog.washingtonpost.com/factchecker/2008/02/obamas_weatherman_connection.html#more.

33. abChris Fusco and Abdon M. Pallasch, Who is Bill Ayers?, *Chicago Sun-Times*, April 18, 2008.

34. Illionois State Board of Elections, http://www.elections.il.gov/CampaignDisclosure/ContribListSearches.aspx?NavLink=1.

35. Interview with Bill Ayers: "On Progressive Education, Critical Thinking and the Cowardice of Some in Dangerous Times," *Revolution*, October 1, 2006.

36. http://billayers.wordpress.com/biography-history/.

D.) Wikipedia internet, United freedom front.
Legal Cases
USA v. Patricia Gros: 84-CR-0222
USA v. Raymond Luc Levasseur et al: 86-CR-180
Further Reference
- "Group Hit Other Targets, FBI Believes," Ronald Kessler, 11/09/1983, *Washington Post.*
- "Case-Study of US Domestic Terrorism: United Freedom Front," Phillip Jenkins.
- "After 13 Bombings, FBI Says Terrorists Remain a Mystery," Rick Hampson, 09/27/1984.

E) Wikipedia internet, Cooper-Church Amendment:

References

- Henry Kissinger. *Ending the Vietnam War.* New York: Simon & Schuster, 2002.
- *Encyclopedia of the Vietnam War.* Oxford University Press, 2000.

This article relating to law in the United States, or its constituent jurisdictions is a stub. You can help Wikipedia by expanding it.

This article about the Vietnam War is a stub. You can help Wikipedia by expanding it.

This Cambodia-related article is a stub. You can help Wikipedia by expanding it.

ABOUT THE AUTHOR

JOSEPH P. KEELY IS A former United States Marine with ten years served on active duty and in the reserves. It is here that he would develop a considerable amount of knowledge in fighting wars. During his time in the Marines, he served with Eighth Communication Battalion, Second Marine Division and Third Tank Battalion, Third Marine Division, with whom he served one year eight months and four days in Vietnam. He also served with Eighth Engineer Battalion, Second Marine Division, and Gulf Company Second Battalion, Twenty-Fifth Marines, Fourth Marine Division. He is also a retired New Jersey state trooper with twenty-six years of service prior to retiring in 1995.

After serving four years on the road with the New Jersey State Police at various road station assignments, he was transferred to the crime scene investigation unit and assigned to North Jersey. It is here that he would develop an expertise in investigating major criminal cases from burglary and theft all the way up to and including homicides, of which some of these cases are written of in this publication.